The Economics of the Labour Market

Proceedings of a Conference on the Labour Market, sponsored by Her Majesty's Treasury, the Department of Employment and the Manpower Services Commission.

10–12th September, 1979
at Magdalen College, Oxford

LONDON: HER MAJESTY'S STATIONERY OFFICE

ISBN O 11 630291 7

CONTENTS

PREFACE

The labour market is a subject of considerable importance to almost everyone in the economy. Its workings are central to issues of economic policy but these workings are not always fully understood. Certainly, policy makers would be in a much better position if they had a clearer idea of how the labour market behaved when economic management decisions have to be made.

Of course, at the same time there is no dearth of distinguished economists who have devoted their time to the analysis of one or more aspect of the labour market. Indeed in recent years it has been less than easy to keep up with the flood on new studies which have appeared. Naturally, not all of these have had direct policy implications but a large number—perhaps more than in most other fields of economics—have been directed towards questions which do concern government strongly.

These considerations suggested that it would be mutually beneficial to bring together both government and academic economists to survey existing knowledge and exchange ideas on developments and priorities for research. Consequently in September 1979, the Treasury, in conjunction with the Department of Employment and the Manpower Services Commission, organised a three day conference of about 100 labour market specialists. About a third of these economists were from government and two-thirds from academic life split about evenly between United Kingdom and overseas participants.

Much of the value of the conference came from ad hoc meetings and exchanges outside the formal arrangements of the conference. Nevertheless, the invited papers and comments proved of such widespread interest that we felt the proceedings should be made available to the economics profession as a whole.

Most of the papers are by way of survey of recent theoretical or empirical developments. As such, together they represent one of the most comprehensive appreciations of the state of labour economics which is available.

Perhaps finally a word should be said about the coverage of the conference. No conference, however long, could sensibly expect to cover every aspect of labour economics. Accordingly, we designed the programme to concentrate mainly on macroeconomic topics including forecasting aspects and also deliberately excluded wage determination. While this is obviously a subject of crucial importance, it is so large a topic that it would easily merit a separate conference in its own right.

We would like to thank Magdalen College Oxford for their hospitality which allowed us to hold the conference in the most delightful surroundings.

Zmira Hornstein
Joseph Grice
Alfred Webb

LIST OF PARTICIPANTS

Sir F. Atkinson	*HM Treasury*
C. Azariadis	*Pennsylvannia University*
M. N. Baily	*Yale University*
M. Beenstock	*London Business School*
A. R. Bergstrom	*University of Essex*
E. R. Berndt	*University of British Columbia*
R. Boulton	*HM Treasury*
J. K. Bowers	*University of Leeds*
C. V. Brown	*University of Stirling*
G. Caire	*University of Paris*
A. G. Carruthers	*Department of Employment*
R. Churnside	*Manpower Services Commission*
M. J. Clayton	*HM Treasury*
T. R. Dalton	*University of Northern Illinois*
N. H. W. Davis	*Department of Employment*
J. Dixon	*Department of Employment*
J. H. Drèze	*University of Louvain*
W. Driehuis	*University of Amsterdam*
R. Droitsch	*US Department of Labour*
P. Elias	*University of Warwick*
G. Evans	*Manpower Services Commission*
N. Gardner	*Department of Employment*
K. W. Glaister	*Department of Employment*
C. A. Greenhalgh	*University of Southampton*
J. W. Grice	*HM Treasury*
R. Gronau	*Hebrew University, Jerusalem*
H. I. Grossman	*Brown University*
W. Hamovitch	*University of New York*
T. Hazledine	*Economic Council Canada*
B. Henry	*National Institute of Economic and Social Research*
J. Hibberd	*HM Treasury*
G. Holtham	*OECD*
Z. Hornstein	*Department of Employment*
G. R. Horton	*HM Treasury*
G. Hutchinson	*Queen Mary College, London*
H. Joshi	*London School of Hygiene and Tropical Medicine*
W. Keegan	*Observer Newspaper*
M. Killingsworth	*Rutgers University, New Jersey*
R. J. Lasko	*Manpower Services Commission*
P. R. G. Layard	*London School of Economics*
C. S. Leicester	*IMS, University of Sussex*

D. G. Leslie	*University of Manchester*
R. M. Lindley	*University of Warwick*
A. K. Macleod	*Manpower Services Commission*
A. Maddison	*OECD*
K. Mayhew	*Pembroke College, Oxford*
B. J. McCormick	*University of Sheffield*
B. Meriaux	*University of Grenoble*
D. A. Metcalf	*University of Kent*
A. J. Meyrick	*HM Treasury*
G. Mizon	*University of Southampton*
P. Morgan	*Department of Employment*
S. Nickell	*London School of Economics*
D. G. Connor	*Manpower Services Commission*
W. Y. Oi	*University of Rochester, New York*
J. A. Peat	*Manpower Services Commission*
P. Peisa	*University of Helsinki*
J. Pen	*University of Groningen*
J. H. Pencavel	*Stanford University, California*
G. Penrice	*Department of Employment*
W. Peterson	*DAE, University of Cambridge*
C. Phillips	*London School of Economics*
M. Pokorny	*Civil Service College*
G. L. Reid	*Manpower Services Commission*
D. Robinson	*Magdalen College, Oxford*
B. E. Rodmell	*Manpower Services Commission*
H. Rosen	*Princeton University*
M. C. Rout	*Department of Employment*
R. J. Ruffell	*University of Stirling*
A. Sharot	*Audits of Great Britain*
J. R. Shepherd	*HM Treasury*
R. E. Smith	*National Commission for Manpower Policy, Washington DC*
S. D. Smith	*Manpower Services Commission*
V. H. Stamler	*HM Treasury*
D. Stanton	*Department of Employment*
W. Steinle	*Commission of the European Communities*
N. Stern	*University of Warwick*
G. Stewart	*Manpower Services Commission*
M. Stewart	*University of Warwick*
J. Sutton	*London School of Economics*
R. J. Tarling	*DAE, Cambridge*
J. A. Tarsh	*Department of Employment*
J. Taylor	*University of Lancaster*
A. P. Thirwall	*University of Kent*
G. Tintner	*University of Vienna*
D. Todd	*HM Treasury*
R. Turvey	*International Labour Office, Geneva*

A. B. Tylecote	*University of Sheffield*
D. T. Ulph	*University College, London*
P. Warburton	*London Business School*
A. Webb	*Manpower Services Commission*
Y. Weiss	*University of Tel Aviv*
H. Wills	*London School of Economics*
R. Wilson	*University of Warwick*

Some Problems in Analysing the Labour Market*

Moray Clayton
Her Majesty's Treasury

Zmira Hornstein
Department of Employment

*A large number of people in the Treasury, the Department of Employment and the Manpower Services Commission have helped with the construction of this paper. In particular, we wish to thank Geoff Meen, Marion Rout and Alfred Webb.

SOME PROBLEMS IN ANALYSING THE LABOUR MARKET

Introduction

An important aspect of the work of government economists, particularly those in the Department of Employment, the Manpower Services Commission and the Treasury, is analysis of the labour market. Whatever the emphasis of economic policy it is necessary to form a broad view of the prospects for employment and unemployment in the short and medium term and to consider the likely impact of possible policy changes on these quantities.

It is not easy to understand in retrospect, let alone to forecast, many of the recent changes in the labour market, some of which are shown in Figure 1. Movements in labour supply and in productivity growth are some of the most obvious examples of where analysis and forecasts have been plainly defective. This conference has been set up to throw light on these problems, with the hope that through discussions, both formal and informal, recognizable progress will be made.

The object of this paper is to outline the approaches currently being used or considered by government economists in their work on these labour market aggregates and to set out the problems encountered. The paper falls into three parts, labour supply, employment and unemployment. Within each of these sections there is a description of current procedures and an outline of research that has been done or considered by government economists. In some areas there are fairly detailed results to report; in others there is simply an assessment of the relevant literature. Each section concludes with a short list of problems which may be taken up in discussion here while some aspects will be developed in subsequent sessions.

Labour supply

The last fifty years have resulted in significant changes in the composition of the labour force[1], the most noticeable being the rise in the number of married women. In 1921 there were less than three quarters of a million married women in the labour force; in 1975 there were almost nine times as many, making up 25% of the labour force. This compares with an increase in the total labour force of 6 million to approximately 25½ million in the same period. While the proportion of the population in the labour force has changed only slightly, participation rates of married women have increased sharply.

Long-term projections

The Department of Employment's projections extrapolate trends in activity

[1]Definitions, descriptions and sources are discussed fully in the appendix.

Table 1: Employment, Unemployment, Labour supply and Output; 1969–78 (annual averages)

	Employment						Unemploy-ment[1]	Labour supply	GDP[2]
	Manufacturing		Private non-manufacturing		Non-trading Public				
	000's	%	000's	%	000's	%	Total 000's	000's	000's	1975 = 100
1969	8391	34	12394	50	3823	15	24831	567	25940	91·9
1970	8364	34	12288	50	4130	15	24745	602	24992	93·5
1971	8090	33	12020	49	4259	17	24341	756	25060	94·8
1972	7820	32	12240	50	4417	18	24480	855	25449	97·7
1973	7864	32	12555	50	4547	18	24968	611	25474	103·8
1974	7882	32	12456	50	4720	19	25062	606	25498	101·9
1975	7524	30	12452	50	4938	20	24920	929	25859	100·0
1976	7291	29	12477	50	5002	20	24780	1273	26162	101·6
1977	7354	30	12497	50	4994	20	24858	1378	26433	103·0
1978	7311	29	12576	51	5024	20	24926	1376	26524	105·3

[1] Registered unemployment
[2] Excluding NS Oil

Source: CSO, Department of Employment

Fig 1(a) Labour Supply, Employment, Unemployment and Output, 1969–78

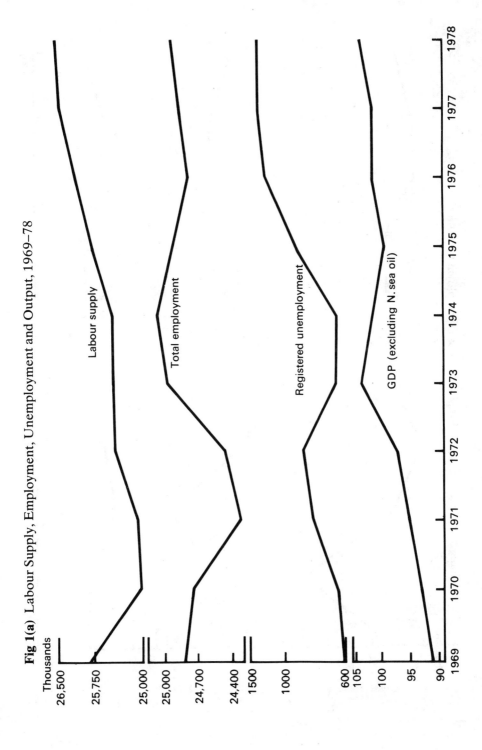

Fig 1(b)   Changes in Labour Supply, Employment & Unemployment: 1969–1978

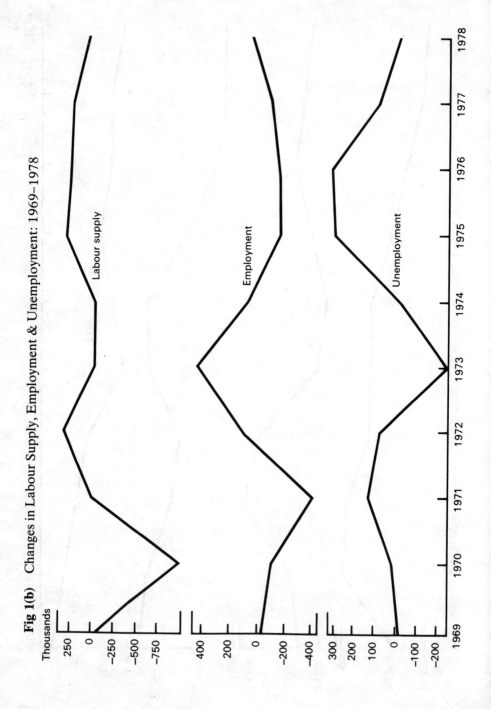

rates calculated from Censuses of Population and Household Surveys. The most recent projections (see Department of Employment, 1977) use data from the 1961, 1966 and 1971 Censuses and the 1975 EEC Labour Force Survey to form the basis of a trend which is projected up to 15 years ahead. Wherever possible the projections take account of research which sheds light on factors influencing the labour force behaviour of different groups of people.

The Department's projections seek to identify longer term trends and do not attempt to take account of the effects of changes in the pressure of demand on the supply of labour. For short-term forecasting and policy analysis these effects must be considered. One approach is the formal model of participation rates recently developed in the Treasury.

Modelling the labour supply decision

There has been a growing recognition of the need to formalize the account taken of the supply side of the economy and in particular to reflect interdependencies between labour supply and other economic variables. Hence work has been undertaken to endogenise the labour supply.

Treasury research has closely followed that of Greenhalgh [1977] and extended her analysis of married women to unmarried women and to males. Because of the lack of time series observations on participation rates, the model utilises regional participation rate data from the 1971 Census of Population to estimate the following equation (derived from the neo-classical income-leisure model), for males, married women and unmarried women, disaggregated by age band.

$$PR = K + \sum_{i=0}^{M} a_i \left[\frac{WM\,(1-MATR)}{CED} \right]_{-i} + \sum_{i=0}^{N} b_i \left[\frac{WF\,(1-FATR)}{CED} \right]_{-i}$$

$$+ \sum_{i=0}^{M} a_i \left(\frac{H}{CED} \right) + \sum_{i=0}^{Q} d_i U_{-i} + \sum_{i=0}^{R} a_i FAM_{-i} + e$$

PR = %age participation rate
WM = hourly wage rate for men
WF = hourly wage rate for women
MATR = average tax rate faced by men
FATR = average tax rate faced by women
CED = consumers' expenditure deflator
H = indicator of nominal wealth (%age of households with exclusive use of hot water, fixed bath and inside wc)
U = unemployment rate
FAM = family structure variable

Full details of the model are given in Grice [1978].

Results and projections

Results from the model are in many respects in line with those of other researchers; for a review see Joshi [1979]. The most satisfactory results are those for married women with only a limited degree of success for males and unmarried females. Overall, the strongest effects come from the real wealth term.

At times of high rates of inflation, the real value of household wealth falls rapidly. One response noted during the seventies has been an increase in the savings ratio as households attempt to restore their real wealth. Another response may be an increase in the number of people willing to work. Grice finds a significant (negative) effect on labour supply from changes in real wealth. But the nature of the indicator of nominal wealth used means that this result must be seen as suggestive rather than definite. This caveat is particularly important when considering the effects on the labour supply of changes in real wealth over time. Partly for these reasons and partly because emphasis is on time series analysis considerable weight is still attached to the DE projections in forecasting and policy analysis.

In forecasts of the labour supply the DE projections are used as a bench-mark, the labour supply model being used to illustrate arguments for adjustments arising from the economic prospects forecast. The relative weight given to each source is reversed in policy analysis particularly when emphasis is on the short term effects. Here the model helps formalise thinking about the effects of eg changes in the pressure of demand on the supply of labour although it does not as yet yield estimates that bear a great deal of weight. 'Feasibility constraints' are provided by the underlying characteristics of the labour force on which DE's projections concentrate.

The male labour force can be divided, roughly, into three age groups with distinct participation rate patterns. For *men* in the prime age-groups (25–54 years) participation rates are high and relatively stable, although there has been a slow but discernible decline since about 1960. For these age-groups, a simple extrapolation yields a further small decline which is constrained to level off in the early 1980's. Among *older workers,* there has been a long run decline in activity rates reflecting the spread of occupational pension schemes and the trends to earlier retirement. This trend is projected to continue. In the last four years the decline has been faster due perhaps to cyclical effects.

For *young men* (those aged 16–24) very nearly all are either in the labour force or in full-time education. The proportion outside these categories is assumed to remain constant and labour force participation may be estimated as the complement to projections of education participation rates prepared by the Department of Education. At present, students in full-time education are excluded from the labour force whether or not they are working. Some may, in the course of the year, contribute as many hours as people counted as fully economically active.

Given these fairly strong trends in male participation rates it is not surprising that, while the model found some evidence of a positive response in participation rates to movements in the own wage rate the response was fairly small, suggesting that among men, the positive substitution effect was almost entirely offset by the negative income effect.

Married women, on the other hand, seem to be much more responsive to economic stimuli. Estimation results show the substitution effect dominated the income effect for each age band and had an elasticity of between a half and unity. Married women's participation rates are also significantly influenced by men's wage rates (a negative coefficient because of the unambiguous income effect), the level of unemployment and the level of real wealth. In principle the unemployment effect may be positive or negative. The latter possibility arises from a discouraged worker effect, as the prospects of securing a job decrease with high levels of unemployment. The former influence stems from the income effect of the husband losing his job. In practice the discouraged worker effect is found to be the more important.

It should be noted that disaggregation by marital status of women proxies child-rearing patterns and family structure which would be more appropriate differentiating factors. The proxy variable is becoming a weaker explanatory factor in the determination of women's labour force behaviour than it was in the past. Women now are unlikely to leave the labour force on marriage, generally continuing to work until the birth of their first child. They may also return to work sooner on completion of their families (or between births) than in the past. An increasing number of single parents has blurred the distinction, in terms of participation rates, between married and unmarried women re-emphasising the need for disaggregation by family structure.

The Department of Employment's projections of the participation rates of married women, while based partly on the factors isolated in the model, are also based on a cohort study (see Department of Employment, 1974) which used information from the count of National Insurance Cards—a source no longer available to us. This material has been up-dated from the EEC Labour Force Survey. Together these lead to an assumption that trend growth in participation rates in the main child-bearing age-groups will abate following the recent up-turn in the birth-rate[2].

Estimation results on participation rates of *unmarried women* were disappointing. Trends are also difficult to interpret as the structure of the group (which includes single, divorced and widowed women) is changing, with a higher proportion of divorced women and single parents than in the past. The labour force behaviour of these different groups varies significantly. However, the net effect has been a decline in participation rates. Their future course will depend, inter alia, on variation in the age of marriage and in divorce rates.

Some directions for improvements

The primary use of a model of the labour supply is for forecasting and policy analysis. As the labour supply model described above has been estimated from cross section data this presents a number of problems. In its present form the model does not say anything about the dynamics of the response of labour

---

[2]This is a gross over-simplification if child-bearing itself is determined by economic factors. The problem of co-determination of family and labour supply decisions is being researched both in the US and in Britain but the development of operational models is at an early stage.

supply to economic changes and fairly arbitrary lag structures have been imposed. Another limitation is in quantifying the impact of tax changes. At any point in time, differences in marginal and average tax rates are fairly small across the country; hence from a cross section model one cannot test the response of labour supply to changes in marginal tax rates or whether the response is different to that from changes in the wage rate. Further, the impact of taxation needs to be looked at in a detailed way as the effects differ between different groups of the population and must take into account the full range of state benefits. There is a great deal of scope for work in these areas and results could have an important bearing on policy.

The trend projections of labour supply could be greatly improved by disaggregation by family structure rather than by marital status. The Office of Population Censuses and Surveys (OPCS) are currently developing a model for population projections based on family formation which could allow a refinement of current methodology. A more ambitious possibility might be the development of a flow model for women's labour force behaviour. Researchers at the University of Warwick are developing a transition matrix of flows into and out of the labour force and between employed and unemployed states within the labour force. Disaggregation by family structure might allow explicit account to be taken of projected birth trends and the decision to return to work may be found to be sensitive to economic factors. Some of the necessary data are available from the OPCS Family Formation Survey and more may be available from the proposed survey of Women in Employment. However lack of data may constrain work along these lines.

Employment

Total employment in the UK has increased only slightly over the last 10 years (Figure 1(a)) but its distribution among sectors of the economy has changed markedly. In the manufacturing sector employment has fallen 13% from its 1969 level while employment in the private non-manufacturing sector increased only slightly. Non-trading public sector employment increased substantially; details are set out in table 1. While these changes are matched by shifts in the pattern of demand, the relation between changes in demand and changes in employment appears to have altered significantly, forcing a reconsideration of the simple model of employment now used.

This section outlines the basis for current practice and then considers two areas still very much at the research stage, models of the simultaneous demand for factors of production and models of non clearing markets. Comments on productivity and technical change and an observation on the possibility of modelling employment in the non-manufacturing sector complete the section.

Employment-output relationships

Most work on the employment-output relationship is confined to that for manufacturing industries as there is data at a disaggregated level and also data

18

on hours worked. For the UK the best known work is that of Brechling [1965], Ball and St Cyr [1966] and Hart and Sharot [1978]. Henry has recent work along similar lines [1978]. These authors derive an employment function[3] by minimising a cost of labour function subject to a production function, with output given. There are differences in the specification of the cost of labour, particularly of adjustment costs, and in the adjustment process. Ball and St Cyr and Brechling focus on the basic wage rate and on the overtime rate; hence costs per hour worked will be minimised when normal hours are worked, irrespective of the level of output. Adjustment of employment to output is by an imposed simple partial adjustment mechanism.

This is the basis of the Treasury model equations. Employment—number of persons employed—is modelled for five sectors; private manufacturing industry, private non-manufacturing industry, nationalised industries, public sector employment and the North Sea oil sector. The biggest problems are in the private sector which accounts for about 70% of total employment. The private sector equations relate numbers employed to a lagged distribution of current and past output of the appropriate sector and to a time trend reflecting technical progress[4]. The time trends and long run elasticities used are not freely estimated, but have been imposed on the basis of plausibility subject to reasonable consistency with recent experience.

While this simple functional form has been used for some time it is well known that estimated coefficients are unstable particularly over the recent past. Equations estimated up to 1974 substantially under-estimate employment in both manufacturing and non-manufacturing industry in the post-sample period. This has been interpreted as a marked fall in underlying productivity growth—a feature common to industrial countries in this period—and qualitatively ascribed to the fall of investment and to slow/no output growth.

Is part of the explanation a fall in hours of work? Probably not. It is thought that changes in normal (or standard)[5] hours of work are not fully reflected in changes in actual hours as more overtime will tend to be worked and output per man-hour may also rise. Such hypotheses are difficult to test formally as normal hours have changed at infrequent and irregular intervals (the last hours reduction in the UK took place in the mid-1960s). Casual empiricism and the few econometric studies that have examined this question suggest that the size of these productivity and overtime offsets may be quite large. However it may be dangerous to apply estimates of this kind to future changes in normal hours; any analysis would need to take account of the circumstances of the time and, in particular, of labour market conditions.

Changes in hours worked are not formally allowed for in the Treasury model of employment. However, changes in the level of output above or below trend

---

[3] Most authors focus on actual employment (numbers of hours) but refer to labour demand. Muellbauer points out that if these are labour demand functions then unsatisfied demand—which might be represented by vacancies—should be considered.

[4] In the last few years the impact of selective employment measures on employment has been assessed separately. Some allowances should be made for these effects when post 1974 data is used.

[5] Normal weekly hours are those laid down for manual workers in national collective agreements and statutory wage orders. Hours worked in excess of normal hours are recorded as overtime.

19

are assumed to affect the level of average weekly earnings; this is based on an implicit relationship between changes in activity and the levels of short-time and overtime working.

Hart and Sharot have tried to formalise this relationship. They extend labour costs to cover hiring and firing costs (so that it may be cheaper to work some overtime than hire additional workers) and—in a development of ideas advanced by Brechling—postulate that hours adjust to changes in output more quickly than numbers employed and that utilisation of labour returns—relatively slowly—to a 'normal' level by changing employment. Their results support these hypotheses but their model, estimated up to 1972(3), is not stable over subsequent years. Morgan [1979] provides a concise survey of these models.

The arguments of the preceding paragraphs, and production functions that include 'hours worked' as well as 'numbers employed', require a measure of *effective* hours. While there is quite a lot of data on hours worked, there is no measure of effective hours. Short run labour demand functions in terms of hours raise a further problem for the supply side. If short-run functions model hours of work demanded it may be necessary to model labour supply in hours, not only in numbers of persons. At present there is no data on hours that would be available for work at various wage rates.

Hazledine [1978] has an alternative approach. He emphasises the desired levels to which employment and hours adjust and constructs his model in terms of deviations from these desired levels. However, these levels are simply taken as trends through past peaks and so cannot explain deviations from these trends such as have been experienced in the last few years. Nevertheless employment functions of this sort are a reasonable description of recent data and are used in the disaggregated model of the Manpower Research Group at the University of Warwick.

Modelling the simultaneous demand for factors of production

All the models just described ignore the availability of other factors. Models of simultaneous demands for factors of production tackle this lacuna. Optimal long run equilibrium demands for inputs are derived by minimising a cost function constrained by a production function and accounting identities. The short run dynamics of most models are ad hoc but utilisation rates of factors are considered. The approach of deriving demand for inputs simultaneously is intellectually satisfying and 'elegant'. Given output and relative prices equilibrium demands for various inputs are derived from a constrained optimizing framework and imply cross equation restrictions. Use of these restrictions helps identify basic parameters, eg of the production function; and also ensure consistency in the firm's actions in the labour and capital markets. In some respects the model is very flexible, allowing consideration of a large number of inputs and their utilisation levels and also a choice in the specification of technology.

There are drawbacks of two sorts, conceptual and practical. Conceptually the firm is constrained to the production function frontier at all times. This is not always consistent with optimal behaviour when there are costs of adjustments; nor is it consistent with the observation that firms do at times hoard labour and pay for more hours than are actually worked. Most available models do not explicitly include adjustment costs and rely heavily on long run equilibrium conditions at the expense of formulating short run behaviour in a more realistic fashion. Realism is also lost in the general assumption that output and prices are exogenous. Even at the level of the firm in perfect competition it can be argued e.g. Fair [1971], that, with the possibility of holding inventories, output is a decision variable. In macro markets and markets in imperfect competition it is even clearer that both output and prices are endogenous and that supply constraints may also be important.

At a high level of aggregation the great reliance on the production function constraint may be a serious weakness of this approach, since the existence of such a function even in an approximate form is unlikely under conditions of varying relative factor costs; [1969, p. 575].

Some of these problems are being faced in the models that try to integrate the optimal flexible accelerator methodology used in studies of investment behaviour (Lucas 1967, Treadway 1974) with the production function restriction approach to the simultaneous demand for inputs (Berndt et. al. 1977, Faurot 1978, Tinsley 1971). Such studies allow explicitly for the cost of adjusting quasi-fixed factors and derive optimal long run demands as well as an optimal path to equilibrium. The models are exceedingly complicated, quite restricted in the choice of production function and cost function and so far have proved tractable only for one quasi-fixed factor, usually capital.

In application the overwhelming drawbacks of estimating models of simultaneous demand are data requirements, the need for sophisticated estimation techniques and the intractability of the more general models. The requirements of even the simpler models include data on stocks of capital and labour and, in most cases, their level of utilisation and the relative user costs of inputs. More realistic models also require measures of overhead costs, adjustment costs and a discounting rate. These are considerable requirements and, though approximations can be used e.g. a functional form for adjustment costs, they cannot be met for the UK.

To make the most of models of the simultaneous derivation of demands, estimation should be by simultaneous methods utilising cross equation restrictions. Such methods are available and have been used, but the larger models are usually non-linear and difficult to estimate.

Results of estimation are interesting but not very successful in establishing some of the basic parameters. Nadiri and Rosen [1969] used OLS estimation to derive demands for manufacturing employment, capital, hours and capacity utilisation. They drew attention to the varying speeds of adjustments, with hours and capacity utilisation changing rapidly, employment adjusting more slowly and capital stocks very slowly. The quasi-fixed property of employment was validated by the data. Cross equation restrictions were not imposed and did not generally hold, though increasing returns to scales of similar magnitude were obtained in both the demand for employment and for capital. The relative cost of labour to capital had the wrong sign in the employment function.

21

The identical model was applied to UK data by Briscoe and Peel [1975] and by Smith [1978]. The results were disappointing. In the Briscoe and Peel study coefficients are not well defined, the patterns of speeds of adjustments are not intuitively sensible and the effect of relative factor costs on the demand for capital is perverse. Smith's estimates show similar weaknesses. It is only fair to say that the unsatisfactory results are at least as much due to unsatisfactory data as to the underlying assumptions of the model. Coen and Hickman's [1970] study concentrated on applying the cross equations restriction on long run demand for employment and capital in the US private non-residential sector. Their results are quite promising but the model is very simple.

For use in forecasting and policy analysis this approach to modelling the demand for labour and capital appears to have some serious faults. These include the great reliance on constrained optimisation by a production function which is not well defined in the aggregate and other restrictions which cannot be clearly formulated. Imposing restrictions derived in such a manner on equations used for short run forecasting is unrealistic. However, much insight on the connection among different sections of a model, as well as indications on adjustment mechanisms, can be gained from the theoretical developments and applications of simultaneous models. More work is needed on costs of adjustments and models with more than one quasi-fixed factor. If the primary aim of a model is to explain short run changes in macro variables then there is a need to concentrate on costs of adjustment, including costs of holding inventories. This will have the effect of endogenizing the determination of output.

Non clearing models of the labour market[6]

In both the short run models and the simultaneous models of factor demands discussed above supply restrictions are ignored; while firms are not always in equilibrium their movement to equilibrium is constrained only by adjustment costs and not by restrictions on the availability of inputs per se. Non clearing models and/or disequilibrium models of the labour market explicitly recognise these restrictions.

The approach to modelling the labour market as a non clearing market is, unlike other models which are based on the firm's and individual's behaviour, essentially macro in nature. It takes on board the observation that much of the time there is involuntary unemployment and unfilled vacancies which indicate that the market does not clear in the short or possibly even in the long run. The theoretical background for this configuration of the labour market has a long

[6] There is some disagreement about the terminology applying to non-clearing markets. It is generally agreed that a non clearing market is not in Walrasian equilibrium (where prices are set to equate quantities demanded and supplied), although the market can be considered to be in equilibrium in the sense that, given prices, the preferred actions of economic agents are mutually compatible, Hahn [1979]. So while these models are often referred to, particularly by econometricians as 'disequilibrium models', e.g. Rosen and Quandt [1978], others refer to them as 'equilibrium models' or 'SR equilibrium models' e.g. Malinvaud [1977]. The terminology used depends upon the view taken of the underlying causes of excess demand and supply, and on whether there is a long run tendency to, or optimal adjustment process which will lead to, Walrasian equilibrium and a cleared market.

history including Keynes' 'sticky wages' and deficient demand, as well as more recent theories developed by Barro and Grossman [1971] and Malinvaud [1977] which incorporate quantity restrictions in the labour and product markets. Rationing theory is one of the tools used to pin this macro theory to some underlying micro behaviour.

If what characterizes the labour market is that observed states are either demand or supply restricted then observations have to be divided into those which lie on the supply curve and those on the demand curve. To do this some hypothesis is needed on a market signal of excess demand or supply. The model in its simplest form includes (i) a demand schedule (ii) a supply schedule (iii) a rationing rule e.g. $Q = \min$ (Q demand, Q supply) and in most cases (iv) a signalling function, usually a real wage formation equation stating that, if after removing the effects of other exogenous variables, $\Delta W_t > O$ the market is in excess demand (supply restricted), and when $\Delta W_t < O$ the market is in excess supply (demand restricted). This wage formation equation assumes a long run tendency to Walrasian equilibrium. Estimation is complicated (see for example Bowden 1978, Fair and Jaffee 1972) and depends on the stochastic specifications of the four equations.

Two applications to the labour market are those by Rosen and Quandt and Muellbauer. Rosen and Quandt [1978] estimated a four equation model along the lines described above using annual data on US total employment 1930–73. The results indicated that the speed of adjustment of wages is slow, strengthening the case for a non clearing market model, but the implied time series of 'excess demand' was not reasonable nor were some of the estimated parameters. An asymptotic test of the disequilibrium model compared to a similar model but with immediate wage adjustment rejected the latter. The model used is, by the authors' admission, crude and further work is needed on the specification and on estimation methods.

Muellbauer and Winter [1978, 1979] under commission to the MSC and HM Treasury are working on a non clearing market model of the UK manufacturing sector. They consider a large number of markets for labour differentiated by skill, location, etc, and distributed about an average which measures excess demand or supply. The indicator of the state of the market relates to direct measures of unemployment and vacancies. In theory, unemployment is a sign of excess supply and vacancies of excess demand for labour. Results are still very tentative and marred by the poor match between *measured* vacancies and unemployment and the *theoretical* concepts.

Non-clearing market models are one possible way of describing a market that yields simultaneous observations of unemployment and vacancies. It is not the only way. Other models, such as models of demand for labour not restricted by supply but taking account of adjustment costs and fixed proportions technologies in the short run also describe disequilibrium in the sense that desired demand is not achieved. It may be that in addition there are also at times supply restrictions. Only further work in this area will show if such supply restrictions are important.

There is a certain attractiveness to the macro model builder in an approach which tackles macro variables directly and concentrates it seems on the causes

23

of unemployment. But in fact the model does not spell out the *causes* of (real or nominal?) wage rigidity and therefore does not give much insight into policy issues.

Productivity and technical progress

The foregoing models analyse labour demand in an essentially static framework. Technical progress is usually incorporated as a simple exponential time trend. While this may be acceptable for short-term projections, longer periods and policy analysis require a more integrated framework, especially in the light of the recent growth in productivity which has averaged less than 1% per annum since 1973, compared to 2½% per annum over the sixties and early seventies; table 2 and figure 2. This fall in productivity growth does not appear to be explicable in terms of either the dynamics of the response of employment demand to changes in the product market, or of a shift along a conventional neo-classical production function.

The neglect of forces shaping productivity growth is puzzling given the central role it plays in determining the natural rate of growth in growth models. There is a substantial literature on the economic factors determining the role of innovation and adoption of new techniques, but most of the empirical work is of the case-study or international cross-section kind and has proved particularly difficult to incorporate into a time series labour demand function. One of the few areas where an attempt has been made is in the field of vintage models which, building on the pioneering work of Salter [1966], highlight the importance of investment and embodied technical progress. Mizon [1974] and Malcolmson and Prior [1979] have applied such models to the determination of output, while Hutton, Stamler and Stern [1978] have estimated a similar model to describe manufacturing employment. However, most applications require drastic simplifying assumptions to make them tractable and highly sophisticated econometric techniques in estimation, which has so far prevented them providing the insights into technical change that might be hoped for.

An extension of the vintage approach was provided by Kaldor [1966] who argued that the internationally observed correlation between productivity growth and output growth could be explained by the presence of embodied technical progress and dynamic economies of scale, wherein rapidly growing firms had both more opportunity and more incentive to develop new techniques and utilize existing equipment more efficiently. Later writers, particularly Rowthorn [1975], have criticised the original work of Kaldor, and it is clear that there is a major difference in opinion in the direction of causality between output growth and productivity growth. In Rowthorn's view labour supply and productivity are the exogenous variables whereas for Kaldor output is given by demand conditions. The existing empirical work does not enable a conclusive verdict to be given, but the generally observed less than unity elasticity of changes in employment to changes in output and the empirical work of Brechling and O'Brien [1967] who in a study of a number of national employment functions found a correlation between the productivity trend and output growth, provide some tentative support for the Kaldorian thesis.

Table 2: Employment, Output and Output per Head; 1969–78 (indices, 1975 = 100)

	Manufacturing			Private Non-Manufacturing			Whole Economy [1]		
	Employ-ment	Output	Output per head	Employ-ment	Output	Output per head	Employ-ment	Output	Output per head
1969	111·5	98·4	88·2	99·5	89·2	89·6	99·6	91·9	92·3
1970	111·2	98·7	88·8	98·7	93·6	94·8	99·3	93·5	94·2
1971	107·5	97·6	90·8	96·5	96·4	99·9	97·7	94·8	97·0
1972	103·9	100·0	96·2	98·3	98·3	100·0	98·2	97·7	99·5
1973	104·5	109·1	104·4	100·8	104·0	103·2	100·2	103·8	103·6
1974	104·8	107·3	102·4	100·0	101·5	101·5	100·6	101·9	101·3
1975	100·0	100·0	100·0	100·0	100·0	100·0	100·0	100·0	100·0
1976	97·0	102·1	105·4	100·2	100·7	100·5	99·4	101·6	102·2
1977	97·7	103·8	106·2	100·4	102·4	102·0	99·8	103·0	103·2
1978	97·2	104·2	107·2	101·0	106·2	105·1	100·2	105·3	105·1

[1] Excluding NS Oil.

Source: CSO, Department of Employment.

25

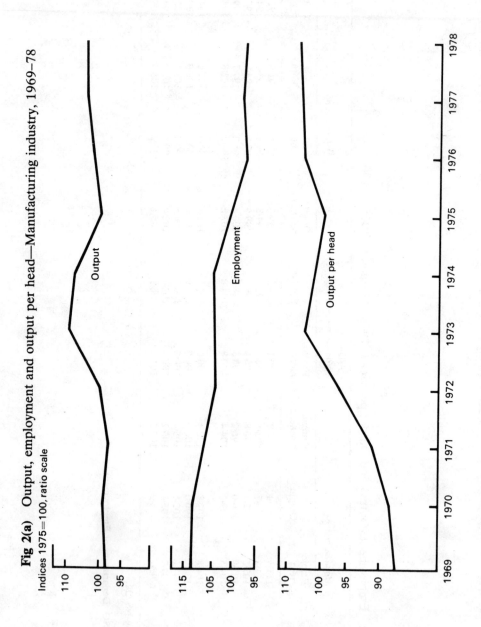

Fig 2(a) Output, employment and output per head—Manufacturing industry, 1969–78
Indices 1975=100, ratio scale

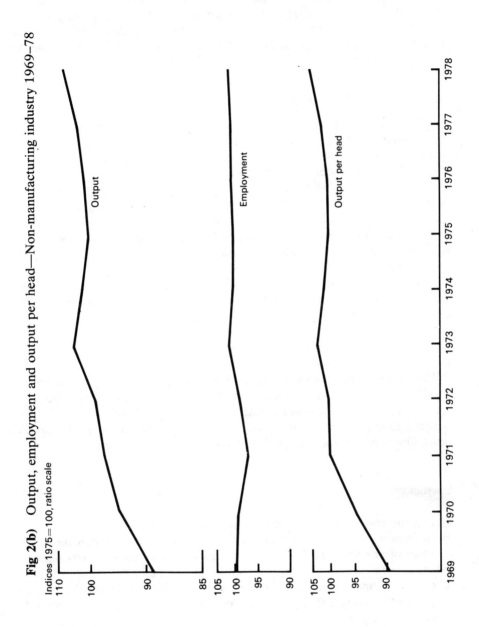

Fig 2(b) Output, employment and output per head—Non-manufacturing industry 1969–78

Indices 1975=100, ratio scale

Aside from these studies there seems to have been little attempt to incorporate the economic factors determining technical progress into the conventional time series employment function. Any work which attempted to shed light on such factors as the importance of profitability in affecting the rate of adoption of new techniques, the role of factor prices in determining the bias of technical progress, and the effect of tax changes on work effort would be particularly welcome.

Modelling employment in non-manufacturing industries

Empirical work on all of these models is confined to employment in manufacturing industry, which now accounts for only just over one third of UK private sector employment. The bulk of employment is in a heterogeneous collection of non-manufacturing industries—agriculture, construction, professional services etc—which have experienced a significant increase in the proportion of women and perhaps part-timers in their work-force. Approximately two million self employed persons are also included in this sector.

Availability of data severely restricts the range of models which may be used for estimating labour demand functions for this sector and the degree of disaggregation possible. In some industries—e.g. services—it may be reasonable at a theoretical level to ignore capital; in others—e.g. construction—the derived demand for output of the industry (housing etc) may have to be explicitly modelled so that non-clearing market theories may be appropriate. For the self employed data is very scarce, their number being accurately determined only at a full Census of Population. Recent surveys have given widely divergent counts.

There are no indications that any achievable disaggregation provides a key to a well behaved employment-output relationship in this sector. It may be that, even with major advances in the manufacturing sector, it will be necessary to continue to impose relationships which reflect (unverifiable) a priori propositions. Obviously verified propositions would be most welcome.

Unemployment

During the recent recession unemployment[7] in the UK rose sharply not so much from an increase in flows onto the register as from an increase in the duration of unemployment. During the past two years the numbers unemployed have fallen steadily, on a month to month basis. (This movement is hidden by the annual averages of table 1 and figure 1.) As the rate of growth of output and employment during this time was low and trend of the monthly figures was puzzling.

The resolution of the puzzle depends partly on the way in which unemployment is analysed. One way is to look at unemployment as a residual, simply as the difference between the number of people in the labour force and those in employment. In the UK attention is focussed on the number of people

[7] Definitions and sources are given in the Appendix.

registered as unemployed; as not all the unemployed register it is also necessary to consider the registration rate. Alternatively, unemployment may be modelled directly.

The Treasury model adopts the residual approach; total unemployment is calculated as the difference between the labour supply and total employment i.e. as the difference between two large aggregates[8]. Registration behaviour is modelled by a logistic curve with a marginal registration rate of between 30–80%, the upper rate applying when registered unemployment rises above 1.0 million. This is an approximation to known behaviour but not one that has been tested directly. Unemployment among school leavers is assessed separately by applying a decay rate that varies with the level of registered adult unemployment to the stock of school leavers.

Forecasts using this fairly crude framework have not performed well in recent years. This is due less to poor specification of registration behaviour than to the difficulties in modelling employment and labour supply which have been discussed above. However those who have adopted the alternative approach of modelling unemployment directly have not found more robust relationships and a study of registration behaviour did not provide an improvement on the logistic curve now used.

Modelling unemployment directly

Okun's law provides a framework for direct estimation of the unemployment rate, a framework extended by Friedman and Wachter [1974]. In the UK work in this vein has focussed on the impact of unemployment benefits on the numbers registered as unemployed. Maki and Spindler [1975][9] argue that the rate of registered unemployment is primarily determined by the ratio of unemployment benefits to income while in work and by the deviation of GDP from its trend. This is a cursory treatment of the demand side and avoids the question of determining *total* unemployment and the subsequent decision of whether to register or not. (It seems quite reasonable to suggest that what Maki and Spindler observe is an increasing willingness to register as unemployed when benefits increase rather than an increasing willingness to become unemployed[10]) Morley [1974] has a different focus relating registered unemployment to the proportion of company and public corporation profits in GNP. A regression on quarterly data for 1970(1)–77(4) has a high R^2 but a large standard error and strong serial correlation. This probably reflects the weakness of this approach.

While it is possible to model separately each of labour supply, total in employment and registered unemployed, the causality surely runs from labour supply and demand decisions to unemployment. Hence it is preferable to

---

[8] The impact of selective employment measures designed to reduce unemployment directly is assessed separately. The measures were discussed at a joint US Department of Labour/Manpower Services Commission conference in May 1979.

[9] And subsequent contributions by Cubbin and Foley [1977], Sawyer [1979] and Spindler and Maki [1979].

[10] Work on this question is discussed later.

model the supply and demand decisions treating unemployment as a residual and modelling registration behaviour.

Modelling registration behaviour

The only study that explicitly models registration behaviour is Hornstein's [1977]. She derives a simple relationship between registered unemployed and total ('true') unemployment and finds this a reasonable description of cross section data; in particular the registration rate increases as total unemployment rises. But as 'true' unemployment is only observed at census dates some other relation is needed for forecasting. Hornstein suggests relating the proportion registering as unemployed to the unemployment rate i.e. to registered unemployed divided by employees in employment plus the registered unemployed. In estimation, simultaneity is overcome by using instrumental variables and reasonable results for unemployment among men are obtained.

Hornstein's model, is, she admits, inadequate when applied to female unemployment. The factors that have influenced women's participation rates may also influence their attitude to registering as unemployed and the change in NI contribution rules (discussed in the Appendix) is expected to increase married women's propensity to register as unemployed. Hence a model of registration behaviour may have to treat men, married women and unmarried women separately.

Influence of unemployment benefits

A person out of work may be eligible for a bewildering array of social security benefits and entitlements. These range from (past) earnings related benefits to (current) income supplements, free school meals for children, rent and rate rebates and so on. Most of these benefits etc. are means tested and are lost at income levels well below average. Hence marginal tax rates on 'family income' (income from employment plus benefits) may exceed 100% at relatively low levels of income, a situation described as 'the poverty trap'. Consideration of the impact of these benefits must cover their effects on the level of unemployment and also those on the propensity to register as unemployed. It is widely held that as the ratio of 'benefits to income' (the replacement ratio) rises, unemployment rises. The most careful study of this hypothesis is Nickell's [1979]. He explains the probability of leaving unemployment in any period (conditional upon being unemployed at the beginning of the period) by four sets of factors, the pertinent ones here being an indicator of pressure in local labour market and the ratio of real income while unemployed to real potential income in work. (Because of lack of data wealth and income from investments are ignored but may be assumed negligible for the unemployed.) On individuals cross section data Nickell concludes:

(a) 'that evidence against the hypothesis that the replacement ratio has no 'cet par' impact on the probability of leaving unemployment, is overwhelming';
(b) that the impact of the replacement ratio is very much lower ('more or less negligible') for those unemployed for 26 weeks or more;

(c) that the elasticity of duration with respect to the replacement ratio is between 0·6 and 1·0.

Applying the cross section results—with necessary caution—to aggregate time series data, Nickell estimates that of the 92% rise in registered unemployment during 1964/5–1973, 14% (35,000) may be attributed to the rise in benefits. The replacement ratio has not risen since 1973. A similar estimate was given in an earlier study by the Department of Employment [1976]. They suggested that the introduction of the earnings related supplement[11] contributed less than 50,000 to the increase in unemployment between 1966 and 1974.

Atkinson and Flemming [1978] make a similar, although qualitative, assessment of the impact of changes in the replacement ratio on unemployment; they point out that in November 1977 well under half of the registered unemployed were receiving work related (NI) benefits at all. They suggest that benefits act more on the duration of unemployment (rather than on prompting voluntary withdrawal of labour) and that marginal tax rates may be a particularly important aspect of the decision. For example, a man with a wife and two young children was, in November 1977, slightly better off in the 3rd–28th week of unemployment than in work earning £55 per week gross. When marginal tax rates are considered, the break-even point rises to £70 per week; because of tax allowances the 'income maximising' strategy would be a mix of employment and unemployment. While such a working of the system is considered unlikely—it is difficult to plan spells of employment and unemployment—Atkinson and Flemming feel that the disincentive effects of high marginal tax rates may lead to an increase in the duration of unemployment although such an effect would be quantitatively small. Because marginal tax rates vary greatly with the composition of the tax paying unit the effect may be difficult to capture in empirical work.

The number registered for unemployment benefit is a matter of interest for policy and planning and is an indicator of the pressure of demand in the economy. An improved understanding of recent experience would be a valuable contribution to policy analysis and forecasting. If the residual approach is favoured then work on registration behaviour can only complement work in the areas of employment and labour supply. Direct modelling of unemployment may be a shorter route but adequately specified demand and supply effects could swamp what may be important timing decisions which are influenced by the range of replacement ratios that face different groups of the working population.

Implications for micro markets

The discussion so far has treated unemployment at a macro level, disaggregated at most by sex. But the co-existence of unfilled vacancies and unemployment suggests that consideration of micro-markets may be necessary. These markets may be occupational or regional, with substitution between them depending, among other things, on the clearing of the housing

[11] The ERS is paid in addition to unemployment benefit to some registered unemployed.

market and various institutional factors. The persistence of rates of unemployment in regions of the UK well above and below the national rate, and the co-existence of skill shortages and high levels of total unemployment, suggest the need for such an approach.

Following these lines leads to a cluster of questions concerned with the existence and stability of micro labour market equilibria. For example:

(i) How responsive are labour market participants to quantity signals? How quickly do individuals move from markets in excess supply to markets in excess demand in response to information about unemployment and vacancies, and abstracting from relative earnings effects? Work in this area has mainly concerned inter-regional migration e.g. Weeden [1973] but moves within the industrial and occupational dimensions are also worth considering.

(ii) Are there institutional factors which obstruct movement to a market clearing equilibrium? Such factors could include the increasing 'professionalisation' of certain occupations which demand high academic qualifications and other entry requirements; trade union enforcement of pre-entry closed shops, opposition to 'dilution', and other 'restrictive practices'; and various contracts and regulations in the rented sector of the housing market which restrict mobility.

(iii) How responsive are participants in the various labour markets to price signals? Do individuals switch between micro markets in response to changes in earnings relativities, as well as move into and out of a wider labour market?

The work of Pissarides [1978] is suggestive. His study of 14 industrial sectors in the UK found that, between 1963 and 1975, relative wages were more rigid than relative vacancy and unemployment levels (taken as an indicator of excess demand) so that perceived job availability had been an important factor in determining flows of labour between sectors. Relative wages also play a role; a 0·5% increase in a sector's share of total employment could be obtained by a 4% increase in wages in the sector or by a 40% increase in the number of vacancies in the sector.

The implication is that rather than one market which is not clearing there is a set of markets which are failing to clear within and between themselves except in the very long run. This view has a number of implications both for the balance between macroeconomic and microeconomic employment policies and for the design of various micro measures. For if it were believed that the wage in each of the labour markets would adjust to its market clearing level fairly rapidly, then there would be little justification for micro measures, other than information improvements. However the conventional view is that non-market clearing is likely to persist, in the sense that there are groups of unemployed who would be willing to accept employment at, or even below, the level of real earnings received by similar individuals in employment. This provides the justification for micro measures, such as training and assistance to improve occupational and spatial mobility, or policies to assist those discouraged by unsuccessful job search, albeit with the caveat that these policies must be designed to cause the minimum disruption to market adjustment processes.

The non-clearing view is one which will not be left unquestioned as many of the important trends in the literature, particularly those dealing with rational expectations, job-search and contract theory either explicitly assume that all markets clear, or that they would do fairly rapidly in the absence of external interference and/or unexpected shocks, see for example Lucas [1975]. An implication that could be drawn is that all of the unemployed are engaged in 'optimal job search'. Obviously a clear-cut resolution of this question may have profound implications.

Summary

This paper has ranged over a number of topics and raised many questions. But its theme may be stated quite simply. Until the mid 1970s the labour market was a world of stable functions which, if not linear, were continuous and twice differentiable. Now things are somewhat different in ways in which we are groping towards understanding. We hope that this conference will take us further towards that goal.

APPENDIX

Labour supply projections

Labour supply is currently defined to include those in employment (whether employed or self-employed) and those out of work and actively seeking employment. More specifically, the following categories of people aged 16 and over are included:
1. Those in employment, taken in this country as paid employment, including:
    (a) those at work, i.e. those who performed some work for pay or profit during the reference week;
    (b) those with a job but not at work during the reference week for reasons of illness or injury, industrial dispute, vacation or temporary dislocation attributable to bad weather or mechanical breakdown.
2. Employers and the self-employed classified in the same way as employees.
3. Members of HM Forces.
4. Those unemployed in the reference week including:
    (a) people available for and seeking work for pay or profit whose previous contract of employment has been terminated;
    (b) people available for and seeking work for the first time or after an absence;
    (c) those available for, but temporarily prevented from seeking, work because of minor illness;
    (d) those waiting to take up a specific job.
Students in full-time education are *excluded* from the labour force in the UK although some may be employed for part of the year.

Measurement is based on self-assessment by each individual of his current situation and there are, inevitably, problems of definition at the margin where attachment to the labour force may be weak. This will apply to both those in employment for only a few hours a week and those who are seeking work of a very limited kind. Participation is measured primarily on the basis of 'in' or 'not in' the labour force, not in terms of actual hours supplied. In particular, the labour supply of some married women, pensioners and students poses problems for definition, measurement and interpretation.

The principal instruments of measurement are the decennial Censuses of Population the most recent being in 1971. A mid-term sample census was carried out in 1966. In recent years, this information has been supplemented by data from household surveys and, in particular, by that from the EEC Labour Force Survey. The UK has participated in this survey since accession and results are now available for 1973 (although these results are thought to be unreliable), 1975 and 1977. Information on similar lines is available from a small annual survey, the General Household Survey, begun in 1971. The size of sample makes this survey unsuitable as a basis for projection but it is used for corroboration of trends and it yields useful material for cross-section analysis of participation variation.

It is these sources which give information conforming with labour force definitions and coverage currently used in the UK and described in the first paragraph. These conform, broadly, with international definitions. The labour force projections are prepared on the basis of these definitions.

The Censuses of Population and labour force sample surveys cover almost all workers and potential workers and give measures which are not unduly influenced by changes in legislation and administrative practice. They allow analysis of relationships between activity variables and characteristics of the population. The majority of countries now use—or are planning to use—household surveys as the primary source of labour force information. However, in the UK, such information is available infrequently and is unsuitable, therefore, for monitoring and projecting short-run changes in labour market behaviour.

Alternative sources of information, based on surveys of establishments and on administrative records, give more frequent and up-to-date measure of parts of the labour force. The Annual Census of Employment and related quarterly sample surveys give estimates of employees in employment based on employers' pay records. This quarterly series gives an indication of recent trends in this group which forms a large proportion of the labour force. However, interpretation of these trends, in particular of small changes over time, is made difficult by incompatibility with the usual labour force definitions. The sampling frame may exclude those employers who have never operated a PAYE system; it may also exclude those employees paid in cash who do not appear on the employer's pay-roll; it specifically excludes people in domestic employment. It will count twice those people who have jobs with different employers and would include students on an employer's pay-roll.

Information on the numbers registered as unemployed with the employment services is also available on a frequent and up-to-date basis. (This measures the number of people registered on a particular day each month who are out of work and available for—usually full time—employment.) Again, this measure does not conform with that used in labour force surveys. The unemployment register includes some people not included in the labour force—in particular those with occupational pensions registering for National Insurance purposes only. It will also include some people who would be classified as 'employed' in surveys as they have had some employment in the week, although they were registed as unemployed on that day of the count. Those actively seeking work, but not registered at an Employment or Careers Office will be excluded. This latter group—the 'unregistered unemployed'—is notoriously difficult to measure. It includes a large number of married women who are ineligible for benefit and thus have less incentive to register.

Interpretation of trends in the numbers of women registered as unemployed is difficult at present. Prior to April 1977, married women (and widows) in employment were able to opt out of full participation in the NI Scheme. Under the rules, married women (and widows) could opt to pay a reduced NI contribution when in work. They then lost entitlement to a number of flat-rate national insurance benefits; in particular they were ineligible for unemployment benefit.

A particular result of the rule was that women who opted to pay at the reduced rate (estimated to be about 40% of married women in employment in 1976) and who subsequently became unemployed had no incentive to join the register though in the labour force and seeking work. However, legislation consequent to the White Paper 'Better Pensions' [Cmnd 5713] has changed this. The reduced contributions option was abolished for any women marrying on or after 6 April 1977. For those married women who had opted before April 1977 the reduced contributions could continue unless those women left employment for two full tax years. The change in rules will clearly make more unemployed married women eligible for benefits and so will encourage a greater number to register as unemployed.

For forecasting and policy analysis an agreed, if very uncertain, estimate of this change is that the proportion of married women paying the full NI rate will rise from 22% in 1976 to 36% in 1981 and perhaps to 80% in 1991.

Taken with (infrequent and survey-based) measures of the self-employed and of the numbers in HM Forces, these series (employees in employment and registered unemployed) form the 'working population'. As noted, the definitions and coverage of the constituent series mean that interpretation of movements in the working population series is difficult. Differences in concept, coverage and measures also make it difficult to reconcile this short-run measure with the less frequently measured labour force. Indeed, as at present, it appears that the trends shown by the two series are not compatible although some of the recent data is subject to revision. Similar problems have arisen in other countries.

In general, the working population measure gives more cyclically sensitive estimates than the survey-based labour supply measure. This may suggest that unregistered unemployment moves counter-cyclically. Data on this are sparse, but there is some evidence that this is the case for men.

The theme of lack of data runs through all attempts at analysis of labour force trends in this country. There is an urgent need for consistent measures of labour force variables for individuals on a frequent or continuous basis. Effort at present is consumed in attempts to reconcile incompatible sources of data, rather than in analysis of trends and changes in labour market behaviour. In theory, the General Household Survey gives quarterly estimates of labour force variables, albeit in a series of 'snapshots' rather than in the time-series form. However, the small size of the sample precludes any weight being put on this data.

REFERENCES

Atkinson, A., Flemming, J. [1978]. 'Unemployment, Social Security and Incentives'. *Midland Bank Review*, Autumn.
Ball, R. J., St. Cyr. E. B. A. [1966]. 'Short Term Employment Functions in British Manufacturing Industry' *Review of Economic Studies*, Vol. 33.
Barro, R. J., Grossman, H. I. [1971]. 'A General Disequilibrium Model of Income and Employment'. *American Economic Review*, Vol. 61.

Berndt, E. R., Fuss, M. A., Waverman, L. [1977]. 'Dynamic Models of Industrial Demand for Energy' Economic Research Group Ltd., Project 683–1.

Bowden, R. J. [1978]. 'Specification, Estimation and Inference for Models of Markets in Disequilibrium' *International Economic Review,* Vol. 19.

Brechling, F. P. R. [1965]. 'The Relationship between Output and Employment in British Manufacturing Industry' *Review of Economic Studies,* Vol. 32.

Brechling, F. P. R., O'Brien, P. [1967]. 'Short-run Employment Functions in Manufacturing Industries: An International Comparison' *Review of Economic Studies,* Vol. 34.

Briscoe, G., Peel, D. A. [1975]. 'The Specification of the Short Run Employment Function' *Oxford Bulletin of Economics and Statistics,* Vol. 37.

Coen, R. M., Hickman, B. G. [1970]. 'Constrained Joint Estimation of Factor Demand and Production Functions' *Review of Economic Studies,* Vol. 37.

Cubbin, J. S., Foley, K. [1977]. 'The Extent of Benefit-induced Unemployment in Great Britain: Some New Evidence' *Oxford Economic Papers,* Vol. 29.

Department of Employment, [1974]. 'Female Activity Rates'. *D. E. Gazette.*

Department of Employment, [1976]. 'The Changed Relationship between Unemployment and Vacancies'. *D. E. Gazette.*

Department of Employment, [1977]. 'New Projections of the Labour Force'. *D.E. Gazette.*

Fair, R. C. [1971]. 'The Joint Determination of Production, Employment and Investment Decisions'. Princeton University Research Memo 128.

Fair, R. C., Jaffee, D. M. [1972]. Methods of Estimation for Markets in Disequilibrium' *Econometrica,* Vol. 40.

Faurot, D. J. [1978]. 'Interrelated Demand for Capital and Labour in a Globally Optimal Flexible Accelerator Model' *Review of Economics and Statistics,* Vol. 60.

Fisher, F. M. [1969] 'The Existence of Aggregate Production Functions' *Econometrica,* Vol. 37.

Friedman, B. M., Wachter, M. L. [1974]. 'Unemployment: Okun's Law, Labour Force and Productivity' *Review of Economics and Statistics,* Vol. 56.

Greenhalgh, C. A. [1977]. 'A Labour Supply Function for Married Women in Great Britain' *Economica,* Vol. 44.

Grice, J. W. [1978]. 'An Operational Model of the Labour Supply' Unpublished Treasury Paper.

Hahn, F. [1979]. 'Unemployment from a Theoretical Viewpoint' Mimeo.

Hart, R. A., Sharot, T. [1978]. 'The Short Run Demand for Works and Hours: a Recursive Model' *Review of Economic Studies,* Vol. 45.

Hazledine, T. [1978]. 'New Specification for Employment and Hours Functions' *Economica,* Vol. 45.

Henry, S. G. B. [1978]. 'Employment and Hours in British Manufacturing 1963–1977' Unpublished.

Hornstein, Z. [1977]. 'The Propensity to Register when Unemployed' Unpublished.

Hutton, J., Stamler, V. H., Stern, J. [1978]. 'Employment in a Vintage Capital Model' *Government Economic Service Working Paper No. 10.*

Joshi, H. [1979]. 'The Incentive to Work; a Brief Review of Some Recent British Research' Paper presented to the Anglo-French Colloquium on Taxation and Incentives.

Kaldor, N. [1966]. 'Causes of the Slow Economic Growth of the U K' Cambridge University Press.

Lucas, R. E., Jnr [1975] 'An Equilibrium Model of the Business Cycle' *Journal of Political Economy,* Vol. 83.

Lucas, R. E., Jnr [1967]. 'Optimal Investment Policy and the Flexible Accelerator' *International Economic Review,* Vol. 8.

Maki, D., Spindler, Z. A. [1975]. 'The Effect of Unemployment Compensation on the Rate of Unemployment in Great Britain' *Oxford Economic Papers,* Vol. 27.

Malinvaud, E. [1977]. *The Theory of Unemployment Reconsidered* Blackwell.

Malcolmson, J. M., Prior, H. J. [1979]. 'The Estimation of a Vintage Model of Production for U K Manufacturing' *Review of Economic Studies,* Vol. 46.

Mizon, G. [1974]. 'The Estimation of Non-Linear Econometric Equations: An Application to the Specification and Estimation of an Aggregate Putty-Clay Relationship for the U K' *Review of Economic Studies,* Vol. 41.

Morgan, P. L. [1979]. 'Employment Functions in Manufacturing Industry' *Government Economic Service Working Paper No. 24.*

Morley, R. [1974]. 'The Rate of Unemployment and the Share of Profit in National Income: 3 Hypotheses' *Durham Working Paper No. 14.*

Muellbauer, J., Winter, D. [1979]. 'Unemployment in British Manufacturing' Progress Reports, Birkbeck College.

Nadiri, N. I., Rosen, S. [1969]. 'Interrelated Factor Demand Functions' *American Economic Review,* Vol. 59.

Nickell, S. [1979]. 'The Effect of Unemployment and Related Benefits on the Duration of Unemployment' *Economic Journal,* Vol. 89.

Pissarides, C. A. [1978]. 'The Role of Relative Wages and Excess Demand in the Sectoral Flow of Labour' *Review of Economic Studies*, Vol. 215.

Rosen, H. S., Quandt, R. E. [1978] 'Estimation of a Disequilibrium Aggregate Labour Market' *Review of Economics and Statistics,* Vol. 60.

Rowthorn, R. [1975]. 'What Remains of Kaldor's Law?' *Economic Journal*, Vol. 85.

Salter, W. G. [1966] *Productivity and Technical Change,* Cambridge University Press.

Sawyer, M. C. [1979]. 'The Effects of Unemployment compensation on the rate of unemployment in Great Britain: a comment' *Oxford Economic Papers,* Vol. 31.

Smith, R. [1978]. 'Estimating Joint Factor Demand Models' Unpublished Treasury paper.

Spindler, Z. A., Maki, D. [1979]. 'More on the Effects of Unemployment Compensation on the Rate of Unemployment in Great Britain' *Oxford Economic Papers,* Vol. 31.

Tinsley, P. A. [1971]. 'A Variable Adjustment Model of the Labour Demand' *International Economic Review,* Vol. 12.

Treadway, A. B. [1974]. 'The Globally Optimal Flexible Accelerator' *Journal of Economic Theory,* Vol. 7.

Weeden, R. [1973]. 'Inter-regional Migration Models and their Application to the U K' *N I E S R Regional Paper No. 2.*

Labour Supply in Great Britain: Theory and Evidence*

Christine Greenhalgh
St. Peter's College Oxford

Ken Mayhew
Pembroke College, Oxford

*We are grateful to many academic colleagues and to government economists and statisticians for help and advice in the preparation of this survey.

LABOUR SUPPLY IN GREAT BRITAIN: THEORY AND EVIDENCE

I. Introduction

This paper surveys recent work on labour supply in Britain. Section II is concerned with describing trends in participation and hours; and with outlining suggested explanations and major uncertainties, particularly in a forecasting context. Section III discusses the analytical work done by mainly academic economists, and assesses its contribution both to explaining the past and to improving forecasting procedures. Section IV covers a rather different aspect of labour supply—its quality and composition, both of which are important in determining the effectiveness of a labour force of any given size.

II Trends in Participation and Hours

Table 1 shows trends in the participation rates of three groups—men, single women, and married women—during the post-war period.[1] Amongst men there were large falls in the rate for the 15–19 age group and for the over 65's. There was a smaller fall for the 20–24 group, though this was not monotonic, there being a slight increase between 1961 and 1966. The participation rate of single women aged 15 to 19 behaved in much the same way as that of men in the corresponding age group. This was not the case for single women in the over 65 group. Their rate remained roughly constant and then rose in the early 1960's, only to fall thereafter; the fall was much less than that for older men. The 20–24 group showed a much more substantial fall than the equivalent male group, whilst the participation rates of single women aged between 25 and 64 were stable. The participation rates of married women of all ages showed dramatic increases.

The survey of the next section will attempt to assess the relative magnitudes of the various possible determinants of these trends. Pending that, we can suggest some explanations. For men the main development has been a contraction of working life, and rising wealth is probably the main cause of this. For the young this means that short-term cash flow problems are less likely to constrain education on a full-time basis beyond the school-leaving age. For the old greater provision for retirement during working life makes full-time retirement possible. However in both instances state intervention has had an impact, though this area has been relatively under-researched. What, for example, has been the effect of the rising real values of state pensions?

A further important influence on the behaviour of older men during the last decade may have been long duration unemployment leading to 'discouraged workers' withdrawing from the labour force. Unemployment rates for older workers have increased dramatically in the 1970's.

---

[1] For greater detail on trends see Department of Employment [1976b], [1977a] and [1979c].

41

Table 1: Post-war Trends in Participation Rates

	1951	1961	1966	1971	1976
Men					
15–19	83·8	74·6	70·6		
16–19				69·7	64·7
20–24	94·9	91·9	92·6	89·9	88·5
25–34	]98·3	98·2	98·2	97·5	97·6
35–44				98·3	98·3
45–54				97·6	97·6
55–59	]95·2	97·6	95·1	95·3	95·0
60–64				86·6	86·6
65–69	]31·1	24·4	23·5	30·6	26·5
70+				11·0	8·4
All ages	87·6	86·0	84·0	82·6	80·6
Single Women					
15–19	80·7	73·2	68·4		
16–19				65·6	58·8
20–24	91·0	89·4	86·7	81·2	76·7
25–34	]81·2	84·2	84·2	80·8	79·1
35–44				80·0	78·7
45–54				78·1	77·5
55–59	]50·5	57·4	60·0	67·2	66·5
60–64				33·7	32·0
65+	6·6	6·5	7·4	6·3	4·5
All ages	55·0	50·6	49·2	44·4	41·6
Married Women					
15–19	38·1	41·0	43·6		
16–19				44·2	51·9
20–24	36·5	41·3	43·5	46·7	54·6
25–34	]25·1	33·6	41·8	38·4	47·8
35–44				54·5	66·4
45–54				57·0	66·3
55–59	]19·0	29·6	41·4	45·5	49·8
60–64				25·2	26·6
65+	2·7	3·3	5·5	6·5	5·4
All ages	21·7	29·7	38·1	42·3	49·0

Sources: 1951 to 1966, *British Labour Statistics: Historical Abstract;* 1971 and 1976, *Department of Employment Gazette,* June 1977.

The striking increase in the participation of married women is partly the result of a change in tastes making more women work regardless of the trend in wages. But it probably also reflects the substitution effect of higher wages dominating the income effect both of the woman's own wage and of her husband's wage. It is difficult to discern the relative strength of these two general influences. Also important is the trend towards smaller families and the greater certainty of completion of families, as techniques of birth control have improved, which allow plans to return to work to be formulated and implemented. More uncertainty is involved in evaluating the relative importance of the 'added worker' and the 'discouraged worker' effects. Is, for example, the added worker only operative when the husband is unemployed?

Or, do wives react to uncertainty about their husband's job tenure and anticipate probable unemployment?

When considering single women, both the sets of influences we have described as affecting the decisions of men and married women apply, since this group is composed partly of women who are single and behave like men, and of women who are divorced or separated or cohabiting and who behave like married women. The trend is towards a greater proportion of the latter type, as divorce rates and stable non-married partnerships increase.

These changes in participation rates combine with demographic changes to give the movements of labour supply, which are shown in Table 2. The labour force grew by 14% between 1951 and 1976. The major development was the greater representation of married women, with an increase of 153% during these years. The male labour force reached a peak in 1961, the numbers then fell slightly until the mid 1970's, when they started to rise again. Over the 25 years as a whole, there was an increase of just over 1½%. The number of unmarried women in the labour force fell until the mid 1970's, since when there has been a slight increase; but taking the period as a whole there was a fall of 25%.

As well as considering the number of people in the labour force we need to consider the number of hours they work. Actual hours worked by men and by full-time women have fallen since the war, but not by as much as would be implied by the reduction in standard hours, which (for manual workers) fell in discrete steps to 44 in 1945–7, to 42 in the early 1960's and to 40 in 1964–66. In other words, the relative importance of overtime working has increased. Amongst women the proportion of part-timers has increased, but the average number of hours worked by this group has remained more or less constant.

Table 2: The Labour Force, 1951–76 (thousands)

	1951	1961	1966	1971	1976
Males	15,649	16,071	16,994	15,993	15,914
Married females	2,658	3,886	5,063	5,799	6,731
Single females	4,303	3,853	3,799	3,286	3,225
TOTAL	22,610	23,810	24,857	25,018	25,868

Sources: As for Table 1.

Section III surveys the econometric work on the determinants of hours, but a number of issues can be raised here. Firstly, when considering labour supply in terms of efficiency units, it is necessary to know whether a reduction in the number of hours and in their composition has an impact on efficiency per hour. The balance of the evidence indicates that the productivity of an overtime hour is not significantly different from that of a standard hour, whilst an overall reduction in hours is associated with a rise in output per hour.[2] Perhaps the explanation of this latter finding is that such reductions have provided a way for employers of absorbing the effects of technical progress without a reduction in the labour force, whilst simultaneously allowing workers to supply their prefered hours under a situation of changing economic circumstances. Secondly, it is necessary to ask to what extent individuals can make *unconstrained* decisions about the number of hours they work. This is particularly important given the significance of part-time working among married women and older workers. Empirical studies cannot always make an accurate assessment of the extent to which workers are constrained by a lack of suitable job opportunities, because of a lack of suitable evidence on desired hours of work. Nevertheless it is sometimes possible to make inferences by comparing different labour markets, (see below section III).

Turning to forecasts of labour supply, the latest official projections are for an increase of just over 2¼ million or 9.0% between 1976 and 1991.[3] The male labour force is expected to increase by ¾ million or 5%, unmarried women by 450,000 or 14% and married women by 1 million or 15%. This projected growth is not large in comparison with long-run trends, but, except for married women, it is large by the standards of the recent past. The rates of increase are expected to be particularly great in the first half of the 1980's. These projections are the result of assumptions about future demographic trends and about activity rates. The population of working age will increase substantially to make a bulge in the late 1970's and early 1980's. This is a consequence of low birth rates in the First War and the 1920's and of high birth rates between 1956 and 1964. A very slight fall in the overall activity rate of men is overwhelmed by these demographic factors, as is a similar fall in the activity rates of unmarried women. The proportion of women not married is expected to rise for a number of reasons, including an older average age of marriage and higher divorce rates. The activity rates of married women are expected to increase, but at a slower rate than between 1971–76.

It is difficult to assess the value of such projections, since the forecasting procedure is not specified in detail. There are two generic sources of uncertainty. The first involves possible changes in government policy. Quite sensibly the official projections are on the basis of unchanged policies. But changes in policy towards the school-leaving age or the introduction of public subsidies or grants to those still at school would reduce the activity rates of younger workers. Similarly the rates of older workers would be reduced by lowering the official retirement age. Though there has been some discussion of this Department of Health and Social Security, 1976 and 1978) the costs make such a decision unlikely. However, the government is continuing to encourage early retirement as a means of job sharing,[4] and at the same time the real value of state pensions and occupational pensions are likely to improve relative to

[2] For the history of hours of work and overtime, see Clegg [1962], Whybrew [1968], and Leslie [1977]. For recent work on the productivity of hours, see Leslie [1978a].

[3] Outline projections are given in Department of Employment [1979c]. The latest detailed official projections are in Department of Employment. [1978c]; these in turn were updates of figures in Department of Employment [1977a].

[4] See, for example, Department of Employment [1978b]. See also Incomes Data Services [1977].

pre-retirement incomes. The other source of uncertainty concerns whether the right economic variables have been taken into account.

As an illustration we examine a recent official approach to married women's activity rates. 'The three main causes of the recent sharp rise in activity rates are thought to have been:

(a) the very sharp fall in the birth rate . . .

(b) equal pay and equal opportunities . . .

(c) the increased opportunities for part-time work.'

[*Department of Employment Gazette,* June 1977, p. 589]

No justification is given for the selection of these factors rather than others, such as changes in real earnings and employment of their husbands. In the projections it is assumed that the fall in the birth rate . . . will continue but at a slower rate that previously. The Equal Pay Act and other anti-discrimination legislation will continue to have an effect in the future, but it is thought that these measures may have exerted much of their effect by now. The increase in job opportunities, particularly part-time jobs, over the period 1971–5 is assumed not to be matched by similar increases in the future.' (p. 592).

This exercise somehow yields components of change in the married female work force due to changes in activity rates of 67 thousands in 1977–81 and 115 thousands per annum in 1981–6, despite the observed value of 201 thousands in 1971–5. No attempts are made to conduct a sensitivity analysis, which would involve varying each of the assumptions to give different projections. Such alternatives would give the sceptical reader an opportunity to make his own judgements about uncertain future events and to select his preferred estimates. This would represent a significant advance even though remaining within the simple projection model. On the basis of econometric studies discussed below it would seem that for men or women a closer examination should be made of the potential effects of the participant's own wage, his/her spouse's wage and family unearned income.

Much less attention has been paid to the forecasting of hours of work. There has been some discussion—partly in the context of worksharing—of a reduction in the standard working week for manual workers to 35 hours (Department of Employment [1978d], TUC [1978], Trade Union Research Unit [1978a], [1978b]). Though such a reduction may not be generally imminent, it is quite probable during the next decade. Since the standard work week is a minimum work week for most male manual workers, this fall is unlikely to be reflected in a corresponding reduction in actual weekly hours. Although fewer full-time women workers engage in overtime, the impact of changes in the standard work week on women is reduced by the large amount of part-time working. Thus the prediction of working hours requires more than an estimate of future standard work weeks and requires the assistance of the economic models discussed below.

III Econometric Studies

All the papers discussed in this section estimate labour supply equations which have their basis in the utility-maximizing individual choice model. In this model

45

both participation and total hours of work are determined by the individual's wage rate, unearned income and preferences between income and leisure. These preferences are proxied by means of personal characteristics and family circumstances, such as numbers and ages of children, education, health and race.

When aggregate data are used, further variables are introduced to account for differences in composition of the labour forces under comparison (Metcalf, 1976, Leslie, 1978b, Greenhalgh, 1977, 1978a). It also becomes necessary to consider the simultaneity between wages and supply which occurs at the aggregate level, and this may require the specification of a two equation model of supply and demand (Metcalf, 1976, Leslie, 1978b).

The individual choice model has been adapted to estimate labour supply functions for individuals of different age group, sex and marital status, by defining the appropriate budget constraint and by entering relevant variables to proxy work-leisure preferences. Thus for married men, the presence of children is likely to increase the utility of money income compared to leisure, whereas, given the existing specialization within the family, the reverse would hold for their wives. Older persons are likely to have a different set of concerns and it has been shown that, in addition to financial variables, health is the most important factor influencing the decision to retire, (Clark *et al.*, 1978, Zabalza *et al.*, 1979).

Econometric studies using aggregate cross-section data

This section analyses the findings of three British studies which have used aggregate data to estimate supply functions. In the first of these, Metcalf *et al.* [1976] use inter-industry cross-section data for 1966 to estimate a simultaneous supply and demand model for hours per week and average hourly earnings for male manual workers in 1966. Control variables in the supply functions are skills, race, age, location, unionization and establishment size. The wage variable has a small positive coefficient, but there is some evidence to suggest the function becomes backward bending at high wages. Higher skills appear to lead to lower hours; race and age yielded no significant effects; those in conurbations and in the South East and Midland regions supplied less hours; unionization and concentration both encouraged shorter hours. It was not possible to control for earnings by other family members nor for unearned incomes, so that the implied positive wage elasticity must be treated with caution[5]. In addition the comparison across industries may reflect a sorting procedure, whereby individuals with a taste for leisure choose industries which typically do not work overtime and vice versa for those who have stronger preferences for income. Preference variables are not easily obtained for inter-industry workforces; for example the presence of dependent children is a relevant but omitted variable (Layard, 1978).

The Metcalf model is re-estimated by Leslie [1978b] on 1971 data, with some minor amendments to the specification, and using data sets for male and

---

[5] If these omitted variables were uncorrelated with participant's own wages then no biases would arise. However this seems rather unlikely.

female manual workers. Leslie obtains positive elasticities of weekly hours with respect to hourly earnings for both men and women, with men having the larger elasticity.

Census participation rates of men and married women in 1971 have been used to estimate single equation models by Greenhalgh [1977, 1979a] with comparable data from the New Earnings Survey providing wage variables. Unearned income could only be proxied by an asset variable reflecting quality of housing. Preferences were proxied by dependency ratios, calculated using census data on children in three age groups, and marital status in the regressions for men. Other variables included were race, location and the unemployment variables discussed below[6]. The analysis was conducted for all those of working age and also separately for 5 year cohorts. For both men and women, participation was found to be positively related to own wage and negatively related to wages of the opposite sex, whilst the asset variable had a negative coefficient. These results are consistent with the economic theory and with earlier US results.

The effects of children on participation of men and women are to increase male participation and decrease that of wives. It should be noted that the relevant coefficients reflect marginal effects of higher or lower dependency ratios. Thus the effects of average family size is also reflected in the constants of the regressions by age group, which are about 16% lower for 16–34 than 35–55 year old wives, implying a reduction in participation of this order of magnitude during the childbearing years. If the mean values of the children variables are used to compute the loss of participation as compared to a situation of no dependent children, the total effect including constants can be estimated at about 30% on average for 16–34 year old married women. For men of the same age the added participation due to children compensates for most of this, leaving very little net loss in participation. (It should be emphasized that these are bound to be rough estimates since they are projections far outside the usual range of variation in the independent variables). This suggests that the main effect of children may be to encourage specialization between husband and wife, rather than inducing more or less total participation per family. If this is the case, then changes in family size will have rather weak effects on total participation, although the composition of the workforce will obviously be affected.

Econometric studies using individual cross-section data

The lack of adequate data on individual characteristics for the 'typical individual' and the greater complexity arising from aggregation in these studies have led British researchers to use individual data obtainable from household surveys (Brown *et. al.*, 1976, Layard, 1978, Greenhalgh, 1978b, Layard *et. at.*, 1979). A selection and summary of similar American research is presented by Cain and Watts [1973]. Individual data are typically used to estimate single equation models of labour supply, assuming that wages are exogenously determined at the market level. The methods of specifying and estimating these

---

[6] See the section which is concerned with cyclical fluctuations, pp. 54–56 *infra*.

equations for various types of workers were converging into a standard practice until further considerations revealed several major difficulties, some of which have yet to be fully resolved.

For primary workers, who mostly participate, hours of work functions were often estimated for the whole sample including non-participants, setting hours of the latter to zero. For secondary workers, the accepted practice until recently was to estimate a participation function for individuals using a 0, 1 dependent variable and then to estimate an hours of work function for participants only. From these two functions the overall effect on labour supply of a change in any variable could be assessed by a weighted average of the effects on participation and hours of participants. The relevant parameters of the budget line facing the individual were derived by adjusting gross wage rates and unearned incomes to net values using tax schedules. Where wages were not observed (non-participants), or could only be estimated by dividing earnings by hours, then predicted wage rates were used from an auxiliary wage function, which provided an unbiased estimate of the mean wage facing an individual of given personal characteristics.

The criticisms of these procedures which have been raised can be classified as more or less serious in terms of the likely bias to the estimates. Participation at the individual (or aggregate) level generates a dependent variable with a limited range of variation, for which simple regression methods and linear models are not entirely appropriate, because of the need for predicted values to lie within the 0, 1 range. Whilst the simple estimates are inefficient they may not be seriously biased, and the linear approximations often work reasonably well for groups with average participation rates not close to zero or unity. The selection of participants only, when estimating hours of work functions (and auxiliary wage equations) for secondary workers, can generate biases due to the fact that the residuals are truncated. This has been discussed extensively by Heckman [1976], but whether the degree of bias is sufficient to justify recourse to the very complex econometric methods necessary to resolve these problems has to be determined for each data set.

A very serious problem is that the majority of existing US and some UK studies (Brown *et. al.*, 1976, McGlone and Ruffell, 1978, 1979, Glaister and Ruffell, 1979) treat the marginal net wage as exogenous to individual supply whereas, because tax rates are dependent on hours of work via earnings limits (and because of the existence of various rates for part-time, full-time and overtime working), the marginal net wage is strongly endogenous. There is evidence that the biases arising from these problems are large, possibly even sufficient to reverse the direction of effect for key variables such as wage rates and income in hours of work functions for married women (Hurd, 1976, Greenhalgh, 1979b). Various methods of approach have been suggested (Hurd, 1976, Wales and Woodland, 1977, Ashworth and Ulph, 1977a, Greenhalgh, 1979b) each of which has some disadvantages, so that estimates of hours functions for the UK to date must be treated as approximate. The above problems are much less serious for male workers who are mainly full-time workers paying standard rates of tax. Nevertheless, the existence of overtime rates creates a parallel problem to that of taxation, so that even for men estimation problems remain.

The most satisfactory approach (from an econometric standpoint) to the above difficulties is to specify the underlying decision model in full, rather than attempting to directly estimate a labour supply equation derived from such a model. This requires a specific utility function to be posited and the complete set of constraints reflecting the opportunities facing the individual to be formulated. The parameters of the non-linear model can then be estimated via maximum likelihood techniques. This procedure is computationally expensive for large samples of data, or when large numbers of parameters are involved because of the inclusion of preference variables. The studies which have used this approach to date (Wales and Woodland, 1977, Ashworth and Ulph, 1977a) utilise small data sets and comparatively few variables, so that the advantages of the method may be outweighed by lack of precision and by mis-specification.

Other authors (Hurd, 1976, Layard *et. al.,* 1979, Greenhalgh, 1979b) have continued in the tradition of earlier studies by estimating the labour supply function, but modifying the specification and method of estimation in various ways. Hurd and Layard use predicted tax parameters from a subsidiary equation, thus essentially taking an instrumental variable approach to the simultaneity problem. However Greenhalgh [1979b] argues that this is unlikely to be effective in eliminating the correlation between included variables and the error on the equation due to the tax structure facing British wives and prefers to adopt a reduced form specification. Both of these approaches involve linear approximations to non-linear functions, but have the advantage of being computationally simple, allowing the use of large data sets and rich specifications.

A compromise is attempted by Zabalza *et. al.* [1979a] using data for older workers. Their model follows the utility function approach but reduces the opportunity set to three points: full-time work, part-time work and retirement, instead of allowing variation across the whole range of hours of work. This trade-off between econometric and computational efficiency cannot be evaluated at present and awaits estimation of the unrestricted model.

Summary of results from cross-section studies

A summary of the existing estimates of wage and income elasticities of labour supply for men and women are presented in Table 3.

For men, the small positive elasticity of participation for own wage reflects the behaviour of younger workers, who are less likely to engage in further education when wages are high. This is not inconsistent with the small negative hours elasticities estimated by three studies using individual data, which suggest that the average male worker has reached the backward bending portion of the supply curve. However, industry data yield a small positive elasticity of hours, (Metcalf, 1976, Leslie, 1978) for workers in manufacturing industry.

Looking at other financial variables shows the effects of spouse's wage and unearned income on male labour supply to be consistently negative. Over time, if all three independent variables rise together in the long run, then their total effect on participation and hours can be obtained by summing the elasticities with respect to wages and incomes. The predicted trends implied are generally negative for male participation and hours, with greater reductions in hours of work, which seems consistent with the evidence. These negative trends would be enhanced by falling birth rates, because of the positive effects of children on participation (discussed above) and on hours of work (Layard, 1978). In contrast, for older men, Zabalza *et. al.* [1979a] obtain a small positive elasticity with respect to wages; this, together with the considerably larger negative income elasticity, emphasises the different position of older men compared with prime age workers.

All but one of the female studies yield positive own wage elasticities and negative spouse's wage and income elasticities, but there is very little consistency in the magnitudes of the parameters across the various studies. Firstly there is a considerable difference between own wage and income elasticities of participation, when estimated for married women using aggregate and individual data, the latter yielding smaller values. This has received no attention in the literature, but two possibilities suggest themselves. The aggregate data may overestimate supply response if supply is only revealed when job opportunities are numerous and the number of jobs is correlated with level of wages across areas. However, the use of unemployment variables to capture these effects should be sufficient to ensure that the estimates are unbiased. Hence it is necessary to ask whether the estimates from individual data are too low.

It is possible that downward bias arises if the use of a predicted wage from an auxiliary equation averages out much of the wage variation arising from demand differences between areas, (because of the lack of sufficient detail relating to location) which is necessary to identify the supply function. For individuals of a given labour quality there is thus observed variation in supply but little variation in predicted wage. Differences in predicted wages arise mainly from labour quality (experience, qualifications, etc.). When these variables are included separately in American supply functions (in addition to predicted wages) as proxies for preferences, they generally have negative coefficients, although many UK studies omit them entirely[7] (e.g. Brown, 1976, Layard, 1978, Layard *et. al.,* 1979).

The typical result in many studies using individual data is a very poor fit and apparently inelastic supply. This may reflect the fact that tastes for leisure increase with education, whilst for individuals of a given educational level the identifying wage variations due to demand factors are lost in the wage prediction procedure. These comments apply equally to the hours functions, and it is interesting to note that the only study of wives which included education proxies for preferences (Greenhalgh, 1979b) obtained a large positive wage elasticity of hours worked. The difficulties surrounding the use of

---

[7] Zabalza *et. al.* [1979a] found that educated workers were more likely to retire if male, but less likely to retire if female; however this result must be seen in the context of involuntary retirement discussed below, since it is likely that educated women are more able to resist pressures to retire.

Table 3: Supply Elasticities with Respect to Wage Rates and Incomes

Participation		Men			Women		
		Own Wage	Spouse's Wage	Unearned Income	Own Wage	Spouse's Wage	Unearned Income
Greenhalgh [1977, 1979a]	Town data, small sample, aggregate, all men, married women, Census 1971.	0.09	−0.08	−0.07*	1.35	−0.88	−0.23*
Greenhalgh [1979b]	Large sample, individual, married women, GHS 1971.				0.36	−0.35 (spouse's & unearned)	
Layard et. al. [1979]	Large sample, individual, married women, GHS 1974.				0.49	−0.28	−0.04

Hours of work

		Own Wage	Spouse's Wage	Unearned Income	Own Wage	Spouse's Wage	Unearned Income
Ashworth & Ulph [1977a]	Small samples, individual, married men and women, 1971.	−0.06	n.a.	−0.004	−0.07	n.a.	−0.10
Brown et. al. [1976]	Small sample, individual, married men, manual workers, 1971.	−0.10	n.a.	−0.02			
Greenhalgh [1979b]	Large sample, individual, married women, GHS 1971.				0.68	−0.18 (spouse's & unearned)	
Layard [1978]	Large sample, individual, married men, GHS 1974.	−0.13	−0.10	−0.02			
Layard et. al. [1979]	Large sample, individual, married women, GHS 1974.				0.08	−0.10	−0.00
Leslie [1978b]	Industry data, small sample, aggregate, 1971.	0.2	n.a.	n.a.	0.08	n.a.	n.a.
Zabalza et. al. [1979b]	Large samples, individual, older men and women, OPCS Survey 1977.	0.06	n.a.	−0.26	0.42	n.a.	−0.44

Notes 'Small sample' = hundreds.
'Large sample' = thousands.

* = Proxy variable.
n.a. = not available.

predicted wages suggests that cross-section area studies of hours worked might yield useful results, although currently none are available.[8]

Differences between the existing studies may also result from their alternative approaches to the problems of estimation, (see above pp. 16–18), which would tend to affect wage and income parameters more than those relating to preferences variables, such as family structure. Certainly there is much closer agreement about the effects of children on female labour supply. There are large negative coefficients for children aged 0–5, smaller negative effects for ages 6–10, and non-significant or small positive effects for 11–16 in the individual participation and hours functions of both Greenhalgh and Layard. Greenhalgh estimates that total lifetime effects of a reduction in family size by one child would be to raise participation by 4% and lifetime hours by 12·5%, (Greenhalgh, 1979b).

In the short run, however, the postponement of the birth of a child would have much larger effects on participation and hours, of the order of at least 60% on participation and annual hours of work in the relevant age-group (Layard *et. al.* [1979]). Cross tabulations presented in Joshi [1979] confirm that young children present a major deterrent to labour force participation, but it is worth noting that this is likely to be tempered by financial considerations. In Joshi's tabulations by cohorts it is significant that the youngest group of married women (18–24) does not have lowest participation rate, even though they have the highest proportion with a youngest child aged under 5 years.

These studies imply that in order to forecast accurately the participation of married women of childbearing age it is necessary to predict both exit and re-entry. The number of first births and also the total family size, will affect withdrawals most strongly; whereas the number of families whose youngest child is reaching school age and the numbers with dependents reaching the expensive teenage period are most relevant to re-entry into the labour force. If these variables were smoothly trended, labour force projection would be simplified, but the timing of births and the magnitude of completed family size are themselves decision variables which may be influenced by economic events.

The economics of fertility is a controversial and relatively new area which has been pursued in America but not, to any great extent, in the UK, an exception being Ermisch [1979]. Pioneering work by Becker [1961] has been extended by several authors; this work has been recently surveyed in articles by Leibenstein [1974] and Sanderson [1977]. Whilst a detailed survey of this area is beyond the scope of this paper, it is relevant to summarise the main issues in view of the close links between fertility and labour supply.

If decisions to bear children are influenced by their cost (i.e. 'price', including opportunity costs of foregone earnings) and by income levels, as argued in some of these studies, it is evident that over time family structure cannot be treated as a completely exogenous variable determining labour supply. Decisions relating to family creation and labour supply are simultaneous to some degree, although clearly there is no freedom to reverse a decision

---

[8] As noted above (p. 46), cross-section industry data used by Metcalf *et. al.* [1976] yielded a negative effect on hours if a higher proportion of the workforce was skilled and positively sloped supply curve.

to bear children. Thus an economic boom may result in fewer first births due to the higher opportunity cost facing young wives who are thinking of starting a family, but at the same time it may encourage more additions to families with children and non-working wives whose skills have depreciated, because of the increased incomes earned by husbands. A recession is likely to have reverse effects. The net effects on the number of births, on their spacing and on completed family size will depend on the relative strengths of price and income effects for different age-groups of women. The final outcome will then be, *ex post*, an exogenous constraint for future labour supply for those who have completed their family (and will not be persuaded to reverse their decision by any economic fluctuations). Therefore the economics of fertility creates particular difficulties for the projection of the labour supply of younger married women in the short run and for all women in medium term annual projections (of the kind attempted by the Department of Employment). A recent paper by Ermisch [1979] attempts to estimate the elasticity of the total fertility rate with respect to men's and women's earnings using UK data for 1951–75. Since the results presented are not free of serial correlation bias they cannot be held to give definite support for economic influences on fertility. However, it is worth noting that the elasticities obtained are positive for men's wages and negative for women's wages.

Although financial variables and family responsibility are the most important determinants of labour supply, for older workers poor health becomes increasingly important in determining withdrawal from the labour force. Findings for all ages (Layard 1978, Greenhalgh 1979b), indicate that substantial proportions of the population suffer from some kind of illness which limits their activity by a significant amount.[9] Wives also have to take on extra responsibility if other members of the family have long term ill health. Thus Greenhalgh found that ill health of wives (relevant to 12% of the sample) reduced their own participation by 15%, and poor health of dependents (relevant to 9% of the sample) reduced wives' hours of work by 11%.

In their study of older workers, Zabalza et. al. [1979a] found that poor health (relative to others of the same age) increased the probability of retirement by 0.56 and 0.75 respectively for men and women who were five years below the official retirement ages. Both men and women with poor health were virtually certain to have retired by age 65 and 60 respectively, whereas about one quarter of their healthier counterparts were still working. Thus any improvement in the health of the population could have a significant impact in releasing those workers who are at present directly or indirectly inhibited by illness.

Throughout this survey little attention has been paid to institutional factors influencing labour supply. In many of these studies there was little information on these factors, but for their older workers Zabalza et. al. were able to test for the effects of losing a job involuntarily on the probability of retirement. These effects were substantial for both men and women, but greater for the latter. Retirement proportions for those affected were 6% higher for men aged 60 and 16% higher for men aged 65. For women of 55 and 60 more than a quarter

[9] More single persons than other groups are so affected (about 15%), presumably due to the selection process inherent in decisions to marry.

were affected; by age 65 the percentage was still about 20%. If these results are correct, then proposals to lower the statutory retirement age for men to achieve male-female equality should perhaps be dropped in favour of raising the retirement age for women, to encourage employers to keep willing workers on their payrolls.

Another issue which might be termed 'institutional' is the question of whether workers are free to choose their desired hours, as most studies generally assume. Zabalza *et. al.* are an exception, arguing that workers are limited to part-time or full-time work schedules; this is reflected in their econometric methodology, but the authors present no empirical justification for collapsing continuously measured hours data to three points.

A recent article by King [1978] tests for the effects of greater potential choice in hours of work on female labour force participation. The greater choice is proxied by the standard deviation of hours of work, and this variable is tested against an industry mix variable relating to types of jobs available, as reflected in a measure of industrial structure. The variability of hours appears to be important for mothers with pre-school children but not for other women, whilst the structure of industry in the area is significant for women without children or with children of school age.

Economic studies using aggregate time-series data

Studies in this category are concerned with evaluating the response of labour supply to variations in labour market conditions. It is obviously important to distinguish between labour market developments which are the result of short-run cyclical variations and those which reflect long-run changes. Thus, evidence from these studies about the influence of particular demand variables may be useful to an analysis of trends.

High unemployment in a period of depression leads to 'discouraged workers', who drop out of the labour force since the high costs of job search exceed their expected gains (because of the low probability of finding a job). At the same time, in families with an unemployed worker, 'added workers' may be generated as wives or children attempt to bolster the family income. The net relationship between labour supply and pressure of demand depends on which of these two effects dominates.

Many American studies (surveyed in Mincer, 1968) have examined the relationship between the total labour force and unemployment in order to investigate these effects. In Corry and Roberts [1970] an attempt is made to present this kind of analysis using British data. Unfortunately the lack of an adequate time series for the total labour force, because of the existence of a variable amount of unmeasured unregistered unemployment, means that their results cannot be used to draw any conclusions about added and discouraged workers. The authors recognize this in their subsequent article (Corry and Roberts, 1974). A recent analysis by Joshi [1978] tries to formulate explicitly the relation between registered and unregistered unemployment for secondary workers, but again cannot circumvent the measurement problem.

The findings of Corry and Roberts suggest that a 1% rise in registered unemployment is associated with decreases of $\frac{1}{3}$% (and 1%) in male (and female) activity rates (defined as employed plus registered unemployed divided by population).[10] These results undoubtedly exaggerate the elasticity of the labour force with respect to demand pressures, since their time series measures of labour supply would unavoidably be negatively correlated with registered unemployment over the cycle. As demand rises workers are drawn into jobs from both registered and unregistered unemployment and thus the measured value of supply rises whilst unemployment falls. This happens even if the total available work force is constant, merely as a result of the measurement procedures. Thus it may give insights into the size of the pool of hidden unemployed, (this is a larger proportion of total unemployment for women, hence the greater 'elasticity'), but yields no insights into the behaviour of workers at the participation margin. The recent increase in the propensity of women to register as unemployed would be likely to change the behaviour of female 'activity rates', making them more stable over the cycle.

Evidence from American studies shows much less cyclical sensitivity for a more comprehensive time series measure of labour supply (Mincer, 1966), but cross section studies still indicate a significant negative relationship between labour supply and unemployment which has to be explained. In a more recent article Fleisher and Rhodes [1976] hypothesize that the negative relationship across local labour markets arises because of geographical variation in the characteristics of the work force and the industrial environment, which simultaneously increases unemployment and decreases labour force participation. They argue that this relationship does not change when aggregate demand rises or falls as a result of cyclical fluctuations. The authors specify and estimate a three equation model which helps to verify their interpretation, although their model is not without weaknesses, since these 'characteristics' of the labour market are not amenable to direct measurement.

Returning to the studies discussed above, cross-section evidence relating to added and discouraged workers is contained in Greenhalgh [1977, 1979a], who uses 1971 census data from which a local unemployment rate including the unregistered can be derived. Both local and regional unemployment rates are used as explanatory variables in explaining participation, and these variables have effects of opposite sign, being respectively negative and positive. A rise in both these rates simultaneously (due, say, to a general deflation) would yield predicted changes in participation of zero for men and nearly +$\frac{1}{2}$% for married women, indicating the possibility of a dominant 'added worker' effect for the latter group over the business cycle. The negative relationship between local unemployment rates and participation is stronger for married women than men ($\frac{3}{4}$% and $\frac{1}{4}$% falls in activity respectively for a 1% rise in unemployment) and stronger for older men than younger men. These could be interpreted as 'discouraged worker' effects reflecting differences between areas in the level of employment generated by a given level of aggregate demand, which leads some of these more immobile and marginal workers to become permanent non-participants. However, Fleisher and Rhodes prefer to

---

[10] Corry and Roberts, [1974], Appendix Table 11, contains the only results corrected for autocorrelation in the error components, which seriously mars their other estimates.

interpret this type of result from the supply side, putting the blame on the unemployability (lower skills and motivation) of such workers, rather than the demand side (lack of jobs) as interpreted by Greenhalgh.

The implications of these studies for forecasts of available labour supply thus seem to be that there is a cyclically stable aggregate labour supply, if correctly measured to include the unregistered unemployed and holding constant wage rates and income, although there may be some labour reserves of secondary workers in local labour markets who could be drawn into the labour force if employment could be redirected to low demand areas. The cyclical rise and fall of real wages would of course directly induce movements of workers into and out of the labour force in the case of groups such as married women with positive wage elasticities of supply, but these effects would be partly offset by real wealth effects. There is also the possibility of wives timing the birth of their children to minimise costs, as suggested above in the discussion of economic determinants of fertility. This could lead to further variations of a pro- or counter-cyclical nature in wives' labour supply.

Extension of the simple model

The simple model of individual choice between income and leisure has been extended to provide more complex specifications. In these models it is often possible to utilize the predictions of economic theory to obtain more efficient econometric estimates and also to ensure that the correct economic interpretation is placed on coefficients of wage and income variables.

The first issue to be examined in detail was the inter-relationship between individual decisions caused by the pooling of family resources. The extension of the individual model of income/leisure choice to a typical modular family of two adults and children does not present any major difficulties, providing a family welfare function can be defined; i.e. interpersonal comparisons of utilities can be made (and agreed upon) by those concerned. The labour supply of husband and wife can then be derived as a function of each person's wage and the family's unearned income, whilst, as before, work/leisure preferences are proxied. The empirical testing of such a model by Ashenfelter and Heckman [1974] yields fairly small cross-substitution effects, so that the main impact of the husband's earnings on the wife's labour supply is seen to be an income effect rather than a relative price effect. This suggests that studies which use the impact of husband's earnings (rather than a measure of unearned income) to determine income effects are not commiting too great an error.

Ashworth and Ulph [1977b] question the compatibility of work-leisure choices by husbands and wives and attempt to estimate a model which allows each to have a separate utility function. Unfortunately in pursuing this issue using individual data they are unable to deal with the tax and overtime problems described above, so that their results are unlikely to give a true test of alternative models.

Further extensions of the simple work-leisure model are possible by defining preference functions over a whole set of commodities and leisure rather than over total income and leisure, which implicitly constrains the form of the preference function over various commodities. Very little work of this kind is available. An example is Abbott and Ashenfelter [1976], who use US time series data and find evidence that housing, transportation and services are complementary with leisure, whilst durables are substitutable. Thus, over time, changes in relative prices of these items could be expected to influence labour supply even if real wages and incomes happened to remain constant. Work on an integrated model of consumer demand and labour supply has recently been done by Atkinson and Stern [1979], who use cross-section Family Expenditure data for 1973 relating to households with working male heads. To simplify the problems of the non-linear tax structure, they select a sample of full-time workers with wage rates in a range likely to make them standard rate tax payers, for whom a linear tax structure is a good approximation.

In addition to extending the standard model to allow consumers' choices of several goods and leisure to be simultaneously determined in the manner of Abbott and Ashenfelter, Atkinson and Stern formulate further extensions which permit the estimation of the time necessary for consumption of different goods. Each of the models is an adaptation of a linear expenditure system and many of the results can only be obtained by careful use of the implied restrictions of the model, e.g. price elasticities are obtainable even though a single year cross-section of data is used. The labour supply equation is obtained using such cross-equation restrictions and is not directly estimated. The authors admit that the results obtained so far are not completely satisfactory; in particular the estimated amount of time available for work is less than hours actually worked. However, this approach should ultimately prove more fruitful for long-run projections than the standard one good and leisure model.

At present, the only detailed work on forecasting from the empirical estimates described above is contained in Grice [1978]. This paper attempts to utilize cross-section estimates based on Greenhalgh's Census participation rate studies to construct forecasting equations for the Treasury model. It is possible that these will provide a better basis for projection than the simple extrapolation methods currently being used, especially for the more volatile groups such as married women. However, to the extent that measurable variables do not explain past trends satisfactorily, the residual trend factors will have to be estimated by extrapolation and then combined with the systematic variations predicted by the economic and demographic models to give the total projection. Thus for women, there appears to have been a greater influx of participants than would have been predicted, which may have a sociological explanation (changing roles of men and women), a demographic link (earlier and more certain family completion as modelled in fertility studies), or an economic cause (falling relative prices of goods which substitute for domestic labour as modelled by Atkinson and Stern, 1979). The current state of knowledge does not permit us to estimate exactly the relative weight of each of these factors.

IV The Composition and Quality of the Labour Force

This section is concerned with the quality and mix of labour supply, and especially with likely developments during the next decade. This may be of vital importance in assessing whether the needs of the economy will be met by a labour force of any given size.[11] In particular the occupational and geographical 'flexibility' of the labour force are important indicators of how well the economy will cope with technological change, productivity growth and changes in the structure of demand. We lay no claim to the level of expertise on these issues possessed by many of those attending this conference, but it seems worthwhile briefly to outline the important topics of debate as we see them.

In terms of formal qualifications the quality of the labour force has improved.[12] Of those leaving school, 22% go on to some form of full-time further or higher education. This compares with only 14% in 1961, but with 20% in 1967. In other words, there has been very little change in the last decade, though the proportion of girls continued to improve. Similarly, the percentage of school-leavers going on to university has remained pretty constant (at about 6%) over the last ten years. The number of qualified school-leavers has risen, but it was only in the early 1960's that the proportion of leavers who had A levels or 5 or more O levels increased by very much. The *total* number of people obtaining A levels has continued to rise, because of those obtaining them in further education. Indeed the number of students in full-time further education has more than doubled in the last ten years, whilst higher education is producing 80,000 graduates (those with first degree or equivalent standard) per year, as compared with 50,000 per year in the 1960's.

The proportion of the labour force with no academic qualifications has, therefore, fallen. As for the future,[13] the proportion of school leavers with one or more A level passes is expected to have risen only slightly above the 1976 level of 16% by 1991. The proportion of leavers with five or more O level passes at grades A to C, but with no A levels, is also expected to remain pretty steady at about 9%. Some growth is projected in the proportion of leavers with CSE or lower grade O level passes. Thus although there is expected to be no dramatic change in the proportion of school-leavers with 'qualifications' entering the labour market in any one year, the *stock* of such people is expected to increase, as the less qualified older generations retire. As for highly qualified manpower (those with first degree or equivalent qualifications), there has been great debate[14] about the projections of numbers in higher education. Such projections depend of demographic movements and on forecasts of 'age participation rates' (the percentage of various age groups who actually enter higher education). The latter is in turn both a function of government policy and of the preferences and choices of individuals and their families. The projections suggest that the numbers in higher education will reach a plateau by the mid 1980's, and that thereafter there will be a fall. The extent of that fall is

[11] The Warwick group [1978] have done regional, occupational and industrial projections of employment demand. The question is whether the appropriate supplies of labour will be forthcoming.

[12] Work giving details of recent developments includes Cribbins, Department of Employment [1974, 1976a, 1978a], Department of Employment [1978e, 1979c], Hutt Parsons and Pearson [1978].

[13] The latest official thinking of this is given in Department of Employment [1979c].

[14] An official consultative document (Department of Education and Science, 1978) received much critical attention (e.g. Times Higher Education Supplement, 1978). Revised projections appeared in Department of Education [1979].

highly uncertain, but it seems very likely that there will be no more, and possibly less, students in higher education in the early 1990's than today. Nevertheless the stock of highly educated manpower will continue to increase. To give an example, by 1986 the total stock is expected to be nearly 60% above its 1976 level of 1½ million (Department of Employment 1979c).

The stock of *formally* qualified manpower has, therefore, grown, and it will continue to grow. But the important question concerns the extent to which this represents a gain in terms of socially useful quality. A number of interconnected issues are involved here. First is the phenomenon of occupational 'filtering down'—individuals taking jobs which some time ago would have been regarded as 'beneath' their level of qualification. Second is the question of whether the 'subject' mix of the qualified group is appropriate for the economy's needs. Third is the more general issue of the role of off-the-job training vis-a-vis on-the-job training. Finally, and perhaps over-riding all the other issues, is the 'flexibility' of the labour force. How effectively can potential entrants to the labour force adjust their educational plans to signals about what is needed by the economy? Similarly how effectively can employers adjust their own plans and training programmes, and how effectively can those already in the labour force switch their jobs?

The basis of concern about filtering down revolves around the rapid expansion of the number of graduates in the labour force, and the belief that it is unlikely that the number of jobs traditionally done by graduates has expanded at an equivalent rate. Surprisingly little hard information is available on this; perhaps the best source is the information collected by the UGC for last decade on the first destination of university graduates. This, together with other sources, suggests that some 'filtering down' has been going on since the 1960's (Cribbins, Department of Employment, 1974 and 1976a). Employers are looking for graduates to fill posts formerly filled by school-leavers; graduates are looking for posts for which employers do not specify a degree as a necessary or even desirable qualification; graduates on average take longer to find their first job. (Dean and Prior-Wandesforde, 1977); the relative earnings of some of the highly qualified groups have declined (Department of Employment, 1978a). Certainly there is some suspicion that *social* benefits derived from expenditure on higher education are less than they used to be. It would be useful to be able to test how relevant employers find the educational training received by their recruits. This would provide a partial answer to the second and third questions listed above. Relatively little direct evidence exists on this, and what does is based mainly on hearsay. It is difficult—if not impossible—to get at the answers through even a well-designed questionnaire. For example, how could an employer be made to distinguish between the innate qualities of a man and those acquired through schooling?

Some limited, but mainly indirect, evidence was summarised in a recent Department of Employment Gazette article (Department of Employment 1979a). Industry did not complain about the number of graduate applicants nor about the quality of the arts graduates; but manufacturing industry was worried about a growing proportion of lower quality scientists and engineers. This decline was noted in 'academic ability, motivation, creativity, flexibility and communicative skills.' The main criticism, however, was about poor personal or industrial motivation rather than academic qualities. A final point to note in this context is that on present projections the output of graduates in the arts and social sciences will increase more rapidly than in the sciences.

Very little quality work has been done on how far the higher educational system should cater for the needs of industry, and how far it in fact does so. The same is basically true of school-industry liaison (Engineering Industry Training Board, 1977, Department of Education and Science 1976 and 1977), though a number of recent initiatives have been made in this direction (Department of Employment, 1978f). This is an area in which more research is needed.

There is great uncertainty about both the timing of and the size of the effect of progress in microprocessors lasers and fibre optics, energy related technologies and biotechnologies on the demand for labour. It seems likely, however, both that new skills will be needed in existing employment, and that there will be some shedding of labour which will have to find employment in other sectors. This will demand flexibility of the labour force not only in terms of industrial (and possibly regional mobility), but also in terms of its occupational composition. This will determine both the levels of unemployment and the ability of the economy to adapt successfully to technical change. Britain's record on this score has not been good, but our failures have been masked to some extent by changes occurring in a reasonably buoyant macroeconomic environment. Even if the future pace of technological change is no greater than in the past, it may well take place against a much less favourable backdrop and be more concentrated by sector. The consequences of lack of flexibility would be correspondingly greater.

By itself, simple industrial mobility would not seem to be a problem. Over half of all job changes involve a change of industry, and in the past 20 years we have seen substantial change in the industrial distribution of labour. But this is not to say that the 'right' industry can easily obtain labour, or at least, the best sort of labour. Very little is known about this, but it is clear that particular difficulties are involved with a change of industry which also implies a change of region and/or occupation. A fair amount of work has been done on regional mobility. It indicates that geographical movement is sensitive to economic signals, but that state intervention is probably needed. Much more important than geographical mobility is the need for occupational mobility and skill flexibility. This involves both individual workers and potential entrants being willing and able to react quickly. It also involves employers making adequate plans.

Given the likely developments in microprocessing and other industries, it is possible to pick out particular areas where more labour will be needed. Those are the areas of computing sciences, systems design, information sciences and skills related to engineering and production design. In the same way there are other areas where current developments suggest problems for the future—for instance, the lack of new entrants into coal mining. In our view, however, such an exercise is of limited use for a number of reasons. First, it is difficult, if not impossible, to make overall predictions about the specific composition of commodity demand, and therefore of demand for particular skills. Second, within any skill category, the skill requirements of any firm are so specific that forecasting such requirements and ensuring that they are met is to a large extent best left to the firm itself. This is not to say that guidance, encouragement and financial help from the government are not needed, and that the state does not have a role to play in ensuring that the products of our educational system should have some relevance for the needs of society; but it would be foolish to pretend that state intervention on its own would be sufficient.

Perhaps we can gain some insight into the sort of problems which might be faced by an examination of current skill shortages. Increasing evidence of skill shortages is forthcoming.[15] Though 'skill' most often refers to manual craftsmen, other categories of labour (e.g. draughtsmen and technicians) have also been found to be in short supply. Two methodological points are important. The first is the need to define a 'shortage'; Hunter [1978] defines it as excess demand at prevailing relative wages. Many other sources fail to give any precise definition. The second involves the nature of the evidence. Some work analyzes vacancies. Most of the evidence comes from surveys. The problem here is that the response rate might be expected to be biased towards employers who are in difficulty. A number of studies concentrate specifically on engineering. A report on the toolmaking industry (Engineering Industry Training Board, 1976) made use of vacancy data as well as a survey (1973) of employers. A survey of employers was also used in the Leicester inquiry in 1970 (Department of Employment, 1971). By contrast the NEDO 1977 study used a survey of employees. A series of pieces commissioned by the MSC cover a wider range of industries than just engineering, as do the NEDO SWP Progress Reports. The latter presumably reflect the 'impressions' of the participants rather than quantitative analysis. The MSC also commissioned surveys by IFF and the TSA, which are described in Manpower Services Commission [1976b]. The latter, as well as the SWP Progress Reports, are as concerned with possible future shortages as with present difficulties. It is hard to be sure how many industries are affected by such shortages, how far they are global or how far they represent relatively localized mismatching. Further evidence has recently been published by the Department of Employment (Department of Employment 1979b)—some of it making more sensible use than hitherto of vacancy data.

It is impossible to rank the factors affecting skill shortages, but the various authorities cited above suggest a whole number of possible reasons. These include low skill differentials, low starting rates for apprentices, lack of security, limited prospects for advancement and the poor quality of applicants. But it is clear that much can be laid at the door of inadequate and short-sighted planning by private sector employers. For example, it seems that their apprenticeship intake is over-sensitive to cyclical movements of demand and that many employers are poor at encouraging and developing flexibility of skills. It is also likely that conditions of training and employment encourage a high quit rate of young apprentices, whilst there is an often-voiced (but

---

[15] Department of Employment [1971], Engineering Industry Training Board [1975, 1976], Manpower Services Commission [1975b, 1976a, 1977c, 1977d, 1978a, 1978b], NEDO [1977, 1978].

ill-documented) feeling that inadequate or inappropriate use is made of skilled labour.

Though, as we stressed earlier, the main responsibility for ensuring an adequate and appropriate supply of skills rests with the employers themselves, the government has an important supporting and exhortatory role to play. Government training policy is described briefly in Department of Employment [1979b]. A main thrust of the programmes should, we argue, be concerned to encourage flexibility and mobility. In this light there are a number of encouraging developments. Flexibility is now one of the keynotes of TOPS as it is of the MSC's proposal in *Training for Skills* [1977]; the first full programme based on this is due to start in the autumn of 1979. The following aims are stressed: improve the amount and quality of training in skills; discourage employer stop-go attitudes to recruiting apprentices; prevent persistent shortages because of traditional restrictions on flexible or adaptive training; encourage adaptability. At the same time a number of schemes exist or are being experimented with in order to redress skill imbalances through retraining and geographical mobility. Concern[16] that the secondary education system might do more to meet the needs of industry is leading to attempts to achieve better school-industry liaison. Presently at the more contemplative level is the Grouping of Skills project (Manpower Services Commission, 1975a, Townsend and Freshwater, 1978, Holland *et al.* 1977). The main aim of this project is to identify and better understand the underlying skills needed to carry out jobs so that they can be compared and grouped to shed light on manpower mobility and training. Rather less encouraging has been the apparent failure of the Engineering Industry Training Board to win acceptance for its Review of Craft Apprenticeships, IP 49, [1978]. A modular system of training was introduced in 1968. Each module teaches separate but complementary skills. The suggested scheme builds on that innovation. Whereas present apprenticeship schemes last four years, the new scheme envisages vocational education during the last two years at school, one year off-the-job training in two modules, and one year on-the-job training. The authors of the scheme stress that 'late entrants' should be encouraged. This together with the module system is meant to encourage flexibility.

V. Concluding Comments

This survey has attempted to cover the main areas of work which have recently been undertaken in Great Britain. In view of the rapidly burgeoning literature on econometric estimation of labour supply functions, it seems likely that we shall shortly see a change in the methods of projecting the labour force. This will take the form of supplementing simple extrapolation with the use of complex models which are more sensitive to changes in the economic system. Such models are likely to be of most use in short- and medium-term forecasting.

Whilst this will represent an advance in our knowledge, it may be that an analysis of the quantity of labour supplied is insufficient. Perhaps of equal (or

[16] In, for example, Engineering Industry Training Board [1978], Coventry Engineerng Employers Association [1976].

greater) importance to the British economy is an analysis of its quality and flexibility of use. The marginal productivity of research effort applied to these issues may be greater than that applied to further estimates of participation and hours, given the existing state of knowledge in each field.

SELECT BIBLIOGRAPHY

Trends in Participation and Hours

Clegg, H. [1962]. *Implications of the Shorter Working Week for British Management,* British Institute of Management.
Department of Employment, [1976b], Unit for Manpower Studies, *The Changing Structure of the Labour Force.*
Department of Employment, [1977a]. 'New projections of the future labour force'. *Gazette,* pp. 587–592.
Department of Employment, [1978b]. 'Measures to alleviate unemployment in the medium term: early retirement', *Gazette,* pp. 283–5.
Department of Employment, [1978c]. 'Labour force projections: further estimates', *Gazette,* pp. 426–427.
Department of Employment, [1978d]. 'Measures to alleviate unemployment in the medium term work-sharing', *Gazette,* pp. 400–402.
Department of Employment, [1979c]. 'The changing composition of the labour force', *Gazette,* pp. 546–551.
Department of Health and Social Security [1976]. *Pension Age.*
Department of Health and Social Security, [1978]. *A Happier Old Age.*
Incomes Data Services. [1977]. 'Early Retirement', *IDS Study,* No. 152.
Incomes Data Services. [1978a]. 'Subsidising Jobs', *IDS Study,* No. 173.
Incomes Data Services. [1978b]. 'Occupational Pensions', *IDS Study,* No. 182.
Leslie, D. and Hughes, B. [1975]. 'Hours of work in British manufacturing industries', *Scottish Journal of Political Economy.*
Leslie, D. [1976]. 'Hours and overtime in British and US manufacturing', *British Journal of Industrial Relations,* July.
Leslie, D. [1977]. 'Overtime: the institution that will not die', *Personnel Management,* July.
Leslie, D. [1978a]. 'The productivity of hours in UK manufacturing and production industries', mimeo.
TUC [1978]. *Economic Review,* February.
Trade Union Research Unit [1978a]. 'Now is the time for the 35 hour week'.
Trade Union Research Unit [1978b]. *Technical Notes,* Nos. 43, 46 and 47.
Warwick Manpower Research Group [1978]. *Britain's Employment Prospects.*
Whybrew, E. G. [1968]. *Overtime Working in Britain,* Research Paper No. 9, Royal Commission on Trade Unions and Employers Associations.

Analytical Work on Labour Supply and Demography British

Ashworth, J. and Ulph, D. T. [1977a]. 'Estimating labour supply with piecewise linear budget constraints', University of Stirling, mimeo.
Ashworth, J. and Ulph, D. T. [1977b]. 'On the structure of family labour supply decisions', University of Stirling, mimeo.
Atkinson, A. B. and Stern, N. H. [1979]. 'On labour supply and commodity demands', (mimeo). Paper presented to the NBER-SSRC Conference on Econometric Studies in Public Finance.
Bowers, J. [1970]. 'The anatomy of regional activity rates', *National Institute of Economic and Social Research, Regional Papers I.* Cambridge University Press.
Bowers, J. [1975]. 'British activity rates: a survey of research', *Scottish Journal of Political Economy,* Vol. XXII (I), pp 57–90.
Brown, C. V., Levin, E. and Ulph, D. T. [1976]. 'Estimates of labour hours supplied by married male workers in Great Britian', *Scottish Journal of Political Economy,* Vol. XXIII (3), pp 261–278.

Corry, B. A. and Roberts, J. A. [1970]. 'Activity rates and unemployment: the experience of the UK 1951–66', *Applied Economics*, 2, pp 179–201.

Corry, B. A. and Roberts, J. A. [1974]. 'Activity rates and unemployment. The UK experience: some further results', *Applied Economics*, 6, pp 1–21.

Ermisch, J., [1979]. 'The relevance of the 'Easterlin Hypothesis' and the 'New Home Economics' to fertility movements in Great Britian', *Population Studies*, 33(1), pp 39–58.

Gales, K. E. and Marks, P. H. [1974]. 'Twentieth century trends in the work of women in England and Wales', *Journal of the Royal Statistical Society*, Series A (General), Vol. 137(1), pp 60–74.

Glaister, K. E. and Ruffell, R. J. [1979]. 'Single workers: labour supply and preferences', Department of Economics, University of Stirling, Discussion Paper No. 66.

Glaister, K. E., McGlone, A. and Ulph, D. T. [1979]. 'Labour supply responses to tax changes—a simulation exercise for the UK', (mimeo). Paper presented to the NBER-SSRC Conference on Econometric Studies in Public Finance.

Greenhalgh, C. A. [1979b]. 'Participation and hours of work for married women in Great Britain', *Economica* Vol. 44, No. 175, pp 249–265.

Greenhalgh, C. A. [1979a]. 'Male labour force participation in Great Britain', *Scottish Journal of Political Economy*, forthcoming.

Greenhalgh, C. A. [1979b]. 'Participation and hours of work for married women in Great Britian', *Oxford Economic Papers*, forthcoming.

Grice, J. [1978]. 'An operational model of the labour supply', Treasury Paper AP (78) 11.

Joshi, H. [1978]. 'Secondary workers in the cycle', Government Economic Service Working Paper No. 8, DHSS.

Joshi, H. [1979]. 'Employment flows and fertility of married women in Great Britain 1970–1974'. (mimeo), Centre for Overseas Population Studies.

Layard, P. R. G. [1978]. 'Hours supplied by British married men with endogeneous overtime', LSE Centre for Labour Economics, Discussion paper No. 30.

Layard, P. R. G., Barton, M. and Zabalza, A. [1979] 'Married women's participation and hours', *Economica*, forthcoming.

Leslie, D. [1978b]. 'A supply and demand analysis of the structure of hours of work for UK production industries', mimeo.

Metcalf, D., Nickell, S. and Richardson, R. [1976]. 'The structure of hours and earnings in British manufacturing industry', *Oxford Economic Papers*, Vol. 28(2), pp 284–303.

McGlone, A. and Ruffell, R. J. [1978]. 'On preferences and the labour supply of married women', SSRC Public Sector Study Group, Seminar Paper 1. Also in *Economics Letters* 1 (1978) pp 167–168.

McGlone, A. and Ruffell, R. J. [1979]. 'Preferences and the labour supply of married men', Department of Economics, University of Stirling, Discussion Paper No. 65.

Zabalza, A., Pissarides, C. A., Piachaud, D. and Barton, M. [1979a] 'Social security and the choice between full-time work; part-time work and retirement', (mimeo). Paper presented to the NBER-SSRC Conference on Econometric Studies in Public Finance.

Zabalza, A., Pissarides, C. A. and Piachaud, D. [1979b]. 'Social security, life-cycle saving and retirement', (mimeo). Paper presented to the Colston Symposium on Income Distribution.

American

Abbott, M. and Ashenfelter, O. [1976]. 'Labour supply, commodity demand and the allocation of time', *Review of Economic Studies*, Vol. 43, pp. 389–411.

Ashenfelter, O. and Heckmann, J. J. [1974]. 'The estimation of income and substitution effects in a model of family labor supply', *Econometrica*, Vol. 42(1), pp. 73–86.

Barzel, Y. and McDonald, R. J. [1973]. 'Assets, subsistence and the supply curve of labor', *American Economic Review*, Vol. 63(4), pp. 621–633.

Becker, G. [1961]. 'An economic analysis of fertility', in NBER, *Demographic and Economic Change in Developed Countries*, (Princeton).

Bowen, W. G. and Finegan, T. A. [1969]. *The Economics of Labor Force Participation*, Princeton University Press, Princeton.

Cain, G. and Dooley, M. [1976]. 'Estimation of a model of labor supply, fertility and wages of married women', *Journal of political Economy*, 84, pp. S179–199.

Cain, G. G. and Watts, H. W. (eds.) [1973]. *Income Maintenance and Labor Supply*, Markham Press, Chicago.

Clark, R., Kreps, J. and Spengler, J. [1978]. 'Economics of aging; a survey', *Journal of Economic Literature*, XVI, pp. 919–962.

Fleisher, B. M. and Rhodes, G. [1976]. 'Unemployment and the labor force participation of married men and women: a simultaneous model', *Review of Economics and Statistics,* Vol. 58, pp. 398–406.

Heckman, J. J. [1974]. 'Shadow prices, market wages and labour supply', *Econometrica,* Vol. 42(4), pp. 679–694.

Heckman, J. J. [1976]. 'Sample selection bias as a specification error', University of Chicago, mimeo, (revised February 1977).

Hurd, M. [1976]. 'The estimation of non-linear labor supply functions with taxes from a truncated sample', Research Memorandum No. 36, Centre for the Study of Welfare Policy, Stanford Research Institute.

King, A. G. [1978]. 'Industrial structure, the flexibility of working hours and women's labor force participation' *Review of Economics and Statistics,* 60: 3, pp. 399–407.

Leibenstein, H. [1974]. 'An interpretation of the economic theory of fertility', *Journal of Economic Literature,* 12, pp. 457–479.

Mincer, J. [1966]. 'Labor force participation and unemployment: a review of recent evidence', in *Prosperity and Unemployment,* R. A. and M. S. Gordon (eds.), John Wiley and Sons: New York.

Sanderson, W. [1977]. 'On two schools of the economics of fertility', *Population and Development Review,* 3, pp. 469–476.

Wales, T. J. and Woodland, A. D. [1977]. 'Labour supply and progressive taxes', Discussion Paper No. 77–05, Department of Economics, University of British Columbia.

The Composition and Quality of the Labour Force

Conference of University Administrators [1978]. Group on Forecasting and University Expansion, Final Report.

Coventry and District Engineering Employers Association [1976]. *Literacy and Numeracy in the Factory—Have Standards Declined?*

Cribbins, C. *Qualified Manpower: Follow-up of the 1971 Census.*

Dean, T. and Prior-Wandesforde, G. [1977]. . *Department of Employment Gazette,* February.

Department of Education and Science [1976]. 'The future of the school population', *Reports on Education,* No. 85, June.

Department of Education and Science [1977]. 'Education in schools: a consultative document', July Cmnd. 6860.

Department of Education and Science [1978]. *Higher Education into the 1990s,* February.

Department of Education and Science [1979], 'Future trends in higher education'.

Department of Employment [1971]. *Skilled Engineering Shortages in a High-Demand Area,* Manpower Paper No. 3.

Department of Employment [1974]. *Employment Prospects for the Highly Qualified,* Manpower Paper No. 8.

Department of Employment [1975]. 'Recent trends in apprenticeship training', *Gazette,* pp. 1115–17.

Department of Employment [1976a]. *Qualified Manpower in Great Britain,* Studies in Official Statistics, No. 29.

Department of Employment [1977b]. 'Finding a way to predict wastage of craftsmen and apprentices', *Gazette,* pp. 699–703.

Department of Employment [1978a]. *Employment of the Highly Qualified.*

Department of Employment [1978e]. 'Employment of the highly qualified', *Gazette,* pp. 531–39.

Department of Employment [1978f]. 'Industry and education unit will improve liaison between employers and schools'. *Gazette,* p. 774.

Department of Employment [1979a]. 'Going into industry—trends in graduate employment', *Gazette,* pp. 18–25.

Department of Employment [1979b]. 'Skill shortages in British Industry', *Gazette,* pp. 433–36.

Engineering Industry Training Board [1975]. *The craftsman in engineering: an interim report.*

Engineering Industry Training Board [1976]. *Technological Change, Structural Change and Manpower in the UK Tool-making Industry.*

Engineering Industry Training Board [1977]. *The Relevance of School Learning to Performance in Industry.*

Engineering Industry Training Board [1978]. *Review of Craft Apprenticeship in Engineering,* IP 49.

Holland, G., Pirie, W., Freshwater, M. R. and Townsend, C. [1977]. 'Identifying common skills'.

Hutt, R., Parsons, D. and Pearson, P. [1978]. *Education and Employment.*

Manpower Services Commission [1975a] *Grouping of Skills.*
Manpower Services Commission [1975b]. *Labour Shortages: A Literature Review.*
Manpower Services Commission [1976a]. *The Merseyside Study.*
Manpower Services Commission [1976b]. *Towards a Comprehensive Manpower Policy.*
Manpower Services Commission [1977a]. *Young People and Work.*
Manpower Services Commission [1977b]. *Training for Skills.*
Manpower Services Commission [1977c]. *The Borders Study.*
Manpower Services Commission [1977d]. *Recruitment Problems,* August.
Manpower Services Commission [1978a]. *The South Essex Study.*
Manpower Services Commission [1978b]. *Labour Shortages and Manpower Policy,* (by L. Hunter).
NEDO [1974]. *Shortages of Qualified Engineers.*
NEDO [1977]. *Engineering Craftsmen: Shortages and Related Problems.*
NEDO [1978]. *Sector Working Party Progress Reports.*
Times Higher Education Supplement [1978]. 'DES forced to reduce 1990s forcasts as recruitment falls', 24 November.
Townsend, C. and Freshwater, M. [1978]. 'Manpower mobility and the grouping of skills', *Personnel Management,* June.
TSA *Short-term Labour Market Monitoring for Critical Skills.*

Labour Supply in Great Britain: Theory and Evidence

COMMENT *by C. V. Brown.* (University of Stirling)

My comments are restricted to section III. Despite the title the theoretical issues are not fully explored in this paper. They are however carefully and fully explained in the paper by Heckman et al in this volume. Careful reading of that paper will aid the evaluation of the British work referred to in this paper. This is important because *no* study either UK or US simultaneously solves all of the problems in making labour supply estimates. The reason for this is that as work on labour supply estimates developed authors became aware of various problems and did their best to find ways of tackling them, given the limitations of their data sets. Indeed some of the more interesting developments that have occurred have been designed to overcome deficiencies in data sets (e.g. truncation bias). In most of the more recent papers it is explicitly stated by the authors that they have *not* solved certain problems. Nevertheless these papers have made significant theoretical advances.

The paper could have been considerably strengthened by an expanded discussion of some of these developments as well as by reporting a wider cross section of results in Table 3. The basic data set used in any study determines *both* the estimation problems that need to be faced *and* the possible ways in which these problems can be handled. For this reason the authors should have said more about the data used in the studies they reported. The size of the data set is only one of a number of considerations. In my judgement the theoretical developments which should have received fuller treatment are the incorporation, by Atkinson and Stern [1979—for full references see Greenhalgh and Mayhew], of the demand for goods as well as the demand for leisure into a single model; the treatment of preferences by McGlone and Ruffell [1978 and 1979] who do include an 'education proxy for preferences' (p. 21); and the test for the difference between the Leuthold and Neoclassical household models by Ashworth and Ulph [1977b]. In each of these cases it would have been helpful to report the main results.

From the Treasury's point of view the most serious omission is that of Glaister, McGlone and Ulph [1979]. Greenhalgh and Mayhew are in error in stating that only Grice has undertaken detailed forecasting work based on labour supply estimates. Ignoring the work of Glaister et al is a particularly unfortunate omission because it represents a considerable theoretical advance over the work referred to. Glaister et al demonstrate that supply elasticities of the sort presented in Table 3 are insufficient to predict the effects of tax changes. For example increases in allowances may decrease the labour supply of workers who remain in the same tax band while simultaneously increasing the labour supply of people who stopped work at the old tax threshold. A cut in the basic rate of tax will increase the labour supply of people at the bottom of the basic rate band even if the price elasticity is negative. This means that it is critical to know how people are distributed about their budget constraints and how they will be affected by changes in these constraints. What is required is to re-estimate the model that is used to derive the elasticities in order to estimate the overall effects of any tax change that is under consideration.

Labour Supply in Great Britain: Theory and Evidence

COMMENT *by Peter Elias* (Manpower Research Group. University of Warwick)

It is only four years since Bowers [1975] published his survey of British research on labour force participation rates. These four years have seen rapid developments, both theoretically and empirically, on the estimation of the labour supply function. A comparison of Bowers' paper with this paper by Greenhalgh and Mayhew gives some indication of the enormous burgeoning of the literature that has occurred in this field. Yet, despite this interest, it appears that we still have very little knowledge about some important aspects of the supply of labour in Great Britain. As the authors indicate, the most difficult area of labour supply forecasting relates to the predicted participation of married women and their hours of work. Part-time employment has been growing rapidly, particularly the part-time employment of married women. Female unemployment has also risen quite substantially since 1974 and at a faster rate than male unemployment. Given these rapid developments, it is not surprising to find that the task of forecasting the labour force participation of married women has presented the Department of Employment (DE) with considerable problems.

It is interesting to note that, in 1966, the DE forecasted a 54 per cent participation rate for married women in the 35–44 age group by 1981. In 1974 this forecast was revised to 63 per cent. The latest DE projection of the labour force participation of married women (DE *Gazette,* June 1977) shows a further revision to 70 per cent by 1981. These figures are not quoted to prove how erratic the DE forecasts have been, but rather to indicate that the dramatic increases that have occured have taken most researchers by surprise. This rise in labour force participation has been associated with a rapid rate of increase of part-time working. The part-time employment of women has grown by 1½ to 2 per cent nearly every year this decade. With such changes in mind one must ask, does this survey of the research cast further light upon the labour market processes underlying these developments? In my opinion the answer to this question is negative. The paper is most informative, although there are a number of issues I wish to query, but I feel that its emphasis is misplaced. Very little of the work which is quoted in the paper addresses itself to an understanding of the major compositional changes that are occurring in the labour force. One's expectations are raised upon reading the second section of the paper and deflated upon reading the third. Some redemption is offered in the fourth section, but very little substantial research can be referenced in this section. Much of the research documented in the third section relates to cross-sectional work. This has, I feel, created an undue emphasis on the role of earnings and income in a forecasting context. As an example, there is a substantial interest in the sign and value of cross-sectional wage and income elasticities, yet I remain to be convinced that the expenditure of further time and effort upon their estimation will help produce more reliable forecasts of trends in labour supply. It is only through a better understanding of all the medium-term influences upon the trends in supply that our ability to forecast will be improved.

Turning to some of the conclusions reached within the paper, I wish to query the authors' remarks on the effect of children on married women's labour force participation. In the 1950s the participation rates of married women grew rapidly for women with children of secondary school age. During the sixties and in the first half of this decade, it was the employment of mothers with primary school and pre-school children which experienced the sharpest rise. This coincides with an increase in the provision of nursery school or primary education for 3 and 4 year olds from 16% of the age cohort in 1961 to 36% in 1977. Also, the General Household Survey indicates that there are a substantial number of married women who want to work, but cannot because of the need to look after young children. These facts I find difficult to reconcile with the conclusion of the authors, that changes in family size will have only weak effects upon total participation. Is it being suggested that, as mothers seek and find employment as the provision of child care and education for the under-fives increases, fathers work less? This suggestion cannot be reconciled with the constant rates of labour force participation for males in the 25–50 year age range over the last two decades.

The effect of the provision of such care and education for young children upon the participation of their mothers is clearly an important factor in determining medium-term trends in participation. It is, though, only a part of the link between fertility, family formation and labour force participation. I was most interested to read the authors' comments upon these related areas, but a little disappointed to find that they had not included the work of Easterlin [1978] and Wachter [1977] which considers the effect of the age structure of the population upon labour supply. As the crest of a large population wave reaches the edge of the labour force, one wonders what effect this might have over the next twenty years upon employment prospects, fertility rates and the labour supply decision for different age groups. This is very much an under-researched area in the UK.

There is one important conclusion drawn in this paper which I wish to challenge. It is suggested that the aggregate labour supply is cyclically stable. I would argue that the weight of evidence is to the contrary and that, particularly for married women, high levels of labour demand draw more women into the labour force. I agree that there are problems with defining the supply of labour of the type experienced by Corry and Roberts [1970, 1974], but they are not the only researchers to find a strong negative relationship between female labour force participation and unemployment. McNabb [1977], Berg and Dalton [1977], and Grice [1978] all indicate that a one percentage point increase in unemployment rates can yield a one-half to three-quarter per cent reduction in female labour force participation. Some recent time-series estimates obtained by the author [Elias, 1979] from Family Exenditure

Survey data show that a one percentage point increase in the unemployment rate of husbands in FES households can yield a one-half percentage point reduction in the labour force participation of their wives. Such effects will significantly affect the size and composition of the labour force if, as projected, male and female unemployment continues to rise. The calls being made in some quarters for measures to reduce the participation of married women in the labour force may therefore be answered by married women themselves as they become too discouraged to seek employment.

The final section of the paper attempts to add a further dimension to an assessment of labour supply, that of quality. However, most of the discussion centres around the supply of specific skills. Given the present lack of detail in the published research on the topic of occupational mobility and skill flexibility and the unavailability of time-series data on employment by occupation, I find it surprising therefore that the authors come down so firmly in favour of a 'laissez faire' system for the provision of vital skills. One the one hand they state that the provision of skills should be left to the firm itself. On the other, they state that the government should encourage flexibility and mobility in the provision of skills. Surely the best way for such flexibility and mobility to be developed is through the provision of training, either directly in skillcentres, or through the ITB's. If a high rate of technological change is forthcoming in the British economy, then we cannot afford to wait for the employer to retrain labour as the demand for new products grows; labour with the requisite skill must be available to employers as and when they need it or we stand to lose valuable export orders through an inability to meet delivery dates. This puts government agencies in the forefront of manpower planning and training for vital skills.

Finally, I refer back to the first section of the paper in which the authors argue for more information about the assumptions embodied in the DE projections of labour supply. While the debate continues about the relevant factors which influence the medium-term trends, I can understand the Department's reluctance to spell out the causal relationships embodied in their supply projection. But without this information the task of updating the projections as our understanding of these influences improves or as social and economic circumstances dictate is more a process of guesswork than forecasting.

REFERENCES
Berg, S. V. and T. R. Dalton [1977]. 'United Kingdom Labour Force Activity Rates: Unemployment and real wages'. *Applied Economics,* 9, no. 3, 265–70.
Corry, B. A. and J. A. Roberts [1970]. 'Activity Rates and Unemployment: The Experience of the United Kingdom 1951–1966'. *Applied Economics,* 2, no. 3, 179–201.
—— [1974]. 'Activity Rates and Unemployment. The UK Experience: Some further results'. *Applied Economics,* 6, no. 1, 1–21.
Easterlin, R. A. [1978]. 'Fertility and Female Labor Force Participation in the United States: Recent Changes and Future Prospects'. Paper prepared for the International Union for the Scientific Study of Population Conference, Helsinki. (mimeographed)
Elias, D. P. B. [1979]. 'A Time-Series Analysis of the Labour Force Participation of Married Women in the UK 1968–75'. *MRG Discussion Paper,* University of Warwick. (mimeographed)
Grice, J. W. [1978]. 'A Time-Series Model for the Labour Supply'. *Treasury Working Paper* AP(78)11. (mimeographed)

McNabb, R. [1977]. 'The Labour Force Participation of Married Women'. *The Manchester School*, 45, no. 3, 221–35.
Wachter, M. L. [1977]. 'Intermediate Swings in Labor Force Participation', in Okun, A. M. and G. L. Perry (eds.). *Brookings Papers on Economic Activity*, 2, 545–74.

Empirical Evidence on Static Labour Supply Models: A Survey of Recent Developments

James J. Heckman
University of Chicago

Mark R. Killingsworth
Rutgers—The State University

Thomas MaCurdy
Stanford University

EMPIRICAL EVIDENCE ON STATIC LABOUR SUPPLY MODELS: A SURVEY OF RECENT DEVELOPMENTS

In this paper, we survey recent empirical work on static labour supply models. The message underlying our discussion is simple. First, *theory matters*. The past fifteen years of research on labour supply indicate that careful attention to theoretical issues in specifying labour supply functions pays valuable dividends in empirical work, and that estimates of labour supply and related parameters are of limited value unless they are derived from careful structural analysis rather than *ad hoc* models. Second, *technique matters*. Another important lesson implicit in the research we survey is that the quality of empirical results on labour supply is quite sensitive to choice of estimation technique: least squares may be quite convenient, but it may also be quite unsatisfactory for analytical or policy purposes. Finally, and corollary to the two previous points: *theory and technique make an important practical difference* in enhancing the ability of analysts and policy-makers to understand important features of labour supply behaviour and to evaluate policy measures. It is sometimes supposed that, while attention to theory and technique is desirable in principle, differences in theoretical approaches or in estimation techniques have few if any practical consequences. However, the experience of the past fifteen years of research on labour supply teaches quite a different lesson: at least as far as empirical evidence on the subject is concerned, differences in theory and technique lead to important differences in results, with important implications for practical questions of analysis and policy.

Our discussion below does not survey literally all work on labour supply.[1] Rather, we have limited our focus. First, we concern ourselves primarily with quantitative aspects of labour supply (e.g., hours worked per year) and for the most part ignore important qualitative aspects of work effort (e.g., occupational choice). Second, we have little to say about non-market activity (e.g., the allocation of 'leisure' time to child-rearing) and focus on time supplied to the market. Third, for the most part we shall centre our attention on empirical rather than theoretical work. Fourth, we confine ourselves to analyses of labour supply in a static setting of certainty and complete information.[2]

Even with these self-imposed limitations, there remains a vast body of work for consideration. In analyzing and interpreting it, we have been both historiographic and analytical. We begin in Part 1 by discussing what we call 'first generation' empirical work on static labour supply models, from the 1930's to about 1974. Part 2 is concerned with the underlying analytical

---

[1] Fortunately, a number of recent or forthcoming surveys supplement or extend our discussion here. See Cain and Watts [1973a], DaVanzo, DeTray and Greenberg [1973], Moffitt and Kehrer [1980], Killingsworth [1980] [1981], Borjas and Heckman [1979], Heckman and MaCurdy [1980a] [1980b] and Greenberg [1972].

[2] For discussions of labour supply under imperfect information and risk (with special reference to job search and unemployment), see Burdett and Mortensen [1978] and the survey by Lippman and McCall [1976a] [1976b]. For discussions of dynamic labour supply models under certainty and perfect information, see Heckman and MaCurdy [1980a] [1980b] and Killingsworth [1981].

framework used in what we call 'second-generation' empirical studies, while in Part 3 we discuss the results of a number of these studies. In Part 4 we briefly examine empirical analyses of static labour supply under conditions of rationing, with special reference to unemployment.

I. First-Generation Empirical Studies of Labour Supply

Beginning with the pioneering studies of labour force participation by Schoenberg and Douglas [1937], most empirical work on labour supply and related matters has been based on the neoclassical analysis of individual choice. The individual derives utility from leisure time L and a composite bundle of consumption goods C, receives R per period in real property income and is paid a real wage of W per period; there are no taxes, and no fixed costs (for commuting, uniforms, etc.) associated with entering the labour market. The individual divides his available time per period between leisure time L and work time H, with $L + H = 1$. The individual acts as if he enjoyed perfect certainty and perfect information, and neither saved nor borrowed;[3] hence, utility maximization is subject to the constraint that total real income, $WH + R$, may not exceed consumption in real terms, C. The individual's labour supply function is therefore $H = H(W, R)$, with H positive whenever the wage exceeds a critical value W_r known as the reservation wage, and H equal to zero otherwise.

The model may readily be extended to the case of persons who are family members. In the most widely-used version of such a model, the family maximizes a family social welfare function which depends on total family consumption C and on the leisure times of its m members. In the absence of saving or borrowing, the family maximizes welfare subject to the constraint that total family income $R + \sum_i W_i H_i$ may not exceed total family consumption C in real terms. (Here, W_i is the real wage and H_i the labour supply of the ith family member.) In this case, any given family member i's labour supply function is $H_i = H_i(W_1, \ldots, W_m, R)$. If intra-family, i.e., 'cross-', substitution effects (on i's labour supply of a change in the wage of some other family member j) are assumed to be zero, then i's labour supply function simplifies somewhat, to $H_i = H_i(W_i, R + \sum_{j \neq i} W_j H_j)$. Again, the H_i function for family member i entails positive H whenever the wage exceeds a critical value W_{ri} known as i's reservation wage, and $H = 0$ otherwise.

The structural model can readily be extended to allow for tax and transfer payments. If one assumes that taxes and transfers do not affect the utility function[4] but do alter the budget constraint subject to which utility is

---

[3] For an extension of the simple model to intertemporal decision-making, see Lluch [1973]. Ghez and Becker [1975] and Weiss [1972] discuss intertemporal labour supply decisions. In either case, savings and borrowing are treated explicitly.

[4] This is somewhat stronger than we need for our purposes. All that we actually require is that tax and transfer payments be neutral with respect to the marginal rate of substitution between C and L; that is, an individual's tax or transfer payments may make him feel better or worse off indirectly (e.g., because he believes that they contribute to the purchase of different goods or services by the government), but so long as the position of indifference curves is unaffected, it does not matter that the utility level associated with a given indifference curve may have changed.

maximized, then, in general terms, all that changes is that the budget constraint becomes $R + WH - T \leq C$ for an individual. Here T is the tax payment that the individual makes (and so will itself be negative when, e.g., the individual is a net recipient of transfer payments), and in general T will depend on income and therefore on hours of work. Fig. 1.1 is a geometric representation of an individual's budget constraint both before ($1RF$) and after ($1R'ZF'$) introduction of a specimen T function for which T is determined by total gross income $WH + R$ such that gross income is taxed first at the marginal rate t_1, between $L = 1$ and $L = L_1$, and then at the higher marginal rate t_2, between $L = L_2$ and $L = 0$.

Modifying the basic labour supply function to allow for tax and transfer payments is straightforward. For example, one may write the post-tax budget constraint relevant to an individual by linearizing it at his current equilibrium and then projecting it back to where $L = 1$. For example, someone who has chosen a point on the line segment $F'Z$ of the post-tax budget constraint in Fig. 1.1 has a net wage $\hat{W}$ equal to $W(1-t_2)$ and acts as if he had real property income $\hat{R}$ equal to $\bar{R}$; while an individual who has chosen a point on the line segment $R'Z$ of the post-tax budget constraint has a net wage $\hat{W}$. equal to $W(1-t_1)$ and acts as if he had real property income $\hat{R}$ equal to R'. Hence, using

Fig. 1.1: Taxes in the Simple Model

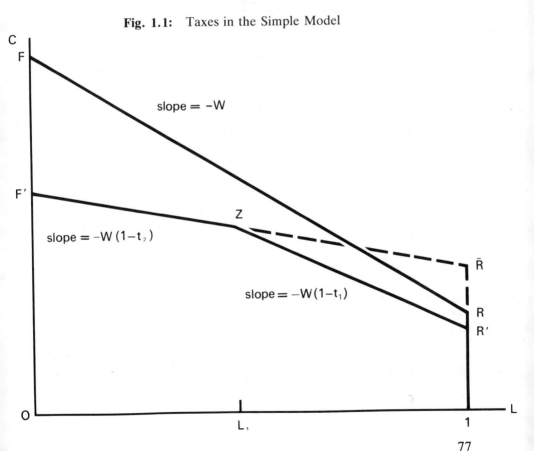

this 'linearized budget constraint' method, one may rewrite the labour supply function as $H = H(\hat{W}, \hat{V})$ —*mutatis mutandis*, very much the same as before. In particular, as before, the individual will have $H > 0$ so long as the net wage $\hat{W}$ exceeds a critical reservation level W_r, and will have $H = 0$ otherwise. On the other hand, one may use an explicit utility function to evaluate the utility of being at any of the segments along an after-tax budget constraint such as $1R'ZF'$ in Fig. 1.1, and then solve for the level of hours of work that yields maximum utility. (We say more about this particular approach in Part 2 below.)

Simple theoretical labour supply models such as the ones just described imply a number of testable propositions: for example, (i) *negativity*—the own-substitution effect (of a compensated change in one's own wage) on leisure time must always be negative; (ii) *symmetry*—cross-substitution effects for any pair of family members (of a compensated change in family member i's wage on family member j's wage, and vice-versa) must be equal; (iii) *homogeneity*—labour supply functions are homogeneous of degree zero in nominal wages, nominal property income and prices, so that labour supply depends only on wages and property income in real terms and on relative prices; and (iv) *continuity*—labour supply functions will be continuous (except perhaps at points such as Z in Figure 1.1, where marginal tax rates change discontinuously) and entail positive or zero hours of work depending on whether the wage exceeds or does not exceed the critical value W_r known as the reservation wage. Finally, since W and R determine the optimal or utility-maximizing levels of C and L, and since utility in turn depends on C and L, W and R indirectly determine maximized utility. This maximized utility may therefore be written as $V(W, R)$; and the function for maximized utility $V = V(W, R)$ is often known as the indirect utility function. By *Roy's identity*, labour supply H may be written as a function of partial derivatives of the indirect or maximized utility function:[5]

$$H = V_W/V_R$$

There are three main kinds of approaches to empirical estimation of labour supply models. First, one may start with an explicit functional form for the utility function; and then derive a specification for the labour supply function by first maximizing the utility function subject to the budget constraint and then solving for the value of H at the optimum. Second, one may start with an indirect utility function and obtain a specification for the labour supply function using Roy's identity. Finally, one may dispense with explicit reference to utility functions as such, and instead use 'free-form' labour supply functions chosen either arbitrarily or on the basis of specific *a priori* considerations. (For discussion of alternative approaches to specification and of the implications of each approach for choice of estimation technique, see Abbott and Ashenfelter [1976].)

---

[5] See Roy [1947]. As Brown and Deaton [1972] observe, this means that one may easily derive a labour supply function that obeys all the restrictions of the neoclassical consumer-worker model by applying Roy's identity to any function that is homogeneous of degree zero in wages, property income and prices. This result often proves to be a considerable convenience, since it means that reference to utility functions *per se* is unnecessary for purposes of deriving specifications for the labour supply function.

Until recently, most work used ordinary least squares regression (OLS) to estimate labour supply functions derived under the third approach; we call such research 'first-generation' research. (For examples of first-generation work and of antecedents to what we describe below as 'second-generation' work, see Cain and Watts, eds. [1973].) Examples of linear specifications that are prototypes of ones widely-used in first-generation research include the following:

(1) $\qquad H = a + bW + cR + \epsilon$

(2) $\qquad H_i = a_i + \sum_j b_{ij} W_j + c_i R + \epsilon_i$

(3) $\qquad H_i = a_i + b_i W_i + c_i (R + \sum_{j \neq i} W_j H_j) + \epsilon_i$

where ϵ (or ϵ_i) is a stochastic term. From the above discussion, (1) refers to the labour supply of a given individual, while (2) and (3) refer to the labour supply of a given family member. (2) allows for non-zero intra-family or cross-substitution effects on i's labour supply, while (3) constrains all such effects to be zero.

A number of remarks of clarification or explanation are useful at this point. First, we either ignore or else treat as parameters the intercept terms in the above expressions. However, in practice they are made a function of various variables such as age, sex, race and the like that may be relevant to labour supply via their effect on, or association with, tastes for work, etc.

Second, we write (1) – (3) as linear in a (or a_i), W and R for convenience only; after all, the a (or a_i) term could be understood to include polynomials in W, R or other variables, and the H on the left hand side of (1) – (3) could just as well be regarded as a transformation (logarithmic, etc.) of the actual level of hours of work.

Finally, the error term ϵ (or ϵ_i) is usually assumed to be randomly distributed in the population of individuals. (The assumption that ϵ is a normally-distributed random variable in the population is convenient, and therefore widely used. However, in contrast with second-generation work, it is not an essential assumption in first-generation studies.) In general, ϵ is implicitly or explicitly assumed to arise from factors known to the individual decision-maker but not to the empirical investigator. In particular, ϵ may arise from unobserved components from *either* side of labour supply equations such as (1). For example, if the dependent variable H is measured with error, the available measure $\hat{H}$ differs from the true or actual value H by the amount of measurement error m, which is usually taken to be comprehended within ϵ. Similarly, omitted right-hand side variables uncorrelated with the included variables are also usually taken to be included within, and to give rise to, ϵ. (Uncertainty as a source of equation error is never explicitly treated in first-generation studies.)

On the whole, questions about the sources of ϵ were ignored or brushed aside in first generation studies. Most of this research proceeded on the maintained assumption that the error term was in fact random, and made no distinction between the different factors that may have generated it. (In contrast, as we indicate later on, this question has become an important concern of more recent second-generation research.)

The empirical results of these first-generation studies of labour supply functions are not particularly encouraging, and often raise more questions than they answer. To document this point, in Table 1.1 we present the rather wide range of first-generation OLS estimates obtained from US data for several key labour-supply magnitudes of particular theoretical or practical interest: the gross, own- and cross-substitution elasticities of labour supply with respect to wages, and the elasticity of labour supply with respect to property income.[6]

Table 1.1: Summary of Empirical Estimates of Labour Supply Elasticities in 'First-Generation' Studies

Labour supply elasticity				
Population group	gross own-wage rate	compensated own-wage rate[1]	compensated spouse's-wage rate[2]	property income[3]
Males	− ·45 to + ·55	− ·05 to + ·96	0 or < 0	0 to − ·16
Females	− ·10 to + 1·60	− ·05 to + 2·00	0 to − ·40	− ·1 to − ·75

[1] 'own-substitution effect' expressed as an elasticity
[2] 'cross-substitution effect' expressed as an elasticity
[3] elasticity of hours of work with respect to property income

Several difficulties in the table are immediately apparent. First, the range of estimates for any given elasticity is typically quite large—in most cases, much too large to be of much use for analytical or policy purposes. For example, Cain and Watts [1973a] observed that the estimates presented in their collection of relatively advanced 'first-generation' empirical studies [1973b] implied that the reduction in work hours attendant upon introduction of a negative income tax scheme could be anything between four and forty per cent, depending on the specific set of estimates used to simulate the effects of such a scheme.

Second, not infrequently empirical estimates of certain labour supply responses have turned out to be inconsistent with basic theoretical predictions derived from the underlying labour supply model. For example, in almost all cases symmetry is rejected by the empirical results; and at times the empirical evidence has proven inconsistent with negativity.

These perceived failures of first-generation studies stimulated a more careful examination of theoretical labour supply models and of econometric methods used to secure labour supply parameter estimates. Second-generation analysis is much more explicit than its predecessor about the economic models underlying estimating equations, and about the way unobserveables enter these models. As a consequence of making crucial assumptions explicit, there has been rapid progress in relaxing and testing some of the more restrictive of

[6] For more detailed tabular summaries of some of the results of first-generation work, see Cain and Watts [1973a], Killingsworth [1980] [1981], DaVanzo, DeTray and Greenberg [1973] and Borjas and Heckman [1979]. Needless to say, the entries in Table 1.1 are approximate and are offered as a summary, not as a comprehensive and exhaustive list of all available results. In most cases, the elasticities reported in first generation work that fit in the range of values shown in Table 1.1 are as reported by the authors of individual studies, but in other cases we have calculated the elasticities ourselves, evaluating them at the means of the samples used by specific authors.

these assumptions, and not infrequently the resulting labour supply estimates conform more closely to predictions of the theory.

Three issues have received particular attention in second-generation work, and in each case this work seems—at least with hindsight—to be a natural response to difficulties revealed in, but not resolved by, first-generation studies. These issues are as follows:

(i) *The nature of labour supply.* Even in purely quantitative terms, 'labour supply' could in principle refer to a variety of different phenomena: the fact of working or not working (i.e., 'labour force participation'), hours worked per week, weeks worked per year, hours worked per year, and so on. In much first-generation work, functions such as (1) – (3) were used to analyze H, 'labour supply,' defined in all of these different ways: weekly hours, annual weeks, participation in a survey week, participation during a year, lifetime participation and the fraction of a lifetime spent working. In contrast, recent work recognizes that (except perhaps in a few very special cases) it is not possible to treat these various phenomena as analytically interchangeable or as being given by the same function. Accordingly, theoretical models of participation and hours of work, of hours per week and weeks per year, of lifetime participation and lifetime hours of work, etc., have recently been developed and empirically implemented.[7] These studies go part way in reconciling persistent differences in empirical estimates of labour supply parameters derived by fitting the same function to data on different aspects of 'labour supply,' H. Other studies consider such phenomena as the standard workweek[8] and the relation between labour supply and unemployment.[9]

(ii) *Functional form and econometric technique.* In implementing the different models of labour supply described above, it is necessary to consider a number of important questions about specification and estimation. In turn, these questions raise further questions about the treatment of unobserveables and the problem of self-selection bias or, more generally, sample selection bias. For example, it is worth noting, at the outset, that equations such as (1) – (3) are not in fact accurate or complete representations of the labour supply function implied by even the simplest theoretical labour supply model. For even the simplest model of this kind implies a labour supply function such as the one shown in Figure 1.1(a), which, for a single individual, may be stated algebraically for purposes of econometric estimation as

(4·1) $\qquad H = a + bW + cR + \epsilon$ $\qquad\qquad$ *iff* $W > W_r$

(4·2) $\qquad H = 0$ $\qquad\qquad\qquad\qquad\qquad$ otherwise

where W_r is the reservation wage, found by setting the right-hand side of (4·1) equal to zero and then solving for W. First-generation empirical studies almost entirely ignored this basic consideration. In some studies, researchers instead

---

[7] For example, Hanoch [1980] treats hours of leisure during working weeks and hours of leisure during nonworking weeks as imperfect substitute in the utility function.

[8] Judging from data on *reported* weekly hours, the standard workweek is widespread. (For example, Rosen [1969, p. 264] reports that 40-hour observations were 49% of all observations in his data set on weekly work hours.) For discussion of the standard workweek, see Part 4 below.

[9] For example, see Ashenfelter [1980] and our discussion in Part 4 below.

proceeded to fit equations such as (1) to a random sample taken from the entire population, with the labour supply of non-working individuals set at zero.[10] In effect, this approach requires the assumption that (1) or its equivalent, (4·1), hold for all values of W, not just for those values in excess of the reservation wage. Hence, this procedure misspecifies the model and so will produce inconsistent estimates of its parameters.

In other first-generation work, researchers obtained OLS estimates of the parameters of functions such as (1) using population subsamples consisting of working individuals only.[11] While rarely stated explicitly, it appears that the justification for this alternative procedure is that, since it fits (4·1) using only observations that do in fact have $W > W_r$, no problem of specification will arise. However, while $W > W_r$ for working individuals, this procedure is still inappropriate. The consistency of OLS estimates of functions such as (1) or (4·1) rests on the assumption that the stochastic term ϵ is random; but even if the randomness assumption is correct as regards random samples taken from the population as a whole, it is necessarily violated, except under very special conditions, when the analysis is restricted to a population subsample of working individuals only. To see this, note that an individual will be included in an estimation subsample of workers if and only if $H > 0$, or, by (4·1), if and only if $\epsilon > - (a + bW + cR) \equiv - J$. So ϵ must necessarily be correlated with W and R in the estimation subsample of working individuals, except for unlikely cases such as $b = c = 0$, even if ϵ is random in samples taken randomly from the entire population. In other words, observations are selected into an estimation subsample of workers not on a random basis, but rather systematically — according to the criterion $\epsilon > - J$ — so that parameter estimates based on applying OLS to that subsample will not provide consistent measures of the labour supply responses to which the model refers.

Of course, if everyone in the relevant *population* works, then everyone has $W > W_r$. In this case, there is no need to worry either about corner solutions (in which $W \leq W_r$) or about the possibility that ϵ may be nonrandom within the 'subsample' of workers: the working 'subsample' and the full population sample will be one and the same, and application of OLS to (4.1) will produce consistent estimates. Initial first-generation research was concerned with populations such as prime-age males, in which virtually everyone did, in fact, work.[12] However, subsequent work on other populations, such as women or teenagers, raised these issues with full force: often, a substantial fraction (at times, over two-thirds) of the persons in random samples taken from such populations were not at work. The need to address the question of corner solutions, and to consider the possibility that the distribution of ϵ within

---

[10] For example, Hall [1973] follows this procedure.

[11] This is the procedure used in all of the studies presented in Cain and Watts, eds., [1973b] except for that by Hall [1973].

[12] One of the earliest examples is Kosters [1966] [1969], but he also considers the labour supply of population groups in which substantially less than all of the population is at work. It is worth noting that the issues discussed here may be important even when almost all the persons in a given population are at work. For example, Garfinkel [1973] found that, when he excluded the seven non-workers that he found in a sample of 3969 males, the estimated coefficient on his R variable took on the 'wrong' sign (implying that leisure is an inferior good) and became statistically insignificant.

working subsamples might not be random, became increasingly clear.[13] Moreover, in doing so, it becomes necessary to distinguish between labour supply as 'participation' (i.e., being or not being at a corner solution) and labour supply as 'hours of work,' as discussed earlier. While generated from the same preference function, the hours of work equation and the participation equation are fundamentally different.

(iii) *Nonlinear budget constraints.* In elementary textbook discussions, the budget constraint facing the individual is a straight line whose slope is equal to the real wage. In the presence of tax and transfer systems, fixed costs of work, employer preferences for minimum hours of work, etc., budget constraints are complex and contain kinks, discontinuities, gaps, nonconvexities, etc. Most first-generation work ignored these phenomena altogether. As a simple illustration of some of the questions raised by complex budget constraints, note that, in principle, the labour supply function implied by the tax system shown in Fig. 1.1 could be written

(5) $\qquad H = a + b\hat{W} + c\hat{R} + \epsilon$

where
$$\hat{W} = W(1-t_1) \text{ and } \hat{R} = R' \text{ if } H \in [0, 1 - L_1]$$
$$\hat{W} = W(1-t_2) \text{ and } \hat{R} = \bar{R} \text{ if } H \in (1 - L_1, 1]$$

However, even in the absence of the econometric problems noted earlier, estimates of (5) obtained using least squares will be inconsistent: since $\hat{W}$ and $\hat{V}$ are a result as well as a cause of the individual's labour supply H, they are necessarily correlated with ϵ.[14]

One of the main reasons for estimating labour supply functions is to use the resulting estimates to evaluate likely responses to alternative social programs. Thus, estimates derived from models that incorporate tax and transfer effects and other phenomena that generate complex budget constraints are especially important: in some cases, persons subjected to social programs face complex budget constraints that influence their response to those programs, while in others, the programs themselves entail complex budget constraints. Much recent research has been explicitly concerned with the effects of various social programs and has been funded by agencies responsible for those programs (the most obvious, though not the only, example in this regard is the US negative income tax experiments). Accordingly, it is not surprising that many second-generation studies have devoted special attention to complex budget constraints that affect and are affected by policy measures of this kind.

In sum, analysis and technique go together, and first-generation work, which glossed over some of the structural aspects of labour supply decisions and used empirical techniques that did not adequately address some of the complexities

[13] See, for example, the studies in Cain and Watts, eds. [1973b]. One extremely important reason why it is essential to consider questions relating to corner solutions is that measures of wage rates are, for the most part, simply unavailable for persons who are not at work, which poses obvious problems for any attempt to fit a function such as (1) in Part 1, and which suggests that it is necessary to use a statistical model to address questions about the joint determination of hours of work *and* wage rates; see, in particular, Heckman [1974].

[14] Of course, in principle this simultaneity between ϵ, W and V could be addressed by choice of appropriate instruments for $\hat{W}$ *and* $\hat{V}$, but in practice, as in Hall [1973], it has been ignored.

of that structure, suffered from a number of serious problems. The results of second-generation work, to which we now turn, suggest that solving these problems makes a considerable difference for estimates of labour supply parameters, with correspondingly considerable implications for analysis and policy.

II. Second-Generation Empirical Studies of Labour Supply: Theoretical Models and Statistical Strategies

In this section, we consider theoretical models and statistical strategies used in second-generation research, most of which has appeared since the early 1970's. In general terms, the methodology underlying this research is as follows: first, to develop theoretical models in which the various structural aspects of labour supply decisions are set out and considered in detail; and, second, to develop statistical procedures for estimation of labour supply parameters that consider the structural aspects of labour supply decisions, and therefore effectively capture the essential features of the process of optimization described by the theoretical model. Roughly speaking, the strategy is to select a functional form for the individual's preference structure (e.g., for the utility function or for some other function related to the utility function, such as the marginal rate of substitution function or the indirect utility function). Explicitly accounting for the budget line confronting the individual, these procedures either explicitly or implicitly evaluate the individual's utility at each point on the budget line (e.g., working at wage W with marginal tax rate t_j, working at wage W with marginal tax rate t_k, not working and so on). For each set of parameters of the utility (or other utility-related) function and a given value of the unobservable variable, there is some equilibrium position, either interior or corner. By checking each point on the budget line (including any kinks, such as the point Z in Fig. 1.1) and choosing the one with the highest utility, one could literally solve the individual's optimization problem for each set of parameter values—though, with enough structure on the problem, this brute-force procedure is unnecessary. As parameter values are changed, the computed optimum changes; the relevant parameters may be estimated by minimising some measures of the discrepancy between the observed and predicted labour supplies of the individuals in the estimation sample (including those individuals who do not work, individuals at kink-points such as Z, etc.). The non-random nature of ϵ for persons at particular points on the budget line (e.g., for workers vs. nonworkers) is explicitly accounted for.

This general strategy, or a shortcut for it, is the basis for much second-generation work. We begin this part by examining general principles and then turn to three leading cases: first, basic models of labour supply without fixed costs of work or taxation; second, models of labour supply with fixed costs of work; and, finally, models of labour supply with both fixed costs of work and taxation (including 'negative' taxation, via transfer programs).

All of the models discussed in this section assume that the individual acts as if he is able to choose any amount of hours of work. After discussing in Part 3 some empirical findings derived from the models discussed in this Part, we briefly turn in Part 4 to some recent models of labour supply rationing. In these models, the individual is constrained not only in terms of the W and V he is eligible to receive but also in terms of the H values he may choose.

A. General Principles: The Basic Index Function Model

The essential statistical notions underlying most second-generation work on labour supply are straightforward. Labour supply decisions may be regarded as a combination of quantitative choices (e.g., the number of hours that will be worked, given that one will work) and discrete choices (e.g., to work or not to work). (Heckman [1974] [1976].) These two kinds of choices are intimately connected. In particular, observed choices constitute evidence on underlying preferences and provide both quantitative and qualitative measures of aspects of those preferences. The preferences themselves may be thought of as latent variables; sometimes, as when labour supply is positive, the latent variables are directly observed, but at other times (as when an individual does not work) the investigator only knows whether these latent variables have crossed some threshold. In any event, qualitative and quantitative data on observed behaviour permit one to construct a function that indexes the basic latent variables—a general 'index function'. By combining statistical methods for discrete choice and quantitative choice (such as probit or other quantal choice models,[15] and regression models) one may estimate the parameters that generate observed behaviour.

In its essentials, the approach used in all of the models considered in this part may be understood most easily by considering a simple binary choice model of the labour supply of individuals who face budget lines such as $1RF$, with real property income R and real wage W, as shown in Fig. 1.1. (Hence, taxes and fixed costs of work are ignored for the time being.) Let the maximum utility attainable by these individuals be $V^w (W, R, \epsilon)$ and $V^n (R, \epsilon)$ when they do or do not work, respectively; and assume that W and R are observed and ϵ is an unobserved random term. (Obviously, W is irrelevant to utility when an individual does not work.) Next, define $Y_1 \equiv V^w - V^n$. Clearly,

(1.1) $Y_1 > 0 \longleftrightarrow H > 0$

(1.2) $Y_1 \leqslant 0 \longleftrightarrow H = 0$

This condition, or closely-related conditions, underlies much second-generation work on labour supply.

If the individual works, then one may use Roy's identity to derive an expression for hours of work:

$$H = V_w^w / V_R^w \longleftrightarrow Y_1 > 0$$

No matter how derived, the hours of work equation may be written as

---

[15] For example, see Amemiya [1975], McFadden [1976] and Domencich and McFadden [1975]. For discussions of the notion of 'index functions' see, e.g., Heckman [1976] [1978] [1980] and Schmidt [1979].

Fig. 1.2(a): Continuous
Labour Supply Schedule

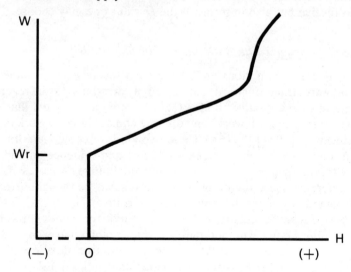

Fig. 1.2(b): Discontinuous
Labour Supply Schedule

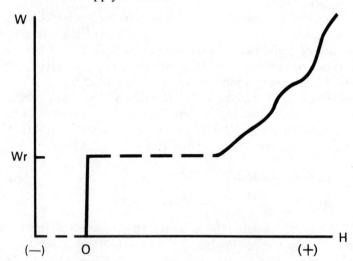

(2) $\qquad Y_2 = H(W, R, \epsilon)$

where, from the above,

$\qquad Y_2 = V_w^W/W_R^w \longleftrightarrow Y_1 > 0$

$\qquad Y_2 = 0 \qquad \longleftrightarrow Y_1 \leqslant 0$

Equations (1) and (2) are a prototype of a class of sample selection conditions that has received considerable attention in the recent econometric literature. To focus on the essential statistical issues involved, suppose that the Y_i in (1) – (2) are given by

(3.1) $Y_1 = Z_1 b_1 + \epsilon_1$

(3.2) $Y_2 = Z_2 b_2 + \epsilon_2$

where ϵ_1 and ϵ_2 are mean-zero random variables with finite second moments. Further, suppose that we desire to estimate b_2, and that we have data on Y_2 only for those individuals in a population sample for whom $Y_1 > 0$. The regression for Y_2 given Z_2 and $Y_1 > 0$ for this subsample of the population is

(4) $E(Y_2 \mid Z_2, Y_1 > 0) = Z_2 b_2 + E (\epsilon_2 \mid Y_1 > 0)$

$$= Z_2 b_2 + E(\epsilon_2 \mid \epsilon_1 > -Z_1 b_1)$$

Now, if ϵ_1 *and* ϵ_2 are independent, then $E(\epsilon_2 \mid \epsilon_1 > - Z_1 b_1) \equiv K$ will be zero, as assumed in conventional OLS regression. However, in all other cases, K depends on Z_1 and, in particular, on the probability that an observation with observed characteristics Z_1 will be found in the subsample of persons who have $Y_1 > 0$.

Therefore, rewrite (4) as

(5) $E(Y_2 \mid Z_2, Y_1 > 0) = Z_2 b_2 + K$

where K is a function of the parameters θ of the joint distribution of ϵ_1 and ϵ_2 and of the Z_1. (In particular, K is a function of the probability that an observation with characteristics Z_1 will be found in the subsample.) Fitting a regression of Y_1 on Z_1 only, as in much first-generation work, omits the term K—that is, it ignores the fact that the subsample is not randomly-selected, but rather is selected according to the rule $\epsilon_1 > - Z_1 b_1$. Hence standard specification-error arguments apply. (Heckman [1976] [1980a].)

For example, consider a variable Z_{2j} that appears in both Z_1 and Z_2. Let Y_2 be hours of work. A regression of Y_2 on Z_2 that does not correct for the nonrandom nature of sample selection (that is, omits the 'sample selection variable' K) will not estimate the coefficient on Z_{2j} consistently. Rather, such a regression will obtain an estimate of b'_{2j}, where, to a first order of approximation,

$$b'_{2j} = b_{2j} + (\partial K / \partial Z_{2j}).$$

The essential point is that, as Z_{2j} changes, so does the effective composition of the subsample of workers. Computed partial derivatives with respect to Z_{2j} combine (1) the *ceteris paribus* effect of changing Z_{2j} while tastes remain unchanged, b_j, and (ii) the association between Z_{2j} and tastes for work *within the subsample*, $\partial K / \partial Z_{2j}$.

The subsample distribution of tastes for work is the distribution of ϵ conditional on (1.1) being satisfied; and this second effect is a consequence of entry into and exit from the subsample of observations under the requirement that (1.1) be satisfied.

Condition (1) compresses two distinct ideas that are sometimes confused in the literature. The first idea is that of self-selection: for example, an individual chooses either to work or not to work, so a subsample of working individuals is not randomly-selected from an initial random population sample but is, rather, self-selected according to condition (1.1). The second idea is a more general concept: that of a sample selection rule of *some* kind (of which self-selection is one special case, though hardly the only one). That is, starting with an ideal random population sample, *some* rule generates an observed subsample of individuals to be investigated. These rules may or may not be the consequences of choices made by the individuals being studied. For example, administrators of negative income tax experiments decided to 'experiment' on low-income populations, and hence to select subsamples for study under the condition that income had to be no greater than some maximum amount. In this case, the 'Y_1' of (1) is the difference between this maximum and actual income and labour supply is the 'Y_2' of (1); since earnings and therefore income, are in part generated by tastes for work, it is likely that ϵ_1 and ϵ_2 are correlated—so that (5) applies with full force. (See, for example, Cain and Watts [1973a, p. 343].)

As this discussion suggests, the index function model can readily be generalized to encompass a variety of different sample selection rules and behavioural functions, or even a multiplicity of such rules and functions. Thus the Y_1 and Y_2 of (1) may be vectors, and the simultaneous satisfaction of a set of sample selection rules can (still) be characterized by the condition $Y_1 > 0$. An important special case of this approach that is useful for the analysis of taxation and fixed costs of work, to which we devote special attention below, treats Y_1 as a scalar random variable. Different samples are generated depending on the boundary points of the random variable. In these models, sample i (e.g., workers and nonworkers; persons facing marginal tax rate t_i; etc.) is generated if

$$C_{i-1} < Y_1 < C_i, \qquad i = 1, \ldots, I$$

where C_j is a boundary value. If Y_1 is normally distributed, then an ordered probit model is generated (see Amemiya [1973], Johnson [1972] and Rosett and Nelson [1975]). Given the sample selection rule, one may then compute the conditional means for the Y_2 functions, a la (5), and hence correct regression estimators for the sample selection bias that would arise if terms such as K in (5) were omitted. In the next sections of this part, we consider application of these general principles to specific questions in the analysis of labour supply.

B. *Labour Supply Without Fixed Costs or Taxes*

First consider a simple model of labour supply that neglects fixed costs of work and taxes. Following Heckman [1974], we write the individual's strictly quasiconcave preference function as $U = U(C, L, \epsilon)$, where ϵ is a 'taste shifter.' The utility function implies a function for the marginal rate of substitution M, i.e., for the ratio $M \equiv U_L(C, L, \epsilon)/U_C(C, L, \epsilon)$ of the partial derivatives of the utility function. Like U, M is a function of C, L and ϵ; in particular, $M = M(C, L, \epsilon) = M(R + W(1-L), L, \epsilon)$. Write the density of ϵ in the population of individuals as $f(\epsilon)$; note that this function induces a distribution on U and M.

Now, an individual will work if and only if his best alternative involving work is better than not working (i.e., having $L = 1$). In the present model, the budget constraint is linear. Therefore, a global comparison between the best attainable utility from working and the utility attainable when $L = 1$ reduces to a local comparison between the marginal value of leisure at the no-work position (= the slope of the individual's highest attainable indifference curve at $H = 0$, i.e., his reservation wage $W_r = M(R, 1, \epsilon)$) and the wage rate W. The reservation wage is defined as the marginal rate of substitution evaluated at $L = 1$ (at which $H = 0$ and $C = WH + R = R$); hence, we have

$$(6.1) \qquad W > M(R, 1, \epsilon) \qquad \longleftrightarrow \qquad H > 0$$
$$(6.2) \qquad W \leqslant M(R, 1, \epsilon) \qquad \longleftrightarrow \qquad H = 0$$

Conditions (6) define a set of values for W, R and ϵ such that individuals do—(6.1)—or do not—(6.2)—work. In terms of the prototype model discussed earlier, $Y_1 = W - M(R, 1, \epsilon)$ and the individual works if and only if $Y_1 > 0$. If (6.1) is satisfied, then the individual's labour supply function may be derived by solving for $H = 1 - L$. From the first order condition for maximum utility, $W = M(R + WH, 1 - H, \epsilon)$ if and only if $H > 0$; thus, if (6.1) holds, then the labour supply function can be obtained by solving the relation $W = M(R + WH, 1 - H, \epsilon)$ for H. Let $H(W, R, \epsilon)$ be the solution of this relation for H. Then one may characterize labour supply behaviour by

$$(7.1) \qquad H = H(W, R, \epsilon) \qquad \longleftrightarrow \qquad W > M(R, 1, \epsilon)$$
$$(7.2) \qquad H = 0 \qquad\qquad \longleftrightarrow \qquad W \leqslant M(R, 1, \epsilon)$$

H_W and H_R are the (uncompensated) wage and property income derivatives for the labour supply function in (7.1); it is crucial to note that these derivatives are computed with ϵ fixed.

Thus far, our discussion has been concerned with *given individuals*. However, the model also has a number of implications about the behaviour of *populations* and *subpopulations*. First, note that, given $f(\epsilon)$, one can derive the density of M evaluated at R and $L = 1$, which we write as $g(M(R, 1, \epsilon))$. Thus, from (7), the fraction of the population that works is given by

$$(8) \qquad P(W, R) = \int_{-\infty}^{W} g(M(R, 1, \epsilon))\, dM = Pr\,[M(R, 1, \epsilon) < W]$$

Let P_w and P_R refer to the derivatives of (8) with respect to W and R, respectively; these two derivatives refer to the effect of changes in W and R, respectively, on the fraction of the population that works.

Further, (7) also implies that the average level of labour supply for the sub-population of persons who work is given by

$$(9) \qquad E(H|M(R, 1, \epsilon) < W, W, R)$$

$$= \int_{\{\epsilon/M(R,\, 1,\, \epsilon)\, <\, W\}} H(W, R, \epsilon)f(\epsilon)d\epsilon \int_{-\infty}^{W} g(M(R, 1, \epsilon)dM$$

This may be called the 'conditional labour supply function,' i.e., labour supply conditional on $H > 0$. Let C_W (C_R) refer to the derivative of (9) with respect to W (R). Clearly, C_W (C_R) refers to the effect of changes in W (R) on the average labour supply of persons who work.

Finally, (7) implies that the average level of labour supply for the entire population—working or not—is given by the expected-value locus:

$$(10) \qquad E(H|W, R) = \int_{\{\epsilon|M(R,\, 1,\, \epsilon)\, <\, W\}} H(W, R, \epsilon)f(\epsilon)d\epsilon$$

Let E_W (E_R) refer to the derivative of this expected-value locus with respect to W (R). E_W (E_R) refers to the effect of changes in W (R) on the average labour supply of the entire population. It encompasses both changes in the labour supply of persons who switch from working to not working, or vice-versa, as given by (8), and changes in the labour supply of persons who continue to work, as given by (9).

Thus, the model (7) permits consideration of four related, but conceptually distinct, questions: (i) the labour supply H of a *given worker*, (7.1); (ii) the proportion P of the population at work, (8); (iii) the average labour supply $E(H|W, R, H > 0)$ of working persons, (9); and (iv) the average labour supply $E(H|W, R)$ of all persons, working or not, (10). Because these four functions (7)–(10) refer to distinct phenomena, it is clear that their partial derivatives with respect to W and R are also conceptually different. For example, the partial derivatives P_W and P_R are not identical to H_W and H_R, respectively. In particular, P_W must be positive, while H_W need not be; and P_R and H_R need not be equal. Likewise, E_W and E_R (or C_W and C_R) will not be equal to H_W and H_R, respectively, unless (6.1) holds for all persons in the relevant population (that is, unless all persons in the population are at work).

Finally, consider estimation of the various derivatives just discussed. The complete model of labour supply as given in (4) of the previous section or in (2) or (7) of the present section might be given a simple explicit specification such as

$$(11.1) \qquad H = a + b \ln W + cR + \epsilon \quad \text{if } a + b \ln W + cR + \epsilon > 0$$
$$(11.2) \qquad H = 0 \qquad\qquad\qquad\quad \text{if } a + b \ln W + cR + \epsilon \leq 0$$

Thus, if ϵ is assumed to be a normally-distributed random variable and wage data are available for all observations, (11) can be estimated using the maximum-likelihood technique of Tobin [1958] or the regression procedures of Amemiya [1973] or Heckman [1976]; for example, see Schultz [1980]. As applied to (11), the Tobit approach proceeds by specifying that H is given by the right-hand side of (11.1) *if* the right-hand side is positive, and that $H = 0$ otherwise. This being the case, it is natural to think of the right-hand side of (11.1) as 'desired' hours of work, and to observe that 'desired' hours will be non-positive (that is, 'desired' leisure $L = 1 - H$ will exceed unity) when, and only when, $W > M(R, 1, \epsilon)$. (Thus, 'desired' leisure is the value obtained by solving the relation $W = M(R + W(1-L), L, \epsilon)$ *without* regard for the constraint $L \leqslant 1$.)

Under the assumptions noted above, these procedures produce consistent estimates of the parameters of (11.1), and thus of structural effects such as H_W and H_R. These are of direct interest for considering issues about the labour supply of given workers (for example, questions about income and substitution effects). However, as is obvious from inspection of (8)–(10), estimates of (11.1) can also be used to answer questions about the other aspects of labour supply mentioned earlier (e.g., about P_W, C_W and E_W). Once estimates of the parameters of (7) have been obtained, they can then be used to evaluate (8)–(10), since (8)–(10) are generated by the same parameters that govern (7). Thus, the advantage of the structural approach outlined here is that it permits estimation of the parameters that are common to all four aspects of labour supply discussed above and that can be used to analyze each of them. (For discussion of this point, see Schultz [1980].)

Of course, in lieu of this approach, one may use a discrete dependent variables technique (e.g., probit) to estimate the parameters of (8) alone; use least squares and data restricted to the working subpopulation (that is, persons with $H > 0$) to estimate the parameters of (9) only; or use least squares and data on the entire population (with the labour supply of non-workers set at zero) to estimate the parameters of (10) only. However, such estimates are measures only of the particular labour supply response with which they are concerned; also, note that least squares estimates of (9) or (10) can hold only as approximations. Moreover, such alternative estimates cannot be regarded as measures of H_W or H_R. This simple point has been ignored in much of the first-generation literature. For example, Hall [1973] obtains least squares estimates of (11) (with nonworkers' supplies set at zero), i.e., obtains approximations of the expected-value locus derivatives E_W and E_R. However, he then interprets these derivatives as if they were measures of H_W and H_R. Others interpret the partial derivatives of (10)—that is, estimates of labour supply functions fitted to subsamples of workers—as estimates of the parameters of (7.1). These interpretations are incorrect[16].

Thus far, we have evaded an important practical problem of estimation: in general, data on wage rates W are available only for persons who are working

---

[16] For nonworkers, H_W *and* H_R are both zero by definition of the term 'nonworker'. It is straightforward to verify that the partial derivative of expected hours with respect to W from (10) exceeds the mean value of H_W in the population. If leisure is a normal good, then the partial derivative of expected hours with respect to R is smaller than the mean value of H_R in the population.

(or, in terms of our previous discussion, only for persons for whom (6.1) holds). In most cases, therefore, direct estimation of (11) *per se* is not possible. Three alternative approaches have therefore been used in the literature. In the first, which may be called the 'imputed wage' approach, one first fits OLS wage equations of the form

$$(12) \qquad W = \beta X + u$$

where u is a random term, to subsamples restricted to working persons. One then uses the OLS estimates of ß, $\hat{\text{ß}}$, to compute 'predicted' or 'imputed' wage rates $\hat{W} = \hat{\text{ß}}X$ for nonworkers; these $\hat{W}$ are then treated as data on W and are used (either with actual W or imputed $\hat{W}$ values for workers) in estimation of (11) by, e.g., Tobit. However, estimates of (12) obtained in this way are subject to the same sort of sample selection bias that infects labour supply functions that are estimated using subsamples restricted to workers (Gronau [1974]).

A second approach is to specify both a wage equation and an hours equation and then 'substitute out' the W in (9) by replacing it with the right-hand side of an expression such as (12). For example, Heckman [1976] writes the reservation wage function at $H = 0$ in semilog form as

$$(13.1) \qquad ln\ M = \alpha_0 + \alpha_1 R + \alpha_2 Z_2 + \epsilon$$

and the market wage function as

$$(13.2) \qquad ln\ W = \beta_0 + \beta_1 Z_1 + v$$

where ϵ and v are mean-zero jointly normally-distributed random error terms. Hours of work for observations for which $ln\ W > ln\ M$ are assumed to be proportional to the difference between $ln\ W$ and $ln\ M$:

$$(13.3) \qquad H = (ln\ W - ln\ M)/\gamma = (\beta_0 + \beta_1 Z_1 + v - \alpha_0 - \alpha_1 R - \alpha_2 Z_2 - \epsilon)/\gamma$$

$$= (\beta_0 - \alpha_0 + \beta_1 Z_1 - \alpha_1 R - \alpha_2 Z_2)/\gamma + (v - \epsilon)/\gamma$$

This 'proportionality hypothesis' may be written in terms of the two-equation index function model as

$$(14.1) \qquad Y_1 = ln\ W - ln\ M = (\beta_0 - \alpha_0 + \beta_1 Z_1 - \alpha_1 R - \alpha_2 Z_2) + (v - \epsilon)$$
$$(14.2) \qquad Y_2 = H = Y_1/\gamma \qquad \longleftrightarrow \qquad Y_1 > 0$$
$$(14.3) \qquad Y_2 = H = 0 \qquad \longleftrightarrow \qquad Y_1 \leq 0$$

Maximum-likelihood methods (Heckman [1974]) or regression methods (Heckman [1976]) may be used to estimate the model; provided that one variable appears in (13.2) that does not appear in (13.1) or given some information about the covariance structure of the model, γ can be identified.

C. *Labour Supply Models with Fixed Costs of Work*

Cogan [1980] extends the Heckman model just discussed by allowing for a nonconvex choice set attributable to the presence of fixed time and money costs of work. (One motivation for such models is the relative thinness near $H = 0$ of hours of work distributions.) To see what is implied by fixed money costs of work, consider Fig. 2.1. If the individual does not work, he has $L = 1$ and income equal to R, his property income. In order to work, he must pay a fixed money cost f (for uniforms, commuting costs, etc.). Thus the individual chooses between the 'no-work' point R and the best point along the budget line $R'F$, where $R' = R - f$. The breakeven wage—at which the individual is indifferent between working (and paying the fixed cost f) and not working—is given by the slope of the line $R'D$. At any higher wage rate, the individual will work; note that 'working' here means working *at least* H_d hours. Thus, the labour supply schedule is discontinuous: the individual either does not work at all (whenever $W \leqslant W_d$, the slope of $R'D$) or else works *at least* H_d hours (whenever $W > W_d$); the slope of the no-work indifference curve at H_d hours, W_d = the slope of $R'D$, is the reservation wage. Thus, the labour supply function for workers is essentially a standard labour supply function, but with property income R

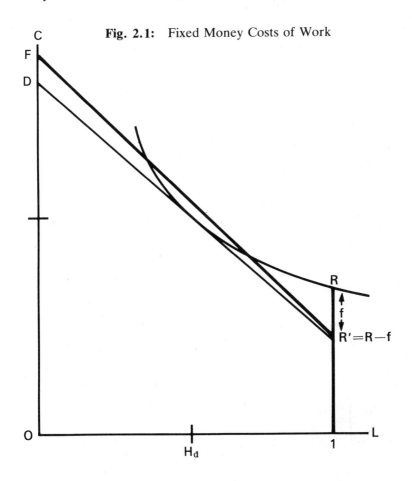

Fig. 2.1: Fixed Money Costs of Work

Fig. 2.2: Alternative Labour Supply Schedules

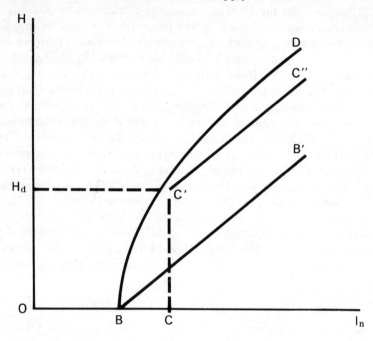

Fig. 2.3: Woodland-Wales Estimation Procedure

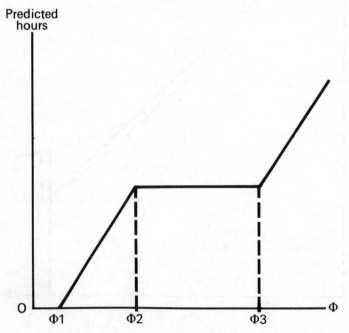

Fig. 2.4: Nonconvex Budget Constraint

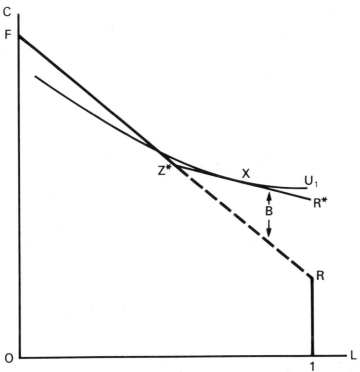

reduced by f, the amount of fixed money costs of work. It is interesting to note that, as Fig. 2.1. implies, an increase in f will have a pure income effect on the labour supply of persons who are working relatively many hours, and so will *increase* their labour supply; while an increase in f will induce at least some persons who are working not much more than H_d to *reduce* their labour supply to zero, i.e., to stop working entirely.[17]

To see how this kind of labour supply model may be estimated, it is convenient to start by solving for W_d and H_d by using the indirect utility function. By definition, W_d is the value of W such that

(15) $\quad V(W_d, R - f, \epsilon) = U(R, 1, \epsilon)$

i.e., W_d is the value of W that, given the amount of fixed costs of work f, makes the individual indifferent between working and not working. (This is the procedure Cogan [1980] uses.) By (15), one can solve for W_d and then use Roy's identity to derive H_d:

[17] The analysis of fixed *time* costs of work (e.g., commuting time) parallels our discussion of fixed money costs of work. If there are fixed time costs, the individual's budget constraint in graphical form includes a horizontal segment at point R of length c, where c is the amount of time required in order to work (e.g., to commute to work). An increase in c or f will cause at least some persons to stop working; however, while an increase in f will increase the labour supply of persons who are working relatively many hours, an increase in c will reduce the labour supply of such persons (if C and L are normal goods). See Cogan [1980] for details.

(16) $\qquad H_d = V_W(W_d, R - f, \epsilon)/V_R(W_d, R - f, \epsilon)$

One may therefore write

$$H_d = H_d(Z, f)$$
$$W_d = W_d(Z, f)$$
$$H = H(Z, f)$$

where Z is a set of exogenous variables. The parameters of the H_d, W_d and H functions are all generated by the parameters of the utility function and by R and f. In general, there are across-equation restrictions on these functions, although, unless an explicit utility function is assumed, they may be difficult to impose.

In practice, f is not observed and may depend on variables that may or may not appear in Z. This leads Cogan (and later Hanoch [1980]) to ignore across-equation restrictions and to work with independently-parameterized H_d and H functions instead. (However, they do note that one can determine the W_d function from estimates of the H and H_d functions.) Further, the individual works if and only if $H > H_d$, so, in terms of the index function model, one may write

$$Y_1 = H - H_d$$
$$Y_2 = H$$

where Y_2 is observed only when Y_1 is positive. Using standard sample selection bias procedures (Heckman [1974] [1976]), the H function may be estimated. Further, adopt appropriate functional forms, write $H - H_d$ in reduced form and assume that one variable appearing in H does not appear in H_d so as to estimate the H_d function (from the reduced-form probability that the individual works) using a random sample of workers *and* nonworkers. Thus, if

$$H = \beta Z + \gamma W + \epsilon_1$$
$$H_d = \phi Z \qquad\quad + \epsilon_2$$

then $H - H_d = (\beta - \phi)Z + \gamma W + (\epsilon_1 - \epsilon_2)$. If $(\epsilon_1 - \epsilon_2) \equiv \delta$ is normally-distributed, then the probability that $H - H_d > 0$ is a probit function. Thus, it is possible to estimate $(\beta - \phi)/[\text{Var}(\delta)]^{1/2}$ and $\gamma/[\text{Var}(\delta)]^{1/2}$. From estimates of β and γ from the hours-of-work function, it is thus possible to estimate ϕ.

In Cogan's work [1980], H_d (measured by evaluating the H_d function at mean values of the Z) is estimated at about 1250 hours per year for workers and 1320 hours per year for non-workers (mean *actual* hours averaged 1418 and 0, respectively); while in Hanoch's work [1980] H_d is estimated at 820 for all workers and about 870 for 'survey-week' workers (i.e., persons who were working during the week that the survey used in constructing Hanoch's data base was conducted).[18] In principle, a simple test for the validity of the fixed

---

[18] As Hanoch [1980] observes, limiting estimation to the subsample of 'survey-week' workers is another form of selectivity bias, since—roughly speaking—it is (only) those persons most likely to work who will be found working in any given survey week.

money cost of work model would be to see whether H_d is significantly different from zero; in practice, the model has usually been tested, and discussions about the presence or absence of such fixed costs have been premised, on a 'baseline' assumption that the relevant model without fixed costs is the Heckman [1974] 'proportionality' specification, equations (14). This particular way of tackling the question, however, confuses issues about the presence or absence of fixed costs with issues about functional forms.

To see this, note that, under the simple Heckman model, the labour supply schedule may be drawn as BB' in Figure 2.2, and that the intercept of this function, B, is the (log of the) reservation wage. The main point of the Cogan analysis is that, with fixed money costs of work, the labour supply function looks like $CC'C''$. The log-reservation wage will be higher than B, a person who works will work at least H_d hours and the labour supply function will lie above the one implied by the simple Heckman model (because the presence of fixed costs, f, is tantamount to a reduction in R for workers and because leisure is assumed to be a normal good). Now, if $CC'C''$ is the true labour supply function and the linear Heckman function is fitted to the data, then labour supply elasticities will be overstated because the intercept in the linear Heckman labour supply curve is the reservation wage. However, the validity of this argument depends crucially on the specific functional form assumed in the simple Heckman model. For example, labour supply schedule BD is also consistent with the Heckman model (see Heckman [1980a]). For all practical purposes, the nonlinearity of BD captures the essential features of the Cogan [1980] model: most persons work some large number of hours if they work at all.

Consequently, evidence for or against Heckman's simple proportionality hypothesis is hard to interpret, and what are treated as tests for the presence or absence of fixed costs are often little more than tests of the simplifying proportionality hypothesis. That is, fixed costs may make a linear model of labour supply into a nonlinear model, but proof that the labour supply is nonlinear does not necessarily constitute proof of important fixed costs of work.

Hausman [1979] extends Cogan's treatment of fixed costs by using across-equation restrictions on the H and H_d functions and by exploiting a key piece of information that Cogan neglects: the position of the indifference curve of nonworkers does not depend on the amount of fixed costs. He is therefore able to estimate income and substitution effects on labour supply H using only data on the employment status of individuals—i.e., on whether H is positive or zero. The necessary price of these remarkable achievements is the imposition of very stringent (and necessarily arbitrary) functional forms for preferences and very stringent assumptions about the way unobserveables enter the model. First, Hausman uses a specific preference scheme (for discussion, see Hausman [1979] and Muellbauer [1980]) to specify the utility of the individual in the no-work state and, via the indirect utility function $V(W, R - f, \epsilon)$, to locate the best work alternative. (The indirect utility function may not be defined for certain values of W, R, f and ϵ, but in such cases, the individual will not work.)

Next, Hausman specifies the unobserved 'heterogeneity' variable ϵ in a manner that, while stringent, leads readily to econometrically useful results: he assumes that utility in the no-work state, $U(R, 1, \epsilon)$, indirect utility V and their difference, $U - V$, are all monotonic functions of ϵ, a scalar random variable. Given W, R and an *exact* function for fixed costs f (so that fixed costs are a function of observed variables *only*), Hausman can divide the domain of ϵ into two regions: a work region, and a no-work region. The boundary of these regions is given by the ϵ^* that satisfies the relation

$$V(W, R - f, \epsilon^*) = U(R, 1, \epsilon^*)$$

Since a common set of parameters generates both U and V, Hausman is able to estimate all of them, and hence can generate estimates of all labour supply parameters—including income and substitution effects on hours of work H—using only data on employment status (that is, on whether H is positive or zero). Thus, Hausman gets as much information on labour supply as Cogan does while using less data, mainly because he assumes that the same linear labour supply function applies to the entire preference map (Cogan uses a linear specification only as an approximation to the labour supply function for workers). However, given hours of work data, Hausman's procedure produces no more information than does Cogan's. A key identifying assumption in the approach outlined above is that fixed costs f are given exactly by a function of observed variables. If this is not so, then a more involved procedure is required; it amounts to solving for ϵ^* given the unobserved component in f and then integrating out over all values of the unobserved component of f. See Hausman [1979] for details.

D. *Taxes and labour supply*

As shown in Part 1, if the tax function with which the individual is confronted generates a continuously differentiable and strictly convex choice set, few analytical difficulties arise when one introduces taxes into the labour supply model.[19] In particular, as noted above, one may treat an expression such as (5) as the structural labour supply equation; if H is measured with error, or if there are omitted labour supply determinants, or if individuals are unable to attain their desired work hours level H, then one must of course use an instrumental-variables procedure. Hall [1973] and Rosen [1969] evaluate marginal wage and adjusted property income terms $\hat{W}$ and $\hat{R}$ at a standard number of hours of work for everyone in their estimation samples, but this will generate inconsistent parameter estimates unless labour supply is exogenously-determined.

[19] There is, however, at least one important caveat: when individuals engage in tax evasion, or when tax authorities exercise discretion in administering tax rules, published tax schedules will not accurately reflect the taxes persons actually pay, even when published schedules fully define all permissible exemptions and deductions. If individuals spend real resources to avoid paying taxes, such tax avoidance costs are properly considered as part of the effective tax. However, with few exceptions (see, e.g., Gould [1979], this problem has more or less been ignored in the literature. Most empirical research has, instead, used published tax schedules to simulate the tax behaviour of individuals on the assumption that individuals fully and scrupulously follow such schedules in paying taxes.

While few *analytical* difficulties arise due to the introduction of taxes (or transfer payments), allowance for taxes does pose several econometric issues that are more complicated than the ones discussed earlier—but which, nevertheless, fit conveniently within the simple index-function framework already described. In describing recent empirical work on labour supply with taxes and transfers, we find it convenient to categorize the issues considered according to (i) the type of budget constraint considered (convex or nonconvex) and (ii) the type(s) of errors ϵ considered (that is, ϵ arising due to right-hand side omitted variables, to left-hand side measurement errors or 'optimization errors', or both). As will become clear presently, this categorization is useful in part because, since after-tax budget constraints such as the one shown in Figure 1.1 typically involve both kink-points and 'flats', or line segments, for positive hours of work, the individual now chooses not simply between not working and a single line segment for working, but rather between not working and two or more different line segments entailing work at different marginal rates of tax t_j.

1. Convex kinked budget constraint; ϵ attributable to 'missing variables' only

We begin by considering the simplest case, in which the budget constraint generated by the tax structure is kinked and convex, as shown in Figure 1.1, and in which errors ϵ are attributable only to 'missing variables'—that is, to right-hand side errors. Thus, H is assumed to be measured without error. Recall that, in Figure 1.1, initial after-tax property income is R'; that the individual faces a kinked tax schedule and a gross wage W such that a marginal tax rate t_1 applies for hours of work in between zero and $H_1 = 1 - L_1$; and that a marginal tax rate t_2 applies for hours of work in excess of H_1. Let the two segments of the post-tax budget line $1R'ZF'$ that involve positive hours of work, $R'Z$ and ZF', be called the first and second segments, respectively; and note that projecting the second segment back to where $L = 1$ would intersect a line perpendicular to the L axis at $L = 1$ at a value $\bar{R}$, where $\bar{R}$ is equal to $\bar{R} = R' + W(1 - t_1)H_1 - W(1 - t_2)H_1 = R' + WH_1(t_2 - t_1)$.

Consequently, the individual may be in equilibrium either (i) at the no-work corner point R'; (ii) at an interior solution along the first segment that entails work, $R'Z$; (iii) at the kinkpoint that entails work, point Z; or (iv) at an interior solution along the second segment that entails work, ZF'. While there are therefore more corners and more interior segments than in the simple Heckman model, specification and estimation issues in the present model are in principle little different. In particular, specification is a matter of describing the conditions under which the individual will pick a given point or segment on the budget line; and in order to avoid sample selection bias in estimating the parameters that generate labour supply behaviour, one must account for the conditioning that generates the observations (i.e., one must account for the particular branch or corner on which an observation is located).

First consider specification, and in particular the determinants of an individual's decision to be at any specific place on the budget constraint. Due to convexity both of preferences and of the constraint set, a *local* comparison between reservation and market wage rates fully determines whether the individual will work. Conditions (6) modified for taxes, become

(17.1) $\quad M(R', 1, \epsilon) < W(1 - t_1) \quad \longleftrightarrow \quad H > 0$

(17.2) $\quad M(R', 1, \epsilon) \geqslant W(1 - t_1) \quad \longleftrightarrow \quad H = 0$

In terms of index function notation, $Y_1 = W(1 - t_1) - M(R', 1, \epsilon)$; the individual works if Y_1 is positive.

If the individual works, then it remains to determine whether he works on the first or second segment of the 'work' portion of the budget line confronting him. He works in the interval $(0, H_1]$ if (17.1) is satisfied and if the marginal rate of substitution at the kinkpoint, Z, is greater than the wage on segment ZF''; that is, if

(18) $\quad M(R' + W(1 - t_1)H_1, 1 - H_1, \epsilon) > W(1 - t_2)$

He will be at an interior solution on this interval if (17.1) holds and if

(19) $\quad M(R' + W(1 - t_1)H_1, 1 - H_1, \epsilon) \geqslant W(1 - t_1)$

while he will be in equilibrium at the kinkpoint Z if

(20) $\quad W(1 - t_1) > M(R' + W(1 - t_1)H_1, 1 - H_1, \epsilon) > W(1 - t_2)$

Next consider estimation. To begin with, follow (5) of Section I and write the labour supply function at interior equilibrium along the first branch $R'Z$ and along the second branch ZF' as

(21.1) $\quad H^I = H^I(W(1 - t_1), R', \epsilon)$

(21.2) $\quad H^{II} = H^{II}(W(1 - t_2), \bar{R}, \epsilon) \quad$ respectively

(Individuals may also be in equilibrium at a kink point.) As noted earlier, one could estimate equations (21) using instruments to correct for the endogeneity of tax rates t_j and property income levels; alternatively, as we now show, one can estimate (21) correcting for sample selection bias. Indeed, in this model, endogeneity of t_j and property income, on the one hand, and sample selection bias, on the other, come to the same thing. To see what is involved, consider the following specific notation. Write $ln\ M(R, 1, \epsilon)$ as

$$ln\ M(R, 1, \epsilon) = m_0 + m_1 R + m_2 + \epsilon$$

The probability of equilibrium on any branch or kinkpoint of the budget constraint may be generated from the ordered probit model. Thus, the probability that the individual works is simply

(22.1) $\quad$ Prob $[H = 0] = $ Prob $[C_1 > \epsilon]$
where $C_1 \equiv ln\ W + ln\ (1 - t_1) - m_0 - m_1 R - m_2$. The probability that the individual is at interior equilibrium in the first segment $R'Z$ is

(22.2) $\text{Prob} [0 < H < H_1] = \text{Prob} [C_1 > \epsilon > C_2]$

where $C_2 \equiv C_1 - m_1 W(1 - t_1)H_1 + m_2 H_1$. The probability of kink equilibrium at point Z is

(22.3) $\text{Prob} [H = H_1] = \text{Prob} [C_2 > \epsilon > C_3]$

where $C_3 \equiv C_2 + ln\,(1 - t_2) - ln\,(1 - t_1)$. The probability of interior solution along branch ZF' is

(22.4) $\text{Prob} [H_1 < H < 1] = \text{Prob} [C_3 > \epsilon]$

If the random variable ϵ is normally distributed, this statistical model is an ordered probit scheme; see Johnson [1972]. Rosett and Nelson [1975] and Amemiya [1975]. (Of course, density functions other than the normal may also be used for ϵ.) Forming the sample likelihood, one can estimate all the parameters of the marginal rate of substitution function and the variance of ϵ.[20] Since the parameters of the M function generate all of the parameters of the labour supply function, the ordered probit analysis suffices to determine the parameters of the labour supply function *without any data on hours of work as such;* all that is required for the analysis is categorical data on the individual's location on the budget constraint (i.e., at the no-work corner point R'; along the first segment; at the kinkpoint Z; or along the second segment). Of course, when quantitative data on actual hours of work are available, this approach wastes information and so is inefficient. However, it is straightforward to use (17) to compute the conditional means of interior solutions of the hours of work function for each branch of the budget constraint, and modify the likelihood function appropriately so as to achieve full efficiency. (See Pellechio [1979], who proposes estimating a model with kink convex constraints in essentially this fashion.)

It is important to note that the validity of this procedure depends crucially on the assumption that hours of work are measured without error. Unless this is so, measured hours of work do not tell the investigator which branch of the budget constraint has been chosen by the individual, equations (22) are inappropriate and we confront a discrete-date version of an errors-in-variables problem. In effect, the ordered probit analysis will estimate the wrong P functions; and generalization of the ordered probit analysis to refer to quantitative data on actual hours of work will estimate both the wrong P functions and the wrong H functions. This question is treated by Wales and Woodland [1979], Burtless and Hausman [1978] and Hausman [1979].

2. Convex kinked budget constraint; ϵ attributable to errors in measurement of H only

First consider Wales and Woodland [1979], who tackle the problem by assuming that the only source of random variation in labour supply ϵ is errors in

---

[20] The variance of ϵ, σ_ϵ^2, is estimated by normalizing by the standard deviation within each probability statement, which makes the coefficient on $ln\,(1 - t)$ and on $ln\,W$ equal to $1/\sigma_\epsilon$. The parameter m_2 is, implicitly, the coefficient on the total number of hours available, set at unity here; m_2 is identified if the kink-point in the after-tax income function comes at different hours of work for different individuals—which, plausibly, is the case.

the measurement of H (or, alternatively, errors of 'optimization' under which actual H and the desired levl of H implied by structural labour supply parameters may differ). Although they ignore the work—no work decision in their analysis, their model can readily be extended to handle this case.

In essence, their procedure is to evaluate utility at each point (including kink-points) of the individual's budget constraint at given values of the relevant structural parameters, and thereby literally solve the individual's maximization problem for each such set of values. Of course, as the parameter values change, the computed equilibrium hours of work changes; estimation proceeds by maximizing the likelihood of observed hours with respect to these parameters. Specifically, begin by defining U $(C, L; \phi)$ as the direct utility function, where ϕ is the vector of parameters to be estimated; and then derive the indirect utility function $V(W, R; \phi)$. When there is an interior solution, labour supply may be written as

$$H = V_W/V_R = H(W, R, \phi)$$

Now, for *each* value of ϕ, one can write the predicted value of labour supply for each branch of the budget constraint, using expressions such as equations (21). If the predicted H lies in the interval comprehended within a given branch (e.g., $0 < H < H_1$ for the first branch in Fig. 1.1), this value of H is taken as the individual's true equilibrium given ϕ; otherwise, the true equilibrium does not lie on that branch; and so on for all branches. From convexity of preferences and constraints, equilibrium can occur on at most one branch, or—if there is a corner equilibrium—on no branch (in which case we never predict an H in the correct interval). In the latter instance, each corner (including the no-work corner) should be checked by evaluating U at each corner and picking the corner with the highest U, which is the equilibrium corner.

This procedure is guaranteed to locate the individual's optimum for each value of ϕ. To illustrate, let ϕ be a scalar and fix the wage, property income and tax parameters; and suppose the preference and labour supply functions are monotonic in ϕ. Then one may depict predicted hours as in Fig. 2.3. For ϕ in the interval $[0, \phi_1]$, $H = 0$. For ϕ in the interval (ϕ_1, ϕ_2) hours of work increase. For ϕ in the interval $[\phi_2, \phi_3)$, hours of work stay constant at kink-value H_1; and so forth. Predicted labour supply is, in general, $H^P = H$ (ϕ). This function is continuous, but may or may not be differentiable at kink-points ϕ_2 and ϕ_3 (it is differentiable if a 'constraint qualification' condition holds at ϕ_2 and ϕ_3). The Wales and Woodland criterion for estimation becomes

$$\text{Min} \sum_{\phi} [H^* - H(\phi)]^2$$

where the summation is over individuals, and H^* is measured hours of work (which may or may not be the same as true hours of work). The analysis can of course be extended to allow ϕ to be a vector rather than a scalar. (Another way to rationalize their procedure is as a process of maximizing a likelihood function of normally-distributed random optimization errors.)

This procedure solves the errors-in-variables problem, but at a cost: the somewhat immodest assumption that the econometrician knows as much about each individual's decision problem as the individual does (or, in more prosaic terms, that there are no 'missing variables' in the model, so that the *only* source of variation ϵ is errors of measurement). This is a very strong assumption: if there are omitted variables, or if ϕ differs across individuals, the procedure generates inconsistent estimates and will allocate individuals to the wrong segment of the budget constraint. The more general case is considered by Burtless and Hausman [1978] and Hausman [1979].

3. Convex kinked budget constraint; ϵ attributable to errors in measurement of H and to omitted variables

In effect, Burtless and Hausman [1978] and Hausman [1979] generalize the Woodland-Wales procedure by allowing both for errors of measurement of H and for omitted variables. To see how to proceed in this more general case, suppose that omitted variables (and random coefficients) are summarized by a scalar random variable ϵ and note that one could repeat the Woodland-Wales analysis for *each* value of ϵ. That is, for each value of ϕ, write the conditional predicted hours of work function as

$$H^P = H^P (\phi, \epsilon)$$

For different values of ϵ, hours of work equilibrium will occur on different segments (or kink-points) of the budget constraint. Assume that the H function is monotonic in ϵ, and draw the analogue of Fig. 2.3, holding ϕ fixed, with ϵ as the variable on the horizontal axis. That is, for each value of ϕ, H is a function of ϵ: For $\epsilon < \epsilon^1$, the individual does not work; for $\epsilon^1 < \epsilon < \epsilon^2$, the individual is at an interior equilibrium along the first segment of the budget constraint; for $\epsilon^2 < \epsilon < \epsilon^3$, true hours of work are at the kink-point Z; for $\epsilon \geqslant \epsilon^3$ hours of work are in equilibrium along the second branch of the budget constraint.

Appropriately modified, the analysis in (17)–(20) serves to determine the boundary values ϵ^1, ϵ^2 and ϵ^3. That is, ϵ^1 is defined by the relation

$$M(R', 1, \epsilon^1) = W(1 - t_1)$$

while ϵ^2 is defined by the relation

$$M(R' + W(1 - t_1) H_1, 1 - H_1, \epsilon^2) = W(1 - t_1)$$

and ϵ^3 is defined by the relation

$$M(R' + W(1 - t_2)H_1, 1 - H_1, \epsilon^3) = W(1 - t_2)$$

A more explicit derivation works with labour supply functions such as (21). Thus, the expected value of 'true' or predicted hours is

$$(23) \quad E(H^P) = \int_{\epsilon^1}^{\epsilon^2} H'(W(1 - t_1), R', \epsilon) \, f(\epsilon)d\epsilon + H_1 \int_{\epsilon^2}^{\epsilon^3} f(\epsilon)d\epsilon$$
$$+ \int_{\epsilon^3}^{\infty} H''(W(1 - t_2), \bar{R}, \epsilon)f(\epsilon)d\epsilon$$

THE ECONOMICS OF THE LABOUR MARKET

Assuming normally-distributed optimization errors v, one may form the likelihood function for $H^* = E(H^P) + v$ and maximize with respect to the parameters of the hours of work function (i.e., the ϕ) *and* the parameters of the distributions of v and ϵ. Alternatively, one may estimate the model using nonlinear least squares. In any event, the reformulated Woodland-Wales criterion becomes

$$\text{Min } \Sigma [H^* - E(H^P) \,]^2$$

where the summation is over individuals, and where the minimization is with respect to ϕ and to the parameters of the distributions of v and ϵ. We note, parenthetically, that the Burtless-Hausman assumption of a normally-distributed v is somewhat unattractive: it permits measured hours of work to become negative. A more general specification would allow for different types of measurement (or optimization) error in recording whether or not someone works and the hours worked by a individual. To date, no one has systematically addressed this issue.

4. Kinked and nonconvex budget constraints

All of our discussion so far has been concerned with tax systems that generate convex budget constraints, in which case a local comparison between the reservation wage and the market wage in the vicinity of $H = 0$ fully determines whether the individual will work. However, certain social programmes, transfer payment systems and negative income tax schemes (Keeley et al. [1978]) generate nonconvex budget constraints. Here a local comparison of M and W cannot completely characterize the work-no work decision. Fortunately, however, the key analytical idea appropriate to analysis of labour supply in the presence of this kind of nonconvexity is, in its essentials, the same as the one used earlier in our discussion of labour supply in the presence of fixed money costs of work.

Fig. 2.4 displays the case we consider here. In the absence of any transfer payments, the individual's budget constraint would be $1RF$; but the government pays the individual benefits B according to the formula $B = G - t(WH + R)$ whenever his gross income $Y \equiv WH + R$ is less than the 'break-even' level $Y_B \equiv G/t$. (B will be zero whenever $Y > Y_B$.) Consequently, the budget constraint relevant to the individual, inclusive of transfer payments, is $1R^*Z^*F$ where the vertical distance between $1R^*Z^*F$ and $1RF$ is the amount of transfer benefit paid to the individual and where the slope of the line segment R^*Z^* is $W(1 - t)$, his wage net of benefit reductions that accompany increases in gross income. (Thus G is usually called the 'income guarantee,' since the transfer payment scheme effectively guarantees that the individual's income net of transfer benefits will be at least B; while t is usually called the 'marginal tax rate,' or more accurately the 'marginal rate of benefit reduction,' since benefits are reduced or 'taxed away' as gross income rises.)

The Woodland-Wales estimation technique may fairly readily be adapted to handle estimation of labour supply parameters in this case. Under this procedure, it is possible to check each segment of the budget constraint for each value of the parameters ϕ to see if an interior solution exists on it. Due to the nonconvexity of constraints, existence of an interior solution on a given segment does *not* necessarily mean that equilibrium will occur on that segment. Thus, for example, point X in Fig. 2.4 associated with indifference map U_1 is a possible interior equilibrium on branch R^*Z^* that is clearly not the individual's global optimum. However, the Woodland-Wales approach can easily be extended to check all admissible optima, including corner optima, and then to select the maximum maximorum of all admissible optima. This would define the $H(\phi)$ function discussed above, and the $H(\phi)$ function could then be used, as before, in estimation of the parameters ϕ.

As before, Burtless and Hausman [1978] in effect extend this approach to the more general case, in which errors arise not only due to mismeasurement of H but also due to omitted variables. The price of this greater generality is the assumption of very specific functional forms: a utility function that is monotonic in the unobserved component ϵ, and that implies that all individuals always work (because the reservation wage at $H = 0$ is equal to minus infinity).

The nature of their utility function is such that at a critical value ϵ^* of the unobserved component, and given the wage rate, tax rate and property income, the individual is in equilibrium on *both* segments of the budget constraint. In terms of the indirect utility function, ϵ^* is implicitly defined by the relation

(24) $\qquad V(W(1 - t), R^*, \epsilon^*) = V(W, R, \epsilon^*)$

where, for their special functional form, a unique solution for ϵ^* is guaranteed to exist. Further, for values of ϵ less than ϵ^*, the individual is in equilibrium on segment one of the budget constraint, while, for values of ϵ greater than ϵ^*, the individual is in equilibrium on segment two.

Given their functional form for V, hours of work equations are defined by Roy's identity. Thus, for segment one, hours of work are defined by

$$H^I = V_1(W(1 - t), R^*, \epsilon)/V_2(W(1 - t), R^*, \epsilon)$$

and for segment two hours of work are given by

$$H^{II} = V_1(W, R, \epsilon)/V_2(W, R, \epsilon)$$

where V_j is the partial derivative of V with respect to its jth argument.

Thus, by imposing very strong conditions on functional forms, Burtless and Hausman are able to avoid the laborious Woodland-Wales maximizing procedure. The 'predicted' or expected value of hours of work, H^P, is simply

$$H^P = \int_{-\infty}^{\epsilon^*} H^I(\epsilon) f(\epsilon) \, d\epsilon + \int_{\epsilon^*}^{\infty} H^{II}(\epsilon) f(\epsilon) \, d\epsilon$$

Allowing for measurement error v in measured hours H^*, they form the criterion

$$\sum [H^* - H^P]^2$$

which is minimized with respect to the parameters of the v and ϵ distributions. (Note that the value of ϵ^* changes with values of wages, tax rates, property income and the parameters of the preference function; thus, ϵ^* must be updated in any computational algorithm that determines the parameters of the model.) If optimization errors v are normally-distributed, this is also a maximum-likelihood procedure.[21]

III. Second-Generation Empirical Studies of Labour Supply: Findings and Results

With the methodological framework of Part 2 above as prologue, we now briefly consider empirical findings and results of several second-generation studies, focusing on two issues. First, do the results of these studies suggest any important regularities or 'stylized facts' about labour supply not apparent in first-generation work? Second, does second-generation methodology really make a difference, in the sense that (say) estimated elasticities obtained using such techniques differ appreciably from those derived using OLS? There is as yet no clear answer to the first question; but the answer to the second question is an emphatic 'yes.'

Taken as whole, most recent second-generation studies avoid many of the mistakes that appear in the first-generation research discussed in Part 1. All of the second-generation research noted below except Burtless and Hausman [1978] treats the gross wage rate W as endogenous in estimating the labour supply function.[22] Also, all such work attempts in one way or another to correct for some of the biases that can arise in samples that are selected in a non-random fashion. Finally, second-generation research explicitly distinguishes the labour force participation function (e.g., (7) in section II) from the labour supply function *per se*.

---

[21] Hausman [1979] extends this procedure to allow for corner equilibrium at $H = 0$; the essential idea here has already been discussed in our section on fixed money costs of work and so will not be repeated here. Note that since marginal calculations of the kind mentioned in our discussion of the ordered probit model (e.g., equations (17)–(20)) do not correctly predict the global optimum when the budget constraint is nonconvex, the ordered probit model is not appropriate to the present case. Finally, note that the Burtless-Hausman analysis depends crucially on their assumptions about functional forms. For a general specification of preferences and unobserved components, the indirect utility function V need not be monotonic in ϵ; furthermore, and more crucially, the ϵ^* defined by (24) may not exist, and even if one exists it may not be unique—which poses obvious problems for attempts to partition the domain of ϵ into regions associated with alternative segments of the budget constraint.

[22] By this, we mean that the unobserveable component in a wage equation such as (13·2), v, is correlated with the unobserveable component in an hours of work equation such as (13·1), ϵ, implying that ϵ is correlated with one of the regressors (W) in (13·1). For discussion of evidence in support of the view that the wage should be treated as endogenous in estimation of the labour supply function, see DaVanzo, DeTray and Greenberg [1973] and Borjas [1980].

For the most part, second-generation work thus far has been concerned with two issues: fixed costs and discontinuities in the labour supply function (Cogan [1980], Hanoch [1980], Heckman [1980a], Hausman [1979] and Schultz [1980]); and taxes and nonlinear budget constraints (Burtless and Hausman [1978], Hausman [1979], and Rosen [1976a].) Except for Hausman [1979], who considers both, these studies focus on only one of these two issues and neglect others. Burtless and Hausman [1978] use samples from negative income tax experiments but ignore the effects of income-related sample selection rules that generated these data. Hausman and Wise [1977], who also use such samples, allow for the nature of sample selection rules but ignore taxes. Cogan [1980], Hanoch [1980] and Heckman [1974] use random samples of married women but ignore taxes.[23] Rosen [1976a] fails properly to take account of the endogeneity of the budget constraint;[24] Rosen [1976a] and Schultz [1980] use 'imputed wages' (i.e., wage equation estimated using the working subpopulation only) but do not correct for the bias that can arise under this procedure.

Hence, no study does everything, and each study differs from other second-generation work in several respects. This makes it hard to draw firm conclusions from comparisons across different studies: in most cases, one does not have *ceteris paribus* situations in which given issues are alternatively ignored and then taken into account. The difficulty is further complicated by differences in samples. For example, Burtless and Hausman [1978] and Hausman [1979] use samples of blacks, making it hard to draw conclusions about the effects of the factors they consider on other population groups.

For these reasons, it is not very surprising that the results of empirical second-generation studies yield few clear conclusions or 'stylized facts' about labour supply behavior as such. Like the results of most first-generation studies, second-generation results suggest that female labour supply is considerably more sensitive to changes in wage rates than is male labour supply; but in other respects second-generation findings are quite diverse in nature. For example, Hanoch [1980] and Cogan [1980] both consider questions pertaining to fixed costs and discontinuities in the labour supply of married white women, and both use a combination of regression, maximum likelihood and weighted regression to estimate labour supply parameters. Cogan's estimate of the uncompensated own-wage elasticity, 0·88, is about double Hanoch's figure (0·44); but Cogan and Hanoch use different samples and different specifications. (In particular, while both fit a labour supply function similar to (3) in section I, Hanoch adds all other family members'

[23] Since a substantial proportion of the US population of married women is not working at any given moment, the labour supply of married women has been of special interest in many second-generation studies; see, for example, Smith, ed. [1980]. In this regard, it seems worth noting that the practice of restricting estimation subsamples to women who are married—as in many second-generation studies—may generate an important sample selection bias if marital status and labour supply are jointly-determined. The importance of this bias is a significant research issue that has not yet been examined; but the same statistical methodology discussed in Part 2 in the context of other kinds of selection biases can be used to tackle this issue as well.

[24] Rosen evaluates the marginal wage function at a constant level of hours of work for all individuals. This is not a valid predictor for the marginal wage rate because it fails to recognize that expected hours of work (which depend on the exogenous variables) vary across individuals.

earnings to property income R, as in (3) in section I, while Cogan ignores both property income and the earnings of family members other than the husband.) Likewise, in Heckman [1976] Heckman's wage elasticity estimate for married women corrected for sample selection bias, 1·23, is higher than his uncorrected estimate (0·94), but in Heckman [1980a] his corrected estimate, (1·35), is lower than his uncorrected estimate (1·68).[25]

Thus, it is difficult to draw hard and fast conclusions about second-generation research *per se*. Of course, as suggested earlier, in large measure this is because there has not yet been much second-generation research, and because the different second-generation studies that have so far become available have often been concerned with quite different questions; it is early days yet, and so far generalizations do not, in most cases, seem either appropriate or necessary.

In one respect, however, generalizations seem both appropriate and important: it is quite clear that, however much they may differ one from another, second-generation studies as a whole differ sharply from first-generation work with respect to magnitudes of labour supply elasticities. In particular, the elasticities obtained using the 'new' methodology are usually greater—sometimes considerably greater—in absolute value than are those obtained using the 'old' methodology. Evidence on this point is of two kinds: first, simulation studies; and, second, *ceteris paribus* comparisons between estimated labour supply parameters derived under first- and second-generation procedures.

The simulation studies, by Wales and Woodland [1978], are sampling experiments using alternative estimators for labour supply and wage equations as applied to artificially-generated data. Their labour supply equation is

(1.1) $\qquad H = \beta_0 + \beta_1 W + \beta_2 X_2 + \epsilon \qquad$ if $\qquad H > 0$

(1·2) $\qquad H = 0 \qquad\qquad\qquad\qquad\qquad$ otherwise

while their wage function is

(2) $\qquad W = \gamma_0 + \gamma_1 Z_1 + \gamma_2 Z_2 + u$

In their sampling experiments, ϵ and u are assumed to be mean-zero normally-distributed random variables with variances $\sigma_{\epsilon\epsilon}$ and σ_{uu} and interequation correlation $p \equiv \sigma_{\epsilon u}/(\sigma_{\epsilon\epsilon}\sigma_{uu})^{1/2}$; wages are observed only if H is positive. In effect, this is a simple version of the labour supply models discussed in Part 2. Wales and Woodland apply alternative estimators to (1) − (2) using constructed data; some of their results are displayed in Table 3.1. Panel (a) presents results obtained from alternative estimators applied to the subsample of working individuals, while panel (b) presents results obtained from

---

[25] This may be because, in Heckman [1976], the dependent variable is a conventional measure of annual hours of work ('normal' hours per week times weeks worked in the year prior to the survey), while in Heckman [1980] annual hours is computed as the ratio of annual earnings to the 'normal' wage rate. (In first-generation work, the definitional relation between this latter constructed labour supply measure and the wage rate would have led to errors-in-variables bias. However, recall that Heckman, like most other second-generation researchers, treats the wage as endogenous.)

alternative estimators applied to data on the entire sample, including nonworkers, for alternative values of $\sigma_{\epsilon\epsilon}$, ρ, etc. In general, OLS is badly biased (though perhaps not as badly in the wage equation as in the hours equation); note that in all cases the OLS parameter estimates are biased towards zero. In contrast, in general the maximum-likelihood estimates, which correct for sample selection bias, are much closer to the 'true' values used to generate the H and W data. (For details, and discussion of the performance of other estimators, see Wales and Woodland [1978].)

The other kind of evidence on the performance of OLS relative to second-generation estimators takes the form of *ceteris paribus* comparisons, in which both kinds of estimators are used to fit a given model to a given data set. Results of this kind for data on women—on whom much second-generation research has been focused—are displayed in Table 3.2. Cogan [1980], Heckman [1976] and Schultz [1980] all obtain larger positive gross own-wage elasticities, and also negative spouse's wage and property income elasticities that are larger in absolute value, using second-generation methods than they do using OLS. In [1980a] Heckman's results have just the opposite properties. (See footnote 25). But in this case OLS is used to estimate a reduced-form system in which the wage rate as such does not appear in the labour supply function (see, e.g., equation (14.1) in section II), unlike virtually all first-generation research.

That differences of this kind should occur is not altogether surprising. What is surprising is the magnitude of the difference: for example, Heckman's maximum-likelihood estimate of the own-wage elasticity for married women, 4.31, is almost three times as large as his OLS estimate obtained for the same reduced-form specification of the labour supply function. Likewise, Schultz' Tobit estimates are usually considerably larger than his OLS estimates of the same parameter.

The results reported in Tables 3.1–2 are all concerned with the labour supply function as such, i.e., with the structural parameters of the labour supply schedule. These describe the labour supply of a *given individual* with (e.g.) given values—assumed equal to zero in the calculations in the tables—of unobserveables in wage and hours of work functions. Of course, these structural parameters also imply a variety of things about average labour supply levels of different groups of persons; recall the discussion above of equations (8), (9), (10) in section I. Thus, it is possible to use structural parameters to derive *average* labour supply elasticities either in unconditional terms (including nonworkers, as with (10)) or conditional on being at work (as with (9)), and for the dichotomy between being at work and not being at work (as with (8)) as well as for hours of work as such. In terms of Fig. 3.1, structural labour supply effects refer to the broken line *abc*, while expected labour supply is the curve *de* and and expected labour supply conditional on being at work is the curve *fg*; the dichotomous variable 'at work-not at work' refers to the proportion of observations with positive H. While OLS estimates of structural parameters appear, on the basis of the results discussed above, to be badly biased, it may be that such estimates are less badly biased if considered as estimates of average labour supply relationships evaluated at sample means.

109

Table 3.1: Selected Results from Wales-Woodland Sampling Experiments Testing Alternative Labour Supply and Wage Equation Estimators (Standard Errors in Parentheses)

Sample used	parameter	"true value"	$\rho = -0.5$ OLS	$\rho = -0.5$ FIML	$\rho = 0.0$ OLS	$\rho = 0.0$ FIML	$\rho = 0.5$ OLS	$\rho = 0.5$ FIML
a) subsample of M Workers			(M = 1626)		(M = 1634)		(M = 1581)	
i) labour supply:	β_0	-1.1854	.860 (.044)	-1.225 (.160)	.359 (.044)	-1.083 (.115)	-.073 (.042)	-1.103 (.093)
	β_1	1.0	.339 (.015)	.969 (.049)	.596 (.017)	.955 (.038)	.822 (.018)	.994 (.033)
	β_2	1.0	.477 (.029)	1.042 (.063)	.625 (.026)	1.011 (.042)	.744 (.022)	1.016 (.027)
	$\sigma^{1/2}_{\epsilon\epsilon}$	*	1.127	1.711 (.057)	.983	1.234 (.034)	.853	1.011 (.026)
ii) wage rate:	γ_0	0	.760 (.048)	-.043 (.068)	.752 (.034)	-.030 (.045)	.783 (.025)	-.006 (.031)
	γ_1	1.0	.827 (.036)	1.002 (.035)	.780 (.026)	.997 (.026)	.794 (.018)	.979 (.018)
	γ_2	1.0	.814 (.037)	.984 (.035)	.821 (.025)	1.019 (.026)	.781 (.018)	.987 (.019)
	$\sigma^{1/2}_{uu}$	*	1.625	1.598 (.031)	1.044	1.160 (.024)	.753	.913 (.019)
b) population of N = 5000 persons (nonworkers' H set at zero)								
iii) labour supply:	β_0	-1.1854	.271 (.015)	-1.207 (.074)	.261 (.015)	-1.168 (.053)	.243 (.015)	-1.217 (.040)
	β_1	1.0	.370 (.009)	.957 (.032)	.398 (.010)	.984 (.023)	.400 (.010)	1.008 (.018)
	β_2	1.0	.321 (.011)	1.024 (.031)	.329 (.011)	1.028 (.027)	.335 (.011)	1.014 (.021)
	$\sigma^{1/2}_{uu}$	*	.889	1.705 (.041)	.906	1.246 (.027)	.909	1.047 (.021)

* = "true" value depends on assumed value for ρ, as follows:

	$\rho = -0.5$	$\rho = 0.0$	$\rho = 0.5$
$\sigma^{1/2}_{\epsilon\epsilon}$	1.7283	1.2472	1.0393
$\sigma^{1/2}_{uu}$	1.6564	1.1455	0.9148

Source: see Wales and Woodland [1978]

Table 3.2: Estimated Elasticities for Hours of Work in 'Second-Generation' Studies

Study	Sample, Procedure used	Estimated elasticity Own-wage	Spouse's wage	Property income
Schultz [1980]	Married women, 1967 SEO: whites 14–24: Procedure A	0·024	0·047	−0·009
	B	1·646	−0·331	−0·001
	blacks 14–24; Procedure A	0·034	0·195	0·015
	B	1·072	−0·995	−0·004
	whites 25–34: Procedure A	0·930	−1·490	0·010
	B	3·950	−5·598	0·030
	blacks 25–34: Procedure A	0·209	−0·334	0·003
	B	0·939	−1·066	0·002
	whites 35–44: Procedure A	−0·045	−0·383	−0·004
	B	0·215	−1·157	−0·015
	blacks 35–44: Procedure A	0·201	−0·058	0·001
	B	0·493	−0·639	0·023
	whites 45–54: Precedure A	0·072	−0·282	−0·005
	B	0·792	−1·077	−0·030
	blacks 45–54: Procedure A	0·271	0·006	−0·006
	B	0·562	−0·810	−0·010
	whites 55–64: Procedure A	0·284	−0·190	0·007
	B	1·886	−1·326	−0·032
	blacks 55–64: Procedure A	0·115	0·297	0·002
	B	0·812	−0·755	−0·018
Heckman [1976]	White married women 30–44, 1967 NLS (n = 2253)			
	Procedure C	1·460	−0·110	−0·005
	D	4·310	−0·120	−0·099
Heckman [1980]	White married women 30–44, 1967 NLS (n = 1735)			
	Procedure C	2·260	−0·090	0·028
	E	1·470	−0·030	0·029
Cogan [1980]	White married women 30–44, 1967 NLS (n = 1829)			
	Procedure D	2·453	—	−0·507*
	D'	1·138	—	−0·148*

*Elasticity with respect to husband's earnings. (Other family income from property or earnings not included.)

Procedure A = estimation of standard labour supply function (using 'imputed wage' calculated from sample restricted to workers only) using OLS. Only workers included in estimation sample.

Procedure B = estimation of standard labour supply function (using 'imputed wage' calculated from sample restricted to workers only) using Tobit. All persons (workers and non-workers) included in estimation sample.

Procedure C = estimation of 'reduced-form' labour supply function (derived by substituting wage function variables in place of actual wage into labour supply function) using OLS. Only workers included in estimation sample.

Procedure D = joint estimation of 'reduced-form' labour supply function and wage function using maximum-likelihood. All persons included in estimation sample.

Procedure D' = estimation of 'reduced-form' labour supply function without correction for sample censoring by OLS. Only workers included in estimation sample.

Procedure E = estimation of 'reduced-form' labour supply function with correction for sample censoring by GLS. Only workers included in estimation sample.

111

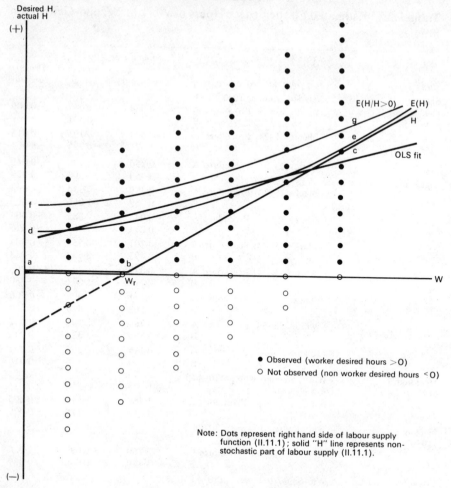

Fig. 3.1: Labour Supply and OLS Fit

Note: Dots represent right-hand side of labour supply function (II.11.1); solid "H" line represents non-stochastic part of labour supply function (II.11.1).

However, as Tobin's remarks in Tobin [1958] suggested long ago, even under this interpretation OLS may provide misleading measures of average elasticities at points far from sample means, or even of overall average elasticities as such in samples where many observations are not close to the relevant sample means.

IV. Rationing, Unemployment and Labour Supply

While the models discussed so far differ in a wide variety of ways, they are all based on a crucial common assumption found even in elementary textbook discussions: that the budget constraint and hence the relevant choice set is defined for all possible hours of work, so that the individual is free to choose the hours he will work. This implies that—except for 'corner' solutions, kinkpoint solutions and errors of optimization—the individual is a 'marginalist' who always attains an equilibrium at which his indifference curve is tangent to his budget constraint. However, there may be some upper (or lower) limit on the number of hours that an individual can work during a given time period (e.g., a year); and even if it is possible to find jobs entailing any number of hours of work during the relevant time period, there may be productivity gains accruing to work at a standard number of hours per period, so that the budget constraint will have a 'spike' at the standard level of hours of work.

The early literature on these questions focused on cases in which, due to technological or other factors, firms decided to offer prospective workers a 'take-it-or-leave-it' choice between working a standard workweek (e.g., 40 hours per week) and not working.[26] Stimulated in part by recent theoretical developments in the analysis of neo-Keynesian macroeconomic models, recent work on this question has stressed unemployment—the fact that one must have a job offer before one can work *any* hours—as a constraint on the individual's ability to choose freely his hours of work.[27] In either case, the fact that individuals are constrained in terms of their ability to choose their hours of work means that the budget constraint confronting them is truncated. For example, suppose that, when an individual is able to work, he is paid a wage W and that he receives property income of R. Absent any constraint on his ability to choose his hours of work H, his budget constraint would appear as $1RF$ in Fig. 4.1, just as in our discussions above. However, 'take-it-or-leave-it' regimes may impose an effective lower bound on the number of hours the individual can work per period, if he decides to work at all; and layoffs and the fact of unemployment may impose an effective upper bound on the number of hours that can be worked per period. Let the lower bound be $\underline{H}$ and the upper bound be $\bar{H}$. Under these assumptions, the budget constraint confronting the individual is not $1RF$, but rather the point R (if the individual decides not to work) and the line segment Z_1Z_2, (entailing hours of work per period in the region $[\underline{H}\,\bar{H}]$).

There are a variety of interesting implications for empirical research in this kind of model. One has to do with absenteeism and its converse, overtime and moonlighting. For example, individual A, shown in Fig. 4.2, finds that it is better to work $\underline{H}$ hours rather than not work at all, given the constraint on his ability to choose his hours of work; but if he could, he would prefer to work fewer hours than the minimum amount $\underline{H}$ required under the 'take-it-or-leave-it' regime he faces. He may therefore attempt to work fewer hours by being absent from work part of the time (e.g., on Fridays); how successful he will be will of course depend on how rigidly his employer enforces the regime.

[26] See Moses [1962], Wilensky [1963], Perlman [1966] [1968], Mossin and Bronfenbrenner [1967], Sherman and Willett [1976], Dankert [1962], Meyers [1965], Whybrew [1968], Bienefeld [1969] and Mabry [1969] and the excellent survey by Perlman in [1969].

[27] See Abowd and Ashenfelter [1979], Ashenfelter [1978a] [1978b] [1980] and Ashenfelter and Ham [1979].

Individual B, shown in Fig. 4.3, finds that it is better to work $\bar{H}$ hours rather than not work at all (or working some amount of hours less than $\bar{H}$, but, if he were free to choose his hours of work, would prefer to work more than the $\bar{H}$ that is available in the face of the layoffs with which he is (likely to be) confronted during the period under consideration. He would therefore be willing to work more than $\bar{H}$ hours—that is, to supply H_s *additional* hours, either on overtime at his present job or else by 'moonlighting' at a second job. Indeed, he would be willing to work additional hours even if the wage paid for those hours were somewhat lower than the wage paid for the $\bar{H}$ hours he now works. (Individual A, in Fig. 4.2, would also be willing to work additional hours, but only if the wage paid for those hours exceeded the wage paid for the $\underline{H}$ hours he now works.) Hence, A is 'overemployed,' in the sense that, at the wage rate available to him, he would prefer to work fewer hours than the minimum he must work; while, by the same token, B is 'underemployed.' Note that B's underemployment could in principle take on a variety of forms. For example, B might be employed year-round, working fewer hours each week than the number he would desire to work were he free to choose his hours of work; or, alternatively, B might be employed part of the year working the number of hours he would desire to work were he free to choose his hours of work, but be unemployed part of the year (and therefore unable to choose his hours of work during that part of the year).

Thus, models of this kind treat questions of overtime, moonlighting and unemployment in a more or less explicit fashion, while the simple model of Part I does not. Several observations about the relation between these two kinds of models therefore seem worth making at this point. First, correctly interpreted, the simple model of Part 1 does not entail any assumption that the individual is free to choose his hours of work at his *present* job; strictly speaking, all that is required for that model is that there be many different jobs, all offering the same wage W, from which the individual chooses the one with the hours-of-work level that best suits his preferences. Hence, in the simple model, changes in hours of work may entail a change of job, something that may not occur immediately. In this sense, models of labour supply rationing are complementary to, rather than competitive with, the 'simple' model of Part 1. That is, they can be interpreted as a description of labour supply decisions at a given job (and therefore, possibly, in the short run), while the simple model is silent about the relation between choice of hours of work and choice of job. A more general approach would analyze the way in which the interplay of firm and employee preferences and decisions establishes a locus of wage-hours combinations—*different* jobs—in the labour market as a whole, and in which an individual chooses one job from among those in the locus.

This view of 'constraints' on hours of work at given jobs—that is, the idea that labour supply decisions entail selecting a job, and hence a wage-hours package, from the locus of jobs generated by the market—is also important for normative analysis. As indicated earlier, the best use of resources in society may dictate a set of 'standard' workweeks that entail jobs in which labour supply appears to be rationed and in which an individual's average wage rate and marginal price of time may not be equal, as in Figs. 4.2–3. But this kind of

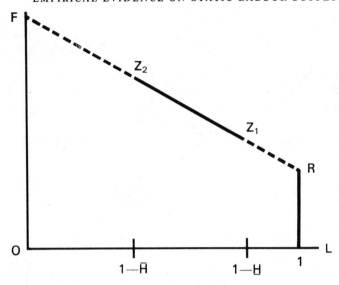

Fig. 4.1: Labour Supply Rationing

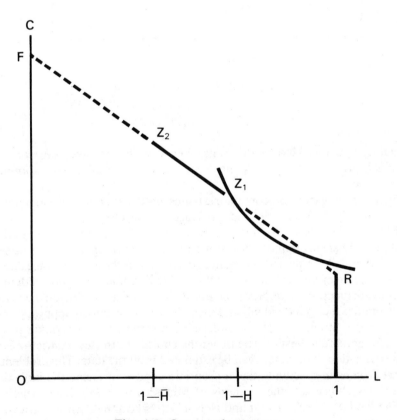

Fig. 4.2: Overemployment

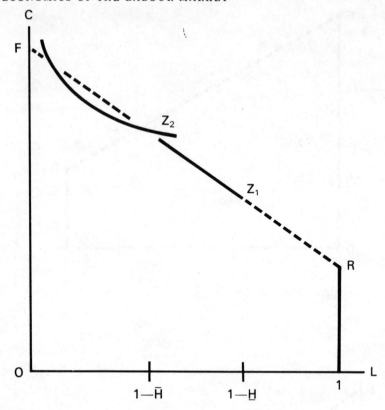

Fig. 4.3: Underemployment

rationing, and this kind of difference between the average wage and the marginal price of time, may have no particular welfare or normative significance.

Finally, with respect to econometric issues, note that empirical estimation of labour supply functions in the presence of rationing involves standard problems in discrete choice analysis, where the discrete choices are the finite (and possibly small) number of distinct hours-of-work opportunities open to the individual. As indicated above, in such conditions the average wage and the marginal price of time will usually differ, so that standard methods of demand analysis are inappropriate. Nevertheless, it is possible to use data on the market opportunities facing individuals and their choices from among opportunities to estimate the parameters of the underlying functions that determine preferences for goods and leisure. The richer the choice set, the less restrictive is the class of functional forms that can be estimated from the data. The problem, of course, comes in specifying the appropriate choice set facing the individual. Given this choice set, the methods of McFadden [1976], Domencich and McFadden [1975] and Rosett and Nelson [1975] can be used to retrieve the parameters of the individual's underlying preference function.

Of somewhat greater interest, both in terms of analytical issues and for policy purposes, is recent work that seeks to test for the existence of Keynesian involuntary unemployment. (See Ham [1979] for a generalization of the model, similar to Figs. 4.1–3, to include overemployment as well.) In this work, unemployment is taken as a constraint on behaviour and is treated as the difference between desired and actual hours worked. Treating unemployment in this way makes it formally equivalent to the optimization error, previously discussed, in the models of Wales and Woodland [1979] and Burtless and Hausman [1978]. Intertemporal considerations are usually ignored (but see Ashenfelter and Ham [1979]). Desired hours of work are assumed to be given by

(1) $H = H (W, R, \epsilon)$

where W is the marginal wage as perceived by the worker who, *ex ante*, assumes that he is free to choose his hours of work according to (1). However, actual hours—that is, hours demanded by the market—are an exogenously-determined amount $\bar{H}$. The possibility that desired hours (labour supply) might exceed actual hours (labour demand) comes as a complete surprise to the individual in each period; whenever $H > \bar{H}$ the individual is said to be involuntarily unemployed, and $U \equiv H - \bar{H}$ is the number of constrained unemployed hours. Note that U need not correspond to any available empirical measure of 'unemployment'; for example, some portion of U may be time spent out of the labour force.

To gauge the significance of unemployment as a constraint on labour supply, Ashenfelter [1980] proceeds as follows. Since desired hours of work H are equal to $\bar{H} + U$, (1) may be rewritten as

(2) $\bar{H} = H (W, R, \epsilon) - U$

Written in this way, it is apparent that Ashenfelter's model is a version of the optimization-error models discussed in Part 3. As noted above, the 'unemployment' of the present model, U, is not observable, and is not (necessarily) measured by available data on 'unemployment.' Let *measured* unemployment be $\tilde{U}$, and assume that $\tilde{U}$ is related to U. Specifically, as a first approximation, suppose that $U = \theta\tilde{U}$. Substitute this into (2) to obtain

(3) $\bar{H} = H(W, R, \epsilon) - \theta\tilde{U}$

If true unemployment U is accurately measured, then $\theta = 1$ and all (measured) unemployment is involuntary; if true unemployment U is zero, then $\theta = 0$ and all (measured) unemployment is voluntary, a consequence of choices rather than exogenous constraints. Fitting (3) and assuming that the *ex ante* marginal wage is the same as the *ex post* average wage, Ashenfelter [1980] and Ashenfelter and Ham [1979] obtain estimates of θ in between 0·36 and 0·96, suggesting that unemployment is indeed a constraint on labour supply.

There have been few attempts to test or estimate well-specified models of disequilibrium behaviour, and, with the exception of the work just noted, no attempts to consider disequilibrium labour supply behaviour of which we are aware. In view of this, such attempts to test for the presence of constraints on labour supply are noteworthy. However, tests such as the one described above do not, in the end, seem particularly convincing evidence that refutes neoclassical analysis, primarily because the rival hypothesis implicit in empirical tests of models such as (3) does not, in fact, capture the essential features of modern neoclassical analysis as applied to questions of 'unemployment.'

In neoclassical models of search unemployment and labour supply (see Burdett and Mortensen [1978] and Lucas and Rapping [1970], respectively), unemployment is a choice variable rather than an exogenous constraint or an error of optimization. In search models, individuals make labour supply decisions in an environment of uncertainty about wage offers and layoff policies (Burdett and Mortensen); in dynamic neoclassical labour supply models, individuals make decisions in an environment in which the relative price of leisure at different dates will be different (due, e.g., to exogenous forces such as the business cycle, or to endogenous forces such as investment in skills and training), giving rise to opportunities for intertemporal substitution of leisure time and consumption and hence affecting *current* labour supply decisions (Lucas and Rapping). In general terms, each kind of model posits a behavioural equation for 'unemployed hours,' and a behavioural equation for (desired) labour supply,

$$(4.1) \qquad H = H(R, S, \epsilon)$$

$$(4.2) \qquad U = U(R, S, \epsilon)$$

respectively, where R and ϵ are as before, and S is a *vector* of variables that represent the *set* of available market wage offers *perceived by the individual*. The components of S may not be recorded in any observed market transaction, and typically refer not only to the current period but also to future periods. In the Burdett-Mortensen model, the individual faces a distribution of potential wage offers at each point in time; when the individual rejects an offer, the offer is not observed and the individual engages in search unemployment aimed at securing a better offer for the next period. Alternatively, in the Lucas-Rapping model, the individual's S is a lifetime profile of wage rates; when the individual declines to work at an 'unacceptably' low wage offer, that offer is not observed and the individual either withdraws from the workforce or is unemployed; in either case, this kind of 'unemployment' is one of the many components of leisure. In the Burdett-Mortensen model, labour supply decisions are made under uncertainty; in the Lucas-Rapping model, such decisions are made under perfect certainty and foresight. In either case, however, U is a choice variable whose determinants are R, ϵ and the relevant components of S.

In contrast, in Ashenfelter's version [1980] of the neoclassical model, workers are free to choose their desired hours of work in the face of the current marginal wage,[28] which in turn is assumed to summarize all the market information required to make labour supply choices. However, this is not consistent with the neoclassical models just described, in which market opportunities are summarized not by a single number (i.e., W) but rather by a vector, S. Under the null hypothesis of no constraint on behaviour ($\theta = 0$) and exogenously-determined unemployment, Ashenfelter's procedure is informative. But suppose that we instead treat as the null hypothesis of equilibrium and no constraint on labour supply behaviour the modern neo-classical analysis represented by equations (4). Then Ashenfelter's estimating equation (3) together with the null hypothesis $H = \bar{H}$ may be written as

$$(5) \qquad H = H(R, S, \epsilon) - \theta \bar{U}$$

A least squares estimate of a suitably parameterized version of (5) in which market opportunity set S is replaced with the *average observed* ('transacted') wage W, as in (3), will estimate a non-zero value of θ solely as a result of misspecification of the effective wage offer set facing the individual. In addition, in view of (4.2), the unobserved components of the labour supply equation in (5) are correlated with the determinants of U. Unless instruments are found for U, θ will be estimated to be nonzero solely as a consequence of ordinary simultaneous-equations bias.[29] Unless the econometrician imposes non-linearities or arbitrary covariance restrictions on unobservables, there is no way to identify θ. The usual exclusion restrictions are inappropriate here: modern neoclassical theory suggests, as in (4), that any variables that appear in the equation for unemployment, (4.1), also appear in the hours of work equation, (4.2). Hence there are no valid instruments.

To be sure, Ashenfelter's procedure is useful as a test of neo-Keynesian theories and models of labour supply under conditions of rationing against a naive neoclassical model that ignores intertemporal considerations. Considered as a test of rationing models against modern neoclassical theories of unemployment that explicitly incorporate intertemporal considerations, however, estimates of the parameters of (3) are much less informative. This is so for two reasons: (i) using the current average price of observed labour market transactions, W, does not summarize the relevant market opportunities considered in modern dynamic neoclassical models; and (ii) even if the relevant market opportunity set S for each individual were available for empirical analysis, identification of the parameter θ in (5) seems difficult to achieve.

[28] In his empirical work, Ashenfelter uses the actual (mean) wage received by labour (e.g., mean hourly earnings in a given year) as his measure of W. As we imply below, this measure of W is subject to various sample selection biases, since not all wage offers (the relevant W here) are accepted.

[29] As Ashenfelter is careful to emphasize, measured unemployment $\bar{U}$ and 'true' unemployment U are not necessarily the same thing. If $\bar{U}$ is used as a proxy for U, then Ashenfelter's test amounts, in operational terms, to a determination of whether $\bar{U}$ is a determinant of hours of work; thus the key test is for $\theta = 0$. An important issue ignored in the analysis is why U and $\bar{U}$ differ. Given institutional features of unemployment insurance programs, $\bar{U}$ reflects choices made by consumers that depend on the same variables that influence desired hours of work H. Thus the measurement error that arises when U is replaced by $\bar{U}$ is much more complicated than the usual kind of measurement error considered in econometrics. If $\bar{U}$ is a consequence of choice, as is likely the case, then replacing U with $\bar{U}$ will, in general, bias θ away from 0, as suggested here.

119

Resolution of these issues raises dynamic questions that are beyond the scope of this survey, but not, we hope, beyond the skills of labour economists.

REFERENCES

Michael Abbot and Orley Ashenfalter, [1976] 'Labor Supply, Commodity Demand and the Allocation of Time,' *Review of Economic Studies* 43, October, 389–411.

John M. Abowd and Orley Ashenfelter, [1979] 'Unemployment and Compensating Wage Differentials,' *Working Paper No. 120, Industrial Relations Section, Princetown University,* March.

Takeshi Amemiya, [1973] 'Regression Analysis When the Dependent Variable is Truncated Normal,' *Econometrica* 41, November, 997–1017.

Takeshi Amemiya, [1975] 'Qualitative Response Models,' *Annals of Economic and Social Measurement 4,* Summer, 363–372.

Orley Ashenfelter, [1978a] 'Unemployment as a Constraint on Labour Market Behaviour,' in M. J. Artis and A. R. Nobay, eds, *Contemporary Economic Analysis,* London: Croome Helm.

Orley Ashenfelter, [1978b] 'What is Involuntary Unemployment?' *Proceedings of the American Philosophical Society* 122, June, 135–138.

Orley Ashenfelter, [1980] 'Unemployment as Disequilibrium in a Model of Aggregate Labor Supply,' *Econometrica* 48, April 547–564.

Orley Ashenfelter and John Ham, [1979] 'Education, Unemployment and Earnings,' *Journal of Political Economy 87,* October, S99–S116.

Yoram Ben-Porath, [1973] 'Labor Force Participation Rates and the Supply of Labor,' *Journal of Political Economy* 81, May-June, 697–704.

M. A. Bienefeld, [1969] 'The Normal Week Under Collective Bargaining,' *Economica* 36, May, 172–192.

George Borjas, [1980] 'The Relationship Between Wages and Weekly Hours of Work: The Role of Division Bias,' *Journal of Human Resources* 15, Summer.

George Borjas and James J. Heckman, [1979] 'Labor Supply Estimates for Public Policy Evaluation,' *Proceedings of the Thirty-First Annual Meeting of the Industrial Relations Research Association,* 320–331.

Michael J. Boskin, [1973] 'The Economics of Labor Supply,' in Cain and Watts, eds. [1973b]

Alan Brown and Angus Deaton, [1972] 'Models of Consumer Behaviour: A Survey,' *Economic Journal* 82, December, 1145–1236.

Gary Burtless and Jerry Hausman, [1978] 'The Effect of Taxation on Labor Supply: Evaluating the Gary Income Maintenance Experiment,' *Journal of Political Economy* 86, December, 1103–1130.

Kenneth Burdett and Dale Mortensen, [1978] 'Labor Supply Under Uncertainty,' in Ronald G. Ehrenberg, ed, *Research in Labor Economics, Volume 2,* Greenwich, Connecticut: JAI Press.

Glen G. Cain and Harold W. Watts, [1973a] 'Toward a Summary and Synthesis of the Evidence,' in Cain and Watts, eds. [1973b]

Glen G Cain and Harold W. Watts, [1973b] eds, *Income Maintenance and Labor Supply,* Chicago: Markham.

John Cogan, [1980] 'Labor Supply with Time and Money Costs of Participation', in Smith, ed [1980]

C. E. Dankert, [1962] 'Shorter Hours—in Theory and Practice,' Industrial and Labor Relations Review 15, April, 323–349.

Julie DaVanzo, Dennis DeTray and David Greenberg, [1973] 'Estimating Labor Supply Response: A Sensitivity Analysis,' *Report R-1372-OEO, The Rand Corporation,* Santa Monica, California, December.

M. Domencich and D. McFadden, [1975] *Urban Travel demand: A Behavioral Analysis,* Amsterdam: North-Holland.

Irwin Garfinkel, [1973] 'On Estimating the Labor Effects of a Negative Income Tax, in Cain and Watts, eds [18].

Gilbert Ghez and Gary S. Becker, [1975] *The Allocation of Time and Goods Over the Life Cycle,* New York: Columbia University Press.

William Gould, [1979] 'Taxes and Female Labor Supply,' *unpublished PhD dissertation, University of California at Los Angeles.*

David M. Greenberg, [1972] 'Problems of Model Specification and Measurement: The Labor Supply Function,' *Report R-1085-EDA The Rand Corporation,* Santa Monica, California, December.

Reuben Gronau, [1975] 'Wage Comparisons—A Selectivity Bias,' *Journal of Political Economy* 82, November-December, 1119–1144.

Robert E. Hall, [1973] 'Wages, Income and Hours of Work in the U S Labor Force,' in Cain and Watts, eds [1973b]

John Ham, [1979] 'Rationing and the Supply of Labor : An Econometric Approach,' *Working Paper No. 103A, Industrial Relations Section, Princeton University,* August.

Giora Hanoch, [1980] 'Hours and Weeks in the Theory of Labor Supply,' in Smith, ed [1980]

Jerry A. Hausman, [1979] 'The Effect of Wages, Taxes and Fixed Costs on Women's Labor Force Participation,' *Massachusetts Institute of Technology,* May.

Jerry A. Hausman and David A. Wise, [1976] 'The Evaluation of Results from Truncated Samples: The New Jersey Negative Income Tax Experiment,' *Annals of Economic and Social Measurement* 5, Fall, 421–446.

Jerry A. Hausman and David A. Wise, [1977] 'Social Experimentation, Truncated Distributions and Efficient Estimations,' *Econometrica* 45, May.

James J. Heckman, [1974] 'Shadow Prices, Market Wages and Labor Supply,' *Econometrica* 42, July, 679–694.

James J. Heckman, [1976] 'The Common Structure of Statistical Models of Truncation, Sample Selection, and Limited Dependent Variables and a Simple Estimator for Such Models,' *Annals of Economic and Social Measurement* 5, fall, 475–492.

James J. Heckman, [1978] 'Dummy Endogenous Variables in a Simultaneous Equation System,' *Econometrica* 46, July, 931–961.

James J. Heckman, [1980] 'Sample Selection Bias as a Specification Error,' in Smith, ed [1980]

James J. Heckman and Thomas MaCurdy, [1980a] 'A Life Cycle Model of Female Labor Supply,' *Review of Economic Studies* 47.

James J. Heckman and Thomas MaCurdy, [1980b] 'Recent Developments in Labor Supply: A Survey with Special Reference to Statistical and Dynamic Issues', in Ronald G. Ehrenberg, ed, *Research in* Labor Economics, Volume 4, Greenwich, Connecticut: J A I Press.

Thomas Johnson, [1972] 'Qualitative and Limited Dependent Variables in Economic Relationships', *Econometrica* 40, May, 440–455.

Michael C. Keeley *et. al.,* [1978] 'The Labor-Supply Effects and Costs of Alternative Negative Income Tax Programs,' *Journal of Human Resources* 13, Winter, 3–36.

Mark R. Killingsworth, [1980] 'A Survey Of Labor Supply Models: Theoretical Propositions and Empirical Problems,' in Ronald G. Ehrenberg, ed, *Research in Labour Economics, Volume 4,* Greenwich, Connecticut: J A I Press.

Mark R. Killingsworth, [1981] *Neoclassical Labor Supply Models,* Cambridge: Cambridge University Press, forthcoming.

Marvin Kosters, [1966] 'Income and Substitution Effects in a Family Labor Supply Model,' *Report No. P-3339, The Rand Corporation,* Santa Monica, California, December.

Marvin Kosters, [1969] 'Effects of an Income Tax on Labor Supply,' in A. C. Harberger and M. J. Bailey, eds, *The Taxation of Income from Capital,* Washington, DC: The Brookings Institution.

H. Gregg Lewis, [1967] 'On Income and Substitution Effects on Labor Force Participation,' *University of Chicago.*

Steven A. Lippman and John J. McCall, [1976a] 'The Economics of Job Search: A Survey, Part I,' *Economic Inquiry* 14, June, 155–189.

Steven A. Lippman and John J. McCall, [1976b] 'The Economics of Job Search: A Survey, Part II,' *Economic Inquiry* 14, September, 347–368.

C. Lluch, [1973] 'The Extended Linear Expenditure System,' *European Economic Review* 4, April 1973, 21–32.

Robert E. Lucas and Leonard Rapping, [1970] 'Real Wages, Employment and Inflation,' in E. S. Phelps *et. al., Microeconomic Foundations of Employment and Inflation Theory,* New York: W. W. Norton.

Daniel McFadden, [1976] 'A Quantal Choice: A Survey,' *Annals of Economic and Social Measurement* 5, Fall, 363–390.

Bevars Mabry, [1969] 'Income-Leisure Analysis and the Salaried Professional,' *Industrial Relations* 8, February, 162–173.

F. Meyers, [1965] 'The Economics of Overtime,' in C. Dankert, F. C. Mann and H. L. Northrup, eds, *Hours of Work,* Harper and Row, Inc.

Robert A. Moffitt and Kenneth C. Kehrer, [1980] 'The Effect of Tax and Transfer Programs on Labor Supply: The Evidence from the Income Maintenance Experiments', in Ronald G. Ehrenberg, ed, *Research in Labor Economics, Volume 4,* Greenwich, Connecticut: J A I Press.

Leon Moses, [1962] 'Income, Leisure and Wage Pressure', *Economic Journal* 72, June, 320–334

Jan Mossin and Martin Bronfenbrenner, [1967] 'The Shorter Work Week and the Labor Supply', *Southern Economic Journal* 33, January, 322–331.

John Muellbauer, [1980] 'Linear Aggregation in Neoclassical Labor Supply', *Review of Economic Studies* 47.

121

Anthony Pellechio, [1979] 'The Estimation of Labor Supply Over Kinked Budget Constraints: Some New Econometric Methodology', *Working Paper No. 387, National Bureau of Economic Research,* Cambridge, Massachusetts, August.

Richard Perlman, [1966] 'Observations on Overtime and Moonlighting', *Southern Economic Journal* 33, October, 237–244.

Richard Perlman, [1968] 'Moonlighting and Labor Supply—Reply', *Southern Economic Journal* 35, July, 82–84.

Richard Perlman, [1969] *Labor Theory,* New York: John Wiley and Sons, Inc.

Harvey S. Rosen, [1976a] 'Taxes in a Labor Supply Model with Joint Wage-Hours Determination', *Econometrica* 44, May, 485–507.

Harvey S. Rosen, [1976b] 'Tax Illusion and the Labor Supply of Married Women', *Review of Economics and Statistics* 58, May, 167–172.

Sherwin Rosen, [1969] 'On the Interindustry Wage and Hours Structure', *Journal of Political Economy* 77, March-April, 249–273.

Richard N, Rosett and Forrest D. Nelson, [1975] 'Estimation of the Two-Limit Probit Regression Model', *Econometrica* 43, January, 141–146.

R. Roy, [1947] 'La Distribution du Revenue Entre les Divers Biens', *Econometrica* 15, July, 205–225.

Peter Schmidt, [1979] 'Estimation of a Generalized Structural Probit Model', *Michigan State University.*

Erika Shoenberg and Paul H. Douglas, [1937] 'Studies in the Supply Curve of Labor: The Relation Between Average Earnings in American Cities and the Proportion Seeking Employment', *Journal of Political Economy* 45, February, 45–62.

T. Paul Schultz, [1980 'Estimating Labor Supply Functions for Married Women', in Smith, ed [1980].

Roger Sherman and Thomas D. Willett, [1976] 'The Standardized Work Week and the Allocation of Time', *Kyklos* 25, 65–82.

James P. Smith, ed, [1980] *Female Labor Supply: Theory and Estimation,* Princeton: Princeton University Press.

James Tobin, [1958] 'The Estimation of a Model with Limited Dependent Variables', *Econometrica* 26, January, 24–36.

T. J. Wales and A. D. Woodland, [1978] 'Sample Selectivity and the Estimation of Labor Supply Functions', University of British Columbia, November.

T. J. Wales and A. D. Woodland, [1979] 'Labor Supply and Progressive Taxes', *Review of Economic Studies* 46, January, 83–95.

Yoram Weiss, [1972] 'On the Optimal Lifetime Pattern of Labour Supply', *Economic Journal* 82, December, 1256–1272.

E. Whybrew, [1968] *Overtime Working in Britian,* Research Paper No. 9, Royal Commission on Trade Unions and Employers' Associations, London: HMSO.

Harold Wilensky, [1963] 'The Moonlighter: Product of Relative Deprivation', *Industrial Relations* 3, October, 105–124.

Empirical Evidence on Static Labour Supply Models: A Survey of Recent Developments

COMMENT *by Yoram Weiss* (University of Tel-Aviv)

As is apparent from the size of this excellent survey by Heckman, Killingsworth and MaCurdy the economics of labour supply is an active area of research. The expansion of redistributive policies has generated demand for precise estimates of the labour supply parameters. We now witness a concentrated research effort in the area of labour economics which is comparable to the developments in the theory and estimation of the consumption function following the Keynesian revolution. This research effort has spawned important developments in the theory of labour supply, innovations in estimation techniques and new bodies of data.

In their survey the authors, perhaps justly, do not make any judgments concerning the direction of recent research. I would like to make two such remarks:

(1) There is in my view too much emphasis on the quantity of work as measured by hours, weeks and participation rates and a neglect of the more qualitative aspects of work. It seems that, at least among males, much of the response to changing economic circumstances is reflected in the type of job rather than in the quantity of work. For instance, the effect of non wage income or hours of work of fully employed males may indeed be negligible while its effect on the kind of work which they choose may be substantial. Similarly, high wage rates need not induce more hours if they represent a compensation for unpleasant work characteristics.

The empirical findings which repeatedly show little response in hours of work among males suggest to me that it is time to look elsewhere. Both the measurement and the theory of job amenities and wage fringes are at a rudimentary stage with considerable scope for potentially useful research.

(2) Most of the research summarized in the survey is based on cross section data. The theory applies only to single units and the researcher has to make some assumption on differences in individual budget sets and preferences. There is increasing recognition in 'sample heterogeneity' and it is not at all obvious which distributional assumptions are valid. The availability of individual time series allows one to test some of these identifying assumptions but considerable arbitrariness remains. For instance, some authors who work on dynamic labour supply assume fixed (i.e. time independent) individual effects. The presumption is that all individuals have equal access to the (perfect) capital market and have the same (fixed) subjective discount rate. Other researchers allow individual growth components. Which is the correct specification? Should we go further and assume, say, different future expectations? We could have perhaps sidestepped some of those questions had we been satisfied with the predictions of average response. However, for the policies under evaluation the distributional impacts are of major importance.

Since many key variables, even of the simplest models, are unobserved, it is unlikely that we shall be able to fully resolve these issues. I am afraid that the big research effort currently under way will not yield clear cut policy prescriptions.

Let me note, finally, that the authors omit from their survey an explicit discussion of the negative income tax experiments. These controlled experiments produced exogenous shifts in both the wage rate and non wage income and the affected individuals were observed over a period of time. The problems of endogeneity in wages and property income as well as the problem of heterogeneity in tests towards work were at least partially relieved (though new problems due to sample selection emerged). My general impression is that the estimated labour supply parameters from these experiments fall within the (wide) range of non-experimental results. The interesting question is whether we have reason to consider the experimental findings as the best available point estimates.

Modelling the Simultaneous Demand for Factors of Production

Ernst R. Berndt
University of British Columbia

MODELLING THE SIMULTANEOUS DEMAND FOR FACTORS OF PRODUCTION

Introduction

The purpose of this paper is to survey developments of the past decade in the theory of cost, production, and derived demand for factors of production, with particular emphasis on empirical applications to labour markets. In the first section, I trace theoretical developments, and comment on empirical aspects such as the choice of representation of technology and the important role of behavioural assumptions. In the second section I summarize a number of particularly interesting empirical factor demand studies, and comment on the changing interpretations of several classical empirical issues. I also note that in the context of models with many factors of production, considerable care must be taken in interpreting 'substitution elasticities'. Finally, I present my own views on current and future directions for research on modelling the simultaneous demand for factors of production.

I. Theoretical Background

Although concern over the derived demand for domestic factors of production has occupied the minds of political economists since at least the time of the physiocrats, modern treatments of factor demands draw heavily on the classic works of Allen [1938] and Hicks [1939, 1946].

Typically the more modern treatment begins with the assumption of an at least twice differentiable production function

(1) $\qquad y = f(x_1, x_2, ... x_n)$

relating the flow of gross output y to the services of n factor inputs, $x_1, x_2, ..., x_n$. Often, but not always, it is then assumed that factor prices $p_1, p_2, ..., p_n$ are exogenous and that firms choose inputs so as to minimize costs of producing a given level of output, or that in addition, firms select the profit maximizing level of output. Given these assumptions, one obtains derived demand functions for the factors of production

(2) $\qquad x_1 = g_1(p_1, p_2, ..., p_n, y)$
$\qquad\quad x_2 = g_2(p_1, p_2, ..., p_n, y)$

$\qquad\quad \cdot$

$\qquad\quad \cdot$

$\qquad\quad \cdot$

$\qquad\quad x_n = g_n(p_1, p_2, ..., p_n, y).$

This set of simultaneous demand functions for factors of production relates the optimal (i.e., cost minimizing or profit maximizing) derived demand for each input to the parameters of technology, input prices, and the level of output.

In order to implement the basic theory outlined above for purposes of empirical research, it is necessary to make additional decisions regarding an appropriate, functional form for f (and hence for the g_i), and the level of aggregation. I now discuss these two issues.

In 1928 Charles Cobb and Paul Douglas published the results of a study relating output in the aggregate private U.S. economy to the aggregate inputs of capital (K) and labour (L) services. The particular functional form employed by them was the geometric mean function

(3) $\qquad Y = A_o K^\alpha L^\beta$

which is of course known today as the Cobb-Douglas production function. In this representation of technology, returns to scale equal $\alpha + \beta$, the Hicks-Allen partial elasticity of substitution is unity, and the constant cost-minimizing factor cost shares are $\alpha/(\alpha + \beta)$ for K and $\beta/(\alpha + \beta)$ for L. With output Y fixed, the own-price elasticities for K and L are also constant (α-1 for K and β-1 for L), as are the cross-price elasticities.

The restrictive nature of the Cobb-Douglas function has been quite obvious to empirical researchers. In 1961, Kenneth J. Arrow, H. B. Chenery, B. Minhas, and Robert M. Solow proposed and estimated a constant elasticity of substitution (CES) production function in which the Allen partial elasticities were constant but not necessarily equal to unity. With constant returns to scale, the CES function took the form

(4) $\qquad Y = [dK^{-p} + (1-d) L^{-p}]^{-1/p}$;

this mean value function, incidentally, was proposed earlier in the economic literature by A. Bergson [1936].

The development of the CES functional form, which took the Cobb-Douglas as a limiting case (as $p \rightarrow 0$), provided the basis for numerous econometric studies and policy debates. A debate carried on for some time on whether the Hicks-Allen partial elasticity of substitution between K and L,

(5) $\qquad \sigma = 1/(1 + p)$

was in fact different from unity. In the United States this debate related to the policy issue of the effectiveness of investment incentives (such as changes in the rate of corporate income taxation, investment tax credits, and accelerated depreciation allowances); for surveys of this literature, see Marc Nerlove [1967] and Dale W. Jorgensen [1971, 1974].

It is worth noting here that even with the choice of the CES function for f, there are numerous alternative equations for estimating σ. Six basic estimating equations have appeared in the literature (see E. R. Berndt [1976] for further discussion):

(6) $\qquad ln(Y/K) = a_1 + \sigma \, ln(P_K/P)$ $\qquad$ (i)

$$ln(Y/L) = a_2 + \sigma\, ln(P_L/P) \quad \text{(ii)}$$
$$ln(K/L) = a_3 - \sigma\, ln(P_K/P_L) \quad \text{(iii)}$$

and the corresponding three reciprocal equations[1]

(7) $ln(P_K/P) = a_4 + (1/\sigma)\, ln(Y/K)$ (i)
$ln(P_L/P) = a_5 + (1/\sigma)\, ln(Y/L)$ (ii)
$ln(P_K/P_L) = a_6 - (1/\sigma)\, ln(K/L)$ (iii)

Empirical researchers seeking to estimate the extent of factor substitutability between K and L therefore often found themselves with considerable discretion in choosing among alternative estimates of σ; incidentally, Berndt [1976] showed that least squares estimates of σ based on 6-i, ii, and iii must always be less than or equal to those based on 7-i, ii, and iii, respectively.

The rather restrictive Cobb-Douglas and CES functional forms have been generalized considerably in the last decade to representations that place no *a priori* restrictions on the Hicks-Allen partial elasticities of substitution, and that also allow for more than one output and two inputs. W. Erwin Diewert [1971] introduced the generalized Leontief function, while L. R. Christensen, D. W. Jorgensen, and L. J. Lau [1973] proposed the transcendental logarithmic (translog) representation[2]; the generalized Box-Cox function of E. R. Berndt and M. S. Khaled [1979] takes the generalized Leontief translog, and other functions as special or limiting cases.

Given all these possible functional forms, the empirical investigator has numerous alternatives available for estimating parameters of the factor demand functions (3). Choice among the various forms could be based on a number of criteria: (i) ease of estimation, (ii) goodness of fit, (iii) agreement of results with basic postulates of demand theory, (iv) approximation properties and robustness of the various functional forms.[3] At the present time, there appears to be no basis in general for preferring one flexible functional form over another; preferred forms are likely to vary with the data, computational costs, and judgments of the researcher. Moreover, comparative small sample properties of these forms have not yet been sufficiently investigated.[4]

In my view, however, there are several reasons favouring use of derived demand equations based on a cost function rather than first order conditions based on a production function. First, under cost minimization it is assumed that output is predetermined, while under profit maximization it is also generally necessary to specify how output price and output quantity are jointly determined. With perfectly competitive input and product markets, the additional assumption of profit maximization may be relatively innocuous.

[1] The constant terms a_1 to a_6 are a combination of p and σ. Relations (i) and (ii) in (6) and (7) are based on the assumption of profit maximization, while (iii) in (6) and (7) relies on the weaker assumption of cost minimization.

[2] Earlier, the translog-type form was discussed by Z. Griliches and V. Ringstad [1971], J. D. Sargan [1971], and S. F. Chu, D. G. Aigner, and M. Frankel [1970] as a generalization of Jan Kmenta's [1967] approximation to the CES production function.

[3] See E. R. Berndt, M. N. Darrough, and W. E. Diewert [1977] for further discussion on choice among flexible functional forms.

[4] See N. M. Kiefer and J. G. MacKinnon [1976].

This is not the case, however, when output markets are imperfect, for in such a case price will not equal marginal cost. Hence if one wishes to model the simultaneous demands for factors of production, use of the profit maximization assumption and the associated production function requires specification of the relationship between output price, output quantity, and the costs of production; by contrast, the utilization of a cost minimization assumption (along with the dual cost function) entails a much simpler (albeit perhaps somewhat unrealistic) exogenous output assumption.

A second consideration concerns the nature of the first order conditions. Under profit maximization and the use of a production function, the normalized input price for each factor is set equal to the marginal product, i.e.

$$(8) \qquad \frac{P_i}{P} = \frac{\partial f(x_1, x_2, \ldots, x_n)}{\partial x_i} \, , \, i = 1, \ldots, n$$

where P is output price. The marginal product $\partial f / \partial x_i$ is of course a function of the technological parameters and the level of all inputs. Hence, for any particular functional form of f, the right hand side of (8) involves quantities of all the endogenous inputs; thus estimation of the entire equation system (8) would involve formidable simultaneous equations problems. One possible way of circumventing this problem is to solve analytically for each of the x_i as a function of only the P_i, Y and the parameters of technology; as soon as f becomes general (more flexible than the CES function) and the number of inputs increases beyond two, this procedure encounters considerable mathematical complexity and becomes virtually intractable. It is precisely for this reason that the use of a cost function is so attractive; all one must do is specify (not derive) a functional form for the cost function satisfying certain regularity conditions (at least locally), partially differentiate it with respect to each input price, and then by Shephard's Lemma set each partial derivative equal to x_i. The resulting set of factor demand functions have input prices and output quantity as right hand variables, and thus estimation does not entail the severe simultaneity problems encountered in (9).

A third and final consideration favouring use of first order conditions based on cost minimization involves aggregation over firms.[5] Assuming that all firms face the same technological constraints, for the representative firm the first order condition estimating equations based on the cost function have input prices as right hand variables, whereas those based on the production function have input quantities as regressors. When aggregating over firms, therefore, one would want to compute 'average' or 'mean' factor demands given certain input prices. It may not be too unreasonable to assume that the input prices facing each firm are approximately equal while input quantities and output differ, but it is more difficult to justify the assumption that input quantities demanded are approximately equal across firms. Hence it is not surprising that, for example, D. F. Burgess [1975] obtained rather different results when estimating first order condition equations based on the translog production

---

[5] This argument has been developed in the consumer demand context by E. R. Berndt, M. N. Darrough, and W. E. Diewert [1977], p. 660.

function and the translog cost function.

To summarize: Although there is generally little basis to choose among alternative 'flexible' functional forms, for empirical research the first order conditions based on a cost function are generally preferable to first order condition equations based on a production function.

Earlier I noted that initial studies of factor demands were typically based on two aggregate inputs—capital and labour—but that the recent development of 'flexible' functional forms permits estimation of demand functions for more than two inputs with no *a priori* restrictions on the Allen partial elasticities of substitution. This raises the issue of how one determines the extent of input disaggregation. In the context of labour markets, for example, in principle one could disaggregate labour by sex, age, occupation, education, etc., or one could simply assume the existence of an aggregate labour input.

The benefits of disaggregation are considerable. Frequently policy initiatives by governments are aimed at particular segments of the labour force; obviously specification and estimation of disaggregated labour demand functions facilitates evaluation of such policy initiatives. Other policies—such as investment incentives or energy taxes—may affect the various labour types differentially, and assessment of such differential impacts requires sufficiently disaggregated labour inputs. The costs of disaggregation, however, are also considerable. The most important obstacle to extensive input disaggregation is frequently simply data availability; it is difficult and costly to obtain reliable data on hours worked (as distinct from hours paid for) for various groups of workers, along with data on compensation per hour worked, where compensation includes all supplementary benefits. Not surprisingly, the quality of the data often declines as the extent of disaggregation increases. Another cost of disaggregation involves computational considerations. With flexible functional forms, the number of parameters to be estimated increases much more rapidly than the number of inputs. This increase in parameters raises computational costs, and as the number of estimated parameters increase the appropriateness of asymptotic distribution theory in small samples is reduced. To the best of my knowledge, no Monte Carlo research has yet been done on assessing the robustness and small sample properties of parameter and elasticity estimates as the extent of input disaggregation increases.

Hence in general there seem to be few hard and precise answers to the question of how extensively the inputs should be disaggregated. If data permit, a useful procedure for reducing estimation complexity is to 'nest' the production or cost function into weakly separable subsets; for example, under the assumption of homothetic weak separability, one could specify a labour production sub-function which produces an 'output' called 'aggregate labour' from the services of a number of distinct labour types. The optimal mix of disaggregated labour inputs within this labour production sub-function depends only on the relative labour input prices, and in particular does not depend on the prices of non-labour inputs or the quantity of output. In turn, the optimal demand for aggregate labour is determined in the second stage of the model, based on optimization of the 'master' production or cost function.[6]

[6] For examples of such nested models in non-labour contexts, see E. A. Hudson, D. W. Jorgensen [1974] and M. A. Fuss [1977].

A few other remarks are in order here. The use of an aggregate labour index does not require the assumption of perfect substitutability among labour types. As discussed in greater detail by E. R. Berndt and L. R. Christensen [1973, 1974], the assumption of the existence of an aggregate labour index is equivalent to assuming that the distinct labour inputs are homothetically weakly separable from all other inputs, which implies that the Allen partial elasticities of substitution between each labour input, say $L_1, L_2 ..., L_l$, and any non-labour input, say $x_2, x_3,..., x_n$, are equal, i.e.

$$(9) \qquad \sigma_{L_1 x_2} = \sigma_{L_2 x_2} = \ ... \ = \sigma_{L_\alpha x_2}$$
$$\sigma_{L_1 x_3} = \sigma_{L_2 x_3} = \ ... \ = \sigma_{L_\alpha x_3}$$

$$\sigma_{L_1 x_n} = \sigma_{L_2 x_n} = \ ... \ = \sigma_{L_\alpha x_n}$$

Moreover, the choice of how to index aggregate labour (assuming that such an index exists) is equivalent to specifying a particular functional form for the labour production sub-function. For example, as shown by W. E. Diewert [1976], if one forms an aggregate index of labour using a Törnqvist discrete approximation to the Divisia index, then one is implicitly assuming that the labour production sub-function is constant returns to scale translog.[7]

Until this point I have avoided making distinctions between static and dynamic optimization. If all inputs are viewed as variable which can be purchased at constant marginal costs, then static and dynamic optimization yield identical solutions. A great deal of empirical literature on demand functions for labour inputs has in fact been based on models with static optimization, constant marginal factor costs, and instantaneous adjustment of factors to their equilibrium level. This literature, and its results, has often been criticized for ignoring adjustment costs which inhibit firms from adjusting input demands instantaneously to their long-run equilibrium levels. Let us denote the long-run equilibrium level of demand for K and L by K^* and L^* respectively. According to the partial adjustment hypothesis, the actual change in demand for K between time periods t and t-1 is a proportion λ_K of the 'desired' change, i.e.

$$(10) \qquad K_t - K_{t-1} = \lambda_K (K^*_t - K_{t-1})$$

Similarly for labour, partial adjustment has been represented as

$$(11) \qquad L_t - L_{t-1} = \lambda_L (L^*_t - L_{t-1})$$

There are a number of problems with this approach. First, there is no economics to the adjustment process; parameters λ_K and λ_L are assumed predetermined and exogenous, rather than endogenous choice variables. Second, because of the absence of a general theoretical framework, it is not

[7] For a discussion of input aggregation and indexing in a non-labour context, see E. R. Berndt [1978].

clear how 'disequilibrium' in the capital demand factor market affects, for example, demand in the labour market. Clearly production of an increased level of output is not feasible if *all* inputs adjust only partially to their long run equilibrium levels. M. I. Nadiri and S. Rosen [1969, 1973] have generalized the Koyck partial adjustment specification to allow for interrelated or 'general disequilibrium' so that, for example,

$$(12) \qquad L_t - L_{t-1} = \lambda_{LL}(L^*_t - L_{t-1}) + \lambda_{LK}(K^*_t - K_{t-1})$$

$$K_t - K_{t-1} = \lambda_{KK}(K^*_t - K_{t-1}) + \lambda_{KL}(L^*_t - L_{t-1})$$

whereby the demand for labour depends not only on the size of the desired labour gap, but also on the extent of 'disequilibrium' in the capital factor market. Although this generalization permits 'overshooting' in the short run and in principle allows for factor demands to be interrelated during the adjustment process, it is still essentially *ad hoc;* there is no economic optimization underlying the adjustment process.

A much more attractive modelling procedure, in my judgment, is to introduce adjustment costs explicitly into the dynamic optimization process. In the theoretical work by R. E. Lucas, Jr. [1967a, b] and A. B. Treadway [1971], a distinction is made between variable and quasi-fixed inputs; a quasi-fixed input is one whose optimal demand at time t depends on its actual demand level at time $t-l$. Typically, quasi-fixed inputs are assumed to be purchased at increasing marginal cost due to costs of adjustments. These adjustment costs could be external (as additional investment is undertaken, borrowing rates increase) or internal (as additional investment is undertaken, due to problems of installation and learning, a certain amount of output is foregone). The optimization problem is then characterized as one of maximizing the present value of profits or minimizing the discounted costs subject to price and technology constraints, including increasing marginal costs of adjustment. A particularly interesting feature of this research is that the derived optimal partial adjustment coefficients for the quasi-fixed inputs are endogenous and variable rather than exogenous and fixed, as in (10), (11) and (12). It has also been shown that a variant of the Koyck adjustment specification can be interpreted as a linear approximation to the optimal accumulation path for quasi-fixed inputs.

Although capital plant and equipment can obviously be viewed as quasi-fixed inputs, labour inputs—especially high skill labour—can also be envisaged as quasi-fixed. Such a view has been articulated by Walter Oi [1962], and is reflected in the employment and manhours models of F. P. R. Brechling [1965, 1975]. To the best of my knowledge, however, the only econometric study that treats capital and certain labour types as quasi-fixed inputs within an explicit dynamic framework is that by Catherine J. Morrison-White and E. R. Berndt [1979].

Once one introduces explicit dynamic optimization into a model of simultaneous factor demands, one must deal with the rather messy issue of price and output expectations, and the process by which those expectations are formed. Since dynamic optimization models have seldomly been applied to labour markets, very little work has been done on comparing alternative models of expectations. Some useful general theoretical results have been reported by J. P. Gould [1968] and S. J. Nickell [1977]; one possible approach incorporating expectations yet remaining analytically and empirically tractable is that of J. Helliwell and G. Glorieux [1970], who allow for non-static output expectations but impose static-myopic factor price expectations.

In the above paragraphs I have briefly surveyed some of the important economic considerations in modelling the simultaneous demand for factors of production. With this general background, I now turn to a discussion and brief evaluation of some of the more interesting empirical applications in labour markets.

II. Review of Empirical Studies

As was noted earlier, frequently government policy initiatives are directed at a particular group of labourers. To the extent that various labour types are substitutable or complementary, the policy thrusts may have unintended spillover effects, or might even be dissipated. Knowledge of labour cross-price elasticities is therefore important. In the last two decades there has appeared in the literature a number of empirical studies attempting to assess the extent to which the various labour factors are substitutable in production. Some of these studies have looked only at labour-labour substitutability and ignored labour-nonlabour interactions (Welch [1970], Johnson [1970], Dougherty [1972], and Bowles [1970]), while others have looked at labour-labour substitutability in the context of labour and capital inputs (Griliches [1969, 1970], Berndt-Christensen [1974], and Kesselman-Williamson-Berndt [1977]). Although these and other related econometric studies have recently been surveyed by Daniel Hamermesh and James Grant [1978], there still remains I believe a serious problem in comparing the various elasticity estimates.

More specifically, suppose the constant returns to scale production function of a firm using three inputs—capital (K) and two labour types $(L_1$ and $L_2)$ is of the form

(13) $Y = f(K, L_1, L_2)$

and that the two labour types are weakly separable from K so that

(14) $Y = f(K, L_1, L_2) = f^*[K, g(L_1, L_2)] = f^{**}(K, L)$

where aggregate labour L is the 'output' of the production sub-function

(15) $L = g(L_1, L_2)$

The weak separability assumption (14) is implicit in the numerous labour-labour substitutability studies cited above that examine only the sub-function

134

(15) and ignore K. Price elasticity estimates based on (15) must, however, be interpreted very carefully.

Define the *gross price elasticities* between L_1 and L_2 as

(16)
$$\epsilon_{12}^* = \frac{\partial \ln L_1}{\partial \ln P_2}\bigg|_{L=\bar{L}}, \qquad \epsilon_{21}^* = \frac{\partial \ln L_2}{\partial \ln P_1}\bigg|_{L=\bar{L}}$$

$$\epsilon_{11}^* = \frac{\partial \ln L_1}{\partial \ln P_1}\bigg|_{L=\bar{L}}, \qquad \epsilon_{22}^* = \frac{\partial \ln L_2}{\partial \ln P_2}\bigg|_{L=\bar{L}}$$

For example, ϵ_{12}^* represents the cross price elasticity between L_1 and L_2 along an $L = \bar{L}$ isoquant; notice that this elasticity measure does not allow for any interaction between K and L_1 or L_2. In particular, ϵ_{12}^* accounts for the effect of an increase in P_2 on the derived demand for L_1 holding aggregate L fixed, but does not reflect the effect of increased P_2 on the price of aggregate labour, which would reduce the derived demand for aggregate L (increase demand for K) and hence reduce demands for *both* L_1 and L_2. Define the *net price elasticities* as follows:

(17)
$$\epsilon_{12}^* = \frac{\partial \ln L_1}{\partial \ln P_2}\bigg|_{Y=\bar{Y}}, \qquad \epsilon_{21}^* = \frac{\partial \ln L_2}{\partial \ln P_1}\bigg|_{Y=\bar{Y}}$$

$$\epsilon_{11}^* = \frac{\partial \ln L_1}{\partial \ln P_1}\bigg|_{Y=\bar{Y}}, \qquad \epsilon_{22}^* = \frac{\partial \ln L_2}{\partial \ln P_2}\bigg|_{Y=\bar{Y}};$$

these net elasticities allow not only for movement along the $L = \bar{L}$ isoquant, but also allow this isoquant to shift, although aggregate output Y is still fixed. The net price and gross price elasticities can be related to each other as follows:[8]

(18)
$$\epsilon_{12} = \epsilon_{12}^* + S_2\epsilon_{LL}, \quad \epsilon_{21} = \epsilon_{21}^* + S_1\epsilon_{LL}$$
$$\epsilon_{11} = \epsilon_{11}^* + S_1\epsilon_{LL}, \quad \epsilon_{22} = \epsilon_{22}^* + S_2\epsilon_{LL}$$

where S_1 and S_2 are the cost shares of L_1 and L_2 in total labour costs and ϵ_{LL} is the price elasticity of demand for total labour L along a $Y = \bar{Y}$ isoquant. Since S_1, S_2 are positive and ϵ_{LL} is negative, it follows that net cross-price elasticities are always smaller than gross cross-price elasticities, but that the absolute value of the net own-price elasticities is larger than that of the gross own-price elasticities, i.e.

---

[8] This analytical framework has been developed in greater detail by E. R. Berndt and D. O. Wood [1979].

(19) $\epsilon_{12} < \epsilon_{12}^{*}, \quad \epsilon_{21} < \epsilon_{21}^{*}, \quad |\epsilon_{11}| > |\epsilon_{11}^{*}|, \quad |\epsilon_{22}| > |\epsilon_{22}^{*}|$

The importance of this result in the labour context is as follows: empirical studies of labour-labour substitutability based on the analysis of labour subfunctions like (15) which ignore K in fact estimate gross rather than net price elasticities. This implies that the resulting ϵ_{12}^{*} and ϵ_{21}^{*} estimates over-estimate ϵ_{12} and ϵ_{21}, while ϵ_{11}^{*} and ϵ_{22}^{*} underestimate (in absolute value) the net own-price elasticities ϵ_{11} and ϵ_{22}.

By analogy, if additional inputs were introduced into the production function (13)—say, for example, energy, non-energy domestically produced intermediate materials, and imports—and if the resulting gross output (rather than value added, Y) were denoted as Q, the resulting net price elasticity estimates along a $Q = \bar{Q}$ isoquant would bear an inequality relationship to gross elasticity estimates along the $Y = \bar{Y}$ isoquant similar to (19).

What this all means is that great care must be taken in comparing labour-labour elasticity estimates from various econometric studies, for in fact the various price elasticities measure quite different phenomena, i.e. they correspond to different partial derivatives. Surveys on labour-labour substitutability such as that by Hamermesh-Grant can easily mislead readers; the apparently disparate econometric elasticity estimates may in fact be reasonably consistent with one another, once one recognizes that different 'outputs' are being held fixed. Although desirable, space and time limitations prohibit presentation here of an appropriate comparison of the various empirical labour-labour substitutability studies.

One empirical finding of the past few decades, however, merits special attention. Although noted earlier by Edwin Kuh [1965b, p. 247], Finis Welch [1969] and Zvi Griliches [1970] have presented empirical evidence suggesting that physical capital is more complementary with skilled than with unskilled labour. Welch has suggested that capital-skill complementarity was partly responsible for the evidence (prior to 1970) that average rates of return to education had apparently failed to decline even with large increases in average education levels. Since investment grew at very high rates in the 1960's, capital-skill complementarity increased the derived demand for high skill labour. Griliches employed the complementarity hypothesis as a partial explanation for the related evidence that skilled and unskilled income differentials through the 1960's had remained stable in spite of large increases in the supply of skilled labour. More recent evidence is also consistent with the capital-skill complementarity hypothesis (see, for example, E. R. Berndt and L. R. Christensen [1974], and J. Kesselman et. al. [1977]), even when skill categories are broken down into several distinct educational categories (James Grant [1979]).

Two implications of the capital-skill complementarity issue are worth special mention. First, if capital and high skilled labour are complements while capital and less skilled labour are substitutes, then investment incentives (such as accelerated depreciation allowances and investment tax credits) have rather differing impacts on the two labour types; in particular, these investment incentives can be viewed as regressive, since they benefit high skill workers more than low-skill labourers. A less regressive way of stimulating employment would involve use of employment tax credits rather than investment tax credits; further discussion of this issue is in Kesselman *et. al.* [1977]. Second, an implication of the Berndt-Christensen [1973] substitution-aggregation theorems is that, in this context, a consistent aggregate index of labour exists if and only if the Allen partial elasticity of substitution between high skill labour and capital equals that between low skill labour and capital. Hence empirical evidence supporting the notion of capital-high skill complementarity and capital-low skill substitutability can also be interpreted as suggesting that the two labour inputs cannot be aggregated in a consistent way.

In addition to the two empirical issues of labour-labour substitutability and capital-skill complementarity, a most interesting and important empirical finding of the last two decades is the so-called paradox of short-run increasing returns to labour.

A classic finding of Thor Hultgren [1960], Edwin Kuh [1960, 1965a,b], Frank Brechling and Peter O'Brien [1967] and others is that in the short run as output increased (decreased), manhours and especially employment increased (decreased) less than proportionally. Kuh showed that this cyclical phenomenon of short run increasing returns to labour (hereafter, SRIRL) was the principal cause of the procyclical variation in the profit share of national income. Additional significance was attributed to the SRIRL empirical finding by Arthur Okun [1962], who demonstrated that SRIRL formed one of the links underlying 'Okun's Law' which stated that for each percentage point of reduction in unemployment above four per cent, GNP would rise about three percentage points.

The classic SRIRL findings by Hultgren, Kuh, Okun and other based on US data have been replicated for other countries, for various levels of disaggregation and for manhours as well as employment. Today the SRIRL phenomenon figures importantly in calculations of potential GNP and in the estimated value of short run employment multipliers with respect to various monetary or fiscal policy instruments.

The empirical finding of SRIRL was at first viewed as being inconsistent with the simple theory of the firm. Consider, for example, a firm producing output with two inputs—a variable input labour and a fixed input (in the short run) capital. If the short run production function is of the normal shape with diminishing returns to the variable factor labour, then as output increases, the short run elasticity of demand for labour with respect to output should be greater than unity, and both marginal and average costs should be rising with output. However, the empirical evidence of SRIRL—a labour elasticity less than unity, and smaller in the short than in the long run—directly contradicts this simple theory.

Several possible explanations have been offered to resolve this paradox. The most common rationale involves labour hoarding. According to the labour hoarding argument, there are substantial increasing marginal costs associated with rapid changes in the level of employment or average weekly hours. The dynamic cost minimization solution for the firm may then be to hoard labour in the downturn of the business cycle, and to realize increasing productivity of labour in the upswing; see Robert M. Solow [1968] for further discussion. A closely related human capital rationale for the firm to hold on to its highly trained employees during the downturn of the business cycle was developed originally by Walter Oi [1962]; another possible cause of labour hoarding involves implicit contracts between employers and employees.

Additional theoretical and empirical underpinings to the SRIRL phenomenon have recently been developed by Catherine J. Morrison-White and E. R. Berndt [1979]. Using a dynamic cost-minimizing model of the firm with a single quasi-fixed input capital and several (more than one) variable inputs, they express the short-run (capital fixed) output elasticity of demand for aggregate labour as

$$(20) \qquad \epsilon_{Ly}^{S} = \left[\frac{Y}{L}\right]\left[\frac{\partial L}{\partial Y}\Big|_{K=\overline{K}}\right]$$

and the corresponding long run elasticity as

$$(21) \qquad \epsilon_{Ly}^{L} = \left[\frac{Y}{L}\right]\left[\frac{\partial L}{\partial Y}\Big|_{K=\overline{K}} + \frac{\partial L}{\partial K^*}\frac{\partial K^*}{\partial Y}\right]$$

where K^* is the long run equilibrium level of demand for capital services. It follows immediately that the difference between ϵ_{LY}^{L} and ϵ_{LY}^{S} which by the SRIRL finding must be positive, is simply

$$(22) \qquad \epsilon_{Ly}^{L} - \epsilon_{Ly}^{S} = \left[\frac{Y}{L}\right]\left[\frac{\partial L}{\partial K^*}\frac{\partial K^*}{\partial Y}\right] > 0$$

Assuming that capital is not an inferior input, $\partial K^*/\partial Y > 0$. Hence $\epsilon_{LY}^{L} > \epsilon_{LY}^{S}$ if and only if $\partial L/\partial K^* > 0$, i.e. if and only if capital and aggregate labour are complementary inputs. Hence labour hoarding is not necessary for the existence of SRIRL; all that is required is that aggregate labour be complementary with the quasi-fixed input capital.

Although aggregate K-L complementarity is theoretically permissible when there are more than two inputs, it is commonly thought that K and L are substitutes rather than complements. Morrison-White and Berndt therefore hypothesize that the SRIRL phenomenon is partially an aggregation phenomenon. Suppose aggregate labour were disaggregated into high-skill (nonproduction) and lower-skill (production labour) workers. If the complementary relationship between high skill labour and the quasi-fixed capital input dominated substitutability between lower skill labour and capital, short run returns to aggregate labour would be increasing, and $\epsilon_{LQ}^{S} < \epsilon_{LQ}^{L}$. To the best of my knowledge, this is the first explicit synthesis of these two different strands of empirical research in labour demand—capital skill complementarity and SRIRL. Morrison-White and Berndt find empirical evidence supporting this interpretation of SRIRL. They also extend their model to allow for two quasi-fixed inputs—physical capital and high-skill labour, thereby explicitly taking labour hoarding into account, and again are able to derive conditions for SRIRL. A principle conclusion of their empirical research therefore, is that SRIRL can be viewed as the natural outcome of a dynamic cost minimization process.

Before leaving this discussion, I should point out that SRIRL has typically not been analyzed in the context of other inputs. In the Morrison-White and Berndt framework, the two labour types and capital as well as energy and non-energy intermediate materials are incorporated as inputs into the firms production process. This permits a much richer specification of simultaneous or interrelated factor demands throughout the adjustment process. An interesting empirical finding (based on their annual US manufacturing data, 1952–71) is that there are short run decreasing returns to some inputs, and increasing returns to others. Specifically, in response to an exogenous increase in output, the dynamic cost-minimizing firm increases its demands for non-energy intermediate materials and semi-processed goods (M) more than proportionally, increases its demand for unskilled labour (U) about proportionally, and raises its derived demand for K, energy (E), and skilled labour (S) less than proportionally. Gradually, however, as the firm adjusts K to K^* and S to S^* it 'produces' the intermediate goods internally, increasing demand for E, K and S and reducing demand for M (including imports). Hence it is optimal for the firm to have short run 'overshooting' of M, and 'undershooting' of S, K and E.

III. Concluding Remarks

In this paper I have surveyed contributions of the last two decades in the theory of cost and production which relate to modelling the simultaneous demand for factors of production. I have also attempted to show how several classical empirical issues in labour markets—labour-labour substitutability, capital-skill complementarity, and short run increasing returns to aggregate labour—are now being reinterpreted. This survey has admittedly been less than exhaustive, yet still reflects I hope the essential flavour of much recent research. One issue not discussed (given space constraints) is the modelling of the rate and bias of technical change in the context of many factors of production, a topic clearly meriting attention. Another neglected but important issue is consideration of data quality and availability.

In concluding this survey, I should like to suggest areas particularly worthy of additional research. First, I believe the modelling of dynamic factor demands is a very exciting and promising recent development. Although the specification of models with many quasi-fixed factors can easily become cumbersome mathematically, very recent suggestions by L. Epstein [1979] may provide the basis for useful empirical research. Specifications of expectation formation can, I think, proceed gradually; for example, it would appear useful first to undertake empirical research where there are myopic expectations on factor prices, but where the expectations on output quantity were slightly more sophisticated—say, adaptive or pseudo-rational. Second, the proliferation of empirically implementable functional forms with many inputs permits much greater examination of labour inputs in the context of other factors of production. In particular, I have in mind energy-labour issues, such as the extent to which E and L are substitutable in the short and long run, and how energy quantity constraints affect marginal and average costs of production. To the best of my knowledge, hardly any research has been done on the effects of the recently enacted massive Social Security tax increases in the U S on demand for labour and non-labour inputs, especially capital and energy. Another energy-labour issue worthy of attention is that of the income redistribution effects of rising energy prices. Although there is ample evidence showing that in terms of final demand by consumers, the budget share directly expended on energy decreases with income, thereby implying that energy price increases are regressive, there has been very little analysis on the production sector effects of rising energy prices.[9] Finally, also in the context of labour as one of many inputs, it appears particularly important to model the inventory accumulation and decumulation process, since this buffer role of inventories has important implications for the cyclical behaviour of manhours and employment.

REFERENCES

Allen, R. G. D. [1938], *Mathematical Analysis for Economists,* London: MacMillan.
Arrow, K. J., H. B. Chenery, B. Minhas, and R. M. Solow [1961], 'Capital-Labour Substitution and Economic Efficiency', *Review of Economics and Statistics,* August, pp. 225–250.
Bergson (Burk), A. [1936], 'Real Income, Expenditure Proportionality, and Frisch's 'New Method of Measuring Marginal Utility', *Review of Economic Studies,* Vol. 4, October 1936.
Berndt, E. R. [1976], 'Reconciling Alternative Estimates of the Elasticity of Substitution, '*Review of Economics and Statistics,* Vol. 58, No. 1, February, pp. 59–68.
Berndt, E. R. [1978], 'Aggregate Energy, Efficiency, and Productivity Measurement', *Annual Review of Energy,* Vol. 3, pp. 225–273.
Berndt, E. R. and L. R. Christensen [1973], 'The Internal Structure of Functional Relationships: Separability, Substitution, and Aggregation', *Review of Economic Studies,* Vol. 40, July, pp. 403–410.
Berndt, E. R. and L. R. Christensen [1974], 'Testing for the Existence of a Consistent Aggregate Index of Labour Inputs', *American Economic Review,* Vol. 64, No. 3, June, pp. 391–404.
Berndt, E. R., M. N. Darrough, and W. E. Diewert [1977], 'Flexible Functional Forms and Expenditure Distributions: An Application to Canadian Consumer Demand Functions' *International Economic Review,* October, Vol. 18, No. 3, pp. 651–676.
Berndt, E. R. and M. S. Khaled [1979], 'Parametric Productivity Measurement and Choice Among Flexible Functional Forms', *Journal of Political Economy,* Vol. 87, No. 6, December, pp. 1220–1245.
Berndt, E. R. and Catherine J. Morrison-White [1978], 'Income Redistribution and Employment Effects of Rising Energy Prices', University of British Columbia, Department of Economics, Programme in Natural Resource Economics, Resources Paper No. 30, December.
Berndt, E. R. and D. O. Wood [1979], 'Engineering and Econometric Interpretations of Energy-Capital Complementarity', *American Economic Review,* Vol. 69, No. 3, June, pp. 342–354.
Bowles, S. S. [1970], 'Aggregation of Labour Inputs in the Economics of Growth and Planning: Experiments with a Two-Level C E S Function', *Journal of Political Economy,* January/February, Vol. 78, pp. 68–81.
Brechling, F. P. R. [1965], 'The Relationship Between Output and Employment in British Manufacturing Industries', *Review of Economic Studies,* Vol. 32, pp. 187–216.
Brechling, F. P. R. [1975], *Investment and Employment Decisions,* Manchester: Manchester University Press.
Brechling, F. P. R. and P. O. O'Brien [1967], 'Short Run Employment Functions in Manufacturing Industries: An International Comparison', *Review of Economic Studies,* Vol. 32(3), No. 95.
Burgess, D. F. [1975], 'Duality Theory and Pitfalls in the Specification of Technologies', *Journal of Econometrics,* Vol. 3, No. 2, May, pp. 105–121.

[9] For results of some preliminary research, see Berndt and Morrison-White [1978].

Christensen, L. R., D. W. Jorgenson, and L. J. Lau [1973], 'Transcendental Logarithmic Production Frontiers', *Review of Economics and Statistics,* February, Vol. 55, pp. 28–45.

Chu, S. F., D. J. Aigner, and M. Frankel [1970], 'On the Log-Quadratic Law of Production', *Southern Economic Journal,* Vol. 37, No. 1, July, pp. 32–39.

Cobb, C. and P. H. Douglas [1928], 'A Theory of Production', *American Economic Review,* Supplement to Vol. 18, pp. 139–165.

Diewert, W. Erwin [1971], 'An Application of Shephard Duality Theorem: A Generalized Leontief Cost Function', *Journal of Political Economy,* Vol. 79, May/June, pp. 481–507.

Diewert, W. E. [1976], 'Exact and Superlative Index Numbers', *Journal of Econometrics,* Vol. 4, January, pp. 115–145.

Dougherty, C. R. S. [1972], 'Estimates of Labour Aggregation Functions', *Journal of Political Economy,* Vol. 80, November, pp. 1101–1119.

Epstein, Larry [1979], 'Duality Theory and Functional Forms for Dynamic Factor Demands', Institute for Policy Analysis, University of Toronto, Working Paper No. 7915, July.

Fuss, M. A. [1977], 'The Demand for Energy in Canadian Manufacturing: An Example of the Estimation of Production Structures with Many Inputs', *Journal Of Econometrics,* January, Vol. 5, pp. 89–116.

Gould, J. P. [1968], 'Adjustment Costs in the Theory of Investment of the Firm', *Review of Economic Studies,* Vol. 35, January, pp. 47–55.

Griliches, Zvi [1969], 'Capital-Skill Complementarity', *Review of Economics and Statistics,* November, Vol. 51, pp. 465–468.

Griliches, Zvi [1970], 'Notes on the Role of Education in Production Functions and Growth Accounting', in W. Lee Hansen, ed., *Education, Income and Human Capital,* New York, 1970, pp. 71–115.

Griliches, Zvi and V. Ringstad [1971], *Economies of Scale and the Form of the Production Function,* Amsterdam: North-Holland.

Grant, James [1979], 'Labour Substitution in US Manufacturing', Unpublished Ph.D. dissertation, Department of Economics, Michigan State University.

Hamermesh, Daniel S. and James Grant [1978], 'Econometric Studies of Labour-Labour Substitution and their Implications for Policy', Lansing, Michigan State University Workshop Paper 7709 (Revised), December; forthcoming, *Journal of Human Resources.*

Helliwell, J. and G. Glorieux [1970], 'Forward-Looking Investment Behaviour', *Review of Economic Studies,* Vol. 37, October, pp. 499–516.

Hicks, J. R. [1939, 1946], *Value and Capital,* Oxford: Oxford University Press. First edition, 1939; Second edition, 1946.

Hudson, E. A. and D. W. Jorgenson [1974], US Energy Policy and Economic Growth, 1975–2000', *Bell Journal of Economics and Management Science,* Vol. 5, pp. 461–514.

Hultgren, Thor [1960], 'Changes in Labour Lost During Cycles in Production and Business', New York: National Bureau of Economic Research, Occasional Paper 74.

Johnson, George E. [1970], 'The Demand for Labour by Educational Category', *Southern Economic Journal,* Vol. 37, October, pp. 190–204.

Jorgenson, Dale W. [1971], 'Econometric Studies of Investment Behaviour: A Survey', *Journal of Economic Literature,* Vol. 9, No. 4, December.

Jorgenson, Dale W. [1974], 'Investment and Production: A Review', in M. Intirligator, and D. Kendrick. Eds., *Frontiers of Quantitative Economics,* Vol. 2, Amsterdam: North-Holland.

Kesselman, Jonathan, Samuel H. Williamson and Ernst R. Berndt [1977], 'Tax Credits for Employment Rather than Investment', *American Economic Review,* June, Vol. 67, pp. 339–349.

Kiefer, N. M. and J. G. MacKinnon [1976], 'Small Sample Properties of Demand System Estimates', in S. M. Coldfield and R. E. Quandt, eds., *Studies in Nonlinear Estimation,* Cambridge, MA: Bailinger Press.

Kmenta, Jan [1967], 'On Estimation of the CES Production Function', *International Economic Review,* Vol. 8, June, pp. 180–189.

Kuh, Edwin [1960], 'Profits, Profit Markups, and Productivity', Washington, D.C.: Study of Employment, Growth and Price Levels, Joint Economic Activity, Paper No. 15.

Kuh, Edwin [1965a], 'Cyclical and Secular Labour Productivity in United States Manufacturing', *Review of Economics and Statistics,* Vol. 47, No. 1, February, pp. 1–12.

Kuh, Edwin [1965b], 'Income Distribution and Employment over the Business Cycle', ch. 8 in J. Duesenberry, G. Fromm, L. Klein, and E. Kuh, eds. *The Brookings-SSRC Quarterly Econometric Model of the United States Economy,* Rand McNally-North-Holland Publishing Company, pp. 227–277.

Lucas, Robert, E., Jr. [1967a], 'Adjustment Costs and the Theory of Supply', *Journal of Political Economy,* August, pp. 331–344.

Lucas, Robert E., Jr. [1967b], 'Optimal Investment Policy and the Flexible Accelerator', *International Economic Review,* Vol. 8, No. 1, February, pp. 78–85.

Mork, Knut Anton [1977], 'Aggregate Cost, Productivity, and Prices in the Short Run', Ph.D. thesis, Department of Economics, Massachusetts Institute of Technology, May.

Morrison-White, Catherine J. and E. R. Berndt [1979], 'Short Run Labour Productivity in a Dynamic Model', Paper presented at the Summer Meetings of the Econometric Society, Montreal, June.

Nadiri, M. I. and S. Rosen [1969], 'Interrelated Factor Demand Functions', *American Economic Review,* Vol. 59, No. 4, Part I, September, pp. 457–471.

Nadiri, M. I. and S. Rosen [1973], *A Disequilibrium Model of Demand for Factors of Production,* New York: National Bureau of Economic Research, General Series, No. 99.

Nerlove, Marc [1967], 'Recent Empirical Studies of the CES and Related Production Functions', in M. Brown, ed., *The Theory and Empirical Analysis of Production,* Studies in Income and Wealth, No. 32, New York: Columbia University Press, pp. 55–122.

Nickell, S. J. [1977], 'The Flexible Accelerator Model with Non-Static Expectations', London School of Economics, Mimeograph.

Oi, Walter [1962], 'Labour as a Quasi-Fixed Factor', *Journal of Political Economy,* Vol. 70, December, pp. 538–555.

Okun, Arthur M. [1962], 'Potential GNP: Its Measurement and Significance', American Statistical Association, Proceedings of the Business and Economics Section, pp. 98–104.

Sargen, J. D. [1971], 'Production Functions', Part V of P. R. G. Layard, J. D. Sargen, M. F. Ager and D. J. Jones, *Qualified Manpower and Economic Performance,* London: The Penguin Press, pp. 145–204.

Solow, Robert M. [1964], 'Draft of Presidential Address on the Short Run Relation of Employment and Output', World Congress of the Econometric Society, Vienna, unpublished.

Solow, Robert, M. [1968], 'Distribution in the Long and Short Run', in Jean Marchal and Bernard Ducrois, eds., *Proceedings of a Conference Held by the International Economics Association at Palermo,* New York: St. Martin's Press, Chapter 17, pp. 449–466.

Treadway, A. B. [1971], 'On the Multivariate Flexible Accelerator', *Econometrica,* Vol. 39, No. 5, September, pp. 845–855.

Welch, F. [1970], 'Education in Production', *Journal of Political Economy,* January/February, Vol. 78, pp. 35–59.

Modelling the Simultaneous Demand for Factors of Production

COMMENT *by J. Pen* (University of Groningen).

This is an impressive paper; a scholarly piece of work. I feel honoured that somebody thought that I am fit to discuss it. I am strongly motivated to criticise Mr Berndt's position because his results—numerical results—are embarrassing to those people, like myself, who have vested interest in income equalization. I am in favour of levelling politically, but I also have to explain the income equalization that has taken place in the last forty or fifty years. With Mr Berndt's elasticity that job becomes a difficult one. I'll come back to this point.

But there is a second reason why the paper is embarrassing: it has a strong neo-classical smell. The whole accent falls on substitution. Keynesians, like myself, are not pleased by the idea that investment is bad for employment—blue-collar employment, that is. The theoretical point is that the paper suggests a certain type of investment behaviour which is contrary to the Keynesian ideology and also contrary to casual empiricism.

So my criticism is the criticism of an income leveller, a Keynesian and a casual empiricist. But I do not deny that this paper is an excellent exercise in elasticity searching.

My first point of criticism is about income distribution. Here two issues are involved, and two elasticities. The first issue concerns the share of capital in the national income. In most countries this share has been diminishing. A strong example is the Netherlands: in 1938 dividends interest plus interest plus rent stood at 23% of national income against 5% now (profits are not included). This dramatic decline ought to be explained. Part of it can be explained by simple neoclassical reasoning. Capital intensity goes up, the share of capital goes down. That is Hicks' Law. But the reasoning rests upon the elasticity of substitution between labour and capital being smaller than unity. Berndt's paper suggests the opposite, at least for blue collar workers. That bothers me, because if Hicks' Law works in the opposite direction then we are stuck with the paradox that a more capital-intensive or capitalistic production leads to a more labouristic distribution. It is not easy to explain that paradox. One might think of the power of trade unions, but that does not work either: a high elasticity of substitution makes the unions powerless. Wage inflation works empirically the wrong way: it makes labour's share smaller.

Berndt's paper does not mention this consequence of his elasticity of substitution between labour and capital. Of course, we can't blame the author for saddling us with problems but I'd like to have his opinion. He has explained SRIRL but created an unsolved problem.

Moreover, sometimes you don't know what to believe. On page 45 of Morrison-White-Berndt we read that K-S complementarity may dominate K-U substitutability. And that means that *aggregate labour may be complementary with quasi-fixed capital*. So now investment is the worker's friend. That conclusion is certainly different from Kesselman-Williamson-Berndt. I take it that the first paper gives the more recent information but still I feel a bit baffled.

And perhaps I may refer to some recent research by Tinbergen who used a translog function on American data (going back to 1900 I think) and found an elasticity of 0.6.

Income equalisation has a second aspect and that is levelling within the wage structure, in particular between blue collar and white collar wages. This type of levelling is going on in most countries. It can be explained partly by shifts in scarcity between skilled and unskilled compartments of the labour market. Tinbergen's model of 1971 is perhaps the most daring specification.

Here the paper (by Morrison-White and Berndt) brings a combination of good and bad news. The elasticity of substitution between skilled and unskilled labour is low—which means that more education in the KUSEM model leads to more equalisation. Even limited amounts of Government spending will do. But on the other hand, investment has the opposite effect. It increases the demand for complementary skilled labour and decreases the demand for unskilled labour. The net balance of these two tendencies is difficult to estimate but casual empiricism tells me that the investment boom of the sixties and the early seventies led in Europe to a certain compression of the wage structure and to an influx of unskilled foreign workers. The latter points to complementarity between capital goods and unskilled labour.

So I remain sceptical about the high elasticity of substitution between capital and unskilled labour. I also wonder what will happen to this type of analysis when Berndt decides to take more than two types of labour into account. Once somebody asked Jacob Mincer what he thought of the dual labour market and he said: 'Well, two is better than one but it's still a small number.' So there is room for more research.

Now for the anti-Keynesian tendency of the paper. It is all about substitution. The combination of K and L is dominated by the search for the least-cost combinations. This search is certainly a strong underground current in the economy. The high elasticity implies that if the wage rate goes up, firms try to increase their capital intensity by *either* firing blue collar workers *or* buying new capital goods. The former possibility leads to a high elasticity of demand—own price elasticity of demand—for blue collar labour. This is not confirmed by the Kesselman-Williamson-Berndt paper ($E_B = 0.3$), but it *is* confirmed by Morrison-White-Berndt where in KUSEM $E_{BB} = 1.14$ or 1.15. Mind you, these are elasticities of employment with respect to real wages. Now here again my question about these estimates is: whom should we believe? Hazledine, when speaking of the employment function, reports about the same issue. He tells us that the literature contains several scattered but not very clear indications about the impact of wages on employment.

So far, my argument rests upon a vague kind of scepticism. That is feeble. But there is one possible conclusion from Berndt's paper—which he does not draw himself—that arouses my critical sense; that conclusion is that higher wages provoke a higher capital intensity not be firing people but by buying new equipment. This is not a nonsensical proposition—I am sure that wage inflation has this particular effect on the investment decision in the sixties. But there is an opposing tendency at work. Here we are at the heart of one of the most burning practical questions of the coming decade. That is: what is the impact of continuous wage inflation—increases in money wages of say, 10%, 15%—on investment, on employment, on productivity, on real wages?

It is quite easy to dramatize the influence of what has been called the 'wage grab'. It is not my intention to do that. But the whole subject is so conspicuously absent from Berndt's paper—and also, to my surprise from the other conference papers!—that I feel compelled to repeat a few of the pedestrian arguments one hears in business circles.

When wages go up at a higher rate than average labour productivity, the cost of production increases. If these costs are shifted *fully* into prices there is still a profit squeeze. It only disappears if the profit margin goes up too, that is, if the relative profit margin is a constant. The Treasury Model *(Technical Manual 1978)*, keeps the markups constant. But in practice shifting is less than complete. That means a profit squeeze. That means *lower investment, a lower capital intensity,* a lower growth rate and more unemployment.

These gloomy things are simply non-existent in Berndt's neo-classical world. The word profit is not even mentioned. The profit squeeze—which threatens future employment in Britain—is not mentioned. Future readers of this paper will wonder, why not? Berndt's answer may be: the reason lies with my neo-classical methodology—cost minimization with given output. But then the next question is: what is the relevance of the neo-classical 'simultaneous modelling' for really *burning real world* employment problems?

'Employment Functions' and the Demand for Labour in the Short-Run

Tim Hazledine
Queens University Ontario

'EMPLOYMENT FUNCTIONS' AND THE DEMAND FOR LABOUR IN THE SHORT-RUN

1. Introduction and Summary

This paper is an interpretative survey of the findings of empirical work concerned to explain the determinants of fluctuations of the level of employment. Those wishing an *ab initio* introduction to employment functions should also consult the various survey papers and chapters in the literature [Fair, 1969; Killingsworth, 1970; Hughes, 1971a; Roberts, 1972; Hazledine, 1974], as well as what are, I suppose, the three 'classic' papers of Brechling [1965], Ball and St. Cyr [1966], and Nadiri and Rosen [1969]. For those with a more passing interest, I will attempt to provide in this section an outline of what has become the orthodox model, and a summary of the findings of the other sections.

The orthodox model, due to Brechling and Ball and St. Cyr, assumes that employers have in each time period a 'desired' level of employment, E_t^*, (the demand for labour), given as a function of the demand for output, Y_t, and other factors such as capital stock, 'technology', and, possibly, input prices:

$$(1) \qquad E_t^* = f(Y_t,...)$$

However, because of 'adjustment costs' of actually achieving the desired level of employment when this does not equal the level, E_{t-1}, on hand at the start of the period, employers in general end up making an incomplete change in their labour forces towards E^*:

$$(2) \qquad E_t - E_{t-1} = g(E_t - E_{t-1})$$

E^* is not usually directly observable, so (1) is substituted for it in (2):

$$(2') \qquad E_t - E_{t1} = g(f(Y_t ...) - E_{t-1})$$

The adjustment function, g, is usually specified to be simply a proportional constant, λ, between 0 and 1:

$$(3) \qquad E_t - E_{t-1} = \lambda[f(Y_t,...) - E_{t-1}]$$

It was expected that this formulation would resolve the apparent 'paradox' of employment fluctuating less than output in the short-term, which seemed to imply increasing returns to labour. If the employment levels actually observed were not, because of adjustment costs, equal to the desired levels determined by input costs and production function constraints, then the relationship between actual employment and output was not to be interpreted as returns to labour. The model has seemed to be quite econometrically successful, in that both demand and lagged employment variables have usually shown statistical significance, and the overall goodness-of-fits have been quite high—however, there are problems with the economic interpretation of the parameters, and with the precise *a priori* specification of the function f.

In section 2, the specification of the output demand variable Y_t is examined. Current-period actual output is the most commonly used measure, and is mostly significant, but there are both econometric and economic reasons for expecting that a purer demand-side variable is preferable. This is supported by some results.

Prices, of inputs or of output, might be expected to affect employment either through factor substitution, or under competitive conditions, by affecting the amount of output firms wish to supply. Many employment function studies do not include any price variables; of those that do (section 3), insignificant or 'wrong'-signed coefficients are quite common. Even when the coefficients have the expected sign, they tend to be rather small compared to the coefficients found on the output variable, and are not always easy to interpret clearly.

Section 4 completes the examination of the E^* equation (1) by looking at the forces that affect the shape of, and shifts in, the function f. The shape of the function has typically been assumed to be determined by a constant-elasticity production function such as the Cobb-Douglas, and shifts modelled by including a series for the capital stock, or, failing that, a simple time trend. It is argued in section 4 that neither assumption is valid—that production technology in the short-term is best represented by a variable-elasticity function capable of generating U-shaped average cost curves, and that the technology does not, in general, change smoothly over the entire course of our sample periods.

In section 5 we look at the supply side of the story. A problem with the usual specification of (3) is that we cannot be sure that the lagged dependent variable term is uniquely picking up supply-side adjustment costs. In particular, product-market expectations factors could also be involved. There is some evidence of adjustment speed being affected by the degree of 'tightness' of the labour market, but none of wages paid affecting the availability of labour.

The most striking empirical finding of the first employment function studies was that, even after allowing for incomplete employment adjustment, apparently increasing returns to labour remained (in fact returns estimated from employment functions were sometimes higher than those found by direct estimation of the production function). In section 6 it is suggested that this puzzle can be resolved by adopting the variable-elasticity specification favoured in section 4. This specification is also easily able to deal with the tendency for estimates of returns to labour to fall as recent observations are added to databases.

Section 7 looks at some attempts to disentangle the specification (3) by estimating demand and supply equations separately. Although not yet successful, these attempts do indicate a possibly fruitful direction for future employment function research. Another direction, discussed in section 8, leads to using pooled time series-cross section databases in which the coefficients of the employment model can themselves be explained as functions of various structural and cyclical variables.

In section 9 we examine the notion of 'inter-related adjustment'—of the change in one input towards its equilibrium level being affected by the degree of disequilibrium in the levels of other inputs. It is argued, probably not uncontroversially, that inter-related adjustment is not very relevant to the employment decision. On the one hand, adjustments of capital appears to be so slow relative to employment that levels of capital stock have their influence in the E^* relation, not directly on adjustment speeds; on the other hand, adjustment of the other short-term variable inputs, such as materials and hours per worker may be fast enough, relative to employment levels, for it to be not worthwhile considering, say, hours 'disequilibrium' in the employment-change equation. The converse, of course, does not hold—employment level disequilibrium is likely to be an important determinant of short-term changes in hours per employee, given the relative ease with which the latter is adjustable—and this, and other determinants of hours worked are discussed in section (10). Sections 11 and 12 note some implications of these results for economic theory and for future research.

2. Demand Side (1): The Role of Output

Before the introduction of the notion of employment adjustment costs it was natural enough to make the current level of employment a function of just current levels of output and of any factors fixed in availability during the time period.[1] If employment can be costlessly varied, only the amount of labour needed to produce the particular output rate desired in each period will be hired in that period. Current output was retained in the first partial adjustment models (Brechling, Ball and St. Cyr), and, in much of the work that followed, in which it almost always shows strong statistical significance.[2]

However, there are a number of objections that can be raised to its use. First, there is the fundamental theoretical objection (from the neo-classical point of view) that the proper exogenous variables for a factor demand equation are prices, not quantities. This position is considered below in section 3.

Secondly, accepting for the moment the validity of incorporating some sort of 'quantity' demand constraint, there are three reasons why the best proxy for this will not, in general, be current output:

(1) If employment cannot be costlessly varied within a period, it will pay employers to consider the likely demand for their output in periods beyond the current one, so that they might reduce adjustment costs by smoothing-out fluctuations in employment. That is, future as well as current expected demand

---

[1] Such a function would not simply be the inverse of the production function, so long as there are any other inputs (such as utilization rates) that also are variable within the time period (cf. Section 4 below).

[2] Studies in which current output is the major determinant of changes in employment include those by Brechling & O'Brien, Smyth & Ireland, Nadiri & Rosen [1969], Coen & Hickman, Hazledine [1974, 1978a], Briscoe & Peel, Phipps. Nerlove [1967] has a survey of the early macro-econometric models.

151

should matter. The principle of this point was, in fact, explicitly recognized in the original employment function studies.[3] Kuh notes [1965b, p. 238] that 'changes in output must persist for some time before belief in their continuation is firmly established', and Ball and St. Cyr suggest that adjustment speed will be determined 'by expectations of the permanency of a shift in output' (p. 183), as well as by labour supply conditions. Brechling made a similar point [1965, p. 192]. This should lead to a search for a measure of 'permanent demand', analogous to the permanent income concept of consumption theory, as has been urged, in the context of investment functions, by Eisner and others. In fact, not a lot has been done. Kuh [1965b] and Brechling [1965] both tried including lagged as well as current output, as, more recently, did Friedman and Wachter, and Hart and Sharot.[4] Fair suggested using the *actual* values of future output, and he, and Hazledine [1974], found that actual future output was better than lagged output at helping explain current employment changes. In contrast, Sims has found past values to contain more information.

The notion of adjustment costs has also prompted some theoretical activity, aimed at using the Calculus of Variations to solve multi- or infinite-horizon optimal decision problems. Solow [1968] found, however, that only by making very undesirable assumptions about unchanging parameter values could 'optimal' values for inter-temporal employment adjustment be derived. One might have hoped that this discovery would have brought this line of inquiry to a dead end; not so—the economist's Achilles Heel—our propensity to make economic analysis as difficult as possible, whatever the costs in realism and relevance—has shown itself in a number of attempts to 'solve' the dynamic optimal employment adjustment problem (e.g. Mortenson, Wickens, Ehrenberg).[5] Not only does this approach fail, in my opinion, to contribute interesting theoretical insights, it is empirically misconceived, given the evidence, of Fair and Belsley, that the relevant time horizon for the employment decision is typically no more than about six months. Attention should therefore be focused on what determines their activity *within* this time horizon, and I expect that, to this end, closer consideration of the separation of demand into its 'permanent' and 'transitory' components would be fruitful.

(2) When producers can hold stocks either of goods or of unfilled orders, output is not synonymous with 'demand'. In response to a change in product market demand conditions firms will, in general, trade-off the costs of varying employment levels with those associated with changing inventories or the queue of unfilled orders. That is, output is not an exogenous variable in the employment decision. This point was made by Kuh, [1965b] and is supported

---

[3] These papers are rather more subtle and wide-ranging than the studies that they inspired, which tend to be mechanistic extensions of the barebones partial adjustment model to new samples of industries or countries.

[4] Brechling actually used the *change* from past to current output, and found it to be statistically insignificant, but notes that for the US Kuh found the change in output to be significant for production workers, but not for overhead workers. Brechling's UK data are for all workers (*cf.* [1965, p. 203], fn. 2).

[5] It is surely not valid to argue, as does Nickell in the context of intertemporal investment paths, that the constant parameters can be interpreted as expected values to which firms respond as though true indefinitely, until such time as events force their revision. The *knowledge* that expectations are not, in general, fulfilled should affect decision-making.

by Miller's [1971] findings. Thus, we should prefer a variable such as sales or, better still, orders, rather than actual output, as the proxy for product market demand conditions in the employment function.

Some empirical progress has been made on this. In later work, Nadiri and Rosen [1973] use sales rather than output as their independent demand variable (and, apropos of point (1) above, found signs of future sales mattering), and Mortenson for the US, and Hazledine [1979a] for Canada, succeeded with a variable for new orders (it performed better than current output). We may note the success of an orders variable in helping explain investment behaviour [Evans, Chapter 5].

(3) If there is 'error' in the partial adjustment process, so that the actual change in employment differs, in general, from the planned change, a relationship estimated between current output and desired employment may appear to be more (or less) precise than it really is, due to the fact that the level of employment *actually* achieved will affect, through the production function, the observed level of current output. In Hazledine [1979b, Appendix] it is suggested that an instrumental variable for current demand (that is, a variable untainted by errors from the adjustment process and the production function) could be constructed in the absence of sales or orders data, by regressing current output on its value in the same quarter one year ago and the change since then in output price and in real disposable income. This instrumental variable did perform better than actual current output.

An advantage of estimating the demand variable independently of the employment function[6] rather then imbedding it in that function as is done in those studies which include current and lagged output variables as determinants of employment levels, is that the effects of lags, and of the past in general, on demand expectations can be explicitly disentangled from their influence through adjustment costs. Some conjectures on the possible biases introduced by failing to sort out these effects are made below in section 5.

3. Demand Side (2): The Role of Prices

There are two channels through which the prices of inputs and output might affect the demand for labour; (1) through the level of output, and (2) through factor input substitution. We will discuss these in turn.

(1) *Effect on Output*

In the discussion of the previous section, it was implicitly assumed throughout that output, and thus the demand for inputs, is determined by *demand* conditions in product markets; that is, that firms adjust their output passively in response to changes in the flow of sales or orders that they receive. If the world were neo-classical (by which I mean that all agents are price-takers), this assumption would not be valid—firms would *choose* their output rate to

[6] For firms producing intermediate products, changes in the output of their clients will be an appropriate demand variable. Glickman [1977] has used intermediate demand variables in employment functions estimated for a regional economic model.

maximize profits at a given set of prices. That is, output would be *supply-determined*, and would only alter, in the short-run, with a change in output or input prices such that the intersection point of marginal costs and price shifted. There have been a few attempts to test for the neo-classical supply effect by the inclusion in an employment function of a variable measuring the real wage—the ratio of wage rate to output price. Black and Kelejian, for the US, found a real wage coefficient with a t-ratio of -1.9. Brechling [1975] could get no sensible (negative) price effects for the US. Rosen and Quandt did estimate a real wage coefficient that is both large (elasticity around one) and strongly statistically significant (t greater than 10), but there are some puzzles with their results.[7] Phipps, for his sample of four UK industries, did not find a real wage coefficient with a t-ratio above 2. Norton and Sweeny, for Australia, minimized the standard error of their estimate when they assumed that the elasticity of employment in response to a change in the real wage was slightly less than half the output-employment elasticity. For Canadian manufacturing industries, I found [1979a] a *positive* real wage coefficient.

As a whole, these results do not in themselves suggest that the real wage has a strong effect on employment levels. But, even if a tendency for some non-zero elasticity to emerge be granted, there are problems in giving this a neo-classical interpretation. Most estimating equations in which price terms appear also include terms for product demand (usually current output) which always show up with relatively large and significant coefficients. But if the world were really neo-classical, output itself would be a function of prices, and should not appear as an exogenous variable. An equation including both price and output should suffer from multicollinearity—if output were dropped, the coefficient on price would become more significant, and the corrected goodness of fit would probably rise. Yet, there are very few published attempts to estimate a purely price-dependent desired employment function, and these [Hazledine 1979a, Brechling 1975] do no find sensible results. It seems to be just not possible to get good fits without including a quantity demand variable. This curious practice of specifying hybrid demand- and supply-constrained relationships seems to have originated in the field of investment functions with Jorgenson [e.g. 1963]. My interpretation is that the output variables are included so that the factor demand equation will show a reasonable R^2, and the price term is there to give an apparently neo-classical gloss to the specification. The resulting state of methodological confusion is well-illustrated by Gaudet *et. al.*, who explain that relative price variables are in their investment function by the 'assumption of perfect competition' (i.e., the neo-classical assumption), and output is included 'in conformity with the usual practice' (p. 270).

Another problem with the neo-classical model is that one of the necessary conditions for supply-determined output—that the short-run marginal cost curve cuts the price from below—is contradicted by the almost ubiquitous

---

[7] Rosen and Quandt estimate 'excess demand' series which imply that labour was in relatively short supply for each year from 1930 to 1946, and in excess supply from 1954 to 1973. It seems possible that their assumption of an unchanging economic structure over the forty years of their sample is too strong, and their real wage variable is serving as some sort of trend effect, rather than as an indicator of year-to-year fluctuations in product market supply conditions. *Cf.* also Section 7, below.

finding of increasing returns to variable factor inputs at the output margin. *Cf* section 6 below.

Is there, then, a plausible non-neo-classical rationalization available for those cases when a significant real wage effect on employment is apparently observed? It is possible that an increase in price may follow a shift in the product demand curve, because stronger demand gives sellers an increase in market power which they can use to raise their profit margins. If so, the association that would be noted between the change in price and employment is spurious, and price should not be retained in the employment function.

A demand-side association between price and employment could be tested for by separating the product price and nominal wage components of real wage, and allowing their coefficients to differ. If the demand effect predominates, only the price variable will turn up with a significant coefficient.

(2) *Effects On Factor Substitution*

More common than the full neo-classical 'profit-maximizing' framework is the assumption of 'cost-minimizing' behaviour, under which firms take output (or sales) as given, and attempt to produce it at lowest-possible cost, this depending on the prices of all factors whose input levels can be adjusted within the time period. Thus, the ratio of nominal wage to the price of capital goods (w/c) may be included as an argument in the employment function. Such a variable does not always 'work' econometrically—Nadiri and Rosen found a *positive* coefficient in their original joint study [1969], though later, disaggregating US manufacturing into fifteen industries, they did achieve moderately significant negative coefficients in six cases. Estimated elasticities of employment with respect to w/c tend to be small—in a survey of US results, Hamermesh settles on a 'medium' estimate of 0·15 for the effect on employment after four quarters of a one per cent change in the wage rate, holding the cost of capital constant. For Canada, Woodland found 'very low elasticities of demand for labour with respect to all factor rewards' [1972, p. 25]. For the UK, Briscoe and Peel did manage to estimate a negative, though small and only marginally significant ($t = 2·3$) w/c coefficient in an employment function for quarterly UK data [1975, p. 135].

There is a puzzle in the interpretation of w/c coefficients. The *investment* functions estimated by Nadiri and Rosen, and by Briscoe and Peel, in fact indicate that *no* significant adjustment of the capital stock actually takes place within a quarter (*cf.* section 9), so that changes in w/c cannot, presumably, be affecting the demand for labour through capital/labour substitution. It is possible that just the numerator of w/c has an effect in the short run (Brechling, 1975, in fact found l/w to be significant when w/c was not), working through trade-offs between the *number* of employees and the *hours worked* by each of them. This would imply that w/c also be significant, and with a positive sign, in the equation estimated to explain variations in hours per worker; however, in Briscoe and Peel's results, this is not so. Perhaps there is an omitted factor which varies in response to wage rate or capital cost changes—this possibility will be discussed further in the next section. Nadiri and Rosen [1969, p. 464,

155

Table 1] do find a positive w/c coefficient in their hours equation, but then the variable also has a positive coefficient in their employment equation.

In conclusion, it may be *a priori* desirable to include price variables in employment demand models, but their econometric performance should be scrutinized more critically than has been the usual practice. Ratio variables should be decomposed to see if either numerator or denominator is doing all the work,[8] and the results should be tested for robustness by experimenting with dropping extreme observations from the sample.

4. The Demand Side (3): The Role of Other Factors and 'Technology'

The treatment in employment functions of other factor inputs depends on whether they can be varied significantly within the time period over which the employment decision is being examined. A factor that is variable is not exogenous to the determination of employment and should not be included (just as output should not be included along with prices in the neo-classical context)[9]. However, the presence of such variable factors should be known and understood if inferences are to be made about the constraints underlying the employment decision. In particular, making an inference linking the elasticity between desired employment and demand with the 'production function' elasticity of output with respect to employment requires that any elasticities between demand and other variable factors be taken into account (*cf.* section 6).

Factors which are not significantly variable within the time period over which employment decisions are made are exogenous to the demand for labour, and can and should (if relevant) be included in the desired employment function. These factors can be called the 'technology' available in the short-term, which determines the rates of output achievable with combinations of variable inputs. We will distinguish two issues; (1) the shape of the technology at any particular time, and (2) how technology changes over time.

(1) *Short-term Technological Constraints*

How responsive is output to changes in employment in the short period when scale and quality of the capital stock, and the body of technical knowledge associated with its operation, are fixed? That is, what are the effects on labour productivity of short-term fluctuations in employment? The answers differ by the degree of *ex-post* capital-labour flexibility that they assume. Three positions have been taken in the literature:

[8] The positive real wage coefficient that I estimated with my Canadian manufacturing sample [1979a] turned out to be entirely due to the price component of the ratio. This, I suggested, might be explainable by movement *along* the demand curve.

[9] This is not just a matter of simultaneous equation bias—of including as predetermined in one equation a variable which is endogenous elsewhere in the system. The point is that the demand for two variable inputs is jointly determined by the *same* economic agents—employers—so that it makes no sense to include one as a predetermined variable in the equation explaining the demand for the other.

(a) Full Flexibility

The standard procedure is to assume that productivity in the short-term is determined by a fixed, constant elasticity production function—usually the Cobb-Douglas[10]—which is the same (barring an exponential trend term) as the long-run or *ex ante* production function constraint relevant to decisions concerning changes in the capital stock. There are three assumptions being made here—fixity, constant elasticity, and *ex ante* = *ex post*—which, despite their near-ubiquity in studies by economists of the employment decision, seem to me to be fundamentally and implausibly 'uneconomic' in their implied dismissal of the notion of 'trade-offs' as constraints on economic behaviour. In turn: (i) The assumption of a fixed production function (that is, a function with unvarying parameters) implies a view of the plant and its work-force as an automaton which needs only to be switched on in the morning for it to deliver a steady stream of output through the working day. In fact, capital and labour both need to be co-ordinated and controlled ('monitored' in the terminology of Alchian and Demsetz). Thus, the occasional tendency, noted in section 3, for productivity to fluctuate with wage costs, may reflect the stimulus imparted to managers by changes in labour costs to economize on the use of labour by varying the closeness of shop-floor supervision. Though we cannot expect to directly measure this, it might be possible to allow for it by making the parameters of the short-term production function dependent on changes in the appropriate prices. So far as I know, this has not yet been attempted. (ii) Assuming a constant elasticity short-term production function is tantamount to proposing that, when new plant is designed, there is no trade-off between going for maximal productivity at a particular output rate and giving up some flexibility to alter operating rates *ex post*, in the sense that labour can be added to or subtracted from the plant once installed with a constant-elasticity effect on output. It seems more intuitively plausible, and certainly more 'economic', to follow Stigler [1939] and suggest that there may be costs attached to the degree of flexibility of plant, which will show up in the form of the short-term production functions that we observe firms to have actually chosen. (iii) Having the *ex post* and *ex ante* production functions congruent implies that there is no advantage, in terms of output per worker from a given book-value of capital per worker, in extending the time period to allow a choice from a wider range of techniques. The assumption can be relaxed, in the context of the constant-elasticity model, simply by allowing a lower elasticity of substitution between labour and capital *ex post*; this creates no problems in those models, such as that of Ball and St. Cyr, in which the capital stock is supposed to be fixed in the short-term, but it does, as we shall see below in section 9, complicate the derivation of 'inter-related' factor demand models in which it is supposed that labour and capital are variable jointly, though at different speeds.

(b) Limited Flexibility

Wilson and Eckstein [1964] proposed a model of labour demand based on the 'Marshall-Viner' theory of the firm, in which distinctions are made between the

[10] Since the elasticity of substitution is not identified by variations in employment with respect to changes in output (*cf.* Ireland and Smyth's equation (8), which does not include this parameter, although derived from a CES function), it does not matter which CES formulation is used. The Cobb-Douglas is the easiest to work with.

short and the long-run, and allowances given to divergences between actual output and the output rates expected when new plant is installed. In the long-run they have costs proportional to output, which is consistent with an *ex ante* CES production function with constant returns to scale, but in the short-run they suppose that productivity behaves so as to generate the U-shaped average cost curve found in standard microeconomics texts—output *can* be varied above or below the operating rate planned when the plant was ordered, but only at the cost of a fall in productivity. That is, output per worker *increases* with output up to the plant's most efficient operating rate, and *falls* thereafter. This property contrasts with the prediction of CES functions that productivity is either an increasing or a decreasing function for *all* output rates. Later, I suggested a model different in detail, but similar in spirit to that of Wilson and Eckstein.[11] The inverted-U productivity function assumed in these models has been estimated directly on data for UK manufacturing industries [Hazledine and Watts, 1977], and I have since estimated employment functions, based on the specification with data from a number of industries in Canada and the UK [1978, 1979a, b].

(c) No Flexibility

Fair [1969] proposed a model with *ex post* fixed coefficients—*no* variation possible in the ratio of labour to installed plant, and attributed fluctuations in measured productivity to 'labour hoarding'. Fair does not test the fixed coefficients model directly, and I do not expect that it would be supported if he did, given the evidence of at least limited *ex post* variability of Hazledine and Watts.

(2) *Technology In The Long-Run*

The short-term production function shifts over time with changes in the capital stock and technical knowledge, and these shifts should be built in to the expression for the demand for labour. Within the constant-elasticity approach this has been done by assuming unchanging production function parameters, (that is, parameters such as output-labour elasticities are assumed not to change over the long-run as well as over the cycle) with the function shifted period-by-period by an exponential trend term, to capture technological change, and by changes in the capital stock. In practice, capital stock variables do not work very well econometrically (*cf.*, for example, Briscoe and Peel, p. 135), and most researchers have been willing to follow Ball and St. Cyr in assuming that it is 'sufficient to absorb the influence of capital and technical progress by a simple exponential trend' [p. 180]. Is it plausible to assume that period-by-period shifts in the short-term function are sufficiently steady and unidirectional to be satisfactorily captured by a simple trend term? Plotting productivity over time for a number of industries, Hazledine and Watts [1977] found that, typically, the 'trend' path of productivity changed direction two or

---

[11] Hazledine, [1974]. My main influence was the article by Stigler, but I should have paid more attention to the Wilson & Eckstein paper. I should also have noted that Brechling [1965, p. 204] drew a cubic-type production function. It is a pity his example was not followed.

three times over a decade in each industry. This implies that it is not correct to force the production function to shift smoothly.

An alternative procedure is to make use of plots of productivity or 'capacity' over time to search-out what appear to be peak-productivity periods, and then to join these periods by interpolation to construct series which trace directly shifts in the production relation. Something like this was done by Wilson and Eckstein, and in my own papers [1978,79a, b]. It is not coincidental that these are also the models which propose limited *ex post* capital-labour substitutability, since (a) only in the limited-substitutability context do we expect to find a series for peak-productivity employment levels, and (b) the difference between peak and actual values is crucial in these models for determining short-term labour demand fluctuations; but these differences may be rather small relative to the levels of the variables, and so would probably be obscured by measurement error if some indirect method, such as exponential trending, were used to estimate the peak-value series.

Wilson [1978] has compared the forecasting performance of my model with the standard Ball and St. Cyr specification for a sample of UK industries, and finds that mine does better in predicting employment outside the sample estimation period, using observed values of exogenous variables. While I am naturally encouraged by this, I must admit to doubts about how well my model, as it presently stands, would do in genuine 'front-line' forecasting of employment demand next year or in 1981, given that then the exogenous variables need to be forecast, too. It *is* easier to 'forecast' a time trend than a series for peak productivity which has shown a habit of changing direction every few years!

The moral, though, is not that we should return to the simple constant-elasticity demand for labour specification (since this seems clearly to be wrong), but rather to replace the crude peaks-plus-interpolations technique in the limited-substitutability model with a proper explanation of production function shifts as functions of the scale and quality of investment.[12]

5. The Supply Side

The previous three sections were concerned with equation (1); the determinants of the desired level of employment—that is, the level that employers would *like* to achieve in each period. Whether they actually get to this level depends on whether there are constraints limiting their ability to freely adjust their labour forces up or down—constraints arising from the *supply* side of the labour market. The standard procedure quoted in the introduction is to suggest that a fixed proportion (either linear or logarithmic) of the discrepancy between the desired level and the number of employees on hand at the beginning of each period is actually done away with. That is, the function g of equation (2) is specified as a multiplicative coefficient whose value is expected to lie between zero and one. This specification (equation (3))—known as the

[12] For some not fully successful attempts to do this, *cf.* Ando, [1974], and Peterson [1976], discussed by Wilson [1978].

'partial adjustment' model—almost always does rather well econometrically, but the use of such a simple representation of the supply side of the labour market does, as one might expect, spur a number of queries and objections:

(1) *Is the adjustment process ad hoc?*

In fact, the simple partial adjustment model can, rather grandly, be rationalized as a 'linear decision rule', following the work of Holt *et. al.,* [1960]. If the costs on the demand side of not ending up with desired employment are a quadratic function of the discrepancy between actual E and E^*, and if the costs of changing E are a quadratic function of the magnitude, $E-E_{-1}$, of the change, then the optimal trade-off, as Griliches showed [1967] results in always adjusting a constant proportion of the discrepancy E^*-E_{-1}. Since quadratic costs in this context seem to be plausible (*cf.* Hazledine, 1974 fn16, p. 182, for a brief attempt to support this), so too may be the partial adjustment model, provided, of course, that it is well-formulated in the first place. This qualification leads to:

(2) *Is the process underlying partial adjustment identified?*

It is well known, though usually ignored in the employment function literature, that equations identical to a linear form of (3)—that is, containing a term in the lagged dependent variable—can be derived, through the Koyck transformation, from a true model in which only lagged values of the exogenous variables appear (*cf.* Evans, P. 83). Thus, if desired employment is determined by something called 'normal output', which is a Koyck distributed lag of present and past values of output, then equation (3) will work econometrically, even if there are *no* supply-side adjustment costs. In general, the lagged dependent variable may be picking up a mixture of product and labour market factors; a point recognized early on by Kuh [1965b, p. 28], and Ball and St. Cyr [1966, p. 183], but since neglected.[13]

To sort out the interpretation of the partial adjustment process, we would need to distinguish in our models between product and labour market factors, and estimate their separate effects. This would involve (a) trying harder to get a better proxy for output demand, as recommended above in section 2, and (b) looking for labour market variables that could be shown to affect adjustment speeds directly. On (a), it is perhaps worth noting that I found adjustment speed increased as more sophisticated specifications of output demand were introduced, for a Canadian sample [1979b]. The evidence on (b) we discuss next, in (3) and (4):

(3) *Should upward and downward adjustment be assumed symmetrical?*

The model of equation (3) makes no distinction between upward and

---

[13] Even though 'adjustment speeds' seem rather implausible. Estimates that less than half a desired employment change is achieved over two quarters are common. *Cf.* for example, Briscoe and Peel.

downward adjustment of the labour force, but, in general, the costs involved may differ. Increases in a firm's labour force involve dealing with the 'external' labour market of people not at present working for the firm, and various recruitment costs—advertising, screening, etc.—may be incurred in getting these workers onto the payroll. Decreases, however, are a matter for the 'internal' labour market, and involve the costs of breaking any explicit or implicit contracts promising employment stability (*cf.* Okun, 1975) as well as the costs of on-the-job training.[14] The distinction between upward and downward adjustment costs is not as clear-cut as this, because, for example, of the possibility of having to incur firing costs *in the future*, should an increase in demand be reversed. However, future costs will be given less weight since (i) they possibly will not be incurred, and (ii) future events may be discounted somewhat anyway.

For a sample of Canadian food manufacturing industries, I found [1979b] that upward adjustment was, on average, more than three times faster than downward adjustment, though for manufacturing as a whole [1979a] no significant difference in speeds could be discerned, implying either that the food industry is unusual, or that aggregation bias is a problem. Brechling did not find a significant difference in upward and downward adjustment [1965, p. 208].

Sorting-out differences in adjustment behaviour would be easier if demand variables distinguished between permanent and transitory components. Any lag in responding to a permanent increase in demand could only be attributed to external labour market adjustment costs, since, with a permanent increase there can be no fear of having, in future periods, to incur layoff costs. Conversely, a permanent decrease involves only these internal market costs, given that there is then no expectation of ever wishing to re-hire the laid-off workers.

(4) *Is the adjustment coefficient constant over the cycle?*

It is natural to suggest that recruitment, and, possibly, layoff costs, are not independent of the general labour market situation, so that adjustment speed should vary over the business cycle. Several attempts have been made to estimate cyclical effects:

(a) Hawkins [1971] and Fair [1969] made the adjustment coefficient a function of the unemployment rate. Ball and St. Cyr did not try to include the unemployment rate in their time-series regressions, but did find a positive correlation in a cross-sectional comparison of estimated adjustment speeds and average sample-period industry unemployment rates for their disaggregated U K sample. For Canada, I discovered that, in the disaggregated food manufacturing sample, downward employment adjustment appeared to be *slower* when the national unemployment rate was higher (perhaps reflecting the increased costs of breaking contractual agreements with workers when the

[14] Training is a sunk cost for current employees, but the possibility of demand picking-up in the future will give employers an incentive to carry some of their workforce over a slack period, rather than firing them now and risk having to train a new lot of workers a few quarters hence.

opportunities for alternative employment are fewer), and that upward adjustment was unaffected. For the all-manufacturing sample, however, I could not pick up any upward and downward differences, but did find a significant but very small positive relationship between unemployment rate and adjustment speed in each quarter [1979, a, b]. Briscoe and Peel [p. 133] try including the unemployment rate as an independent variable (i.e. not as a modifier of the adjustment coefficient). As such, it probably is just acting as a cyclical proxy.

(b) Hazledine [1972] and Muellbauer [1978] looked for an effect of vacancies on adjustment speed. The econometrics of using this variable are not very sound—since vacancies are not just an indicator of labour market conditions but also an instrument used by firms to effect changes in their labour forces, the variable is likely to be strongly correlated with the other explanatory variables in the employment function. This probably explains why both of these studies found a positive correlation between vacancies and the change in employment, and why Muellbauer's output coefficient was very sensitive to the inclusion of vacancies in his estimating equation (Table 1, p. 15).

(c) McCarthy [1972] reports that the Wharton model makes adjustment speed a function of the length of the work week—the more overtime being worked, the more pressure on employers to increase their workforces. This is one way of dealing with inter-related employment and hours adjustment (cf. section 9), and it may be valid, although one might expect that, if the desired employment function is properly specified, disequilibrium in the length of the work week will show up as a discrepancy between E^* and E_{-1} and thus induce a change in employment; that is, disequilibrium in factor input levels should be picked up in the exogenous variables, not in changes in coefficients.

(5) *The role of wage rates*

Do wage rates play a part on the supply side of the labour market? Rosen and Quandt estimated an insignificant supply elasticity of labour with respect to wages; a result which, they noted 'is common in virtually all time series and many cross-section studies' [1978, p. 375]. It appears either that changes in wage rates do not affect the supply of labour, or that there are reasons why wages are not in fact used as a supply-side instrument.[15]

(6) *Is the lag structure too simple?*

In sharp contrast to empirical studies of investment behaviour, the literature on employment functions reveals very little concern with the estimation of more complicated lag structures than those compatible with the Koyck or partial adjustment models. I expect that this is just as well. Apart from the cyclical variability of adjustment costs discussed above, we must expect that institutional and technical factors affecting the adjustment decision will change over

---

[15] The recent literature on implicit contracts [cf. Barro, 1979, Okun, 1975] is concerned to find rationalizations for the 'rigidity' of wage rates which they suppose is what prevents labour markets from 'clearing'. (They do not doubt the *potential* effectiveness of wage changes on both the demand and supply of labour).

our sample time periods. If so, then it is surely wise to attempt only to answer 'first-order' types of questions; such as 'do conditions in the labour market at the end of the previous quarter have *any* noticeable effect on what happens in the current quarter'? Of course, strenuous mining of the data through fitting a variety of lag distributions will always increase the sample-period goodness of fit of an equation, but at the cost of decreasing the value of the estimated models for forecasting and policy analysis.[16]

This recommendation that lag structures be kept simple does not imply that the econometrician should not think carefully about the timing of the phenomena to be explained, and check that the data are consistent with this. This is obviously particularly important to the analysis if investment in fixed capital, given the long lags between spending decisions and the actual installation of new plant, but it may also matter for employment functions, if, for example, the output data recorded for a period actually measured payments received for past output rather than output physically produced within that period.

6. The Increasing Returns Affair

As noted in the introduction (section 1), the original stimulus for the modern literature on employment functions was the apparent puzzle of the pro-cyclical behaviour of productivity. The analytical innovation that was expected to resolve this was the notion of adjustment costs, which would rationalize observed employment levels not fluctuating as much as output over the business cycle.

The most striking finding of the early studies was that, even though the partial adjustment model seemed to be econometrically successful, the values for the returns to labour that it implies were almost always *still above one,* indeed, they were sometimes larger than those estimated directly from a production function without lags.[17]

This result has disturbed economists for two reasons, as put by Sims [1974, p. 697]:

(a) there is 'no strong long-run evidence of aggregate increasing returns' (e.g. from long-run factor productivity studies)

(b) it is 'difficult to reconcile with the standard competitive model'.

Some studies, using more recent data, find evidence of constant or decreasing returns (for the U K, *cf.* Briscoe and Peel, who found much higher returns to labour when they truncated their data base at 1968 than from the full 1955-72 sample [1975, p. 132], but even if stable, this result leaves the phenomenon unexplained for earlier periods nor does it explain what has changed for returns to labour to have changed.

[16] For a discussion of the general question of simple versus complicated econometric models, *cf.* the paper by Armstrong [1978] and the comments following it.

[17] Ball and St. Cyr found [Tables VI, p. 192] estimates of returns to labour from direct production function estimates lower than those from their employment functions in six of eleven industries. *Cf.* Hazledine [1974], and Hamermesh [1978] for surveys of estimated returns to labour.

We will examine the increasing returns finding from the point of view of the criticisms made in previous sections of the orthodox employment function model. Three possible sources of error will be discussed—(1) mis-specification of the short-term production function, (2) omission of relevant inputs, (3) mis-specification of product demand and labour market adjustment costs.

(1) *Mis-specification of the Production Function*

The constant elasticity production function (such as the Cobb-Douglas) that is typically assumed in employment function specifications has the following implications:

(a) the derived elasticity of desired employment with respect to output *must* be interpreted as the inverse of the returns to labour elasticity in the production function. This is because the desired level of the only other factor assumed variable in the short-term—hours per worker—is constant, given reasonable assumptions about the wage payment system (*cf.* section 10 below).

(b) the elasticity must be assumed to hold no matter how much output is varied up or down, since the production function is 'constant elasticity'.

In section 4 I argued that a more economically plausible short-term production function would have the property of variable elasticity, such that labour productivity rises with output to a peak rate, representing the technically efficient operating rate, and falls thereafter, with further increases in employment and output. The implications of this function are:

(a) Desired hours will, in general, vary in the short-term with output, so that the desired labour-output elasticity cannot be interpreted as a production function parameter [Hazledine, 1974, pp. 177-9]. Indeed, the elasticity of E^* with respect to output could be less than one even where the marginal productivity of employment was falling.[18]

(b) Even if, after netting-out somehow the effect of varying H^* (desired hours per worker) we found that firms were operating at rates such that returns to labour were increasing, such returns will not hold for all output rates—decreasing returns set in eventually.

(c) If, indeed, E^* elasticities have increased recently, this can be explained as a trend towards operating rates that are higher relative to efficient-capacity rates. Thus, there is no need to assume a drastic change in the properties of the production function, as would be necessary with the CES function.

(d) Assuming that input elasticities are variable, given the capital stock, does not rule out the long-run, no-factor-fixed production from having the properties of constant elasticities and/or constant or decreasing returns to scale.

Thus, in addition to its *a priori* attractiveness, the variable elasticity short-term production function has the desired property of being able to make sense of the 'paradox' of increasing returns to labour.

---

[18] We might even expect to observe this, at least for a range of output values, since if returns to hours worked per employee are about constant, employers may tend to shift more into longer work-weeks, and less to larger labour forces, at output rates that are high relative to the designed capacity of plant.

(2) *Other Omitted Variable Inputs*

Apart from hours, are there other factors whose input levels might vary pro-cyclically in the short-term? Kuh noted [1965a] that 'the work force may be capable of short spurts of increased effort for short periods of time'. Variations in effort may be determined by the keenness of management or by informal work-sharing amongst production employees. If these variations exist, and if they are short-term in the sense that a *sustained* period of high output rates would eventually lead to a falling-away in productivity, then omission of the effort input (and, of course, we are not likely to be able to measure this independently of its presumed effects) will bias upwards our estimates of the short-term returns of other variable inputs.

Ireland and Smyth [1970] suggested that the returns to labour from short-term employment functions should properly be interpreted as returns to scale—that is, as returns to labour and capital varying together. In the sense that variations in the number of employees may involve variations in the scrappage rate of marginally high-cost plant and that changing the number of hours worked by employees each day necessarily involves too changes in the hours over which plant is utilized, this interpretation is obviously reasonable (though these short-term returns to scale are not the same as long-term returns when new capital can be installed).[19]

(3) *Mis-interpretation of Adjustment Lags*

The usual practice of interpreting the coefficient of E_{-1} solely in terms of labour market adjustment costs can lead to a biased estimate of the employment-output elasticity. For example, suppose that there are no labour market adjustment costs and that employment responds to 'nominal' output, which is a weighted average of current and lagged output. Then the employment

$$(4) \qquad E_t = \alpha + \beta\, Y_t + (1\text{-}\beta)Y_{t\text{-}1} + \epsilon_t$$

function is (4) where ϵ_t is the random error term. Suppose that the researcher in conformity with the usual practice, estimated the model

$$(5) \qquad E_t = a + bY_t + cE_{t-1}$$

From (4) we can get

$$(6) \qquad E_{t-1} = \propto + \beta Y_{t-1} + (1 - \beta)Y_{t-2} + \epsilon_{t-1}$$

$$\text{or} \qquad Y_{t-1} = \frac{1}{\beta}E_{t-1} - \frac{\propto}{\beta} - \frac{1-\beta}{\beta}Y_{t-2} - \frac{\epsilon_{t-}}{\beta}\,1$$

[19] This does not imply that we need separate 'capacity utilization' variables. *Cf.* Section 9, below.

so $\qquad E_t = \propto + \beta Y_t + \dfrac{1 - \beta E_{t-1}}{\beta} - \dfrac{(1 - \beta)}{\beta} \propto$

$$(7) \qquad - \dfrac{(1 - \beta)^2}{\beta} Y_{t-1} + \dfrac{(1 - \beta)}{\beta} \epsilon_{t-1} + \epsilon_t$$

Thus if (5) is estimated, we may get significant coefficients on Y_t and E_{t-1} (though if the Y series is serially correlated, (5) will have problems both with serially correlated errors and with the non-independence of Y_t and the error term) which would be interpreted, wrongly, as giving support to the partial adjustment model and as implying a long-run output-employment coefficient of

$$(8) \qquad \beta/(1 - \dfrac{1 - \beta}{\beta}) = \dfrac{\beta^2}{2\beta - 1}$$

which may be larger or smaller than the true value, 1.

7. Other Approaches

(1) *Direct Specification of Desired Employment*

A particular feature of the standard model is that the desired level of employment, E^*, is not estimated directly, but rather is inferred from the specification of equation (3) combining E^* and the partial adjustment mechanism. It might well be asked of those who believe in constant elasticity production functions why they do not estimate directly these functions, and then make use of the result of Ball and St. Cyr that desired hours are constant and equal to the maximum normal-time workweek to insert this value into the production function and then solve for E^*. Then the adjustment process could be *directly* estimated, making the actual change in employment a function of the difference between E^* and E_{-1}, as in equation (2). The answer (for this approach has not, to my knowledge, been adopted in any of the major employment function studies) is probably that, although a belief in something called the production function as a constraint holding exactly at all times is sometimes professed (e.g. Nadiri and Rosen, [1969, p. 459]), faith is not strong enough to sustain an attempt to actually *use* an estimated production function. When estimated (for example by Ball and St. Cyr) they show increasing returns to the labour input, which is usually blamed on 'labour hoarding'—on employers holding some labour surplus to their requirements at low points in the business cycle, for the sort of reasons discussed above in section 5. Ball and St. Cyr tried to adjust the measured labour input series for labour hoarding by adding a term in one minus the unemployment rate, but did not get very sensible results. One solution might be to estimate a production function using data only from the upper halves of business cycles. For New Zealand, which is a country with persistently very low unemployment rates, so that it might be taken to be always in a labour-shortage situation, Hazledine and Woodfield did succeed in estimating a reasonable-looking Cobb-Douglas function, with returns both to employees and to hours of about one, and did then construct an E^* series.

Another approach that is possible is to insert *a priori* values for the parameters of CES production functions, and then to compute E^*. Such has been done for the macroeconometric models of the Bank of Canada and the Reserve Bank of Australia, in which a 'grid' of parameter values was searched for the set that gave the best fitting employment function, though the best fit (in the Australian model) was yielded by the highest *a priori* value tested for returns to scale—1.6, [Hawkins, 1971].

The variable-elasticity production function proposed in section 4 does not seem to lend itself to precise analytic solutions of cost-minimizing input levels, so that we are forced to stay with the indirect method of equation (3). I expect that this may be just as well, since taking something like a production function seriously enough to differentiate it, etc., is probably a good example of misplaced concreteness.

(2) *Demand and Supply Functions Specified Separately*

We should note the attempts, most recently by Rosen and Quandt, to build a formal supply and demand model, with both sides of the labour market assigned its own equation. Actual employment in each period is assumed to be the smaller of labour supply and labour demand ('short-side always wins'). Information on which is the short side in each period is not available *a priori,* however, and Rosen and Quandt make use of a maximum likelihood procedure to estimate their system indirectly. Though I have admiration for the ingenuity embodied in this approach, and make no claims to understand the econometrics involved, it seems to be unsuccessful—the estimated equations imply that there was excess demand for labour in the US from 1930 to 1946, and excess supply continuously from 1954 to 1973.

Rosen and Quandt's own results suggest that their methodology is basically mis-conceived, since they really do not find any evidence of an even potentially operative supply constraint—the wage rate is not significant in the supply equation, and a variable for unearned income has a positive coefficient, contrary to expectations. These results do not, I feel, justify altering the approach to the supply side implied by the use of partial adjustment coefficients, which are consistent with there being no such active constraint as a *given* total available labour supply in each period (or even a total supply dependent on the wage rate), but with the constraint of adjustment costs applied to the *speed* at which the employed labour force is increased or decreased.

(3) *No Attempt to Disentangle Demand and Supply*

The procedure which antedated the model of equations (1), (2), and (3), and which is still made use of in some macro-econometric models involves specifying employment functions with lags, often of both dependent and exogenous variables, but making no attempt to identify explicitly the underlying behavioural model (*cf.* Kuh's papers, for example; as well as the other references cited by Brechling, [1965, p. 187]). It may be that the methodological modesty of this approach is appropriate to the limitations of our theory and data, though my own judgment is that the achievements of the Brechling-Ball and St. Cyr model are at least encouraging enough to justify further work developing their basic distinction between the levels of employment firms *desire,* and the levels that they actually *get.*

To summarize these alternative approaches: (1) and (2) imply that the standard model be *expanded;* by directly measuring desired employment, and by modelling the supply of labour separately from the demand. I concluded that the first of these is quite desirable in principle, but not possible in practice, given the analytical intractability (from the point of view of the calculus— sensible geometric analytics are quite possible) of plausibly-shaped short-term production functions, and given the likely unreasonableness of supposing that the production function would 'stand still' while we analytically manipulated it, anyway.

The second proposal implies that there is some variable called 'the supply of labour' which will, when it is smaller than 'the demand for labour', constrain employment behaviour of firms. I suggest that it is more realistic to think of labour supply as a *flow* of job applicants coming past employers, who can alter the speed of the flow by varying their expenditures on recruitment and training, rather than as a fixed stock.

Alternative (3) involves *contracting* the standard model, by collapsing it to single equation, with no attempt made to disentangle the different product and labour market processes that underly this. In my opinion, a more ambitious approach is both desirable and feasible.

8. Explaining Differences in Coefficients

This section will be short, as there are not many results to report. Several studies (e.g. Brechling and O'Brien, Ball and St. Cyr, Hazledine [1974–78]) have estimated employment functions for a number of industries or countries. In general, the estimates of employment-output elasticities and adjustment speeds vary across each sample, yet little has been done to explain *why* they differ, with the exception (Ball and St. Cyr, Brechling and O'Brien, and Hughes [1971b]) of attempting to correlate adjustment speeds with average unemployment rates over sample periods. Phipps did compare adjustment speed with both training costs and the proportion of administrative to production employees, but with a sample of just four industries.

All these attempts have involved a two-step procedure—first estimate your employment function parameters from time series data, then try and explain (one of) them in a cross-sectional correlation with other factor(s). In econometric principle, a superior method would be to pool the time-series employment function data and the cross-sectional variables that are expected to affect the employment function parameters, and estimate everything at once. I attempted to do this for my sample of thirteen Canadian food manufacturing industries [1979b], allowing parameters to vary both over time (with the unemployment rate) and across industries (as functions of the 'tightness' of the production function, the variance of output prediction error, and the skill level of each industry's labour force). The results seemed statistically quite successful, but were not always in accord with my *a priori* expectations.

9. 'Inter-related' Demand for Inputs

Probably the only major innovation to employment functions since the introduction of the Brechling-Ball and St. Cyr model has been the notion of inter-related adjustment—the proposition that the response to disequilibrium in the level of employment should be considered jointly with disequilibria in other input markets. This suggestion has been developed along two distinct lines; (1) its implication for the *specification* of input adjustment, (2) its implications for the *estimation* of adjustment functions. We look briefly at each:

(1) *Specifying Inter-related Adjustment*

Suppose that both the number of employees and the hours worked per employee can be varied in the short run, but both at a cost which increases more than proportionately with the size of the change. Then, given desired output and the levels of fixed factors, and thus desired employment and hours, the degree to which each factor is changed to approach its desired level should, in general, depend on a trade-off between the costs of adjusting both. This will not be so if adjustment costs for hours per employee are not significant, since it will then be assumed, when deciding on employment adjustment, that hours will be adjusted to their desired level whatever their level in the previous period.

Nadiri and Rosen [1969,1973], whose idea this is, attempted to test for quarterly inter-related adjustment between no fewer than four factors—employment, hours, capital stock, and capital 'utilization'—using US manufacturing data Briscoe and Peel [1975] replicated their model of the UK. We will evaluate the evidence for inter-relatedness between employment and each of the other factors:

(a) Hours Per Employee

Nadiri and Rosen estimate a positive coefficient on their lagged hours variable in the employment function [1969, Table 1, p. 464]. It is not clear to me that a *positive* coefficient is what we should expect, if inter-related adjustment is behind this variable's significance[20]—it could be that hours is just acting as a proxy for cyclical demand conditions. For the UK, Briscoe and Peel did not get a significant lagged hours coefficient [1975, Table 4, p. 135] for aggregate

---

[20] What is really not clear to me is that the essence of inter-related adjustment is captured by simply adding lagged terms of the other inputs to the employment function. Nadiri and Rosen do not formally derive their expression.

manufacturing; nor did I [1978, Table 1, p. 187], in most cases, for a fourteen-industry disaggregation.

(b) Capital Stock

The results both of Nadiri and Rosen and of Briscoe and Peel imply that the capital stock does *not* vary in the short-term in response to the same factors that affect employment. The only significant variable in their capital stock equations is lagged capital stock.[21] Therefore, capital stock disequilibrium will not affect employment adjustment (so the occasional significance of lagged capital stock in employment functions should be interpreted as picking up changes in the given short term production function. *Current* capital stock would probably do better, statistically).

(c) Capital Utilization Rates

Nadiri and Rosen estimate and equation for a variable they call 'capital utilization', which in fact is the FRB capacity utilization index, computed by interpolating between output peaks. This variable certainly is not a factor input, and should not be included as such in the employment function, in which it would bias the coefficients of the other variables (*cf.* Hazledine, [1974, pp. 167–9]). Briscoe and Peel use a theoretically more acceptable proxy— electricity consumption—but have only annual data, and so have to interpolate to get quarterly numbers. The lagged value of this variable is not significant in their employment function.

If it is reasonable to suggest, as I did in section 6, that in the short-term variations in the services received from the capital stock are closely correlated with variations in the labour input, then we should not need to find separate variables for capital utilization to so into the employment function.

(2) *Inter-relatedness and Estimation*

Coen and Hickman [1970] pointed out that, if we are estimating equations for both employment and investment, and *if* the models underlying both equations include the same production function, then the estimates from each equation of production function parameters should be consistent, and constrained estimation techniques should be used to make sure that this is so. However, the production function constraint relevant to the employment decision will *not* be the same as that which matters to investment—the latter should reflect the wider choice of alternative techniques available over a longer time horizon—so we should *not* constrain employment and investment functions to yield identical production function parameter estimates.

To summarize: although inter-related input adjustment is an interesting idea, and certainly well worth trying-out, it does not in fact turn out to have important implications for the specification of employment functions. At most, we might wish to consider the possibility of hours-disequilibrium mattering, though some care should be taken that lagged hours (if this is how hours

---

[21] Of course, there has been plenty of quite successful work done estimating investment equations, often with quarterly data (*cf.* Helliwell (ed.), for a survey and examples) but this has not been able to get by with the simple, current-period factors that do well in employment functions. In particular, the lags involved in the investment process are clearly much longer (*cf.* Evans, [pp. 95–105]).

disequilibrium should be introduced) are not just proxying product market cyclical conditions.[22]

Nor does the investigator whose interest is only in employment behaviour need to worry about also specifying an investment function in order to extract all the relevant information on production function constraints from the data. Employment and investment can be modelled independently.

10. The Hours Equation

This paper is mainly concerned with the determinants of the level of employment. In discussing these, it has sometimes been relevant (especially in sections 6 and 9) to consider the utilization rate of the employed labour force—the number of hours worked per employee. In this section, hours worked will be treated as a variable of interest in itself.

It is by no means universal practice to separate employment and hours per employee. A number of researchers (e.g. Kuh, Coen and Hickman) actually specify the product of number of employees and hours per employee, which they term 'manhours', as the dependent variable in their labour demand models. To the extent that employment and hours are both influenced by similar exogenous variables—notably product demand or output—a 'manhours' equation may get a good statistical fit, but theoretically it is an awkward hybrid, obscuring the distinctive and important differences between decisions to change the number of employees, and decisions to alter the rate at which employees are utilized. In support of this assertion, we will evaluate the evidence on the returns to hours in the short-term production function; on the specification of the level of desired hours, and on the determination of actual levels of hours worked.

(1) *Returns to Hours in the Short-Term*

In the short-term (that is, given a stock of plant and equipment) changing the level of employment involves changing the labour/capital ratio, whereas changing the number of hours per employee means working a given combination of labour and capital for a different length of time. There seems to be no *a priori* reason for returns to these two activities to be the same. I argued in section 4 that, as the number of employees per unit of capital increased, output per employee will increase up to the point of the 'designed-for' or technically-optimal operating rate, and will decrease thereafter, as the machines get 'crowded' with labour. What will happen to productivity as the length of the working day is increased? A reasonable assumption might be of constant returns—that the marginal hour worked is as productive as the average hour, since working longer hours is likely just to involve 'more of the same'—carrying on doing whatever is done in normal-time hours. Worker fatigue

---

[22] One check on this would be to see if the coefficient on the output or demand variable falls when lagged hours are introduced to the specification.

would tend to make productivity fall; morning 'start-up' time would lead to marginal hours being of above-average productivity.

There have been a few attempts to estimate Cobb-Douglas production functions allowing the returns to employees and to hours to differ. Feldstein [1967] used a cross-section of UK two-digit data as a sample, which assumes that the production function is the same for all industries. Feldstein admits that this assumption is 'subject to serious objection', but suggests that it is no worse than the usual assumption of time-series econometrics that the underlying structure remains unchanged over perhaps several decades. He has a point here, though the implication of it may be that one should estimate *neither* time-series *nor* cross-sectional production functions with the assumption of constant parameters.

Anyway, Feldstein finds highly significant coefficients for capital and employment which sum to about one, and mostly insignificant hours coefficients which are around two in value.

Craine [1972] used a time series of US all-manufacturing data, and found highly significant employment and hours coefficients (though not on capital—a common enough result from quarterly data), with the employment elasticity less than one, and that for hours almost two. These findings of a high hours exponent which is poorly determined by a cross-sectional sample but highly significant in a time-series regression rather suggests to me that the variable is acting as a proxy for one of the factors, such as labour hoarding, which are responsible for the pro-cyclical behaviour of productivity in the short-term. For a discussion of this, *cf.* Leslie and Laing.[23] More direct evidence suggests that the returns to overtime hours are slightly diminishing [Hart, 1973].

In any case, there does not seem to be any justification for having employment and hours lumped together as 'manhours' as the proper labour input for the short-term production function.

(2) *Desired Hours*

As does the employment decision, the specification of the desired number of hours (the demand for hours per employee) involves both a production function constraint and the prices of the various inputs. The wage-payment system is a further source of distinctiveness between the demand for hours and for employees. Whereas there are, in general, no institutional limits on the number of people a firm can take on at the going wage, payments for hours per employee are tightly circumscribed by the almost universal institution of the normal-hours working week, which, if exceeded, results in the payment of overtime premium rates, and which may also (perhaps more frequently in the UK than in the US) set a lower bound on the number of hours that must be paid for, whether or not fewer are actually worked.

As noted in section 4, the implication of this wage payment system in combination with the assumption of a short-term production function that is

---

[23] The results of Craine should be treated with a good deal of caution, since he gets very low Durbin-Watson Statistics, and since the Federal Reserve Board output index that he uses was, for most of his sample period, constructed largely from manhour interpolations (*cf.* Sims, [1974, p. 707]) (!)

constant-elasticity with respect to employment, is, in general, that the number of hours desired by the employer is a constant.[24] This is not so for the variable-elasticity function whose virtues I have defended in this paper—even if hours enter the production function with approximately constant elasticity, their desired level varies with output. This is because, with the output elasticity of employment differing at different employment levels, the ratio of the marginal cost of changing output by changing employment (holding hours constant), to the marginal cost of changing hours (with employment unchanged), is not constant as output varies around its short-term peak-productivity operating rate.

Thus, we should expect to find that output demand affects the demand for hours. As well, as Nadiri and Rosen proposed [1969, p. 460], the ratio of the hourly wage to the 'user cost'[25] of labour should matter to the desired hours (and the desired employment) decision, though they were unable to produce any user cost data.[26]

(3) Incorporating the Supply Side

Are there any supply-side constraints preventing observed levels of hours from simply equalling the level employers would like to demand? We can identify three possibilities: (a) costs of adjusting hours; (b) institutional or 'contractual' constraints; and (c) costs of adjusting other factors.

(a) Costs of Adjusting Hours

The inter-related adjustment model of Nadiri and Rosen includes a partial adjustment process for eliminating any discrepancy between desired and actual hours. It is not obvious to me what costs might be involved in changing hours which would lead to partial adjustment. Nadiri and Rosen do not identify any of these costs, and admit that there is 'some intuitive sense' to assuming full adjustment within the time period [1969, p. 462].

(b) Institutional Constraints

If there are not own-adjustment costs for hours, how is the significant coefficient on lagged hours in the hours equation of Nadiri and Rosen to be explained? It could be that the right of employers to alter hours worked is an all-or-nothing thing—either employers can adjust hours or they cannot—depending on implicit or explicit contractual arrangements between employers and employees. If so, then the coefficient on lagged hours could be interpreted as an approximate estimate of the proportion of the labour force in jobs for which hours do not vary (or, at least, a lower bound for this proportion), and the estimated hours-output elasticity would measure the elasticity of desired hours with respect to output changes multiplied by the proportion of the labour

[24] Ball and St. Cyr demonstrated this for the case of employment and hours constrained to have the same exponent in the production function, but this is true, in most cases, when their exponents are assumed to differ. Cf. Hazledine [1973].

[25] The hiring and training costs relevant to the 'user cost' of labour are those incurred in making good the attrition from quits and firings in order to keep the workforce at some given level. They do not include the hiring and training costs involved in the process of adjusting the workforce to a different level, which are accounted for in the partial adjustment relation.

[26] In my 1973 paper, I made an attempt to explain the long-term trend in labour's utilization rate in terms of changes in some of these costs.

force in hours-variable jobs. Under this interpretation, there would be no distinction between short-term and equilibrium responses of hours to a given change in output.

(c) Adjustment Costs of Other Factors

The major innovation by Nadiri and Rosen of the notion of 'cross adjustment' implies that hours may respond to disequilibrium in the level of employment. Both Nadiri and Rosen and Briscoe and Peel do find significant coefficients for lagged employment in their hours functions, which may support the idea.[27] That is, changes in hours worked are used to smooth out the more costly adjustment of the number of employees to its desired level.

11. Implications for Economic Theory

In contrast with the intense theoretical and empirical attention paid to other components of the Keynesian system, the determinants of the level of employment—arguably the most important macroeconomic variable—have been relatively neglected. Neither the quantity nor the quality of the research surveyed above matches the work done on the consumption function, the demand for money, or even the investment function. Furthermore, the results that we do have have not been scrutinized for their implications for the several new theories of employment and unemployment that have sprung-up in the past decade. To, rather briefly, attempt such a scrutiny is the purpose of this section. We will look, in turn, at models of 'search' behaviour and 'rational expectations', at the 'non-market-clearing' paradigm, at the new contract theories, and at attempts to relate (un)employment and inflation.

(1) Search and Rational Expectations Models

These models have in common the fundamental neo-classical postulate of an economy of atomistic, price-taking agents, to which they add the notion that information about these prices is itself a good, and thus costly. Search models [Friedman, 1968; Phelps et. al., 1970] focus on information costs in the labour market, which suggest a view of unemployment as a voluntary and productive search activity, leading to redeployment of workers in more productive jobs. The direct evidence on the characteristics of unemployment and the behaviour of the unemployed strongly suggest that voluntary search cannot account for much of the mean rate of unemployment. [Clark and Summers, 1979] but does not appear to rule out the possibility of some of the fluctuations in unemployment being due to mistakes (owing to incomplete information) on the supply-side of the labour market.

However, the employment function findings are difficult to reconcile with

[27] Note that it is cross adjustment which justifies the inclusion, in the Nadiri and Rosen model, of output in the hours equation. Given their Cobb-Douglas production function, desired hours are not a function of output, but desired employment is, and it is the difference between desired and on-hand (lagged) employment that is the measure of employment level disequilibrium imbedded in their estimating equation. With the variable elasticity model, the coefficient on output has to be interpreted as a mixture of this variable's influence on both desired hours and desired employment.

search models, with their implication of labour supply-dependent output, which would require estimating the employment-output relationship as a production function constraint, since we know that this usually results in estimates greater than one of returns to labour—not consistent with a neo-classical price-taking equilibrium.

In the 'rational expectations' approach (cf. McCallum, [1979], for a short survey), fluctuations in output and employment are ascribed to employers' perceptions of changes in prices, but this is not supported by the apparently robust finding of employment function research that quantity constraints dominate price constraints (cf. sections 2, 3).

(2) The Non-market-clearing Paradigm

The essence of this approach is to admit that exchange can take place at other than prices which clear markets, in which case either buyer or seller will be 'quantity-constrained'—unable to trade all they wish to at the prices actually charged. It is also noted that quantity constraints in one market can spill-over to other markets, so that there may be supply-demand disequilibrium in the latter even when their prices are actually at the levels that would be observed if all markets were in equilibrium. The employment function literature certainly contains plenty of evidence of product and labour market quantity constraints.

Since the *existence* of a market-clearing set of prices is not doubted, the assumption of sticky prices is problematic—why should not agents, even in the absence of Walrasian 'auctioneers', grope their way to equilibrating supply and demand? The evidence cited above (section 3) on the effects on employment of such changes in wages and prices when they *do* occur rather suggests that a search for market-clearing prices would not be successful; perhaps the non-market-clearing paradigm should be cut entirely away from the neo-classical tradition and focused on the possibility of stable quantity-constrained *equilibria*.

The response to the sticky-price puzzle of two of the major contributors to the paradigm—Barro and Grossman—has instead, been to search for a 'choice-theoretic' rationalization for the failure of prices to adjust. Barro [1979] has adopted the incomplete information assumptions of the search and rational expectations models and Grossman has moved towards the new 'contract' theories.

(3) Contract Theories

Theories of explicit or implicit contracts suggest that people differ in their attitude to risk, such that the less risk-averse become employers, and agree to insure the others, who become their employees, from some of the fluctuations in income that would result if prices were adjusted quickly to maintain continuous equilibria between supply and demand.

The idea of examining the implications for the organization of markets of differential willingness to accept risk seems a good one; less compelling, though, (cf. Baily, [1976]) are the arguments that voluntary risk-trading contracts lead to more variable employment than wage rates. The models have to predict this, since they do not question the neo-classical assumption of the existence of a market-clearing price vector, but, in view of the employment function results it could be more realistic to drop this assumption, so that wage flexibility is no longer to be traded-off against employment flexibility, and then explain, with the contract notion, the phenomenon of 'labour hoarding' which implies that employment levels do in fact fluctuate *less* than would be consistent with full adjustment to short-term product market demand variations.

(4) Models of (Un)employment and Inflation

Some attempts have been made to use the divergence between actual employment and its desired level, E^*, implied by employment functions, as a measure of 'excess demand' for labour to be used as an explanatory variable in equations explaining wage rate changes. Reuber [1970], and Peel and Briscoe [1974] did this for Canada and the UK, respectively, and Taylor [1974] performed a quite similar exercise for the UK and the US.

All these authors found the labour market variable to be significantly related to wage changes, and Taylor found that it wiped out the unemployment rate (the usual Phillips Curve variable) as a significant regressor.

However, these results do not seem to imply that the wage increases associated with high 'excess demand' for labour are inflationary (lead to increases in the product price level) since the magnitude of the estimated coefficients (around 0·5), together with the approximate equality between a percentage change in 'excess demand' and the associated percentage change in labour productivity relative to its trend suggest that these wage increases are less than the amount that could be financed, through the increase in productivity, without a change in the price level.

Therefore, the usual Phillips Curve model of inflation as a *labour market* phenomenon may in incorrect, based on a spurious correlation between two variables—wage changes and unemployment—which are in fact not directly related. Higher levels of real product demand lead both to higher levels of employment and so lower unemployment, and to higher productivity, and thus higher wages. To explain inflation we may need a theory, not necessarily invoking the labour market, of how changes in nominal product demand are divided by firms into changes in real output and changes in prices.

12. Implications for Future Research

Many detailed recommendations for the way employment functions should be specified and estimated have surfaced in the survey section above. The purpose of this final section is to suggest some more fundamental changes in the direction of our research.

My main concern is that employment function modelling has become rather run-down; that the field badly needs injections both of sharp new theoretical insights and of richer databases. We could try and augment the simple microeconomic or firm-based model with input from the fields of industrial organization and labour economics, in order to better incorporate in our models the institutional and market-structure framework of the employment decision; and we should look beyond the usual aggregate or II-digit manufacturing quarterly time-series for data on which to test new theoretical specifications. I will try and illustrate these recommendations for each aspect of the modelling process:

(1) *A Priori Specification.*

The proper use for theory in econometric models seems to me to be as a provider of insights into the economic process, which can lead, if carefully thought through, to a useful decision on which variables should be included and which excluded from the regression specification, and on how the estimated coefficients should be interpreted. Attempts to go further than this, and use 'theory' to generate a precise functional form for the specification, and/or for inferring the parameters of the underlying structural equations from a reduced-form estimating model, seem always (at least in the employment function context) to involve slipping-in concrete empirical assumptions which are either wrong (as in the use of a Cobb-Douglas short-term production function) or so simplified that they end up eliminating much of the important phenomena that should be studied (such as the use of optimal control theory to solve problems assuming static expectations and constant parameters). A return to the modest methodology of Brechling [1965], who did not try to identify 'the' underlying production function, could be appropriate.

(2) *Choice of Variables*

Thus informed by theory, which variables should we include in the basic employment function model? There should be separate equations for hours per employee and the number of employees, since these decisions appear to be quite distinct (that is, 'personhours' should not be used as the dependent variable). As for the explanatory variables, it is important not to include on the right hand side any variables which are themselves decision variables for firms over the time period considered. Thus, other variable inputs, such as hours or capital utilization, should be excluded, as even should be current output, given the inventory decision—firms can vary stocks as well as factor inputs in response to a change in demand. Similarly, neo-classical models cannot be tested by specifications including output along with price variables as regressors.

Specifying changes in the underlying structure of the employment decision, due, for example, to changes in capacity, is a difficult business. Exponential trends are too 'smooth', it appears. Fitting lines to actual series by interpolating between peaks seems to work quite well, but is not very satisfactory if the estimated employment functions are to be used for forecasting. We need to be able to explain the long-term shifts as well as short-term fluctuations, and this will probably involve building a model capable of explaining together employment, investment, and productivity.

(3) *Measuring the Variables*

The main points with measurement seem to be (a) to try and ensure that the data in fact measure what they are supposed to, and (b) to watch out for undesirable statistical side-effects. Thus we should not use (i) 'capacity utilization' variables which in fact measure the relationship between current and peak output; (ii) 'quarterly' hours data that are interpolated from annual or six-monthly data; (iii) output data partially constructed from employment data; (iv) data, such as current output, that have relationships with the dependent variable in other equations in the system, so that simultaneity bias may be introduced (an instrumental variable should be used instead).

(4) *Specifying Lags*

An unsatisfactory feature of the standard employment function model is that the coefficient on the lagged dependent variable does not allow us to distinguish between labour market adjustment costs and product market demand uncertainty as the explanation of the role of past events in current decisions. One solution might be to try and specify a more complicated lag structure, but this would inevitably involve trying-out a number of specifications, and so involve us in data-mining; and still it might not unambiguously identify the different sources of lagged effects. It might be better to try and obtain independent estimates of, say, the permanent and transitory components of product demand, and then plug these estimates into the employment function, in which any remaining lag effects might then reasonably be attributed to adjustment costs (*cf.* section 6 above). With respect to these adjustment costs, there seem to be good grounds for allowing them to differ for upward and downward changes in employment (section 5), and between periods of high and low aggregate economic activity (section 6 (2)). There do not seem to be compelling grounds for including 'inter-related adjustment' between employment and capital (section 9).

(5) *Disaggregating the Model*

Although with a realistic (variable elasticity) production function, it does not seem to be possible to directly compute desired employment, it might be fruitful to look harder for *data* that proxy the demand for labour—notified vacancies being an obvious candidate. In general, employment function research could benefit from attempts to think more in terms of the *gross* labour market flows (layoffs, quits, new hires) rather than being confined to the *net* change in employment. Quite a lot of labour economics research has already been done on some of these variables (*c.f.* for example, Medoff, [1979]).

178

(6) *Disaggregating the Data*

To get more degrees of freedom, and variation in the data, we could use disaggregate time-series data for a cross-section of industries. Having a number of independent time series of data to estimate models on both allows the basic specification to be given a good trial, and for hypotheses about the determinants of inter-industry differences in behaviour to be tested, either by running a second series of regressions explaining the estimated employment function coefficients as functions of various structural and institutional factors, or by including these factors directly in a pooled time-series/cross-section model, as attempted, rather crudely, by Hazledine [1979b]. The pooling method probably allows more efficient econometric use to be made of the information in the database. Some of the interesting disaggregations that could be tried are (i) between industries which produce to order and those which produce to inventory (to distinguish different degrees of demand uncertainty); (ii) between capital- and labour-intensive industries (differences in the flexibility of plant, and in the 'fixity' of labour); (iii) between 'primary' and 'secondary' workers (to test the hypothesis that employment adjustment is *easier* in periods of high activity, since a large proportion of workers being hired and laid-off are then secondary workers); (iv) between high and low parts of the cycle, or between growing and declining industries (to distinguish internal and external labour market adjustment costs).

REFERENCES

Alchian, A. A., and H. Demsetz, [1972], 'Production, Information Costs and Economic Organization,' *American Economic Review*, December.

Ando Albert [1974] 'Some Aspects of Stabilization Policies, the Monetarist Controversy and the MPS Model' *International Economic Review*, October.

Armstrong, J. Scott [1978], 'Forecasting with Econometric Methods: Folklore versus Fact' *Journal of Business* October.

Baily, Martin Neil [1976], 'Contract Theory and the Moderation of Inflation by Recession and by Controls,' *Brookings Papers*, 3: 1971.

Ball R. J., and E. B. A. St. Cyr [1966], 'Short Term Employment Functions in British Manufacturing Industry,' *Review of Economic Studies*, July.

Barro Robert J. [1979], 'Second Thoughts on Keynesian Economics,' *American Economic Review*, May.

Belsley D. A. [1969], *Industry Production Behaviour: The Order-Stock Distinction*, North-Holland.

Black, Stanley, and Harry Kelejian [1970], 'A Macro Model of the US Labour Market,' *Econometrica*, pp. 712–41.

Brechling, Frank [1965], 'The Relationship between Output and Employment in British Manufacturing Industries,' *Review of Economic Studies*, July.

Brechling, Frank [1975], *Investment and Employment Decisions*, Manchester University Press.

Brechling, Frank, and Peter O'Brien [1967], 'Shortrun Employment Functions in Manufacturing Industries: An International Comparison, *Review of Economics and Statistics*, August.

Briscoe, G., and D. A. Peel [1975], 'The specification of the Short-Run Employment Function,' *Oxford Bulletin of Economics and Statistics*, May.

Clark, Kim B., and Lawrence H. Summers [1979], 'Labour Market Dynamics and Unemployment: A Reconsideration, *Brookings Papers*, 1: 1979.

Coen, R. N., and B. G. Hickman [1970], 'Constrained Joint Estimation of Factor Demand and Production Functions,' *Review of Economics and Statistics*, August (reprinted in Helliwell (edd.)).

Craine, R. [1972], 'On the Service Flow from Labour,' *Review of Economic Studies*, October.

Ehrenberg, R. G. (1971) 'Heterogeneous Labor, the Internal Labor Market, and the Dynamics of the Employment-Hours Decision,' *Journal of Economic Theory*, pp. 85–104.

179

Eisner, Robert [1974], 'Econometric Studies of Investment Behaviour: A Comment,' *Economic Inquiry*, March.

Evans, Michael K. [1969], *Macroeconomic Activity*, Harper and Row.

Fair, Ray C. [1969], *The Short-run Demand for Workers and Hours*, North-Holland.

Feldstein, M. S. [1967], 'Specification of the Labour Input in the Aggregate Production Function,' *Review of Economic Studies*, October.

Friedman, Benjamin M., and Michael L. Wachter [1974], 'Unemployment: Okun's Law, Labor Force and Productivity,' *Review of Economics and Statistics*, May.

Friedman, M. [1968], 'The Role of Monetary Policy,' *American Economic Review*, March.

Gaudet, G. O., B. D. May, and D. G. McFetridge [1976], 'Optimal Capital Accumulation: The Neo-classical Framework in a Canadian Context,' *Review of Economics and Statistics*, August.

Glickman, Norman J. [1977], *Econometric Analysis of Regional Systems*, Academic Press.

Griliches, Zvi [1967], 'Distributed Lags: A Survey,' *Econometrica*, pp. 16–49.

Grossman, Herschel I. [1979], 'Why Does Aggregate Employment Fluctuate?,' *American Economic Review*, May.

Hamermesh, Daniel S. [1976], 'Econometric Studies of Labor Demand and Their Applications to Policy Analysis' *Human Resources*, Fall.

Hart, R. A. [1973] 'The Role of Overtime Working in the Recent Wage Inflation Process' *Bulletin of Economic Research*, May.

Hart, R. A., and T. Sharot [1978], 'The Short-run Demand for Workers and Hours: A Recursive Model,' *Review of Economic Studies*, June.

Hazledine, Tim [1972], 'Adjustment Speeds and Labour Market Conditions in NZ Manufacturing Industries: An Apparent Paradox,' presented to NZ Association of Economists Conference Massey University, August.

Hazledine, Tim [1973], 'Dual Labour Markets and the Effect of Investment on Employment and Hours in the UK Manufacturing Sector,' *Warwick Economic Research Paper*, No. 37 November.

Hazledine, Tim [1974], 'Employment and Output Functions for New Zealand Manufacturing Industries,' *Journal of Industrial Economics*, March.

Hazledine, Tim [1978], 'New Specifications for Employment and Hours Functions,' *Economica*, May.

Hazledine, Tim [1979a], 'Constraints Limiting the Demand for Labour in Canadian Manufacturing Industry', *Australian Economic Papers*, June.

Hazledine, Tim [1979b], 'Explaining Differences in Cyclical Employment Behaviour in Thirteen Canadian Food and Beverage Processing Industries,' *Journal of Industrial Economics*, Forthcoming, December.

Hazledine, Tim and Alan Woodfield [1971], 'Adjustment Dynamics and Short-run Employment Behaviour in New Zealand Manufacturing,' presented to the Second Australasian Conference of Econometrician Monash University, August.

Hazledine, Tim and Ian Watts [1977], 'Short Term Production Functions and Economic Measures of Capacity for UK Manufacturing Industries,' *Oxford Bulletin of Economics and Statistics*, November.

Hawkins, R. G. [1971a], 'Short-run Employment Functions: A Review,' presented to the Second Australasian Conference of Economists, Sydney, August.

Helliwell, J. F. (ed.) [1976], *Aggregate Investment*, Penguin Books,

Holt, C. C., F. Modigliani, R. Muth, and H. A. Simon [1960], *Planning Production, Inventories, and Work Force*, Prentice Hall.

Hughes, Barry [1971a], 'Short-run Employment Functions: A Review,' presented to the 43rd Congress of the Australia and New Zealand Association for the Advancement of Science, May.

Hughes, Barry [1971b], 'Supply Constraints and Short-term Employment Functions: A Comment,' *Review of Economics and Statistics*, pp. 393–5.

Ireland, N. J., and D. J. Smyth [1970], 'Specification of Short-run Employment Models,' *Review of Economic Studies*, April.

Jorgenson, D. W. [1963], 'Capital Theory and Investment Behaviour,' *American Economic Review*, pp. 247–59.

Killingsworth, M. R. [1970], 'A Critical Survey of Neo-classical Models of Labour,' *Bulletin of the Oxford Institute of Economics and Statistics*, August.

Kuh, E. [1965a], 'Cyclical and Secular Labor Productivity in US Manufacturing,' *Review of Economics and Statistics*. pp. 1–12.

Kuh, E. [1965b], 'Income Distribution and Employment over the Business Cycle,' in James S. Duesenberry, *et. al.*, *The Brookings Quarterly Econometric Model of the United States*, Rand McNally.

Leslie, Derek, and Clive Laing [1977], 'Labour Hoarding and Hours of Work in the U K, mimeo.

McCallum, Bennett T. [1979], 'The Current State of the Policy Inneffectiveness Debate,' *American Economic Review*, May.

McCarthy, M. D. [1972], *The Wharton Quarterly Econometric Forecasting Model, Mark III*, University of Pennsylvania.

Medoff, James L. [1979], 'Layoffs and Alternatives under Trade Unions in US Manufacturing,' *American Economic Review*, June.

Miller, R. L. [1971], 'The Reserve Labour Hypothesis: Some Tests of its Implications,' *Economic Journal*, pp. 17–35.

Mortenson, Dale T. [1970], 'Short-term Employment and Production Decisions, presented to the Second World Congress of the Econometric Society, Cambridge, September.

Muellbauer, John [1978], 'Employment Functions and 'Disequilibrium' Theory, mimeo, December.

Nadiri, M. I., and S. Rosen [1969], 'Inter-related Factor Demand Functions,' *American Economic Review*, September.

Nadiri, M. I., and S. Rosen [1973], *A Disequilibrium Model of Demand for Factors of Production*, New York, NBER.

Nerlove, M. [1967], 'Notes on the Production and Derived Demand Relations Included in Macro-Econometric Models,' *International Economic Review* pp. 223–42.

Norton, W. E., and K. M. Sweeny [1971], 'A Short-term Employment Function,' in Reserve Bank of Australia Occasional Paper No. 37, Sydney, July.

Peel, D. A., and G. Briscoe [1974], 'Another Look at the Role of Excess Demand Variables in Determining Money Wage Inflation,' CIEBR Discussion Paper No. 53, University of Warwick, May.

Peterson, A. W. A. [1976], 'Employment,' in T. S. Barker (ed.), *Economic Structure and Policy*, Cambridge Studies in Applied Econometrics 2, London, Chapman and Hall.

Phelps, E. S. (ed.) [1970], *Microeconomic Foundations of Employment and Inflation Theory*, New York, Norton.

Phipps, Anthony J. [1975], 'The Relationship between Output and Employment in British Manufacturing Industry', *Oxford Bulletin of Economics and Statistics*, February.

Reuber, G. L. [1970], 'Wage Adjustments in Canadian Industry, 1953–60,' *Review of Economic Studies*, October.

Roberts, C. J. [1972]. 'A Survey of Employment Models,' CIEBR Discussion Paper No. 30, University of Warwick, November.

Rosen, Harvey S., and Richard E. Quandt [1978], 'Estimation of a Disequilibrium Aggregate Labor Market,' *Review of Economics and Statistics*, August.

Sims, Christopher A. [1974], 'Output and Labor Input in Manufacturing,' *Brookings Papers*, 3: 1974.

Smyth, D. J. and N. B. Ireland [1967], 'Short-term Employment Functions in Australian Manufacturing,' *Review of Economics and Statistics*, November.

Solow, R. M. [1965], 'Short-run Adjustment of Employment to Output,' in *Value, Capital, and Growth*, Papers in Honour of Sir John Hicks, J. M. Wolfe (ed.), Edinburgh University Press.

Stigler, G. T. [1939], 'Production and Distribution in the Short-run,' *Journal of Political Economy*.

Taylor, Jim [1974], *Unemployment and Wage Inflation*, Longman.

Wickens, M. R. [1974], 'Towards a Theory of the Labor Market,' *Economica*, August.

Woodland, A. D. [1972], 'Factor Demand Functions for Canadian Industries, 1946–1969,' Dept. of Manpower and Immigration, Ottawa.

Wilson, R. A. [1978], 'Comparative Forecasting Performance of Disaggregated Employment Models,' CIEBR Manpower Research Group, University of Warwick, July, (forthcoming in *Applied Economics*).

Wilson, Thomas A., and Otto Eckstein [1964], 'Short-Run Productivity Behavior in US Manufacturing,' *Review of Economics and Statistics*, February.

'Employment Functions' and The Demand For Labour in The Short-Run

COMMENT *by Ralph E. Smith* (United States National Commission for Employment Policy)*

Dr. Hazledine is to be commended for his careful survey of the empirical literature on the determinants of fluctuations in employment and his identification of several important and unsettled issues in this literature. My discussion is limited to one aspect of the topic that is especially important for the development and assessment of active labour market policies: the responsiveness of employers to changes in the costs of certain categories of labour. To be useful to policy-makers in this area, it is necessary to go beyond the aggregate labour demand estimates that are the focus of most of the literature reviewed by Hazledine.

In the United States, for example, there is considerable interest in finding ways of increasing employment opportunities for young workers, especially youth from poor families. Policy options that have been proposed for doing so include (in addition to macroeconomic stimulation) subsidization of jobs in the public sector, subsidization of jobs in the private sector, and the introduction of a youth differential in the federal minimum wage.[1] Each of these policies, with the exception of the minimum wage differential, has been tried in various forms and there is little doubt that each is capable of increasing youth employment.[2]

Critical questions that arise in assessing such policies involve their impact on the employers' decisions to hire and retain workers with the specified characteristics and other workers. If, for example, the cost of employing teenagers is decreased by $1.00 per hour through a government subsidy, how many more teenagers will firms employ? How many of these additional jobs for teenagers would otherwise have gone to adults? Political support for wage subsidies and minimum wage differentials is often based on implicit assumptions about the elasticity of demand for specific groups of labour. Opposition, such as that by trade unions against a youth differential in the federal minimum wage, is in part based on the assumption of substantial labour-labour substitution.

---

*Options expressed do not necessarily reflect those of the National Commission for Employment Policy.

[1] For example, the Revenue Act of 1978 provides substantial tax credits to firms as inducements for them to hire economically disadvantaged youth, certain military veterans, ex-convicts, handicapped persons receiving or having completed vocational rehabilitation, and recipients of certain income transfer programs. The size of the subsidy is linked to wages paid to qualified workers during the first two years of their employment.

[2] For discussion of the application of demand estimates to these and other policies, see Daniel Hamermesh, 'Econometric Studies of Labor Demand and Their Application to Policy Analysis,' *Journal of Human Resources*, XI (Fall 1976), pp. 507–525.

To be helpful to policy-makers in this area, then, requires that estimates of employment demand be based on sound theory and estimation techniques. In addition—and this is the point that is too frequently ignored by the persons making the estimates—it requires that the estimates be disaggregated in ways that are relevant to the policies under consideration. If the issue is whether to institute a lower minimum wage for workers under age 22, for example, then estimates of labour-labour substitution that include that age break are most helpful.

The estimates that are most likely to be relevant include: (1) employer responsiveness to changes in the costs of employing members of specific groups; (2) estimates of substitution across groups; (3) the extent to which these magnitudes are themselves sensititive to the state of the labour market; and (4) the adjustment paths to anticipate when a change is implemented.

With such information in hand, the debates about the most effective and least costly methods of stimulating various groups' employment would be more likely to lead to sound policy.

'Employment Functions' and The Demand For Labour in The Short-Run

COMMENT *by Gerhard Tintner* (Technical University of Vienna)

This excellent paper, which I have read with great pleasure, gives a most valuable survey of the field. I agree with the authors policy recommendations and his remarks about Keynesians and monetarists. With probably a new great depression coming, they are very much to the point.

It is remarkable that the investigation of monopolistic competition, bilateral monopoly etc. in the 1930s by neo-classical economists like Joan Robinson, Chamberlin, Zeuthen, von Stackelberg etc. have to my knowledge never really been integrated into econometric models. Bilateral monopoly is important for the labour market (Tintner [1939]). We also take into account the Zeuthen [1933] theory of bargaining, later justified by Nash [1950].

Measure output x in terms of units of labour (Keynes). Let p be the price of output (constant coefficients of production) and $p = f(x)$ the demand for the product. Let $w = g(x)$ be the cost or disutility function of labour. W is the wage.

$R(x) = p\, f(x)$ is the total revenue. It is easily seen that $W = R^1(x) = D(x)$ is the demand function for labour. Also, total cost or disutility are $C(x) = x\, g(x)$ and $W = C^1(x) = S(x)$ is the supply function of labour.

Case A: The producers dominate. Then denoting by $\bar{S} = \breve{S}(x) + x\, S^1(x)$ the function marginal to $S(x)$ the equilibrium quantity is determined by $D(x) = \bar{S}(x)$ and the equilibrium price by $W = S(x)$.

Case B: The unions dominate. The equilibrium quantity is determined by $S(x) = \bar{D}(x)$ where $\bar{D}(\ddot{x}) = D(x) + x\, D^1(x)$ is marginal to $D(x)$ and the wage by $W = D(x)$.

Case C: The unions and entrepreneurs maximize their joint profit. This gives $D(x) = S(x)$ and $W = D(x) = S(x)$.

Case AC: Here $S^1 = 0$ and $D = S$. In equilibrium S and $\bar{S}$ coincide.
Case BC: Here $D^1 = 0$ and $D = S$. In equilibrium D and $\bar{D}$ coincide.
Case ABC: Here we have $D^1 = 0$, $S^1 = 0$. $D = S$; $D, \bar{D}, S, \bar{S}$ coincide in equilibrium.

Zeuthen-Nash solution. This theory defines equilibrium as the maximum of the product of the utilities of the two bilateral monopolists. Assuming (as approximations) linear utility functions this implies the maximum of

$$\left[C(x) - C(x_o) \right] \quad \left[R(x) - R(x_0) \right]$$

with respect to x, where x_o is the initial value from which the bargaining starts.

In spite of bad initial results I believe one could use the theory of splines

(Poirier [1976]) in order to estimate the demand and supply functions of labour.

The demand function for labour may have a kink (Sweezy [1939]). This also might contribute to the indeterminacy. Again one might use the theory of splines in order to estimate such a function.

BIBLIOGRAPHY

Tintner, G. [1939]: 'Note on the problem of bilateral monopoly', *Journal of Political Economy* 47
Zeuthen, F. [1933]: *Problems of Monopoly and Economic Warfare*, London.
Nash, J. F. [1950]: 'The bargaining problem.' *Econometrica* 18
Poirier, D. J. [1976]: *The Economics of Structural Change.* Amsterdam
Sweezy, P. M. [1939]: Demand under conditions of oligopoly, *Journal of Political Economy* 47

Employment and Technical Progress in Open Economies

W. Driehuis *

University of Amsterdam

*The author is indebted to K. Jansen for his research assistance to H. F. Smies for typing this paper and to Michael Ellman for his stimulating comments.

EMPLOYMENT AND TECHNICAL PROGRESS IN OPEN ECONOMIES

'*By employing improved machinery, the cost of production of commodities is reduced, and, consequently, you can afford to sell them in foreign markets at a cheaper price. If, however, you were to reject the use of machinery, while all other countries encouraged it, you would be obliged to export your money, in exchange for foreign goods till you sunk the natural prices of your goods to the prices of other countries*', David Ricardo, Principles of Political Economy and Taxation, 1821.

1. Introduction

This is a limited paper on a very complicated subject which has received considerable attention in economics ever since its existence as a science: the relationship between technical progress and employment. The paper starts by giving a bird's eye-view of classifications of technical progress (section 2). In the same section a summary is given of the so-called compensation debate. In the following section a simple macro economic model for an open economy is developed with two types of disembodied technical progress. After having investigated their effects on employment both on a partial and on an integral level, attention is paid to empirical specifications of employment functions (section 4). Afterwards two employment functions for the United Kingdom are estimated, one for the so called capital-using and one for the non-capital-using sector. In section 6 an outsider's view of actual employment developments in the UK is given, largely in macro economic terms. Those familiar with the literature on technical progress will thus miss references to problems such as
– what kind of influence does technical progress have on the supply of labour? what is the importance of the market structure and size of firms?
– what is the relationship between expenditures for R & D and technical progress, and
– what determines the national and international diffusion of technical progress?

2. Some general observations

2.1 Classifications of technical progress

It is not the purpose of this paper to review the great number of studies written on technical progress and its impact on different economic variables. The reader is referred to excellent survey studies such as those by Kennedy and Thirlwall [1973], Heertje [1977] and Boylan [1977]. It is nevertheless necessary to mention some relevant concepts in order to facilitate the understanding of what follows.

First of all it is useful to distinguish between inventions, innovations and technical change or technical progress. Although there is no firm convention in using these terms, *inventions* can be defined as the discovery of new technical knowledge and *innovations* as the application of such knowledge. Innovations may come about by new designs of plants, by applying new materials and energy, new processes or producing new types of commodities. The latter type of innovations—product innovations—will be ignored in this paper. The remaining process-innovations will be called *technical progress,* and will be assumed to be due to changes in the input of capital and/or labour.

Secondly it seems useful to point to differences in *micro* and *macro* approaches. The former lays stress on the causes of technical progress, whereas the latter focusses on its consequences. Since the subject of this paper is the impact of technical progress on employment it falls into the class of macro studies.

A third distinction we are confronted with is the one of *autonomous* and *in-duced* technical progress. The latter is not given by God and the engineers but induced by the movement of relative factor prices. Although a standard subject in growth theories, induced technical progress is not a regular part of macro economic models. This is rather disappointing when technical progress is studied in the economy where it is developed. Recent work by Van de Klundert and collaborators shows that it is possible to endogenize technical progress, for instance, by making it dependent on expenditures for research and development and these in turn on the development of costs, in a complete macro model of a closed economy[1]. One might wonder whether in open economies endogenous technical progress is really an important phenomenon. Alternatively one might assume that international competition would force them to adopt new technical developments applied elsewhere.

If this is the right view, theories regarding technical progress as the result of an international diffusion process would be more realistic than the hypothesis that technical progress per country is induced by the development of relative factor prices.[2]

A fourth distinction relates to *embodied* and *disembodied* technical progress. Technical progress is called embodied when new technical knowledge is applied in the production process by introducing new capital goods. Disembodied technical progress takes place independent of the installation of new capital goods and raises the productivity of labour or capital in use, or both. Such improvements may include plant reorganization, speeding up productive processes and increased labour efficiency by change of the organization of labour, greater skills, the effects of learning by doing, and so on. In the course of this paper we will speak about pure disembodied and embodied labour augmenting technical progress and pure disembodied and embodied capital augmenting technical progress. There is a lot of confusion about these terms and the terms pure labour and capital saving or pure labour and capital displacing technical progress are also used in the literature. In this paper *labour augmenting* technical progress has the meaning of producing a higher output with the same amount of manhours under conditions of full capacity utilization;

[1] See Van de Klundert and De Groof [1977] and Van de Klundert and Van Schaik [1973].
[2] For Studies on the diffusion hypothesis are Gomulka [1971] and Streissler [1979].

capital augmenting technical progress relates to the situation in which a higher growth rate of potential production is obtained with the same rate of investment in terms of machine hours.

Finally it should be noticed that a macro economic study of the impact of technical progress on employment can be undertaken on a *partial* and on an *integral* level. By the partial level we mean the study of the direct relationship between these two variables. It is related to the initial impact of technical progress on employment and ignores all other impacts. On an integral level, however, terminal effects of technical progress are studied by taking into account the possible effects that technical progress may have on other variables determining employment such as output, wages, user cost of capital, the rate of inflation etc., as well as the interrelations between these variables themselves.

The distinction between a partial and an integral impact of technical progress on employment is particularly relevent in the so-called compensation debate.

2.2 *A short summary of the compensation debate*

From the beginning of the discussion of the effects of technical progress on employment onwards there has been the notion that an initial negative impact could and was compensated by positive effects. If technical progress was of the kind that speeded up labour productivity growth, unit labour costs would diminish and that would reduce prices. If the lowering of prices increased either domestic or foreign demand, or both, more demand for labour would compensate the initial 'technological unemployment'. This compensation could be either partial or fully.[3]

In this context a number of criteria have been developed in order to define the degree of compensation. Some authors restrict the degree of compensation to the attraction of labour due to technical progress itself: the so-called endogenous compensation. Others also want to include the compensation which results from factors outside the introduction of the new technology: exogenous compensation. As concerns the latter category we might think of policy measures by the government in order to supplement shortcomings of the endogenous compensation.

In later discussions it has been suggested that the rise in labour productivity might lead to a rise in real wages and therefore to a reduction of the price effects just mentioned. Furthermore it has been put forward that the initial rise in unemployment through the initial reduction in employment might directly reduce the rate of change of (real) wages. Finally, depending on the nature of the production process, any impact on wages might, via substitution effects, also lead to a change in employment. All these secondary wage and price effects, have, via income and demand a further effect on production and therfore on employment.

In obtaining a clear picture of the possible effects of technical progress on employment it is, evidently, not sufficient to consider only labour augmenting but also capital augmenting technical progress. Here also partial and integral effects can be distinguished. Analysing its compensationery working it is

---

[3] A good survey of the compensation debate is given in Heertje [1977], pp. 183–190.

necessary to take its effect on capital productivity into consideration, and thus its effect on prices. In an internationally unknown work, Tinbergen [1940] particularly emphasised the role of capital costs which are influenced by this type of technical progress. He also paid attention to the rate of interest in this context.

In summary, integral effects of technical progress on employment seem to be dependent on:
– the type of technical progress involved;
– the type of production function and thus the degree of substitution between production factors;
– the degree to which wages make changes respond to unemployment (the phillips curve);
– the price setting behaviour of firms (market structure);
– the cost structure of firms;
– the price elasticities of foreign trade and the income elasticity of imports.

In the following section I consider these determinants in more detail in a simple model for an open economy. For computational simplicity, a *direct* impact of relative factor prices, on employment is neglected for the time being. Such an influence is discussed in section 5.

The emphasis will be on endogenous compensation only. It is defined as the compensation that takes place at a given gross investment ratio of firms, a given volume of government expenditure and a given supply of money.[4]

Following Tinbergen I include the user cost of capital and the rate of interest in the analysis.

3. A simple model for an open economy with two types of disembodied technical progress

3.1 *Introduction*

The purpose of the construction of this simple macro model is to show the influence of two types of technical progress on employment. It is a macro growth model consisting of three blocks: a supply block, a demand block and a wages and prices block. There are three sectors: a private sector, a government sector and a foreign sector. The government sector is dealt with in a stepmotherly fashion: there are no transfer incomes; a budget constraint is not specified; and the presently frequently discussed shifting on of direct taxes in wages is ignored.[5]

Furthermore labour supply is growing at an exogenously given rate. Changes in the unemployment rate are therefore determined by changes in employment. For reasons of computational simplicity technical progress is assumed to be disembodied and either capital or labour augmenting. It is furthermore autonomous. The production technique is described by a fixed proportion

[4] This definition is not accepted by everyone. See, for instance, Tinbergen and De Wolff [1939], who calculate compensation effects at given nominal wages.
[5] See, for instance, Jackson, Turner and Wilkinson [1972], Dernberg [1974], Driehuis [1975], OECD [1978].

production function, following a number of recent studies (see section 4). More specific assumptions are given when the individual equations are discussed.

3.2 *The supply side*

The technology does not allow substitution between factors of production. When both capital and labour are written in efficiency units we have for potential output (y^*)

$$y^* = \frac{\bar{K}}{\kappa} = \frac{\bar{L}^*}{\iota} \qquad \text{where } \bar{K} = K\, e^{\tau t}\, d^{\eta_1}$$
$$\bar{L}^* = L^* e^{\chi t}\, h^{\eta_2}$$

$\bar{K}$ and $\bar{L}^*$ are the capital stock and the employment measured in efficiency units respectively and τ and χ are the disembodied rate of capital augmenting and labour augmenting technical progress respectively; κ and ι represent the capital and labour coefficients. Potential employment is defined as employment generated by the fully utilized capital stock. If underutilized, actual employment is lower than potential employment or the number of jobs. Furthermore the time aspect is taken into account. A reduction of machine time reduces capital productivity, except for full continuous production processes. This is expressed by a coefficient $0 < \eta_1 < 1$. A reduction of labour time lowers labour productivity, as far as this is not compensated by a 'spontaneous' increase of output per worker (marginal hours effect). The coefficient $0 < \eta_2 < 1$ brings this into the expression.

$$(1) \quad \dot{y}^* = \tfrac{1}{\kappa}\,(I\, d^{\eta_1}) + \tau - \pi + \eta_1 \dot{d}$$

where $\dot{y}^* = \tfrac{1}{y}* \dfrac{dy^*}{dt}$, I is the exogenously given ratio of gross investment to output, d is machine time, π represents the trend of technical and economic depreciation of capital goods. Changes in the economic lifetime of capital goods are not taken into account (see section 5).

The equation determining the growth rate of jobs in the private sector can now be written as

$$(2) \quad \dot{L}^* = \dot{y}^* - \eta_2 \dot{h} - \chi$$

Actual labour productivity is usually varying more than potential labour productivity. This is expressed in the following employment function:[6]

$$(3) \quad \dot{L} = \dot{L}^* + \lambda\,(\dot{y} - \dot{y}^*)$$

where $\dot{y}$ denotes actual private production. The elasticity coefficient has usually the value $0 < \lambda < 1$ because of labour hoarding. In other words, the utilization of labour fluctuates less than the utilization rate of capacity output due to the following circumstances:[7]

[6] It should be noted that implicit in this function is the idea that labour is relatively abundant. Full capacity utilization would therefore not imply full employment.

[7] See also Oi [1962].

— a minimum number of workers is neccesary to operate the plant and equipment at all;

— a certain amount of labour is needed for supervision;

— laying off specialized workers and later hiring such workers is a costly and risky procedure;

— contractual agreements with respect to the duration of employment may limit the reduction in employment.

Finally a definition equation for the rate of unemployment is needed. For a moderate growth rate of the labour force and an unemployment rate of less than 10% it can be safely approximated by:

$$(4) \qquad U = U_{t-1} + \dot{N} - \beta_1 \dot{L} - (1 - \beta_1)\, \dot{Lg}$$

where $\dot{N}$ denotes the exogenously given growth rate of the labour force and $\dot{Lg}$ is public employment (β_1 is the share of private in total employment).

3.3 The demand block.

In this block private production is determined as the difference between domestic and foreign expenditure on the one hand and imports on the other hand. For the sake of simplicity real private consumption is assumed to be a function of disposable labour income only. Labour income is earned by workers in the private and public sector. The rate of change of real wages is equal for each worker. In relative first differences the consumption function reads:

$$(5) \qquad \dot{c} = \alpha_1 (\dot{w} - \dot{p}) + \alpha_1 \beta_1 \dot{L} + \alpha_1 (1 - \beta_1)\, \dot{Lg} + \alpha_2 \dot{\underline{c}}$$

where (only new variables)
c = real private consumption
w = nominal wage rate
p = general price level
Lg = public employment
$\underline{c}$ = autonomous consumption
α_1 = consumption elasticity of wage income (incl. effect of taxation)

Since the share of investment in output is given, private investment is growing proportionally to output:[8]

$$(6) \qquad \dot{i} = \dot{y}$$

real government expenditure is autonomous:

$$(7) \qquad \dot{g} = \dot{\underline{g}}$$

[8] This is equivalent to saying that the rate of change of gross investment is a fraction of the rate of change of capacity output and the rate of change in the degree of capacity utilization:

$$\dot{i} = \dot{y} + (\dot{y} - \dot{y}^*)$$

Exports of goods and services in volume (b) depends on world demand (mw) and the ratio of the own price to the average price on world markets $(\underline{pw})$, for a given exchange rate. In relative first differences:

(8) $\qquad \dot{b} = \alpha_3 \, \underline{\dot{mw}} - \alpha_4 \, (\dot{p} - \underline{\dot{pw}})$

The volume of imports (m) is dependent on production and the ratio of the price of imported goods to the domestic price. For reasons of simplicity we adopt one price for internationally traded goods:

(9) $\qquad \dot{m} = \alpha_5 \, \dot{y} - \alpha_6 \, (\underline{\dot{pw}} - \dot{p})$

Finally we need a definition for output: a weighted average of expenditure and imports, the weights being the share of the relevant variable in output:

(10) $\qquad \dot{y} = \alpha_7 \, \dot{c} + \alpha_8 \, \dot{i} + \alpha_9 \, \dot{g} + \alpha_{10} \, \dot{b} - \alpha_{11} \, \dot{m}$

3.4 The wage and price block.

The wage equation is of the traditional type: prices increases are indexed to nominal wages, which are furthermore related to labour productivity as well as to the rate of unemployment. An autonomous term is added representing unspecified influences.

(11) $\qquad \dot{w} = \epsilon_1 \dot{p} + \epsilon_2 \, (\dot{y} - \dot{L}) - \epsilon_3 \, U + \epsilon_4 \underline{\dot{w}}$

The price equation is a mark-up specification. Firms are assumed not to respond to fluctuations in demand. Unit wage and capital costs are related to the rate of technical progress rather than to actual labour and capital productivity. Furthermore it is important that prices of internationally traded goods have a direct impact on domestic prices.

(12) $\qquad \dot{p} = \delta_1 \, (\dot{w} - \chi) + \delta_2 \, (\dot{p}_k - \tau) = \delta_3 \, \underline{\dot{pw}}$

Since the unit user costs of capital are part of the price equation, there is need for the endogenization of the user cost itself:

(13) $\qquad \dot{p}_k = \Phi_1 \dot{p} + \Phi_2 \dot{r} + \Phi_3 \, \underline{\dot{pk}}$

An autonomous term $\underline{\dot{p}_k}$ is added representing the impact of policy measures in the form of, e.g. depreciation allowancies. The symbol r denotes the rate of interest. Since the economic lifetime of capital goods is assumed bo be fixed, no such variable occurs in a first difference specification of the user cost of capital. Capital gains are, in agreement with a part of the literature, omitted.

Finally, the rate of interest is made partially endogenous, *viz.* as far as the impact of inflation and the impact of output are concerned. The money supply is thus exogenous as well as other policy influences such as changes in the discount rate. The exogenous variable $\dot{r}$ accounts for these influences.

$$(14) \qquad \dot{r} = \omega_1 \, (\dot{p} - \dot{p}_{t-1}) + \omega_2 \, \dot{y} + \omega_3 \, \dot{\underline{r}}$$

3.5 Reduction of the model

A reduction of the model is helpful in understanding its working. The supply block can be solved for the rate of change of employment in the private sector:

$$(15) \quad \dot{L} = \frac{1-\lambda}{\kappa} \, (\underline{Id}^{n1}) + \lambda \dot{y} - \eta_2 \dot{\underline{h}} + (1-\lambda)\eta_1 \dot{\underline{d}} + (1-\lambda)\tau - (1-\lambda)\pi - \chi$$

It is positively related to the investment ratio, adjusted for machine time, the rate of change of output, the rate of capital augmenting technical progress and the rate of change of machine time, whereas the rate of change of working time, the rate of labour augmenting technical progress and the rate of technical and economic depreciation have a negative impact.

Solving the demand block for the rate of change of output, yields $(\dot{wr} = \dot{w} - \dot{p})$

$$(16) \qquad \dot{y} = \alpha(\dot{wr}) + \beta \dot{L} + \xi \dot{\underline{Lg}} - \psi \dot{p} + \psi \dot{\underline{pw}} + Y \dot{\underline{mw}} + \xi \dot{\underline{g}} + \theta \dot{c}$$

where
$$\alpha = \frac{\alpha_1 \alpha_7}{1 - \alpha_8 + \alpha_{11}\alpha_5}$$

$$\beta = \frac{\alpha_1 \alpha_7 \beta_1}{1 - \alpha_8 + \alpha_{11}\alpha_5}$$

$$\xi = \frac{\alpha_1 \alpha_7 (1 - \beta_1)}{1 - \alpha_8 + \alpha_{11}\alpha_5}$$

$$\psi = \frac{\alpha_4 \alpha_{10} + \alpha_6 \alpha_{11}}{1 - \alpha_8 + \alpha_{11}\alpha_5}$$

$$\gamma = \frac{\alpha_3 \alpha_{10}}{1 - \alpha_8 + \alpha_{11}\alpha_5}$$

$$\xi = \frac{\alpha_9}{1 - \alpha_8 + \alpha_{11}\alpha_5}$$

$$\theta = \frac{\alpha_2 \alpha_7}{1 - \alpha_8 + \alpha_{11}\alpha_5}$$

Important is the condition $(1 - \alpha_8 + \alpha_{11}\alpha_5) > 0$ in which, in addition to the savings and import ratio, the income elasticity of imports (α_5) plays an important part. The higher this elasticity, all other things being equal, the smaller are the reduced-form multipliers in equation (16).

Furthermore a reduced form equation for the changes in the real wage rate $(\dot{wr})$ can be found:

$$(17) \quad \dot{wr} = (\epsilon_1 - 1)\dot{p} + \epsilon_2 \dot{y} - (\epsilon_2 - \epsilon_3\beta_1)\dot{L} + \epsilon_3(1 - \beta_1)\underline{\dot{Lg}} - \epsilon_3\underline{\dot{N}} - \epsilon_3 U_{t-1} + \epsilon_4\underline{\dot{w}}$$

Finally, the reduced form price equation can be written as:

$$(18) \quad \dot{p} = \nu_1 \dot{y} - \nu_2 \dot{L} - \nu_3 U_{t-1} + \nu_4 \underline{\dot{pw}} + \nu_5 \underline{\dot{Lg}} + \nu_6 \underline{\dot{w}} - \nu_7 \chi - \nu_8 \dot{P}_{t-1} + \nu_9 \dot{r}$$

$$+ \nu_{10}\underline{\dot{pk}} - \nu_{11}\tau - \nu_3 \underline{\dot{N}}$$

where

$$\nu_1 = \frac{\delta_1\epsilon_2 + \delta_2\phi_2\omega_2}{1 - \delta_1\epsilon_1 - \delta_2\phi_1 - \delta_2\phi_2\omega_1}$$

$$\nu_2 = \frac{\delta_1(\epsilon_2 - \epsilon_3\beta_1)}{1 - \delta_1\epsilon_1 - \delta_2\phi_1 - \delta_2\phi_2\omega_1}$$

$$\nu_3 = \frac{\delta_1\epsilon_3}{1 - \delta_1\epsilon_1 - \delta_2\phi_1 - \delta_2\phi_2\omega_1}$$

$$\nu_4 = \frac{\delta_3}{1 - \delta_1\epsilon_1 - \delta_2\phi_1 - \delta_2\phi_2\omega_1}$$

$$\nu_5 = \frac{\delta_1\epsilon_3(1 - \beta_1)}{1 - \delta_1\epsilon_1 - \delta_2\phi_1 - \delta_2\phi_2\omega_1}$$

$$\nu_6 = \frac{\delta_1\epsilon_4}{1 - \delta_1\epsilon_1 - \delta_2\phi_1 - \delta_2\phi_2\omega_1}$$

$$\nu_7 = \frac{\delta_1}{1 - \delta_1\epsilon_1 - \delta_2\phi_1 - \delta_2\phi_2\omega_1}$$

$$\nu_8 = \frac{\delta_2\phi_2\omega_1}{1 - \delta_1\epsilon_1 - \delta_2\phi_1 - \delta_2\phi_2\omega_1}$$

$$\nu_9 = \frac{\delta_2\phi_2\omega_3}{1 - \delta_1\epsilon_1 - \delta_2\phi_1 - \delta_2\phi_2\omega_1}$$

$$\nu_{10} = \frac{\delta_2\phi_3}{1 - \delta_1\epsilon_1 - \delta_2\phi_1 - \delta_2\phi_2\omega_1}$$

$$\nu_{11} = \frac{\delta_2}{1 - \delta_1\epsilon_1 - \delta_2\phi_1 - \delta_2\phi_2\omega_1}$$

Two important conditions for $(-\zeta\delta_1\epsilon_1 - \delta\phi_1 - \delta_2\phi_2\omega_1) < 1$ are for ϕ_2 to be small and $(\delta_1 + \delta_2) < 1$. It seems very likely that the denominator in $\nu_1 \ldots \ldots \nu_{11}$ is rather small and thus the multipliers relatively large, the reason being that not only the price-wage spiral but also the price-user cost of capital-rate of interest spiral is taken into account.[9]

The four equations (15) – (18) have four unknown endogenous variables, the rate of change of employment in the private sector, output, real wages and prices and can easily be solved as a function of the exogenous variables $\tau, \chi, \underline{\dot{d}}, \underline{\dot{h}}, \underline{\dot{Lg}}, \underline{\dot{g}}, \underline{\dot{mw}}, \pi, \underline{\dot{c}}, \underline{Id}^{\eta_1,} \underline{\dot{N}}, \dot{w}, \underline{\dot{pw}}, \underline{\dot{p_k}}, \dot{r}$ and the lagged endogenous variables $\underline{U}_{t-1}$ and $\dot{p}_{t-1}$.

3.6 *Solution of the model.*

On page 199 the model is given in matrix notation. In short form it can be written as $AY = X$, where A is the coefficient matrix, Y is the vector of four endogenous variables and X is the vector of exogenous variables. To calculate the effects of changes in the exogenous variables on the values of the endogenous variables, it is necessary to invert the matrix A.

In these equations the term Δ is the determinant of the coefficient matrix. It has the value:
$$\alpha\lambda\nu_2(\epsilon_1 - 1) - \alpha\nu_1(\epsilon_1 - 1) - \alpha\epsilon_2 + \alpha\lambda(\epsilon_2 - \epsilon_3\beta_1) + \nu_1\psi - \lambda\psi\nu_2 - \beta\lambda + 1.$$

It is not easy to determine the sign of this determinant. It consists of several positive and negative influences. An analysis of the sign of Δ is facilitated if it is assumed that $\epsilon_1 = \epsilon_2 = 1$: workers are succesful in bargaining for a full compensation of prices and labour productivity in their nominal wages. Under these assumptions $\Delta = 1 + \alpha\lambda(1 - \epsilon_3\beta_1) - \beta\lambda + \psi(\nu_1 - \lambda\nu_2) - \alpha$.

Important herein are:
— the reduced form real wage elasticity of output (α)
— the reduced form price elasticities of foreign trade (ψ)
— the reduced form output elasticity of the rate of inflation (ν_1)
— the reduced form employment elasticity of the rate of inflation (ν_2)
— the employment elasticity of output (β)
— the responsiveness of changes in nominal wages to unemployment (ϵ_3)

It seems likely that the sign of Δ is dominated by the difference of $(\nu_1 - \lambda\nu_2)$, which is positive for plausible values of underlying coefficients (see eq. 18 and footnote[9]) in which case Δ will also be positive. The multipliers for the four endogenous variables with respect to a change in one of the rates of technical progress can be written as:

$$\frac{\partial \dot{L}}{\partial \tau} = \frac{(1 - \lambda)[1 - \alpha\epsilon_2 + \nu_1\psi - \alpha\nu_1(\epsilon_1 - 1)] - \nu_{11}[\lambda\alpha(\epsilon_1 - 1) - \lambda\psi]}{\Delta}$$

[9] When $\beta_1 = .8$ the value of ϵ_3 should be <1.25 for $\nu_2>0$ if $\epsilon_2 = 1$. For the Netherlands this condition seems fulfilled. If not, the sign of ν_2 becomes positive, but remains very small.

$$A = \begin{bmatrix} 1 & -\lambda & 0 & 0 \\ -\beta & 1 & -\alpha & \psi \\ (\epsilon_2 - \epsilon_3\beta_1) & -\epsilon_2 & 1 & -(\epsilon_1 - 1) \\ \nu_2 & -\nu_1 & 0 & 1 \end{bmatrix} \begin{bmatrix} \dot{L} \\ \dot{y} \\ \dot{wr} \\ \dot{p} \end{bmatrix} =$$

$$\begin{bmatrix} \dfrac{1-\lambda}{\kappa}(\underline{Id}^{\eta_1}) - \eta_2\underline{h} + (1-\lambda)\eta_1\underline{\dot{d}} - (1-\lambda)\tau - (1-\lambda)\pi - \chi \\[2mm] \zeta\underline{\dot{L}g} + \psi\underline{\dot{p}w} + \gamma\underline{miw} + \xi\underline{\dot{g}} + \theta\underline{\dot{c}} \\[2mm] -\epsilon_3 U_{t-1} - \epsilon_3\underline{\dot{N}} + \epsilon_3(1 - \beta_1)\underline{\dot{L}g} + \epsilon_4\underline{\dot{w}} \\[2mm] -\nu_3 U_{t-1} + \nu_4\underline{\dot{p}w} + \nu_5\underline{\dot{L}g} + \nu_6\underline{\dot{w}} - \nu_7\chi - \nu_8\dot{p}_{t-1} + \nu_9\dot{r} + \nu_{10}\dot{p}k - \nu_{11}\tau - \nu_3 N \end{bmatrix}$$

One gets:

$$A^{-1} = \frac{1}{\Delta} \begin{bmatrix} 1 - \alpha\epsilon_2 + \nu_1\psi - \alpha\nu_1(\epsilon_1 - 1) & \lambda & \alpha\lambda & \lambda\alpha(\epsilon_1 - 1) - \lambda\psi \\[2mm] -\alpha(\epsilon_2 - \epsilon_3\beta_1) + \nu_2\psi + \beta - \alpha\nu_2(\epsilon_1 - 1) & 1 & \alpha & \alpha(\epsilon_1 - 1) - \psi \\[2mm] \begin{array}{l} -(1 + \psi\nu_1)(\epsilon_2 - \epsilon_3\beta_1) + \beta\epsilon_2 + \psi\nu_2\epsilon_2 \\ -(\nu_2 - \nu_1\beta)(\epsilon_1 - 1) \end{array} & \begin{array}{l} -\lambda(\epsilon_2 - \epsilon_3\beta_1) + \epsilon_2 \\ -(\lambda\nu_2 - \nu_1)(\epsilon_1 - 1) \end{array} & 1 - \lambda\beta + \psi\nu_1 - \lambda\psi\nu_2 & \begin{array}{l} (1 - \beta\lambda)(\epsilon_1 - 1) + \\ \lambda\psi(\epsilon_2 - \epsilon_3\beta_1) - \epsilon_2\psi \end{array} \\[3mm] \zeta\nu_1 - \alpha\nu_1(\epsilon_2 - \epsilon_3\beta) - \nu_2 + \alpha\nu_2\epsilon_2 & \nu_1 - \lambda\nu_2 & \alpha\nu_1 - \alpha\lambda\nu_2 & 1 - \beta\lambda - \alpha\epsilon_2 + \alpha\lambda(\epsilon_2 - \epsilon_3\beta_1) \end{bmatrix}$$

$$\frac{\partial \dot{y}}{\partial \tau} = \frac{(1 - \lambda) \; [-\alpha(\epsilon_2 - \epsilon_3\beta_1) + \nu_2 \, \psi + \beta - \alpha\nu_2 \, (\epsilon_1 - 1)] - \nu_{11} \, [\alpha \, (\epsilon_1 - 1) - \psi]}{\Delta}$$

$$\frac{\partial \dot{wr}}{\partial \tau} = \frac{(1 - \lambda) \, [- (1 + \psi\nu_1) \, (\epsilon_2 - \epsilon_3\beta_1) + \beta\epsilon_2 + \psi\nu_2\epsilon_2 - (\nu_2 - \nu_1\beta) \, (\epsilon_1 - 1)]}{\Delta}$$

$$- \frac{\nu_{11} \, [(1 - \beta\lambda) \, (\epsilon_1 - 1) + \lambda\psi(\epsilon_2 - \epsilon_3\beta_1) - \epsilon_2\psi]}{\Delta}$$

$$\frac{\partial \dot{p}}{\partial \tau} = \frac{(1 - \lambda) \, [\beta\nu_1 - \alpha\nu_1 \, (\epsilon_2 - \epsilon_3\beta) - \nu_2 + \alpha\nu_2\epsilon_2] - \nu_{11} \, [1 - \beta\lambda - \alpha\epsilon_2 + \alpha\lambda \, (\epsilon_2 - \epsilon_3\beta_1)]}{\Delta}$$

$$\frac{\partial \dot{L}}{\partial \chi} = \frac{- [1 - \alpha\epsilon_2 + \nu_1\psi - \alpha\nu_1 \, (\epsilon_1 - 1)] - \nu_7 \, [\lambda\alpha \, (\epsilon_1 - 1) - \lambda\psi]}{\Delta}$$

$$\frac{\partial \dot{y}}{\partial \chi} = \frac{- [- \alpha \, (\epsilon_2 - \epsilon_3\beta_1) + \nu_2\psi + \beta - \alpha\nu_2 \, (\epsilon_1 - 1)] - \nu_7 \, [\alpha(\epsilon_1 - 1) - \psi]}{\Delta}$$

$$\frac{\partial \dot{wr}}{\partial \chi} = \frac{- [- (1 + \psi\nu_1) \, (\epsilon_2 - \epsilon_3\beta_1) + \beta\epsilon_2 + \psi\nu_2\epsilon_2 - (\nu_2 - \nu_1\beta) \, (\epsilon_1 - 1)]}{\Delta} -$$

$$- \frac{\nu_7 \, [(1 - \beta\lambda) \, (\epsilon_1 - 1) + \lambda\psi \, (\epsilon_2 - \epsilon_3\beta_1) - \epsilon_2\psi]}{\Delta}$$

$$\frac{\partial \dot{p}}{\partial \chi} \quad \frac{- [\beta\nu_1 - \alpha\nu_1(\epsilon_2 - \epsilon_3\beta) - \nu_2 + \alpha\nu_2\epsilon_2] - \nu_7 \, [1 - \beta\lambda - \alpha\epsilon_2 + \alpha\lambda \, (\epsilon_2 - \epsilon_3\beta_1)]}{\Delta}$$

I do not intend to discuss the value of all the multipliers just derived. It may suffice for the moment to discuss the numerators of two of them. Again under the assumption $\epsilon_1 - \epsilon_2 = 1$, the numerator of

$\dfrac{\partial \dot{L}}{\partial \chi}$ reads $- 1 \, \nu_1\psi + \alpha + \lambda\nu_7\psi$.

It falls into two parts. The negative part comes from the direct effect of labour augmenting technical progress and from the inflationary effect of the positive change in output. The positive part is due to compensation. The compensation effect consists of positive effects on output of consumption via increased real wages [10] and via price substitution effects in foreign trade. The final net effect

[10] $\dfrac{\partial (wr)}{\partial \chi} > 0$

depends on the relative strength of the negative and the positive effect. This conclusion becomes more complex when *direct* effects of relative factor prices on employment are taken into account (see section 5). As concerns the effect of capital augmenting technical progress it can be observed that the same influences are at work, but now in the opposite direction. Note that only

$$\frac{\partial \dot{L}}{\partial \chi} = -\frac{\partial \dot{L}}{\partial \tau}$$

in the extreme situation that $(\lambda = 0)$, i.e. complete labour hoarding. In normal circumstances $\partial \chi = \partial \tau$ would on balance yield a negative employment effect, even if $\delta_1 = \delta_2$.

From the foregoing analysis it becomes clear that in addition to the real-wage elasticity of output, the price elasticities of foreign trade play an important role in the magnitude of the compensation effect. The lower, furthermore, the income elasticity of imports, the greater the chance that, initial negative employment effects of labour augmenting technical progress will be compensated. It should be born in mind that a starting point of the analysis was that production capacity was not fully utilized and if so, still unemployment would not completely disappear. In my view this is true for most West-European countries in the seventies. In such a situation a sudden acceleration in the application of new innovations will cause an increase of unemployment because the negative employment effects would occur in the short run, whereas the potential positive effects via foreign trade would take a longer period. In this situation so called technological unemployment would arise.[11]

How can policy makers react? Obviously not by preventing the new innovations from being applied. This would cause a disastrous decline in the international competitive position.If there is overcapacity already in existence there would be in the first instance no reason to speed up demand by stimulating investment instead of consumption.

Alternatively the rise in real wages can be used to increase public expenditures (partly) instead of private consumption. Since the latter has a much higher import propensity than public expenditure, this would enlarge the compensation effect. It is necessary, of course, that no shifting of higher tax rates in wages takes place, so that inflation is not increased. Another alternative is to use the rise in real wages (partly) for a shortening of the working day, a lengthening of holidays, or allowing early retirement and longer education, without reducing the capacity to produce.[12] This requires therefore another distribution of the available amount of work. For all of these alternatives it is necessary that their financing does not disturb the external competitive position, otherwise potential compensation cannot be realized.

If in a country a shortage of jobs exists and this seems to be the case for the UK and other European countries,[13] it is likely that after the rate of capacity utilization has risen the share of gross investment in output will have to

---

[11] Sato [1963] shows that adjustment is faster when technical progress is embodied in new capital goods. See also the following sections.

[12] In terms of the model this would imply a reduction in (h), keeping (d) unaltered.

[13] See Driehuis [1977] and Giersch [1978].

increase, in order to bring the rate of growth of productive capacity in line with the rate of growth of the labour force. This would imply another attack on real wages.

However, it should be born in mind that these conclusions are drawn under the assumption of disembodied technical progress. When it is predominantly embodied in new capital goods they may alter somewhat, also because the user cost of capital becomes more important.

4. Employment functions

The previous section has shown, in addition to its conditional conclusions on an integral level, that the specification of the employment function is important. It is therefore not surprising that much empirical work on the explanation of employment has been undertaken. Important herein is the specification of
—the production technology, i.e. the possibility and degree of substitution between factors of production;
—the type(s) of technical progress;
—the time horizon of firms with respect to the optimization of the profitability of production;
—the adjustment processes involved.
Empirical studies undertaken for the United Kingdom are, broadly, character-ised by[14]
—the use of a neo-classical production function, either Cobb-Douglas or CES, which allows substitution between factor inputs;
—the assumption of a homogenous capital stock;
—pure disembodied labour augmenting technical progress;
—a profit maximizing behaviour of firms, either in the short run (with a given capital stock) or in the long run, under conditions of perfect competition;
—simple and uniform time paths of adjustment for *all* determinants of employment.
In a paper for OECD[15] I have critically discussed most of these assumptions and concluded that the demand for labour functions thus derived with homogenous capital are not likely to stand up against a really thorough confrontation with the data. This is, of course, not a very spectacular conclusion and it has been drawn earlier by many authors. Nevertheless it remains necessary to strive for some empirical support.

It is in this context that work in the Netherlands, but also in Germany and France, has been undertaken to improve the degree of realism of demand for labour specifications.[16] This work has attracted attention in the literature and the discussion on its validity and usefulness is still going on.[17]

A number of its characteristics have been used in the simple model of section 3.

[14] A summary of these studies can be found in Killingsworth [1970].
[15] See Driehuis [1977].
[16] See Den Hartog and Tjan [1976], Görzig [1976] and Benassy, Fouquet and Malgrange [1975].
[17] See Malinvaud [1977], Gruen [1978] and De Klerk, Van der Laan, Thio [1977].

In summary the most important features are
—a fixed coefficients production function;
—the heterogenous character of the capital stock, which consists of profitable vintages each with its own technical characteristics;
—embodied technical progress which is labour augmenting;
—its stress on economic obsolescence of equipment which is assumed to take place in a perfect competition world, where firms scrap vintages of equipment when their real wage costs are above the level of labour productivity of that vintage to reach a new 'equilibrium' condition;
—the attention to differences in lag structure of the determinants of employment;
—its distinction between potential employment (L^*) and actual employment (L), so that full capacity utilization may lead to $L - L^*$, but not necessarily to $L^* = N$ (the labour force). This holds especially in a situation where labour is relatively abundant as compared with capital;
—its macro economic character.

Despite its obvious improvement over the type of neo-classical employment functions which have been estimated for the United Kingdom, there remain, evidently, weaknesses of both an empirical and analytical nature. These have been discussed elsewhere.[18] It may suffice here to mention that it seems more realistic to assume that
—the scrapping rule is not applied in *all* sectors of the economy;
—most firms are operating in imperfect markets where a larger sales volume only can be realized at a lower price.

In the following section a *modest* attempt is presented to estimate an employment function for the United Kingdom on the basis of the aformentioned starting assumptions. Although it is not undertaken at a macro level, its degree of aggregation is still too high.

5. Some empirical results for the United Kingdom

Looking at employment in the private sector it seems useful to distinguish between industries where employment mainly depends on the demand for products and services and which use a rather low amount of equipment per worker, and industries where employment, in the absence of fluctuations in the degree of capacity utilization, is mainly determined by the volume and nature of the stock of equipment. Both categories of industries may, of course, use a varying volume of buildings, depending on the nature of the production process. Industries belonging to the former group are, for example, the building and a number of service industries. The latter group consists mainly of manufacturing industries, the transportation, communication and storage industries and finally the agricultural sector.

This distinction into two groups is roughly the same as the well known distinction between *sheltered* and *exposed* industries, *viz* exposed to competition in world markets or not. In most cases, sheltered industries are confronted

---

[18] See Driehuis [1979] for a summary.

with a relatively high income elasticity and a relatively low price elasticity of demand.

Furthermore, the nature of technical progress seems to be different in the two groups of industries. It is likely to be predominantly embodied and of the capital augmenting and labour augmenting type in capital using industries and predominantly disembodied in non capital using industries. Hereafter I will call the manufacturing sector plus transportation, storage and communication *the capital-using sector;* the building sector and the rest of the services sector is labelled the *non-capital-using sector.* In the context of the distinction between actual and potential employment the *rough* classification developed here has certain consequences. In the group of capital using industries the volume and nature of capital accumulation determine the potential number of workers that can be employed. Actually, fewer persons may be given work when productive capacity is not fully utilized. In the group of non capital using industries the distinction between actual and potential employment seems less relevant. Apart from some temporary labour hoarding and dishoarding, actual and potential employment tend to be equal here.

Following the arguments just given I postulate that a clay-clay vintage model with fixed proportions describes the technology in the capital using sector adequately. In a linearized version the production function is similar to equation (1), but now including a variable which denotes changes in the so-called economic lifetime of equipment. When (t,t) denotes the year of installation of the latest vintage at time t and (v,t) the age of the oldest equipment in use at time t, we may write (suffix 1 indicates the capital using sector)[19]

$$(19) \qquad \dot{y}_1^* = \frac{1}{\kappa}(I_1 d^{\eta_1}) + \eta_3 dA + \eta_1 \dot{d} + \tau - \pi$$

where only new variables, A = economic life time of equipment at time $(t) = t - v$.

A shortening of the economic life time reduces, *ceteris paribus,* the growth rate of productive capacity. As concerns potential employment it is possible to derive an equation similar to (2), but now also including the economic lifetime variable, since its shortening raises labour productivity because a newer vintage has a lower labour intensity.

$$(20) \qquad \dot{L}_1^* = \dot{y}_1^* + \eta_4 dA - \eta_2 \dot{h} - \chi_1 - \mu$$

where the only new variable is μ = the rate of embodied labour augmenting technical progress.

Similar to (3) we also have

$$(21) \qquad \dot{L}_1 = \dot{L}_1^* + \lambda (\dot{y}_1 - \dot{y}_1^*)$$

---

[19] A formal derivation of this equation (20) can be found in De Ridder [1977].

The combination of equations (19), (20) and (21) yields a reduced form specification of employment in the capital using sector:

$$(22) \quad \dot{L_1} = \lambda \dot{y_1} + \frac{1-\lambda}{\kappa}(I_1 h^{\eta_1}) + \{(1-\lambda)\eta_3 + \eta_4\}dA + \{(1-\lambda)\eta_1 - \eta_2\}\dot{h_1} -$$

$$- (1-\lambda)\pi - \mu - \chi_1 + (1-\lambda)\tau$$

where, for the sake of simplicity, I have assumed $\dot{d} = \dot{h}$ and $d = h$.

Employment in sector 1, then, appears to be dependent on output, gross investment ratio, working time, changes in the economic lifetime of equipment, the trend of technical and economic depreciation and the rates of disembodied capital and labour augmenting technical progress, as well as the rate of embodied labour augmenting technical progress.

Apart from problems of measurement, availability of data and econometrics, there are analytical and conceptual problems with the introduction of the change in the economic life time of capital goods. As suggested in the previous section it seems questionable to adopt the frequently used scrapping rule in neo-classical growth theories, where changes in the economic life time of machinery are determined as:

$$(23) \quad dA = \left[\frac{-(\dot{w_1} - \dot{p_1}) + \eta_2 \dot{h_1} + \chi_1}{\mu} + 1 \right]$$

Apart from the fact that this condition may be criticized for its underlying assumption of perfect competition on the market for goods, one might argue that it has little to do with actual business practice. Normally, the entrepreneur would try to maintain the continuity of the firm. In this context there is no reason to separate scrapping from replacement. A new type of machine is in general but a link in a chain of improvements. It is therefore more realistic to assume that firms will compare the total costs per unit output of the new equipment to be installed with the prime cost per unit of the production method actually in use. Instead of the scrapping rule, the replacement rule: equipment of a vintage in use is maintained as long as its wage costs per unit of output are lower than total costs per unit of output of the newest vintage, is to be preferred.

Apart from its use in business practice, this reasoning is not new in economic. theory either: Marx [1867], Schumpeter [1942], Salter [1969], to mention but a few names, have drawn attention to it. Recently Malcomson [1975] has shown this rule to be consistent with long run profit maximization under imperfect competition.

Formally we then arrive at:

$$(24) \quad dA = T\left[\frac{-(\dot{w_1} - \dot{p}k_1) - (\eta_1 - \eta_2)\dot{h_1} + \chi_1 - \tau}{\mu} + 1 \right]$$

where T = share of capital costs in total costs of the newest vintage.

It can be shown that this condition involves a shorter life time of the oldest equipment in use, *ceteris paribus*, and a lower speed of adjustment due to economic obsolescence as compared with the scrapping condition mentioned earlier. In the replacement condition it is the rate of change of relative factor prices rather than the change in real wages in comparison with the respective rates of technical progress which is determining changes in the economic life time of equipment.

Before starting empirical work we should be aware of the possibility that the user cost of capital in the replacement condition may itself be dependent on the economic lifetime of equipment. In this case substitution of equation (24) in equation (25) would not provide a suitable starting point for empirical work. Since there are reasons to assume that in business practice depreciation periods are taken as fixed and much shorter than actual economic life times I have chosen a definition of the user cost of capital with a fixed economic life time, so that the interaction mentioned does not occur.[20]

We then obtain:

$$(25) \quad \dot{L}_1 = \lambda \dot{y}_1 + \frac{1 - \lambda}{\kappa}(I_1 h_1{}^{\eta_1}) - \{(1 - \lambda)\eta_3 + \eta_4\}\frac{T}{\mu}(\dot{w} - \dot{p}k) +$$

$$+ \left[\{(1 - \lambda)\eta_1 - \eta_2\} - \{(1 - \lambda)\eta_3 + \eta_4\}\frac{T}{\mu}(\eta_1 - \eta_2)\right]\dot{h}_1 - \mu -$$

$$- \left[1 - \frac{T}{\mu}\{(1 - \lambda)\eta_3 + \eta_4\}\right]\chi_1 + \left[(1 - \lambda) - \frac{T}{\mu}\{(1 - \lambda)\eta_3 + \eta_4\}\right]\tau +$$

$$+ \{(1 - \lambda)\eta_3 + \eta_4\}T - (1 - \lambda)\pi$$

Before turning to the estimation of a dynamic version of this reduced form employment function for the capital using sector for the United Kingdom a few remarks must be made about its parameters. The negative impact of relative factor prices is interesting, while the underlying production technology excludes direct substitution.

It is furthermore not very likely that a reduction in working hours has a substantial positive effect on employment in this sector, if it is accompanied by a reduction in machine time. The reason is that the decline in labour productivity growth is partly compensated by the decline in capital productivity and partly by a reverse effect on the economic life time of equipment (at given relative factor prices!).

Notice that the impact of disembodied capital and labour augmenting technical progress varies with the rate of embodied labour augmenting technical progress. The higher the latter, the stronger is also, all other things being equal, the impact of the two disembodied technical progress rates. Moreover the opposite effects of disembodied capital augmenting and labour augmenting technical progress are not identical when labour hoarding takes

[20] In a recent empirical study for the Netherlands this was confirmed.

place in a situation of overcapacity. Finally it is of some interest to remember that this fixed coefficients clay-clay employment model allows a simultaneous rise in labour productivity, capital productivity and the capital labour ratio.

A matter not dealt with so far is the dynamics of the demand for labour. Although the requirement to find sophisticated lag structures is less in a medium term employment function based on annual data, there is no reason to assume that there is no lag or a completely identical lag structure for each of the potentially relevant determinants. In line with the view that output responds much quicker than (relative) prices I postulate the following equation to be estimated:[21]

$$(26) \qquad \dot{L}_1 - \Gamma \dot{L}_{1_{t-1}} = \lambda(\dot{y}_1 - \Gamma \dot{y}_{1_{t-1}}) + \frac{1 - \lambda}{\kappa} \{I_1 h_1{}^{\eta_1} - \Gamma(I_1 h_1{}^{\eta_1})_{t-1}\}$$

$$- \Psi(\dot{w} - p\dot{k}) - \Pi(\dot{h}_1 - \Gamma \dot{h}_{1_{t-1}}) + (1 - \Gamma)\, \Phi$$

where $\Psi = \{ (1 - \lambda)\eta_3 + \eta_4 \} \dfrac{T}{\mu}$

$$\Pi = \{(1 - \lambda)\eta_1 + \eta_2\} - \{(1 - \lambda)\eta_3 + \eta_4\} \frac{T}{\mu} (\eta_1 - \eta_2)$$

$$\Theta = -\mu - \left[1 - \frac{T}{\mu}\{(1 - \lambda)\eta_3 + \eta_4\}\right]\chi_1 + \left[(1 - \lambda) - \frac{T}{\mu}\{(1 - \lambda)\eta_3 + \eta_4\}\right]\tau$$

$$+ \{(1 - \lambda)\eta_3 + \eta_4\}\, T - (1 - \lambda)\, \pi$$

It will be clear that this equation can only be estimated when the value of T is fixed at *a priori* values. In regressions T was allowed to have the values $\cdot 1 - \cdot 9$. The final value of $\cdot 7$ was selected on the basis of the minimum squared sum of residuals. For η_1 a value of $\cdot 75$ was used in order to adjust the investment ratio for changes in machine time. The calculation of the user cost of capital is as usual; it suffices to mention that it consisted of the rate of change of the price of investment goods, interest rate and an index of investment incentives supplied by the NIESR. Other data have been found in OECD, ILO and IMF statistics.

The 'optimal' result for the period 1961–1975 reads

$$(27) \qquad \dot{L}_1 = \cdot 70\, \dot{L}_{1_{t-1}} + \cdot 35\, (\dot{y}_1 - \cdot 70 \dot{y}_{1_{t-1}}) + \cdot 42\, (L_1 h_1{}^{\cdot 75} - \cdot 70\, L_1 h_1{}^{\cdot 75}_{t-1})$$

$$(-) \qquad\qquad (4\cdot 9) \qquad\qquad\qquad (2\cdot 0)$$

$$- \cdot 10\, (\dot{w}_1 - p\dot{k}_1) - \cdot 04\, (D - \cdot 70 D_{t-1}) - \cdot 03$$

$$(4\cdot 9) \qquad\qquad\qquad (5\cdot 3) \qquad\qquad\qquad (2\cdot 3)$$

$$R^2 = \cdot 81$$
$$DW = 1\cdot 98$$

[21] For an extensive use of a Koyck lag on one of the explanatory variables, see Driehuis [1972].

As can be easily seen the final impact of relative factor prices is about ·30, the average adjustment lag being 2–3 years. It was not possible to find a significant sign for the hours variable, which has therefore been eliminated. The coefficient of the investment ratio implies an (average) capital-output ratio of 1·6. A dummy variable has been added for the year 1965 in order to account for a change in the statistical registration of employment. The constant term, finally, can be calculated to be about 10%. It is clear from equation (26) that its value allows no conclusion about the distribution over its five underlying factors, μ, χ_1, π, τ and T. The negative term $\mu + \chi_1 + \pi$ exceeds the positive term $\tau + T$.

Looking at the development of the determining factors of employment in sector 1 according to eq. (27) one must conclude that from 1967 onwards the gross investment ratio is declining. This implies a decline in growth rate of potential output and potential employment. Potential labour supply has continued to decline but at a slower rate, so that structural unemployment due to a shortage of jobs decreased. Actual employment decreased also, not least because actual output increased slowly. Considering the whole period the difference between the rate of change of wages and capital costs is almost zero. A remarkable development, because in other European countries [Driehuis, 1977] capital costs, identically defined, rose substantially less than wages. In terms of the model used, this implies that the economic lifetime of equipment has increased in the UK and that the share of replacement investment in gross investment has declined. This seems to have checked the introduction of process (and product) innovations and consequently labour productivity growth.

In this context one might wonder whether the market structure of manufacturing industry has something to do with this lack of modernization. It is frequently argued (see, for instance, Salter, [1969, p. 94]) that '. . . the monopolist is under no external pressure (. . .) to scrap obsolete equipment; while the producer in a competitive industry is forced to do so by the price changes resulting from actions of its competitors'. It is well known that the degree of concentration is much larger in the UK[22] than in Western Europe so that this phenomenon might have worked, particularly in the years before the EEC membership.

As concerns employment in the non capital using sector—the building and the rest of the services industries—we may be short. According to the arguments given before, employment in this sector is mainly determined by demand for its goods and services. Since it is a sector largely sheltered from foreign competition with a high income elasticity and a low price elasticity of demand, it can be assumed that unit labour costs will be adequately covered in prices. It is furthermore assumed that there is an impact of working hours. As regards technical progress, it is assumed to be labour augmenting and disembodied. For the period 1960–1975 I have found:

$$L_2 = 1\cdot05\,\dot{y}_2 - \cdot50\,\dot{h}_2 - \cdot028$$
$$\quad\;\;(2\cdot2)\qquad(-)\qquad(2\cdot2)$$

$$R^2 = \cdot43$$
$$DW = 1\cdot50$$

[22] See Prais [1976].

where the hours coefficient has been fixed at ·50.

More sophisticated lag structures and the inclusion of more specific variables will probably improve this result. At present it shows little more than that the growth of labour productivity in the non capital using sector is about 2%, after correction for changes in working hours, is roughly equal to the rate of disembodied labour augmenting technical progress.

6. An outsider's view of the employment situation in the United Kingdom

When I consider employment growth in the UK over the period 1960–1975 in terms of the two sectors distinguished, the following picture is obtained:

sectors	Share in output		Share in employment		output	employment	labour productivity
	1960	1975	1960	1975	average rate of growth in %		
capital using	45·3	44·6	52·3	47·6	2·3	−1·1	3·4
non capital using	45·7	46·9	37·3	45·2	2·6	·8	1·8
agriculture	3·3	3·2	4·9	3·5	2·2	−2·7	4·9
mining	2·9	1·4	3·7	1·8	−2·4	−5·1	2·7
public utilities	2·8	3·9	1·8	1·9	4·8	− ·5	5·3
total	100	100	100	100	2·4	− ·5	2·9

Although one must be careful in drawing far-reaching and firm conclusions on the basis of these figures and the econometric analysis given in the previous section, I am inclined to interpret them as follows:
—the UK has a moderate rate of labour productivity growth in the labour intensive sector of about 2%, rather similar to that in other West-European countries; also the output growth in this sector is not very unusual; similar also is that its share in output and employment is rising; employment is growing in this sector which is largely sheltered from foreign competition and has possibilities of passing on rising unit labour costs in prices, which increase much more than prices in other sectors.
—the UK has also a moderate rate of productivity growth in the capital intensive sector of about 3·5%, which is low in comparison with other West-European countries; output growth is also much lower (about 50%!) and employment is declining more than in other countries; unit costs in this exposed sector have risen more than in competing countries resulting in a weak export performance and a high import penetration.
—if the hypothesis is adopted that the UK capital intensive sectors have no lower rate of disembodied capital- and labour-augmenting technical progress, compared with other countries, it is the lack of modernization of the capital stock which is an important reason behind the unfavourable development of costs per unit of output.
—in the UK wage costs and capital costs have risen to an almost equal extent during the last twenty years; this seems to point to the phenomenon that the

share of replacement investment in total private investment has declined, whereas it has risen in all other West-European countries; this may also have had an influence on the degree of product innovation in the UK.

—closer inspection of the figures shows that the relatively high growth rate of the cost of capital rather than the increase in nominal wages is responsible for the lack of modernization of the capital stock via accelerated replacement. The industrial structure might have something to do with this.

New best-technique practices are probably developed for a multi-country market, such as the EEC. If a country is not able to follow these developments by replacing old equipment by new equipment, which in addition often involves product innovations, it loses its international export position and it is confronted with import penetration. Although the direct effects of labour augmenting technical progress are negative for employment, these may be substantially compensated by favourable developments on the demand side, through an adjustment in prices, provided firms do not increase their profit margins. Moreover, capital augmenting technical progress may take place which is favourable for employment. David Ricardo presented this message already as long as 150 years ago, but it does not seem to have received the attention it deserved in the UK.

REFERENCES
Benassy, J. P., Fouquet, D., and Malgrange, P. [1975], 'Estimation d'une Fonction de Production a Generations de Capital', *Annales de L'Insee*, nr. 19, pp. 3–53.
Boylan, M. G. [1977], 'Reported Economic Effects of Technological Change' in B. Gold, Research, *Technological Change and Economic Analysis*, Lexington.
Dernberg, T. F. [1974], 'The Macroeconomic Implications of Wage Retaliation Against Higher Taxation', *IMF Staff Papers*, Nov., pp. 758–808.
Driehuis, W. [1972], *Fluctuations and Growth in a Near Full Employment Economy*, Rotterdam.
—[1975], 'Inflation, Wage Bargaining, Wage Policy and Production Structure', *De Economist*, pp. 638–679.
—[1977], 'Capital—Labour Substitution and Other Potential Determinants of Structural Employment and Unemployment'. Paper submitted to OECD. Published in *OECD, Structural Determinants of Employment and Unemployment*, Vol. II, Paris, 1979.
—[1979], 'An Analysis of the Impact of Demand and Cost Factors on Employment', *De Economist*, 127, m2, pp. 255–286.
Gomulka, S. [1971], *Inventive Activity, Diffusion, and the Stages of Economic Growth*, Aarhus.
Gorzig, B. [1976], 'Results of a Vintage Capital Model for the Federal Republic of Germany', *Empirical Economics*, Vol. I, pp. 153–166.
Giersch, H. (ed.) [1978], *Capital Shortage and Unemployment in the World Economy*, Tubingen.
Gruen, F. H. G. [1978], 'Structural Unemployment as a Rival Explanation: A Survey of an Inconclusive Argument', in H. Giersch (*op. cit.*), pp. 59–81.
Hartog, H. den and Tjan, H. S. [1976], 'Investments, Wages, Prices and Demand for Labour', *De Economist*, CXXIV, pp. 32–55.
Heertje, A. [1977], *Economics and Technical Change*, London.
Jackson, D., Turner, H. A. and Wilkinson, F. [1972], *Do Trade Unions Cause Inflation?*, Cambridge.
Kennedy, C. and Thirlwall, A. [1973], 'Technical Progress', *Surveys in Applied Economics*, Vol. I.
Killingsworth, M. R. [1970], 'A Critical Survey of Neoclassical Models of Labour', *Bulletin Oxford University Institute of Economics and Statistics*, XXXII, pp. 133–165.
Kierk, R. A. de, Van der Laan, H. B. M. and Thio, K. B. T. [1977], 'Unemployment in the Netherlands: A Criticism of the Den Hartog-Tjan Vintage Model', *Cambridge Journal of Economics*, I, pp. 291–306.
Klundert, Th. Van de and De Groof, R. J. [1977], 'Economic growth and Induced Technical Progress', *De Economist*, Vol. 125, (nr. 4), pp. 505–524.
Klundert, Th. Van de and Van Schaik, A. [1978], 'Demand and Supply as Factors Determining Economic Growth', *De Economist*, Vol. 126, (nr. 3), pp. 370–389.

Malcolmson, J. [1975], 'Replacement and the Rental Value of Capital Equipment Subject to Obsolescence', *Journal of Economic Theory*, X, pp. 24–41.

Malinvaud, E. [1977], *The Theory of Unemployment Reconsidered*, Oxford.

Marx, K. [1867], *Das Kapital*, Frankfurt (reprinted 1972).

OECD [1978], *Trends in Public Expenditure*, Paris.

Oi, W. Y. [1962], 'Labour as a Quasi-Fixed Factor', *Journal of Political Economy*, LXX, pp. 538–555.

Prais, S. J. [1976], *The Evolution of Giant Firms in Britain*, Cambridge.

Ridder, P. B. De [1977], *Een Jaargangenmodel met vaste technische coefficienten en in kapitaal geincorporeerde arbeidsbesparende technische vooruitgang (A Vintage Model with Fixed Coefficients and Embodied Labour Saving Technical Progress)*, CPB Occasional Paper, No. 14.

Salter, W. E. G. [1969], Productivity and Technical Change, Cambridge.

Sato, K. [1973], 'On the Adjustment Time in Neo-Classical Growth Models', *Review of Economic Studies*, pp. 263–268.

Schumpeter, J. [1942], *Capitalism, Socialism and Democracy*, New York.

Streissler, E. [1979], 'Growth Models as Diffusion Processes: part I, *Kyklos*, Vol. 32, Fasc. 1/2, Part II do Fasc. 3.

Tinbergen, J. [1940], Technical Change and Employment, (in Dutch), Amsterdam.

Tinbergen, J. and De Wolff, P. [1939], 'A Simplified model of the causation of technological unemployment', *Econometrica*, p. 193.

Employment and Technical Progress in Open Economies

COMMENT by A. P. Thirlwall (University of Kent)

What Driehuis has done in this paper is to dress up an old body in some fancy clothes, leaving a few bare patches in vital places. The old body, which will be immortal, because it is an identity, is:

$$(1) \qquad \dot{L} = \dot{Y} - \dot{P}$$

where $\dot{L}$ is the rate of growth of employment; $\dot{Y}$ is the rate of growth of output and $\dot{P}$ is the rate of growth of labour productivity.

Ignoring labour hoarding, which Driehuis does not provide any information on, so that $\lambda = 1$, his equation (15), which is the reduction of the 'supply block' of the model reduces to equation (1) above. $\dot{P}$ depends on the rate of labour augmenting technical progress and an 'hours effect'. The novelty of Driehuis is to dress up $\dot{Y}$ and to make it endogenous.

How does he derive $\dot{Y}$? Output growth is taken as the weighted average of the components of aggregate demand comprising the national income identity. Output growth becomes endogenous because consumption growth is assumed to depend on the growth of real wages and employment; and the rate of growth of exports and imports are assumed to depend on technical progress working through changes in relative prices. Ultimately he ends up with a model of four equations in the four endogenous variables—output growth; employment growth; real wage growth, and price inflation—which can then be used to solve for the effect of changes in the rate of technical progress (and other exogenously given variables) on employment growth etc. etc.

Although I see no alternative to the framework and approach that Driehuis takes to analyse the employment effects of technical changes at the macro level, I think the model is unnecessarily complicated. A much simpler model in the same spirit is quite capable of explaining the historical facts for the UK which are presented at the end of the paper. There are also two serious omissions from the model, the inclusion of which would not only give greater realism but also, in the case of one of the inclusions, help to simplify it.

The first omission concerns the induced effects of output growth on productivity growth, otherwise known as Verdoorn's Law. If the relationship is specified correctly with productivity growth or employment growth as the dependent variable (and not with employment growth as the independent variable as some investigators have done), all the evidence I know suggests a positive relationship between output growth and productivity growth, at least in manufacturing industry. It would be extremely odd if there were not. If all productivity growth was 'autonomous', how could we explain large differences in productivity growth in the same industry over the same period in different countries, or very sudden changes in the rate of growth of productivity from one year to the next? The denial of a relationship (or the belief in reverse causation) would also be a denial of the existence of static and dynamic returns to scale. The Verdoorn coefficient as derived by Verdoorn himself is:

$$1 - \frac{j}{\alpha + \beta(\frac{\dot{K}}{\dot{L}})} \ ,$$

where α and β are the partial elasticities of output with respect to labour and capital, respectively, in the Cobb-Douglas production function.

Thus the Verdoorn coefficient is seen to depend on both the scale parameters of the production function and the rate at which capital is growing relative to labour. Contrary to what is sometimes suggested in the employment function literature, pro-cyclical labour productivity growth is not dependent on short-run increasing returns to labour (i.e. $\alpha > l$), unless, of course, it is assumed that $\dot{K} \leqslant 0$. As far as Driehuis's paper is concerned, ignoring the Verdoorn effect will overstate the employment growth effects of output growth. The incorporation of the effect into the model would be a relatively simple matter. Instead of assuming productivity growth to be autonomous, we could specify:

$$(2) \qquad \dot{P} = \dot{P}_A + \gamma(\dot{Y})$$

where $\dot{P}_A$ is autonomous productivity growth and γ is the Verdoorn coefficient.

Driehuis's later specification of the employment function in which technical progress is embodied partly evercomes this deficiency of the basic specification, but the Verdoorn relation consists of more than just embodied technical progress. It is a macro-phenomenon, to use Allyn Young's phraseology, embracing increasing returns in the widest sense.

The second major omission, which is particularly serious in an open economy model, is that there is no balance of payments constraint on output growth. In taking the growth rate of output as a weighted average of the components of autonomous demand, there is no recognition that the rate of growth of imports generated may exceed the rate of growth of exports, making growth at that rate unfeasible. Why not recognise from the start, at least for ex-post explanation or for the making of long-run forecasts, that growth must approximate to the balance of payments equilibrium growth rate, and recognise the empirical evidence (see Thirlwall, [1979]) that this in turn can be approximated by the rate of growth of exports ($\dot{X}$) divided by the income elasticity of demand for imports (m^*), the dynamic analogue of the Harrod trade multiplier:

$$(3) \qquad \dot{Y} = \frac{\dot{X}}{m^*} \ ,$$

where the rate of growth of exports in volume terms is determined by the income elasticity of demand for exports in world markets and the rate of growth of world income. Thus we have a Hicksian-type model in which the rate of growth of output is governed by the rate of growth of autonomous demand, where exports are dominant and, in the long run, must pay for imports.

In my own view, the main importance of technical progress for growth and employment in an open economy is not that it adds to demand by increasing real wages, or that it improves the trade balance through relative price changes, but that it is the main determinant of the *types* of goods produced which determines the income elasticity of demand for exports and imports in world trade. The more technologically progressive a country the higher the income elasticity of demand for its exports relative to imports, and the higher its balance of payments constrained growth rate will be. There is no recognition of this point in Driehuis's paper.

Turning to unemployment, the change in the percentage level of unemployment is approximately equal to the difference between the rate of growth of labour supply and employment. Here it may be important to relax the assumption that labour supply grows at an exogenously given rate independent of demand. It would certainly be a weak assumption in a regional context or in a country which allowed the free mobility of labour. Even within countries the labour force seems to be remarkably responsive to fluctuations in employment opportunity. Thus let:

(4) $\qquad \Delta\% U = \dot{N} - \dot{L}$

and

(5) $\qquad \dot{N} = \dot{N}_A + \epsilon(\dot{L})$

where $\dot{N}_A$ is the autonomous growth of labour supply and ϵ is the elasticity of labour supply with respect to employment growth.

If we put together the equations of my own simple model we have:

(6) $\qquad \dot{L} = \dfrac{\dot{X}}{m*}(1 - \gamma) - \dot{P}_A$

and

(7) $\qquad \Delta\% U = \dot{N}_A - \left[\dfrac{\dot{X}}{m*}(1 - \gamma) - \dot{P}_A\right](1 - \epsilon)$

Driehuis does not test the explanatory power of his own model against any data but my equation (6) is quite able to explain the facts for the UK in the table at the end of paper. For the whole economy: $\dot{X} = 4.5\%; m* = 1.8; \gamma = 0.4$ and $\dot{P}_A = 1.9$ giving $\dot{L} = 0.4\%$. For the capital using sector, assuming the balance of payments constrained growth of manufacturing output to be the same as that of total output (i.e. 2.5%)[1], with $\gamma = 0.5$ and $\dot{P}_A = 2.2\%$, gives $\dot{L} = -1.0\%$.

In discussing the effects of technological progress on employment in an open economy I am firmly convinced that one needs to work within the framework of a balance of payments constrained model at least for the UK. In my own simple

[1] This will be true if manufacturing output is assumed to be a constant proportion of total output, and is consistent with manufacturing exports growing at 5.0% with an income elasticity of demand for imports of 2.

214

model we need to know the effect of technical progress on $\dot{P}_A, \dot{X}, m^*$ and γ. A particularly important task for research is to understand the relationship between technological progress and the determinants of export and import growth.

Fears are now being expressed about the effect of the technological revolution of micro-processors on the future level of employment and unemployment. History does not support the view that technical progress is the cause of widespread unemployment. Driehuis's model shows very nicely some of the reasons why. There are partial adverse effects but also macro compensation effects (see particularly the model after simplification on p. 200). If anything, micro-processors are capital saving both absolutely and relatively which should bias the distribution of income in labour's favour. Provided that the rate of growth of output can be maintained, therefore, there need be no fear of widespread unemployment. Those who fear for the future must be pessimistic about the possibility of raising the growth rate to match the growth in productivity. If the balance of payments is the major constraint on the growth of output in an open economy the policy message is plain. It is equally plain that, in an open economy constrained by the balance of payments, the labour market consequences of *not* participating in technological revolutions are likely to be far more serious than participating. It is income elasticities of demand for exports and imports that rule the roost in an open economy, and favourable income elasticities for growth are primarily a function of the technological dynamism of nations.

I would conclude by saying that Driehuis's model is an ambitious one which he has yet to test. My own view is that it is unnecessarily complex, but whether he simplifies it or not, it needs incorporated a balance of payments constraint, a Verdoorn relationship an the responsiveness of labour supply to demand.

REFERENCES

Thirlwall, A. P. [1979], The Balance of Payments Constraint as an Explanation of International Growth Rate Differences, *Banca Nazionale del Lavoro Quarterly Review*, March.

Employment and Technical Progress in Open Economies

COMMENT *by Paavo Peisa* (University of Helsinki)

In his stimulating paper, Professor Driehuis combines economic and econometric analysis. In what follows, I shall comment only on some of the theoretical issues.

His main innovation in the paper is the relation of the rate of capital augmenting technological progress to what is called the economic life-time of equipment. In this way, he opens the door for a fruitful discussion of the causes and consequences of technological progress, and breaks out of the blind alley to which the usual procedure of assuming exogenously-given rates inevitably leads.

Driehuis argues that the economic life-time of equipment is regulated not by the well-known Neo-classical, or scrapping, rule that a machine should be scrapped if its variable cost per unit of output exceeds the price of output but by the rule proposed by Salter and others which states that a machine should be replaced if its variable unit cost exceeds the total unit cost of a new machine. Here, I think, Driehuis is right in diverting attention from the Neo-classical rule to the replacement rule, but not in rejecting the former altogether. Strictly taken, it is true, as he says, that the scrapping rule applies only in perfect competition, but this is of no importance because the monopolistic case is easily covered by replacing the word 'price' with the words 'marginal revenue' when stating the rule. In all but the extreme Keynesian case of zero elasticity of demand for output, wages affect the demand for labour through the (optimum) price of output and through the demand for output.

Recognizing both of these two margins does not necessarily mean that the employment function to be estimated must be altered, but it does mean that care should be taken in interpreting the results. In particular, the dependence of output on wages (and also, in the long run, on the prices of capital goods) ought to be taken into account.

Furthermore, the relation of the formal presentation of the scrapping rule in equation (24) to the verbal presentation and to the profit maximization results, is not obvious. Some of the assumptions are not explicitly set forth. Suppose, not unrealistically, that investment decisions, once made, are not fully reversible. In this case, the firm will presumably take into account the effect of investment decisions on future investment opportunities and, in the optimum, should be indifferent to replacement today or replacement tomorrow. A firmly anticipated fall in the price of capital goods will induce the firm to modify speculatively its replacement plans and to extend the lifetime of its oldest equipment. If a fall in the price of capital goods leads to the expectation of further fall, the speculative effect may outweigh the substitution effect considered by Driehuis. If this is the case, utilization period will increase and the rate of modernization of the capital stock decline. A low rate of decrease in the relative price of capital goods does not suffice, in itself, to explain a weak growth performance or lack of modernization of the capital stock, as Driehuis seems to imply in his discussion of employment in the United Kingdom.

My second point is concerned with the effects of exogenous changes in the rates of technological progress on endogenous variables like employment, wages and price change, and more specifically, with the sign of the determinant of matrix A in the equation presented on page 199. Driehuis is very successful in reducing his complex subject matter to a simple linear system of equations, $AX = Y$, and in computing the impact of technological change on the exogenous variables Y. However, the discussion of the sign of the determinant of matrix A is not completely satisfactory, with the consequence that the sign of the comparative statics expressions remains largely undetermined.

One way to eliminate this nuisance is to invoke dynamic considerations. A quite natural dynamic formulation is, in discrete time, $\Delta X = -AX + Y$. For this system, the equilibrium state $X^* = A^{-1}Y$ is stable only if the determinant of A is positive.[1] Hence it suffices, for purposes of comparative statics, simply to postulate that the determinant is positive, provided that the lag structure presented above, or some more complicated one leading to the same result is accepted.

If the determinant is negative, the equilibrium is unstable. I conclude by considering the stability of an open economy identical to the one postulated by Professor Driehuis, except that (1) wages do not depend directly on the productivity of labour and (2) changes in the rate of interest do not affect the prices of capital goods, or alternatively, interest rates do not depend on income, i.e., it is assumed that $\epsilon_2 = \phi_2 \omega_2 = 0$. These assumptions divert somewhat from those made by Driehuis, although they are in line with the general Keynesian flavour of his analysis. Specifically, he assumes that $\epsilon_2 = 1$. In a short run analysis, the assumption $\epsilon_1 = 0$ is reasonable, and moreover, the productivity effect on wages can be combined with the exogenous wage push effect if the exogeneous rates of technological change are regarded as permanent rates. The assumption $\phi_2 \omega_2 = 0$, incidentally, prevents money from having any influence on the equilibrium state.

---

[1] These statements require, perhaps, some justification. The system of equations can be written as $X = (1 - A)X + Y$ which corresponds to the system of equations (15) $-$ (18). If a uniform lag of one period is introduced, this becomes $X_{t+1} = (I-A)X_t + Y_t$ which is the same as above. The dynamic system has a unique equilibrium if A^{-1} exists. Let us assume that the equilibrium is stable. Then the determinant of A is positive by virtue of the Poincare-Hopf theorem for systems of differential equations. Or alternatively, note that the dimension of the system can be reduced from four to three by introducing, for example, $\dot{y} - \dot{y}^*$ (proportional rate of change in the rate of capacity utilization) as a variable and substituting $L^* + \lambda (\dot{y} - \dot{y}^*)$ and $(\dot{y} - \dot{y}^*) + \dot{y}^*$ for $\dot{L}$ and $\dot{y}$ in the system. Let now $\Delta X = -AX + Y$ refer to the system obtained thereby so that A becomes a 3×3-matrix. Let the characteristic roots of $-A$ be λ_1, λ_2 and λ_3, so that $\det(-A) = \lambda_1 \lambda_2 \lambda_3$. It suffices to consider the case where λ_1 and λ_2 are either real or complex conjugates, and λ_3 real. Assuming that the equilibrium is stable, the real parts of the characteristic roots are non-positive. $\lambda_1 \lambda_2$ is positive, and as λ_3 is negative, $\det(-A)$ is negative. Because $\det(-A) = -\det A$, the equilibrium condition can be put as $\det A > 0$.
The determinant of the 3×3-matrix is equal to the determinant of the original 4×4-matrix divided by a scalar $1 - \beta\lambda$ which can be taken as positive, and hence, both the determinants have the same sign.

If $\epsilon_2 = \phi_2\,\omega_2 = 0$, the determinant can be written as $1 - \beta\lambda\,[1 + (v_7(\epsilon_1 - 1) - \psi/\beta + 1)\,\epsilon_3]$.

The equilibrium tends to be stable in the sense that the determinant is likely to be positive, if the marginal propensity to consume out of income is small or if private employment does not respond to fluctuations in demand for output, i.e., if $\beta\lambda$ is small. Two sources of instability can readily be identified, namely the index clause in wage contracts, as reflected in a large value of ϵ_1, and the sensitivity of comparative wage costs to changes in unemployment, as reflected in a large value of ϵ_3. Sufficiently flexible money wages will make any equilibrium unstable, if the elasticity of demand for exports is small and a fall in wages seriously cuts domestic demand. Under the same conditions, a devaluation, which is an alternative way to change comparative wage costs, tends to have a contractive effect on aggregate demand and employment.[2] Contracyclical exchange rate policies, used to attain an 'employment target' in such a manner that the exchange rate is depreciated when unemployment increases and appreciated when it declines, contribute to the instability of the economy.

[2] See Krugman, P. and Taylor, L. [1978] Contractionary Effects of Devaluation, *Journal of International Economics*, Vol. 8.

Implicit Contracts and Related Topics: A Survey

Costas Azariadis *

University of Pennsylvania

* Grants from the National Science Foundation and the Centre for the Study of Organisational Innovation, University of Pennsylvania are gratefully acknowledged.

IMPLICIT CONTRACTS AND RELATED TOPICS: A SURVEY

1. Introduction

The theory of labour contracts is concerned with the allocation of labour services in uncertain environments when opportunities to shed risk are limited by imperfectly developed markets for contingent claims. Economies with contracts are in a sense midway between the ideal construct of Arrow [1971, 1971] and Debreu [1959, ch. 7], which possesses complete claims markets, and recent work on rational expectations, [Muth [1961], Lucas [1970], Radner [1972]] from which claims markets are usually absent. The connection of labour contracts with the Arrow-Debreu and spot paradigms is one of the central themes in this paper and what distinguishes it from related surveys [Gordon [1971], Baily [1976], Calvo [1979]][1]

In Section 2 I trace the intellectual origins of the ideas surveyed here to the work of Adam Smith, Knight, and others, and discuss motives for the contractual exchange of labour services. The next four sections are devoted to labour economics. Sections 3 and 4 restate basic results on wage stickiness, temporary layoffs and unemployment compensation for economies with homogeneous labour. Extensions are discussed in Sections 5 and 6: heterogeneous labour phenomena such as preferential layoffs and the cyclical behaviour of wage differentials; asymmetric information problems including the agent-principal relation and employment-contingent contracts.

Macroeconomics occupies Section 7 which deals with the theoretical under-pinnings of contracts with fixed money wages and discusses the monetary transmission mechanism these contracts are likely to produce. The concluding section reviews some unsolved theoretical issues. The main aim of this survey is expository but not encyclopedic: little attempt is made to present original material (except in Sections 6 and 7), acknowledge historical priority, describe the empirical literature related to labour contracts [Baily [1976], Raisian [1980] Abowd and Ashenfelter [1979], Eaton and Quandt [1979], Taylor [1978]], or cover such macroeconomic applications as indexation.[2]

2. Origins

The subject matter of this survey began in the mid-nineteen seventies [Baily [1974], Gordon [1974], Azariadis [1975]] as part of a continuing—and, to this day, far from successful effort to build up the logical foundations of

---

[1] The incomplete-markets aspect of labour contracts is also stressed in Drèze [1979].
[2] Descriptive indexation theory [Gray [1976], Gray [1978], Phelps and Taylor [1966], Fischer [1977], Barro [1977]], is surveyed ably in Barro and Fischer [1976], while optimum indexation [Azariadis [1978], Eden [1979], Blanchard [1979]] is still insufficiently developed.

macroeconomics, purge the field of its inherited ideological superstructure, and bring it to approximate parity with the more developed areas of economics. The empirical regularities which initially attracted most attention were the twin phenomena of sticky wages and layoff unemployment.

The key new idea in the theory of labour contracts is that in the process of exchanging labour services an incomplete insurance policy is traded as well. Baily, in fact, argues [1974, p. 37]:

'In deciding what wage-employment strategy to set, the firm will be willing to reduce worker risk. By doing so, the firm is offering a joint product, employment plus an insurance or financial intermediation service'.

And my own essay clearly states [1975, p. 1185]:

'. . . in the course of the relationship between employer and employees, enough scope exists for the former to unburden the latter of at least some of the variability that otherwise would accompany wage income.'

This idea is less than entirely novel. Adam Smith's theory of occupational wage differentials [1973, Book I, ch. 10; also 35, ch. 13] recognizes the role of risk in the labour market, predicting in particular that wages in different occupations will vary 'with the constancy or inconstancy of employment' and 'with the probability or improbability of success in them'. Frank Knight went further than Smith in arguing that risks were shared in a specific manner [1921, pp. 269–70]: entrepreneurs, being inherently 'confident and venturesome', were naturally willing to relieve their 'doubtful and timid' employees of all risk in return for the right to make allocative decisions. And Hicks [1932, ch. 3] is not surprised that wages fail to respond to changes in demand conditions which recur with some regularity.[3]

Psychological differences in attitude towards risk are not necessary in explaining long-term attachments of employees to firms. One begins, instead, with the observation that workers are far more dependent on human capital for their livelihood than are stockholders, but far less able to diversify their 'wealth portfolio'. Individuals cannot spread firm-specific risks by holding several jobs simultaneously, nor can they issue claims contingent on their own labour services. We do not observe such claims because of moral hazard and of the illegality of involuntary servitude: delivery of the service specified in them would depend on a state (e.g., 'seller's employment status' or 'income') that is costly to monitor and easy to manipulate; and on the seller's willingness to abide by an agreement he may find unprofitable when he realizes the actual state of nature.

These problems are less serious in the workplace; employers possess substantial information about the status of each employee, control a supervisory apparatus which monitors current job performance, and enjoy superior access to financial markets. It is sensible, therefore, for firms to underwrite the

---

[3] For Leontief [1946], on the other hand, wage-employment contracts have little to do with risk; they are merely price-quantity offers by a monopolist or monopsonist bent on price discrimination.

insurance policies their employees are unable to place directly and, in effect, to become in part financial intermediaries, shifting risk from owners of human capital to owners of financial capital. As we shall see in the remainder of the present survey, this is done when wages reflect not only the marginal product of labour but also an insurance premium or indemnity.

3. Contingent Contracts

Some fundamental results on wage behaviour, layoffs and the role of unemployment insurance are restated in this section for economies with homogeneous labour[4].

We consider a competitive industry in which product price is a random variable s attaining the values $s_1 = 1 - a$ and $s_2 = 1 + a$ $(0 < a \leqslant 1)$, each with probability 1/2. The number of firms in this industry and the economy-wide 'consumer price index' are both normalized to one. There is an inelastic supply of identical, risk-averse labourers specific to this industry: It is zero for wages below their reservation wage k, μ persons per firm for wages above k. Hours of work are fixed institutionally and all current income is consumed; workers' preferences are described by a smooth, increasing, concave function $\mu(\cdot)$.

Firms own a convex technology for converting the input of n labourers and of one entrepreneur-owner into $f(n)$ units of perishable output. We assume that

(1) $\qquad (1 - a)f'(\mu) < k < f'(\mu)$

and hypothesize provisionally that owners are neutral to consumption risk.

The purpose of inequality (1) is to motivate unemployment in the worst state. For instance, if labour services are traded in a spot market, full employment will prevail at a wage w_2^0 in state 2 (point A_2 in Figure 1); in state 1 an equilibrium will obtain (point A_1) with the wage at its reservation level k and $\mu - n_1^0$ individuals being voluntarily unemployed. The numbers n_1^0, w_2^0 are defined from

(2a) $\qquad w_2^0 = (1 + a)f'(\mu)$

(2b) $\qquad k = (1 - a)f'(n_1^0)$

As wages are higher in state 2, workers may clearly benefit from insurance against state 1.

(a) The Role of Claims Markets

Individuals who have the option of trading contingent claims on the output of the industry in question may insure themselves by selling state-2 claims and purchasing state-1 claims. Let q be the price ratio of these two securities, i.e.,

---

[4] A similar construction appears in Sargent [197, ch.8]. More general treatments are in Baily [1974], Azariadis [1975], Baily [1977], Holmstrom [1979].

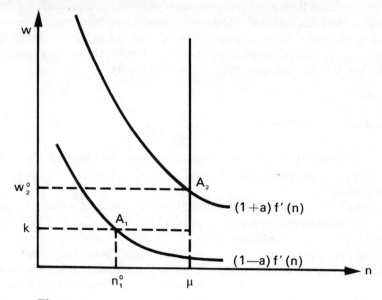

Figure 1

the state-2 price of a claim entitling the bearer to one unit of output in state-1; non-negative costs of administration, state verification, etc., require

(3) $q \geqslant 1$.

The typical worker decides to hold as many units of claims on state-1 output as will maximize over x his expected utility

(4) $V(x,q) = (1/2)[u(w_2^0 - qx) + u(k + x)]$

The solution

(5a) $x^* = \theta(q)$

is a decreasing function of q in the interval $1 \leqslant q \leqslant q^*$, where

(5b) $q^* = u'(k)/u'(w_2^0)$

is the slope of the indifference curve of V through the point $(c_1 = k, c_2 = w_2^0)$. Furthermore, $q = q^*$ implies $x^* = 0$, i.e., no coverage, and $q = 1$ implies $x^* = (1/2)\,(w_2^0 + k)$, i.e., full coverage; these cases correspond to points N and F, respectively on Figure 2. Pursuing the insurance analogy a bit further, $w_2^0 - k$ is the loss to workers, q is the premium and $1 + q$ the indemnity. When $q = 1$, the market for contingent claims supports a Pareto-optimal allocation of resources.

224

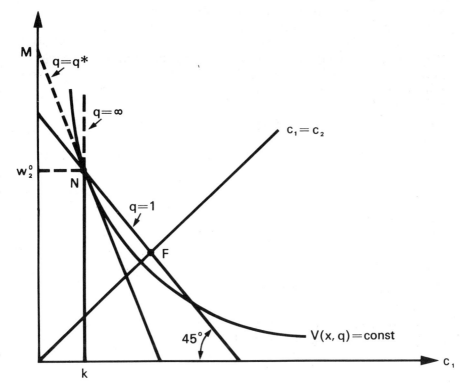

Figure 2

However, the ability of wage earners to trade contingent claims on output is limited by considerations discussed at some length in the previous section. What bears repeating here is that claims on output are ultimately claims on the services of productive factors; courts of law will be less inclined to enforce such claims on human capital then on physical or financial capital. Entrepreneurs may therefore act in part as insurance brokers, tacitly purchasing the claims of workers and issuing others to the general public.

(b) *Wage Stickiness*[5]

We shall consider labour contracts $\delta = (w_1, w_2, \rho)$ specifying the wage paid to a typical worker in each state of nature and the probability ρ of being employed in state 1. The contract is enforceable and all workers are employed in state 2. We assume temporarily that those not working in state 1 are entitled to no direct compensation from their employer but may receive an indemnity from an economy-wide fund set up by the government or all employees acting in unison.

Contracts are combination production plans and insurance policies and must reconcile the requirements of both. A good production plan, for instance,

[5] See also Gordon [1974], Shavell [1976].

requires more workers in state 2 than in state 1 while an ideal insurance policy would guarantee labour income. i.e., eliminate the probability of unemployment and stabilize the wage-rate. 'Good' labour contracts compromise by allowing some unemployment and stabilizing the earnings of employed workers. To see this, suppose the firm offers the contract δ to m workers, employing ρm in state 1 and m in state 2. Expected utility is

(6a) $\qquad V(\delta) = (1/2) [\rho u(w_1) + (1 - \rho)u(k) + u(w_2)]$

for each labourer and

(6b) $\qquad \Pi(\delta, m) = (1/2) (\pi_1 + \pi_2)$

for each entrepreneur. The numbers π_1 and π_2 are profits in each state of nature, viz.

(7a) $\qquad \pi_1 = (1 - a)f(\rho m) - w_1 \rho m$

(7b) $\qquad \pi_2 = (1 + a)f(m) - w_2 m$

In the indifference diagram of Figure 3, tangencies between iso-profit and iso-utility lines occur for any $\rho \in (0,1)$ when

(8) $\qquad w_1 = w_2$

In other words, given $\rho > 0$, any contract off the 45° ray is inferior to some contract on that ray. The superiority of fixed over variable wage contracts is a special case of a well-known result of Borch [1962] and Arrow [1971] according to which the efficient sharing of risk requires that the marginal rates of substitution between consumption in any two states be equal for both parties. If $v(\cdot)$ summarizes the entrepreneur's attitude toward risk, the Arrow-Borch condition is

(9) $\qquad u'(w_2)/u'(w_1) = v'(\pi_2)/v'(\pi_1)$

and simplifies to (8) when v is linear.

Although equation (9) may be consistent with a considerable amount of wage stickiness, that is, with a ratio w_2/w_1 closer to unity than to $(1 + a)(1 - a)$, it makes clear that strict invariance of wages to the state of nature is *not* an essential element in the theory of labour contracts.[6] The essence of these contracts is rather that wages differ from the marginal product of labour by an insurance indemnity in adverse states of nature and by a premium in favourable states.

---

[6] In Japan, for instance, wages are partly paid in the form of a biannual, fluctuating bonus; see Hashimoto [1979].

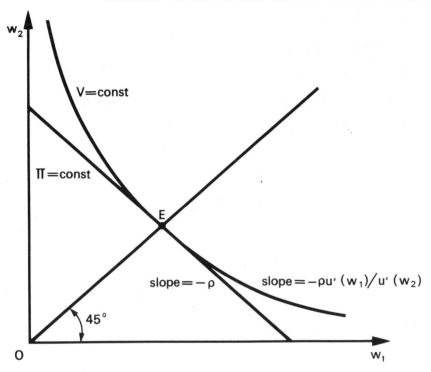

Figure 3

4. Unemployment

(a) *Temporary Layoffs*[7]

To examine whether any unemployment will occur in state 1 we begin with a general fixed-wage contract $\Delta = (w,\rho)$ which commits the firm to pay a wage w to employed persons in each state and nothing to unemployed workers. A fraction $1 - \rho$ of the labour force m which agrees to work on these terms is laid off in state 1 and, since workers are identical, $1 - \rho$ is also the probability that each of them will be unemployed in state 1. Continuing as before, we write

$$(10a) \qquad V(\Delta) = (1/2)\,[u(w) + \rho u(w) + (1 - \rho)u(k)]$$

for expected utility and

$$(10b) \qquad \Pi(\Delta,m) = (1/2)\,[(1 + a)f(m) + (1 - a)f(\rho m) - wm(1 + \rho)]$$

for expected profit.

The best full-employment contract is clearly $\Delta_f = (f'(\mu),1)$ because at $w = f'(\mu)$ the labour force size which maximizes $\Pi(\Delta,m)$ also equals the inelastic

---

[7] In addition to the references in fn. 4, cf. [Feldstein [1974], Mortensen [1978]].

supply, μ, of labourers per firm. Noting that

(11a) $\qquad V(\Delta_f) = u(f'(\mu)) \equiv V_f$

(11b) $\qquad \Pi(\Delta_f,\mu) = f(\mu) - \mu f'(\mu) \equiv \Pi_f$

we draw in Figure 4 two indifference loci for contracts which workmen and entrepreneurs, respectively, find as good as the best full-employment contract Δ_f.

The loci in this figure have slopes

(12a) $\qquad \left(\dfrac{dw}{d\rho}\right)_{V=V_f} = - \dfrac{u(w) - u(k)}{(1 + \rho)u'(w)}$

(12b) $\qquad \left(\dfrac{dw}{d\rho}\right)_{\Pi=\Pi_f} = \dfrac{1}{1 + \rho}\,[(1 - a)f'(\rho\mu) - w]$

where $u(k)$ is value of leisure. Along $V = V_f$, the wage w is decreasing, convex in ρ; the same property holds along $\Pi = \Pi_f$ for values of ρ 'close enough' to 1 to satisfy

(13) $\qquad (1 - a)f'(\rho\mu) < f'(\mu)$ $\qquad\qquad \div$

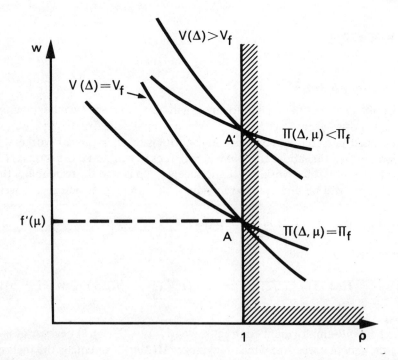

(a) **Figure 4**

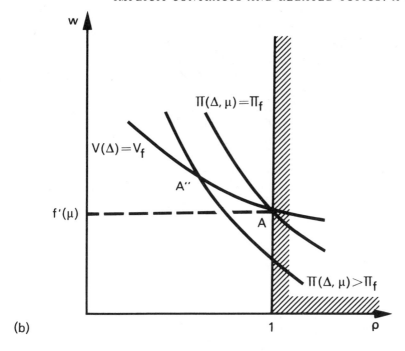

(b)

The contract Δ_f corresponds to point A in either panel. As one moves in a NE direction, the wage rate increases for fixed employment, $\Pi(\Delta,\mu)$ declines and $V(\Delta)$ rises.

Full employment contracts are optimal in panel (a): Given μ and $V(\Delta) = V_f$, there is no feasible $\rho \in [0,1]$, i.e., no feasible contract $\Delta = (w,\rho)$, such that $\Pi(\Delta,\mu) \geqslant \Pi_f$. This argument breaks down in panel (b) where point A'' corresponds to $\rho < 1$ and clearly dominates A. What distinguishes this panel from the previous one is that the iso-profit locus $\Pi = \Pi_f$ is steeper at A than the iso-utility locus $V = V_f$, i.e.,

$$(14) \qquad a > \frac{u(w_f) - u(k)}{w_f u'(w_f)}$$

where the full-employment wage, w_f, equals $f'(\mu)$. Equivalently, we may write

$$(15a) \qquad (1 - a)f'(\mu) < w_f - \phi(w_f,k)$$

where

$$(15b) \qquad \phi(w_f,k) = (u(w_f) - u(k))/u'(w_f) \geqslant w_f - k$$

is the *marginal risk premium* needed to compensate workers for suffering an infinitessimally small probability of unemployment.

When the sum of the risk premium ϕ plus the value of the marginal product of fully-employed labour in state 1 falls short of the full-employment wage, everyone is better off *on average*, that is, before the state of nature becomes public knowledge, if fewer than μ persons work in state 1. This reduction in employment is achieved by temporary layoffs rather than wage cuts; certain workers (selected randomly in this section, more realistically in the richer models of subsequent sections) are simply told to go home for a while and collect unemployment compensation or consume leisure.

As a number of authors (Gordon [1976], Feldstein [1974], Baily [1977], Mortensen [1978]) have pointed out, attitude toward risk plays a crucial role in this argument even though it is neither necessary nor sufficient for layoff unemployment. Aversion to risk is not necessary, for layoffs will occur in any model in which wages are insufficiently flexible because of specific human capital, costs of adjusting wages, or plain old money illusion. It is not sufficient either when hours of work are variable, for then one needs to rule out extensive work sharing, i.e., the possibility that any variation in the derived demand for labour services will be accomodated without layoffs by appropriately changing the number of hours each person works. This will not happen (Azariadis [1975], Feldstein [1974], Mortensen [1978]) if persons and hours are imperfect substitutes in production or preferences suffer from such nonconvexities as set-up costs of going to work.

Nevertheless, risk aversion is a very sensible assumption in economies with incompletely developed markets for contingent claims; to drop it would be logically equivalent to the belief that the effect of market incompleteness on resource allocation is empirically negligible.

(b) *The Nature of Unemployment*[8]

Is the layoff unemployment in (15a) involuntary in the sense of Keynes [1936, ch. 2]? Note that, given state 1, unemployment is *ex post* involuntary; individuals would rather work at a wage w_f than collect the lower sum k which represents the value of non-market activity, i.e., of leisure plus unemployment insurance. On the other hand, the contract itself is freely arrived at, and any unemployment resulting from it is voluntary *ex ante*.

Furthermore, to preserve some semblance of involuntary unemployment, even in the ex-post sense, one needs to appeal to employer risk aversion or some capital market imperfection (e.g., transaction costs) which would prevent firms from offering workers an actuarially fair insurance policy. Imagine, for instance, that workers' evaluate consumption-leisure bundles by the additive utility function

(16a) $\qquad v(c,1) = u(c) + g(1);$

leisure is, as before, indivisible with $g(0) = 0, g(1) = K$; the reservation wage, k, at zero unemployment compensation is still too great to justify full employment in the spot market when $s = 1-a$. In other words, we set

(16b) $\qquad u(w_f) > K = u(k) > u[(1-a)w_f]$

---

[8] See also Polemarchakis and Weiss [1978].

where $w_f = f'(\mu)$.

Suppose now that the firm could offer direct unemployment compensation, z, to its labour force. The contract $\Delta = (w_1w_2,p,z)$ consists now of the wages in the two rates of nature, the probability p of being unemployed in state 1, and the compensation due temporary job losers. One easily shows that an equilibrium contract has the following properties:
   (i) wage is independent of the state of nature, i.e.,

(17a) $w_1 = w_2 = w$

   (ii) workers' welfare is independent of employment status. In particular, the level of unemployment compensation satisfies

(17b) $u(w) = u(z) + K$

   (iii) employment $\bar{n}$ in state 1 is *either* full (i.e., $\bar{n} = \mu$) *or* satisfies the marginal conditions

(17c) $(1-a)f'(\bar{n}) = w - z$

(17d) $(1+a)f'(\mu) = w + z$

In either case, workers are insured at actually fair terms; wage equals the expected marginal product of labour and all unemployment is purely voluntary.

Whatever the ultimate 'nature' of layoff unemployment, it does not generally occur under the same conditions or to the same extent as the purely voluntary unemployment of the spot market depicted in Figure 1 because the insurance aspect of the contract interferes with, and distorts, the hiring decision. The distortion is easiest to perceive if we interpret k strictly as the value of leisure: Then k is the marginal social cost of leisure while the private cost is again k (the state-1 wage rate) in the spot market but less than k, $w_f - \phi(w_f k)$ to be exact, in the market for contracts.

One expects too low a private cost of leisure to result in a socially excessive volume of employment, and this is generally true in the model of this section. If, for instance,

(18a) $w_f - \phi(w_f) \leqslant (1-a)f'(\mu) < k,$

the equilibrium contract $\Delta_f = (f'(\mu),1)$ keeps the labour force fully employed even though it is socially optimal to have $\mu - n_1^0$ persons unemployed in state 1, where

(18b) $(1-a)f'(n_1^0) = k$

The same phenomenon takes place when

(18c) $\qquad (1-a)f'(\mu) < w_f - \phi(w_f).$

In that case the equilibrium contract $\Delta^* = (w^*, \rho^*)$ satisfies (see the Appendix for details):

(19a) $\qquad (1 - a)f'(\rho^*\mu) = w^* - \phi(w^*, k) < k$

(19b) $\qquad (1 + a)f'(\mu) = w^* + \rho^*\phi(w^*, k)$

Workers are paid their marginal product plus the premium ϕ when $s = 1 - a$, and their marginal product minus an indemnity $\rho^*\phi$ when $s = 1 + a$. A comparison of eq. (18b) with (19a) reveals that, in state 1, the contract Δ^* calls for a volume of employment in excess of n_1^0, that is, *stabilizes employment in addition to wages.*

An interesting property of the equilibrium contract is that it will not involve any layoffs if the underlying spot market in Section 3 maintains full employment [Bryant [1978]]. Formally, $k \geq w_f - \phi(w_f, k)$ by (15b); hence $(1 - a)f'(\mu) > k \ (\Rightarrow) \ (1 - a)f'(\mu) > w_f - \phi(w_f, k)$.

This property does not appear very robust. If, for instance, the spot market did maintain full employment while the real wage fluctuated, Pareto improvements could conceivably result from a contract in which the real wage was stabilized at the cost of some unemployment. An example of this kind is the following: Suppose the supply of workers to the industry is infinitely elastic, rather than inelastic, the wage being $w_1 > k$ if $s = 1 - a, w_2 = w_1(1 + a)/(1 - a)$ if $s = 1 + a$. Let w_F be the certainty equivalent of this wage stream, i.e.,

(19c) $\qquad 2u(w_F) = u(w_1) + u(w_2)$

and define m_F, m_0 from

(19d,e) $\qquad w_F = f'(m_F) \ w_1 = (1 - a)f'(m_0)$

Spot employment will clearly be m_0 in each state of nature, and the outcome of the spot market is equivalent to a full-employment contract $\Delta_F = (w_F, 1, m_0)$ with deterministic wage w_F. Since $\phi(w, k) \leq w - k \leq w$, it follows that for every $w_1 > k > 0$, there exists some $a^*\epsilon(0,1)$ such that

(19f) $\qquad a^*w_F = \phi(w_F, k)$

where w_F is given by eq. (19c). Then inequality (14) says that for each $a\epsilon[a^*, 1]$, the equilibrium contract requires layoffs in state 1 even though industry employment would be absolutely constant under the spot arrangement.

(c) *Unemployment Insurance*

The system of compensating job losers now in use in the United States is said to be *partly experience-rated*: A firm's contributions to the system are loosely related to past employment policies but do not generally equal the benefits paid the firm's former employees. According to Feldstein [1974, 1975] and others, this practice in effect subsidizes layoffs, at the expense of such other alternatives as inventory accumulation or cuts in product prices, and increases unemployment unduly during cyclical downturns. The remedy suggested in this argument is a more nearly full experience-rated system in which each firm contributes to unemployment insurance the expected (actuarially fair) value of the benefits collected by its employees.

To highlight these issues, denote by k the value of leisure and by z the exogeneous insurance benefit to each unemployed worker, so that $k + z$ is the value of being on temporary layoff. It will be instructive to compare the performance of an industry with zero experience rating to one with full experience rating. In the former case, the firm's contribution to unemployment insurance is a fixed sum which is not affected by the provisions of the ruling contract: in the latter, it covers the actuarial value, $(1/2)mz(1 - \rho)$, of the benefits claimed by the firm's own employees.

Following (15a), the necessary and sufficient condition for layoffs is

$$(20a) \qquad (1 - a)f'(\mu) < w_f - \phi(w_f, k + z)$$

with zero experience rating, and

$$(20b) \qquad (1 - a)f'(\mu) < w_f - z - \phi(w_f, k + z)$$

with full experience rating. With either practice, an increase in the level of benefits or in the number a (i.e., a decline in state-1 demand) discourages employment in state 1 but the disincentive effect is stronger with no experience rating. If (20a) holds, the employment effect of z is shown in Figure 5 which graphs the solution to eqs. (19a) and (19b), with $k + z$ replacing k on the RHS of (19a).

Specifically, if layoffs are called for, the equilibrium contract satisfies

$$(21a) \qquad (1 - a)f'(\rho\mu) = w - \phi(w, z + k)$$

$$(21b) \qquad (1 - a)\rho f'(\rho\mu) + (1 + a)f'(\mu) = w(1 + \rho)$$

in the unrated system of unemployment insurance, and

$$(22a) \qquad (1 - a)f'(\rho\mu) = W - z - \phi(w, z + k)$$

$$(22b) \qquad (1 - a)\rho f'(\rho\mu) + (1 + a)f'(\mu) = w(1 + \rho) + z(1 - \rho)$$

in the fully rated one. The first equations in each pair set to zero the profit contribution of the marginal worker employed in state 1; the last equations in each pair equate expected profit and expected cost from the marginal member of the labour force.

If $(w = w_N(z,a), \rho = \rho_N(z,a))$ solve (21a,b) and $(w = w_F(z,a), \rho = \rho_F(z,a))$

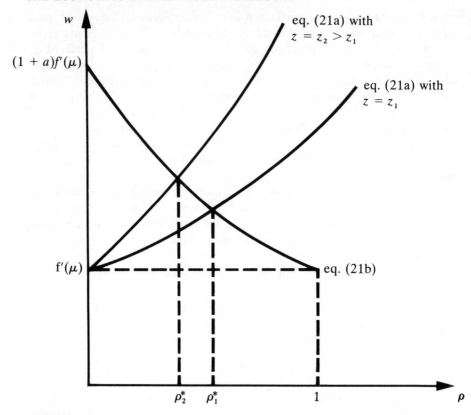

Figure 5

solve (22a,b), then it may be shown (see the Appendix) that, for all $z \geq 0$ and small enough a,

(23a) $\qquad \rho_N(z,a) < \rho_F(z,a)$

(23b) $\qquad w_N(z,a) > w_F(z,a)$

All else being equal, *fewer layoffs will occur in state 1 when firms' unemployment insurance payments match closely their employees benefit claims.*

    The normative implications of this finding are unclear: To justify converting from the current method of financing unemployment compensation to one which approximates actuarially fair insurance, one clearly needs to demonstrate that present practices result in an excessive rate of layoff unemployment in times of low demand. This is clearly not the case in the model we are considering here; in fact just the opposite is true. We saw in Section 4(a) that risk sharing may lower the private cost of leisure below its social cost, and support *too large* a volume of employment in state 1 relative to the optimum n_1^0.

    The marginal private cost of leisure is reduced further, and the distortion becomes even greater, when unemployment insurance payments are fully

234

experience-rated. Note, for instance, that for $z < w - k$ (so that workers prefer working to being laid off) and every strictly concave $u(\cdot)$,

$$\phi(w,z + k) = (u(w) - u(z + k))/u'(w) > w - (z + k)$$

which implies

(24) $\qquad w - z - \phi(w,z + k) < k$

Together with equs. (2b) and (22a), this yields

(25) $\qquad (1 - a)f'(\rho_F \mu) < k = (1 - a)f'(n_1^0)$

Hence, employment under the fully rated system will exceed the volume n_1^0 irrespectively of the level at which the (exogenous to the industry) insurance indemnity is set.

However, from equations (21a) and (21b) one shows fairly easily that there exists a value of z, say z^0, such that

(26a) $\qquad 0 < z^0 < w_N(z^0,a) - k$

(26b) $\qquad w_N(z^0,a) = [n_i^0 k + \mu(1 + a)f'(\mu)]/(n_1^0 + \mu)$

(26c) $\qquad \mu \rho_N(z^0,a) = n_1^0$

To sum up: In economies wish completely homogeneous, risk-averse labour, employment will be too large when insurance premia are fully experience-rated no matter what the level of benefits. For the unrated system, on the other hand, there exists a level of unemployment insurance indemnity which supports the socially optimal volume of employment.

5. Heterogeneous Labour

In this section we examine three durable cyclical regularities: the higher incidence of unemployment in unskilled trades than in skilled ones; the apparent failure of the real wage rate to move countercyclically as diminishing returns to labour would seem to require; and the apparent countercyclical tendency of the unskilled-to-skilled ratio. The exposition draws heavily on Azariadis [1975].

(a) Preferential Layoffs

Skilled workers are both more productive and better remunerated than common labourers. Why should they benefit from seniority rules and receive preferential protection from layoffs? Oi [1962] stresses that the term 'skill' represents investments in specific human capital over a large period of time; the firm is understandably reluctant to jeopardize these by even temporary layoffs. For Grossman [1977, 1978], on the other hand, seniority or length of service are indicators of 'reliability,' a personal trait as desirable as pure technical skill. Reliable workers are valuable because they keep down hiring and training costs: They tend to abide by their contract and stay on the job even though better opportunities (e.g. in periods of high demand) may temporarily beckon elsewhere.

An extension of the model in Section 3 will explain preferential layoffs in a slightly different manner. Using the same symbols as before with superscripts s and u to denote skilled and common labourers respectively, we assume that one of the former is technically equivalent to $\gamma > 1$ of the latter, and that all workers have the same preferences and value of leisure. Then, the marginal private cost of fully employed labour is *higher* and the corresponding product *lower* for unskilled workers, i.e.,

(27a) $w_f^s = \gamma w_f^u = \gamma f'(\mu^u + \gamma \mu^s)$

($\Rightarrow$)

(27b) $w_f^s > w_f^u$

($\Rightarrow$)

(27c) $w_f^s - \phi(w_f^s, k) < w_f^u - \phi(w_f^u, k)$

The meaning of (27c) is that if unskilled labourers differed from skilled workers in nothing but the stock of human capital, then the latter would have a smaller private cost at the margin for they would demand so large an indemnity for bearing unemployment risk as to offset the higher level of their wages.

Therefore, we cannot have an equilibrium with layoffs for skilled workers ($\rho^s < 1$) and full employment for common labourers, for then (15a) would require a contradiction:

(28a) $(1 - a)f'(\mu^u + \gamma \mu^s) \geq w_f^u - \phi(w_f^u, k)$

(28b) $\gamma(1 - a)f'(\mu^u + \gamma \mu^s) < w_f^s - \phi(w_f^s, k)$

In fact a stronger result obtains: *If some of the skilled labour force are laid off in state 1 it must be the case that all of the unskilled labour force is similarly unemployed.*[9] To show this, suppose to the contrary that $0 < \rho^s < 1$ and $0 < \rho^u < 1$. Then ρ^s and ρ^u satisfy the analogue to eq. (21a), i.e.,

(29a) $(1 - a)f'(\rho^u \mu^u + \gamma \rho^s \mu^s) = w^u - \phi(w^u, k)$

(29b) $\gamma(1 - a)f'(\rho^u \mu^u + \gamma \rho^s \mu^s) = w^s - \phi(w^s, k)$

---

[9] Seniority rights in this case are based on differences in skill rather than in length of service with a given firm. Holmstrom [1979] shows in a multiperiod model that length of service helps determine how unemployment will be distributed within a firm: veteran employees get preferential layoff treatment simply because they were the first to join.

This is plainly a contradiction, since eq. (29a) has a smaller LHS and a bigger RHS than eq. (29b).

(b) Cyclical Wage Movements

Older empirical studies failed to detect any significant countercyclical movement in aggregate real compensation per man-hour [Dunlop [1938], Tarshis [1939], Kuh [1966], Bodkin and Klein [1969]], in apparent contradiction of the law of diminishing marginal returns of labour. Explanations of this paradox labour hoarding [Reder [1964]], or cyclical changes in capacity utilization [Lucas [1970]] which tend to shift the demand schedule for labour.

It seems preferable to have empirical investigations of this sort at a less aggregated level [Raisian [1980]]. Aggregate studies fail to capture changes in the composition of output or of the labour force which are by themselves sufficient to induce substantial cyclical movement in economy-wide wages even if the business cycle does not affect the real wage of *any* skill grade in *any* industry.

Consider, for instance, a fictitious economy with homogeneous labour in which all industries experience little cyclical fluctuation except one, the quad industry, that is thoroughly buffeted by the business cycle. If labour mobility is good across industries, quad workers will suffer more layoffs and enjoy a wage higher than elsewhere when employed. The economy-average wage will vary procyclically.

Another phenomenon accounted for naturally by implicit labour contracts is the behaviour of occupational wage differentials (i.e., of the unskilled-to-skilled wage ratio). These have shown a definite countercyclical tendency, widening in contractions and narrowing in booms, both in the US [Bell[1951]] and in the UK [Knowles and Robertson [1961]].

To see why, suppose that we drop the postulate of labour homogeneity in the economy just described and admit two skill grades. For simplicity, assume that the cycle is of such amplitude that there is no unemployment outside the quad industry, while unemployment in the quad industry falls solely on common labourers. These workers are thus the only group in the economy to suffer layoffs; in return they receive a wage above that of common workers outside the quad industry and below that of skilled workers—in the quad industry or out. As the cycle unfolds then, the economy-wide wage average for craftsmen remains unaltered, the one for labourers changes procyclically, and occupational wage differentials follow a countercyclical pattern.

6. Asymmetric Information

The state space over which labour contracts are defined may in principle include all random variables which bear on labour supply and product demand. Observed contracts, on the other hand, turn out to depend on a small number of disturbances, readily (i.e., cheaply) observable by both parties. Richer contingency spaces require, in addition, the maintenance of a complex administrative apparatus to monitor compliance to the terms of the contract [Wachter and Williamson [1978]].

What form the labour contract takes is thus influenced by the availability of information and the cost of transacting; we deal with the first of these factors in this section and with the second one in Section 7. For instance, unless the actual state of nature is (costlessly) observed by both parties, it cannot belong in the contingency space of the contract and must be replaced by other variables (e.g., employment, output) more accessible to both parties.

When information is severely asymmetric, the making of productive decisions may well devolve upon the partner with superior knowledge while the other partner is compensated by a mutually acceptable sum or fee which may depend only on variables observed by both parties. Following Ross [1973], the more informed partner is an *agent* acting on behalf of a less informed *principal*.

Although one can easily conceive of situations involving ability levels [Spence [1973], Riley [1975]] or variable amounts of effort [Stiglitz [1973], Mirrlees [1976]] in which workers are better informed, superior knowledge is possessed by entrepreneurs in what follows here: They know the actual state of nature whereas workers are able to observe only wages in model (a), wages and employment in model (b). We assume that everyone knows the technology of production in either case.

(a) The Null Contingency Space

If workers are unable to observe the state of nature either directly or indirectly (e.g., by computing the firm's state-dependent employment rule and comparing with actual employment), labour contracts must be entirely free of contingencies. Wages will be fixed and employment will be either fixed or left entirely to the discretion of the firm. The former case will result in a full-employment contract Δ_f similar to the one of section 4.

Discretionary-employment contracts consist only of a fixed wage $\Delta_w = (w,.)$ with employment set *ex post* to maximize profit in each state. Equilibrium employment is then n_1 in state 1 and m in state 2, where

(30) $$w = (1 + a)f'(m) = (1 - a)f'(n_1)$$

Whether Δ_f or Δ_w emerges as an institutional regularity in cases of severe informational asymmetry remains to be seen. These contracts are not easily comparable: Δ_f does a better job of allocating risk but overemploys labour in state 1 while Δ_w appears to be a better production plan. Assuming the supply of labour to the industry is perfectly elastic at an expected utility level of $\bar{u}$, it is natural to conjecture that Δ_f will dominate when real risks are small, Δ_w will dominate when real risks are large and/or workers are only slightly risk-averse. Two examples consistent with this conjecture follow immediately.

Example 1: Define w_f, m_f from

(31a,b) $$u(w_f) = \bar{u}, \qquad w_f = f'(m_f)$$

and suppose $a < a^*$, where a^* is given by

(32) $a^* w_f = \phi(w_f, k)$

Then we know the full-employment contract $\Delta_f = (w_f, 1)$ dominates every other contract including Δ_w.

Example 2: Suppose $a = 1, u(w) = w$ for all w. Expected profit and utility from Δ_f are

(33a) $V(\Delta_f) = w_f = \bar{u}$

(33b) $\Pi(\Delta_f) = F(m_f) \equiv f(m_f) - m_f f'(m_f)$

For the discretionary employment contract Δ_w we have, by eq. (30), $n = 0, w = 2f'(m)$, expected utility

(34a) $V(\Delta_w) = \frac{1}{2}(w + k)$

and expected profit

(34b) $\Pi(\Delta_w) = F(m)$

Setting $V(\Delta_w) = \bar{u}$, one obtains $\langle w + k = 2w_f \rangle\ (\Rightarrow)\ \langle 2f'(m) + k = 2f'(m_f) \rangle\ (\Rightarrow)$ $\langle f'(m_f) > f'(m) \rangle\ (\Rightarrow)\ \langle m_f < m \rangle\ (\Rightarrow)\ \langle\ \Pi(\Delta_w) > \Pi(\Delta_f) \rangle$ as $F(\cdot)$ is easily shown to be an increasing function. Hence Δ_w is Pareto-superior to Δ_f.

(b) *Employment-Contingent Contracts*

The principal-agent relation is of special interest when both parties know the payoff from their acts or some quantity which influences that payoff. In such cases, it generally makes sense to share risks by making payments contingent on the observable quantity. Phelps [1977], Calvo and Phelps [1977], and Hall and Lillien [1978] have looked at employment-contingent contracts of the form $\Delta_e = (h(u), \cdot)$ in which wage is a pre-determined function, $w = h(n)$, of employment, and actual employment is left at the discretion of the firm. Suppose entrepreneurs' attitude towards risk is given by the utility-of-profit function $v(\Pi)$, with $v' > 0$ and $v'' \le 0$.

The function h is chosen to allocate risk efficiently and motivate the agent to set a mutually 'acceptable' volume of employment. Given h, employment is picked by the firm with full knowledge of state s, i.e., by solving $sf'(n) = H'(n)$, where the function $H(n) = nh(n)$ is assumed convex, increasing. Solving for n one obtains

(35) $n = n^*(s, h)$

which implies expected utility

(36a) $V(h) = Ev\{sf[n^*(s,h)] - hn^*(s,h)\}$

239

for the entrepreneur, and

$$(36b) \qquad U(h) = E\{\frac{n^*(s,h)}{m}u(h) + (1 - \frac{n^*(s,h)}{m})u(k)\}$$

for each worker.

Proceeding as in Sections 3 and 4, one chooses that h which maximizes $V(h)$ s.t. $U(h) \geq \bar{u}$; equilibrium in the labour market fixes $\bar{u}$.

Although the tools of agency theory [Harris and Raviv [1978], S. Shavell [1976]] should be relevant for this problem, no general solution of it is available at the moment. Yet, that theory suggests that, with risk-neutral employers, *the function h must be a constant*. To see why, we return to the basic two-state model and let employment be n_0 if $s = 1 - a$, m_0 if $s = 1 + a$. Then

$$(37a) \qquad H'(n_0) = (1-a)f'(n_0)$$

$$(37b) \qquad H'(m_0) = (1+a)f'(m_0)$$

Expected payoffs under the function h are now

$$(38a) \qquad V(h) = \frac{1}{2}[(1 + a)f(m_0) + (1 - a)f(n_0) - H(m_0) - H(n_0)]$$

$$(38b) \qquad U(h) = \frac{1}{2}\{u[h(m_0)] + \frac{n_0}{m_0} u[h(n_0)] + (1 - \frac{n_0}{m_0})u(k)\}$$

Suppose now we replace h with a function $\gamma = h$ for all n, except

$$(39a) \qquad \gamma(n_0) = h(n_0) + \epsilon/n_0$$

$$(39b) \qquad \gamma(m_0) = h(m_0) - \epsilon/m_0$$

for some constant ϵ. Clearly, setting $w = \gamma(n)$ will leave employment and expected profit unchanged. The expected payoff to workers becomes

$$(40) \qquad U(Y) = \frac{1}{2}\{u[h(m_0) - \epsilon/m_0] + \frac{n_0}{m_0}u[h(n_0 + \epsilon/n_0] + (1 - \frac{n_0}{m_0})u(k)\}$$

The difference

$$(41) \qquad T \equiv 2[U(Y) - U(h)] = u[h(m_0) - \epsilon/m_0] - u[h(m_0)]$$
$$+ (n_0/m_0)\{u[h(n_0) + \epsilon/n_0] - u[h(n_0)]\}$$

$$> -(\epsilon/m_0)u'[h(m_0) - \epsilon/m_0] + (n_0/m_0)(\epsilon/n_0)u'[h(n_0) + \epsilon/n_0]$$

$$= (\epsilon/m_0)\{u'[h(n_0) + \epsilon/n_0] - u'[h(m_0) - \epsilon/m_0]\}$$

can always be made positive by appropriate choice of ϵ if $h(n_0) \neq h(m_0)$. In particular, if $h(n_0) < h(m_0)$, there exists an $\epsilon > 0$ small enough such that $\gamma(n_0) < \gamma(m_0)$ and $T > 0$; if, on the other hand, $h(n_0) > h(m_0)$, there exists an $\epsilon < 0$ small enough in absolute value such that $\gamma(n_0) > \gamma(m_0)$ and $T > 0$. Hence every undominated contract satisfies $h(n_0) = h(m_0)$.

7. Macroeconomics and fix-wage contracts

In advanced, private ownership economies it is fairly easy to observe product prices and other random variables (e.g., money supply) which are useful descriptions of the 'state of nature' relevant for allocative decisions. Still, labour contracts frequently pre-determine *money* wages for some period of time[10] independently of the state of nature which prevails after agreement is reached. Nominal rigidities of this type motivate in large part contemporary Keynesian macroeconomics, being a key element in an extensive disequilibrium literature [Clower[1965], Barro and Grossman [1971], Benassy [1975], Drèze [1975], Hahn [1978]] and in descriptive indexation theory as well.

There is at present no coherent theoretical account for the emergence of fix-wage contracts as an exchange alternative, or a supplement, to spot markets and state-dependent contracts. Yet some explanation of the arrangements which govern the trading of commodities and labour services is surely of vital importance.

We know, for instance, that real effects from changes in aggregate demand will depend very much on how responsive money wages are to aggregate variables. Conversely, the nature of stabilization policies pursued by the authorities will have some influence on wage responsiveness and, more generally, on the exchange arrangements individuals choose: were policy to become highly volatile, for example, workers would likely become somewhat dissatisfied with fixed money wages.

One useful way to think of fix wage contracts is to exploit their analytic similarity to ordinary forward contracts: both involve the exchange of a given sum of money now in return for a claim on a given amount of a good (or money, if a bond is traded) to be delivered *unconditionally* at a given date in the future. The key advantage of forward claims is that they expand the opportunities to share risks available in a regime of spot markets at a transaction cost which is smaller than that of holding a portfolio of contingent claims. A series of examples, all drawn from a simple partial equilibrium model, will illustrate these issues.[11]

---

[10] Cost-of-living wage adjustments will remind the reader that this practice in not universal.
[11] Townsend [1978] studies the risk-bearing function of future claims in a general equilibrium framework.

(a) *A Simple Exchange Model*

Consider a hypothetical individual who consumes a single commodity, 'bread', is endowed with money income m and a cardinal utility function $u(\cdot)$ which exhibits risk aversion. There are N equiprobable states of nature $(s_1, s_2, \ldots s_N)$ in which this consumer's money income is $(m_1, m_2, \ldots m_N)$ and the spot price of bread is $(p_1, \ldots, p_N)$. Lurking in the background are risk-neutral 'speculators' whose function it is to exploit all opportunities yielding a positive expected profit. Selling insurance to risk-averse individuals is clearly one such activity which can be accomplished by arbitraging between spot bread on the one hand and claims on bread on the other.

We assume there are $N + 1$ types of claims sold before the state of nature is drawn: one has price π and delivers unconditionally a unit of bread; the remaining ones have prices $(q_1, q_2, \ldots, q_N)$ and deliver a unit of bread only in state $(1, 2, \ldots N)$ respectively. A speculator who sells z fix-price claims and $(z_1, z_2, \ldots, z_N)$ contingent claims receives $\pi z + (q_1 z_1 + q_2 z_2 + \ldots + q_N z_N)$ units of money with probability one and delivers $z + z_i$ units of bread in state i. If transaction costs are zero, his expected profit expressed in terms of bread is

$$(42) \qquad \Pi = \frac{1}{N} \sum_{i=1}^{N} \left[\frac{1}{p_i}(\pi z + \sum_{j=1}^{N} q_j z_j) - z - z_i \right]$$

$$= \frac{1}{N} \sum_{i=1}^{N} z_i (q_i \sum_{j=1}^{N} P_j^{-1} - 1) + \frac{1}{N} z(\pi \sum_{j=1}^{N} P_j^{-1} - N)$$

Defining q from

$$(43) \qquad q^{-1} = \sum_{j=1}^{N} P_j^{-1},$$

the arbitrage condition $\Pi = 0$ for all $(z, z_1, z_2, \ldots, z_N)$ requires that

$$(44) \qquad \pi = N_q; \ q_i = q \text{ for all } i$$

The consumer will hold the claims portfolio $(w^*, w_1^*, w_2^*, \ldots, w_N^*)$ which maximizes

$$(45) \qquad c_i = w + w_i + (i/p_i)(m_i - \pi w - q \sum_{j=1}^{N} w_j) \geqslant 0, \text{ all } i$$

Note that we do not directly impose any restrictions in the w's other than the preceding inequality which amounts to a solvency requirement; consumers as well as speculators may sell 'bread' short.

The choice of claims will affect the riskiness of consumption but not its mean, $\bar{c}$; in fact from (43)-(45) one shows readily that

$$(46) \qquad \bar{c} = \frac{1}{N} \sum_{i=1}^{N} c_i = \frac{1}{N} \sum_{i=1}^{N} (m_i/p_i)$$

A first-best optimum portfolio for the consumer removes all risk, that is, satisfies

$$(47) \qquad c_i^* = \bar{c} \quad i = 1,2, \ldots ,N$$

This optimum is achieved with *any* $N = 1$ contingent claims: picking arbitrarily $w_1^* = 0$, eq. (47) holds if we set

$$(48) \qquad w_i^* = \bar{c}(1 - p_1/p_i) + (1/p_i)(m_1 - m_i), \quad i = 2,3, \ldots ,N$$

(b) *Risk Sharing with Fix-Price Claims*

For $N = 2$, one attains the preceding optimum for any values of m and by holding fix-price claims only. To see this, note that the portfolio $w_1^* = w_2^* = 0$, and

$$(49) \qquad w^* = \frac{m_2/p_2 - m_1/p_1}{2(p_1 - p_2)}(p_1 + p_2)$$

yields $c_1 = c_2 = \bar{c}$. A similar result holds for any finite N if money income is fixed, i.e., $m_i = m$ for all i. Then choosing $w_i^* = 0$ for all i, and $w^* = \bar{m}/\pi$, leads to

$$(50) \qquad c_i = \bar{c} = (\bar{m}/N) \sum_{i=1}^{N} p_i^{-1}, \text{ all } i$$

A deterministic spot price, $p_i = \bar{p}$ for all i, on the other hand, destroys the risk-sharing function of fix-price claims for, in that case, $\pi = \bar{p}$. The consumer is as well off purchasing bread exclusively in the spot market.

Unconditional claims on goods sometimes create opportunities to share risk that are intermediate between a spot market and a complete set of contingent claims. These limited opportunities, however, require traders to absorb the costs of operating just one additional market as opposed to the $N - 1$ markets needed to reach the consumption optimum in equation (48).

It is not transparent to me at the moment how to model transaction costs in an appealing way.[12] Nevertheless, I will venture the prediction that these costs

[12] Foley [1966] examines equilibria with transaction costs.

will be an integral part of any plausible equilibrium with long-term contracts in which the money prices of some goods are unaffected by the state of the economy.[13]

8. Conclusions

We have surveyed, especially in Sections 3 and 4, how the sharing of human capital risks affects wages and employment in a competitive, partial equilibrium model of the labour market with complete, symmetric information and zero transaction costs. One might naturally inquire about the connection between layoff and search unemployment (Burdett and Mortensen [1979]), the influence of imperfect competition (Polemarchakis [1979]), and the form of labour contracts when information is incomplete (Azariadis [1978], Blanchard [1979]) or asymmetric (Phelps [1977], Hall and Lillian [1978]). Asymmetric information holds particular promise as a potential explanation why collective bargains usually specify a wage scale, leaving employment at the apparent discretion of firms.

However, the most serious limitation of the theory of labour contracts, as it stands now, seems to be the failure to invent a persuasive story why *money* (as opposed to real) wages are so often invariant to the relevant state of nature, even though that state may be ascertained at a small cost. Economists who, for reasons such as those outlined in section 2, believe that long-term arrangements between the buyers and sellers of some goods or services play an important part in allocating resources, must convince the rest of the profession (or, at least, the more open-minded members of it) that contracts with fixed money wages are occasionally the general equilibrium outcome of a trading process which contains in the opportunity set other exchange arrangements (e.g., spot or state-contingent contracts) as well. It would seem that a similar task faces any serious student of fix-price equilibria.

[13] For a beginning in this direction, see Azariadis [1979].

APPENDIX

1. *Equations (19a), (19b)*

Firms maximize over (w,ρ,m) the expression $\Pi(\Delta,m)$ in eq. (10b) subject to non-negativity, $\rho \leq 1$ and $V(\Delta) \geq \lambda$ where λ is a parameter and $V(\Delta)$ is given in (10a). When eq. (18c) holds, the solution to this problem is

(A1) $(1 - a)f'(\rho m) = w - \phi(w,k)$

(A2) $(1 - a)\rho f'(\rho m) + (1 + a)f'(\mu) = w(1 + \rho)$

(A3) $(1 + \rho)u(w) = \lambda.$

Equilibrium in the labour market requires that the solution $(w(\lambda),p(\lambda),m(\lambda))$ to these equations satisfy $m(\lambda) = \mu$. Substituting this back into (A1) and (A2) produces eqs. (19a) and (19b) of the main text.

2. *Inequalities (23a) and (23b)*

Equations (21a) and 21b) are equivalent to

(A4) $(1 - a)f'(\rho_N \mu) = w_N - \phi(w_N, z + k)$

(A5) $(1 + a)f'(\mu) = w_N + \rho_N \phi(w_N, z + k)$

Similarly (22a, b) lead to

(A6) $(1 - a)f'(\rho_F \mu) = w_F - z - \phi(w_F, z + k)$

(A7) $(1 + a)f'(\mu) = w_F + z + \rho_F \phi(w_F, z + k)$

First we show $w_N > w_F$. Supposing to the contrary that $w_N < w_F$, we have $w_F - z - \phi(w_F, z + k) < w_F - \phi(w_F, z + k) < w_N - \phi(w_N, z + k)$ because, for fixed $z + k$, $w - \phi(w,\cdot)$ is decreasing in w. Hence, from (A4) and (A6) we have $f'(\rho_N \mu) > f'(\rho_F \mu)$ ($\Rightarrow$)

(A8) $\rho_N < \rho_F$

Now, notice that $w + \rho\phi(w,\cdot)$ is increasing in w. Therefore

$$(1 + a)f'(\mu) = w_N + \rho_N \phi(w_N, z + k) \qquad \text{by (A5)}$$

$$< w_N + \rho_F \phi(w_F, z + k) \qquad \text{by (A8)}$$

$$< w_F + \rho_F \phi(w_F, z + k) \qquad \text{by assumption that } w_N < w_F$$

$$< w_F + z + \rho_F \phi(w_F, z + k) \text{ for any } z > 0$$

$$= (1 + a)f'(\mu) \qquad \text{by (A7)}$$

245

This is a contradiction and, therefore, $w_N > w_F$. To demonstrate that $\rho_N < \rho_F$ we note from eqs. (21b) or (22b) that

(A9) $f'(\mu) < w < 2f'(\mu)/(1 + \rho)$

Next note from either (A4) or (A6) that

(A10) $-\phi(w, k + z) > (1 - a)f'(\mu) - w$

Now, for fixed ρ, small a, and $R = -wu''(w)/u'(w)$, the function

(A11) $T'(w) = 2w - (1 - \rho)\phi(w, k + z)$

satisfies

$$T'(w) = 1 + \rho - (1 - \rho)\frac{\phi}{w}R$$

$$> 1 + \rho + (1 - \rho)[(1 - a)f'(\mu)/w - 1]R \qquad \text{from (A10)}$$

$$> 1 + \rho + (1 - \rho)[(1 - a)/2 - 1]R \qquad \text{from (A9)}$$

$$= 1 + \rho - (R/2)[2(1 - \rho) - (1 - a)(1 - \rho^2)] > 0$$

as a, and hence $1 - \rho$, becomes small. Exploiting this result and $w_N > w_F$, we obtain

(A12) $2w_N - (1 - \rho_N)\phi(w_N, k + z) > 2w_F - (1 - \rho_N)(w_F, k + z)$

Suppose now $\rho_N > \rho_F$. Then from (A4) through (A7) we obtain

$$(1 - a)f'(\rho_N\mu) + (1 + a)f'(\mu) < (1 - a)f'(\rho_F\mu) + (1 + a)f''(\mu)$$

or

$$2w_N - (1 - \rho_N)\phi(w_N, k + z) < 2w_F - (1 - \rho_F)\phi(w_F, k + z)$$

$$< 2w_F - (1 - \rho_N)\phi(w_F, k + z)$$

in contradiction of (A12). Hence $\rho_N < \rho_F$,   QED.

REFERENCES

Abowd, J., Ashenfelter, O. [1979], 'Unemployment and Compensating Wage Differentials,' unpublished, Princeton University.

Arrow, K. J. [1971], *Essays in the Theory of Risk-Bearing*, Chicago: Markham.

Arrow, K. J., Hahn, F. H. [1971], *General Competitive Analysis*, San Francisco: Holden-Day.

Azariadis, C. [1975], 'Implicit Contracts and Underemployment Equilibria,' *Journal of Political Economy*, 83: 1183–202.

Azariadis, C. [1976], 'On the Incidence of Unemployment,' *Review of Economic Studies*, 43: 115–25.

Azariadis, C. [1978], 'Escalator Clauses and the Allocation of Cyclical Risks,' *Journal of Economic Theory*, 18: 119–55.

Azariadis, C. [1979], 'Contracts with Endogenous Contingencies,' unpublished, University of Pennsylvania.

Baily, M. N. [1974], 'Wages and Employment under Uncertain Demand,' *Review of Economic Studies*, 41: 37–50.

Baily, M. N. [1976], 'Contract Theory and the Moderation of Inflation by Recession and by Controls', *Brookings Papers on Economic Activity*, 3: 585–622.

Baily, M. N. [1977], 'On the Theory of Layoffs and Unemployment,' *Econometrica*, 45: 1043–63.

Barro, R. J. [1977], 'Long-Term Contracting, Sticky Prices and Monetary Policy,' *Journal of Monetary Economics*, 3: 305–16.

Barro, R. J., Fischer, S. [1976], 'Recent Developments in Monetary Theory,' *Journal of Monetary Economics*, 2: 133–67.

Barro, R. J., Grossman, H. I. [1971], 'A General Disequilibrium Model of Income and Employment', *American Economic Review*, 61: 82–93.

Bell, P. W. [1951], 'Cyclical Variations and Trend in Occupational Wage Differentials in American Industry Since 1914', *Review of Economics and Statistics*, 33: 329–37.

Bodkin, R. G., Klein, L. R. [1969], 'Nonlinear Estimation of Aggregate Production Functions', *Review of Economics and Statistics* 49: 28–44.

Benassy, J. P. [1975], 'Neo-keynesian Disequilibrium in a Monetary Economy', *Review of Economic Studies* 42: 502–23.

Blanchard, O. J. [1979], 'Wage Indexing Rules and the Behavior of the Economy', *Journal of Political Economy* 87: 798–815.

Borch, K. [1962], 'Equilibrium in a Reinsurance Market', *Econometrica* 39: 424–44.

Burdett, K. and Mortensen, D. T. [1979], 'Search, Layoffs and Labor Market Equilibrium', unpublished, Northwestern University.

Bryant, J. [1978], 'An Annotation of 'Implicit Contracts and Under-employment Equilibria', *Journal of Political Economy* 86: 1159–60.

Calvo, G. [1979], 'Quasi-Walrasian Theories of Unemployment', *American Economic Review* 69 (Papers and Proceedings): 102–7.

Calvo, G., Phelps, E. S. [1977], Appendix to [59].

Clower, R. W. [1965], 'The Keynesian Counter-revolution: A Theoretical Appraisal', in *The Theory of Interest Rates* (F. H. Hahn and F. Brechling, eds.), London: Macmillan.

Debreu, G. [1959], *Theory of Value*, New York: Wiley.

Drèze, J. H. [1975], 'Existence of an Equilibrium under Price Rigidity and Quantity Rationing', *International Economic Review* 16: 301–20.

Drèze, J. H. [1979], 'Human Capital and Risk-Bearing', *The Geneva Papers* # 12: 5–22.

Dunlop, J. T. [1938], 'The Movement of Money and Real Wage Rates', *Economic Journal* 48: 413–34.

Eaton, J. and Quandt, R. E. [1979], 'A Quasi-Walrasian Model of Rationing and Labor Supply: Theory and Estimation', unpublished, Princeton University.

Eden, B. [1979], 'The Nominal System: Linkage to the Quantity of Money or to Nominal Income', *Revue Economique* # 1: 121–43.

Feldstein, M. S. [1974], 'Unemployment Compensation, Adverse Incentives and Distributional Anomalies', *National Tax Journal* 37: 231–44.

Feldstein, M. S. [1975], 'The Importance of Temporary Layoffs: An Empirical Analysis', *Brookings Papers on Economic Activity* 3: 725–44.

Feldstein, M. S. [1976], 'Temporary Layoffs in the Theory of Unemployment', *Journal of Political Economy* 84: 937–57.

Fischer, S. [1977], 'Long-Term Contracts, Rational Expectations and the Optimal Money Supply Rule', *Journal of Political Economy* 85: 191–205.

Foley, D. K. [1966], 'Economic Equilibrium with Costly Marketing', *Journal of Economic Theory* 2: 276–91.

Friedman, M. [1976], *Price Theory*, Chicago: Aldine.

Gordon, D. F. [1974], 'A Neo-classical Theory of Keynesian Unemployment', *Economic Inquiry* 12: 431–59.

Gordon, R. J. [1976], 'Recent Developments in the Theory of Inflation and Unemployment', *Journal of Monetary Economics* 2: 185–219.

Gray, J. [1976], 'Wage Indexation: A Macroeconomic Approach', *Journal of Monetary Economics* 2: 221–35.

Gray, J. [1978], 'On Indexation and Contract Length', *Journal of Political Economy* 86: 1–18.

Grossman, H. I. [1977], 'Risk Shifting and Reliability in Labor Markets', *Scandinavian Journal of Economics* 79: 187–209.

Grossman, H. I. [1978], 'Risk Shifting, Layoffs and Seniority', *Journal of Monetary Economics* 4: 661–86.

Hahn, F. H. [1978], 'On Non-Walrasian Equilibria', *Review of Economic Studies* 45: 1–17.

Hall, R. E., Lillien, D. M. [1978], 'Efficient Wage Bargains Under Uncertain Supply and Demand', unpublished, National Bureau of Economic Research # 306.

Harris, M., Raviv, A. [1978], 'Some Results on Incentive Contracts', *American Economic Review* 68: 20–30.

Hashimoto, M. [1979], 'Bonus Payments, on-the-job Training, and Lifetime Employment in Japan', *Journal of Political Economy* 87: 1086–104.

Hicks, J. R. [1932], *The Theory of Wages*, London: Macmillan.

Holmstrom, B. [1979], 'Equilibrium Long-Term Labor Contracts', unpublished Svenska Handel-shogskolan, Helsinki.

Knight, F. H. [1921], *Risk, Uncertainty and Profit*, Boston: Houghton-Mifflin.

Keynes, J. M. [1936], *The General Theory of Employment, Interest and Money*, London: Macmillan.

Knowles, K. G., Robertson, D. J. [1961], 'Differences between the Wages of Skilled and Unskilled Workers, 1880–1950', *Bulletin of the Oxford Institute of Statistics* 13: 109–27.

Kuh, E. [1966], 'Unemployment, Production Functions and Effective Demand', *Journal of Political Economy* 74: 238–49.

Leontief, W. W. [1946], 'The Pure Theory of the Guaranteed Annual Wage Contract', *Journal of Political Economy* 54: 76–9.

Lucas, R. E. [1970], 'Capacity, Overtime and Empirical Production Functions', *American Economic Review* 60 (Papers and Proceedings): 23–7.

Lucas, R. E. [1972], 'Expectations and the Neutrality of Money', *Journal of Economic Theory* 4: 103–24.

Mirrlees, J. [1976], 'The Optimal Structure of Incentives and Authority within an Organization', *Bell Journal of Economics* 7: 105–31.

Mortensen, D. T. [1978], 'On the Theory of Layoffs', unpublished, Northwestern University.

Muth, J. R. [1961], 'Rational Expectations and the Theory of Price Movements', *Econometrica* 24: 315–35.

Oi, W. Y. [1962], 'Labor as a Quasi-Fixed Factor of Production', *Journal of Political Economy* 70: 538–55.

Phelps, E. S. [1977], 'Indexation Issues', in *Stabilization of the Domestic and International Economy* (K. Brunner and A. H. Meltzer, eds.), Carnegie-Rochester Conference Series # 5, Amsterdam: North-Holland.

Phelps, E. S., Taylor, J. B. [1966], 'Stabilizing Powers of Monetary Policy under Rational Expectations', *Journal of Political Economy* 85: 163–90.

Polemarchakis, H. [1979], 'Implicit Contracts and Employment Theory', *Review of Economic Studies* 46: 97–108.

Polemarchakis, H., Weiss, L. [1978], 'Fixed Wages, Layoffs, Unemployment Compensation and Welfare', *American Economic Review* 68: 909–17.

Radner, R. [1972], 'Existence of Equilibrium in Plans, Prices and Price Expectations in a Sequence of Markets', *Econometrica* 40: 289–303.

Raisian, J. [1980], 'Cyclic Patterns in Weeks and Wages', *Economic Inquiry*, forthcoming.

Reder, M. W. [1964], 'Wage Structure and Structural Unemployment', *Review of Economic Studies* 31: 309–22.

Riley, J. G. [1975], 'Competitive Signalling', *Journal of Economic Theory* 10: 174–86.

Ross, S. [1973], 'The Economic Theory of Agency: The Principal's Problem', *American Economic Review* 63 (Papers and Proceedings): 134–9.

Sargent, T. J. [1979], *Macroeconomic Theory*, New York: Academic Press.

Shavell, S. [1976], 'Sharing Risks of Deferred Payment', *Journal of Political Economy* 84: 161–8.

Shavell, S. [1979], 'Risk Sharing and Incentives in the Principal and Agent Relationship', *Bell Journal of Economics* 10: 55–73.

Smith, A. [1973], *The Wealth of Nations*, London: 1776. Pelican Books Edition.

Spence, A. M. [1973], 'Job Market Signaling', *Quarterly Journal of Economics* 88: 353–79.

Stiglitz, J. E. [1975], 'Incentives, Risk and Information: Notes Towards a Theory of Hierarchy', *Bell Journal of Economics* 6: 552–79.

Tarshis, L. [1939], 'Changes in Money and Real Wage Rates', *Economic Journal* 49: 150–4.

Taylor, J. B. [1978], 'Aggregate Dynamics and Staggered Contracts', unpublished, Columbia University.

Townsend, R. M. [1978], 'On the Optimality of Forward Markets', *American Economic Review* 68: 54–66.

Wachter, M., Williamson, O. E. [1978], 'Obligational Markets and the Mechanics of Inflation', *Bell Journal of Economics* 9: 549–71.

Implicit Contracts and Related Topics: A Survey

COMMENT *by John Sutton* (London School of Economics)

Now that implicit contract theories have become fairly familiar ground, it seems timely to try and offer an appraisal of what exactly they do, and do not, offer, on certain traditional problems in the analysis of labour markets. Their achievements have been noteworthy; they provide an interesting way of looking at labour market equilibria, and furnish us besides with a useful mode of analysis which appears to be potentially fruitful in other areas. For the crux of implicit contract theories is an argument of such generality as to suggest a wide range of potential application: that the price (wage) rate is only one dimension of the offer made by a firm to a consumer (worker); and that a competitive equilibrium will correspond not to the lowest price (highest wage), but to that offer which provides the highest level of utility to the individual, consistent with the achievement of 'normal profits' by the firm. In a labour market context, defining the worker's utility over both the wage rate, and the probability of remaining in employment, it suggests that competitive pressures would lead to offers defined, explicitly or implicitly, in terms both of the wage rate, and the worker's security of tenure in the face of fluctuations in the firm's demand for his services. We might equally well apply similar reasoning in a product market context; here, obvious candidates include the offer of optimal price-quality combinations, or the combination of a low average price with a low variance of price over time—the latter notion providing one possible line of attack on the problematic role of 'price-reputation' in markets with imperfect information.

The present survey by Costas Azariadis is doubly valuable, in the light of the potential breadth of application of such ideas, in that it is constructed around an analogy with the literature on contingent contracts. While this is potentially very useful, in yielding new insights into the theory, it does suffer from the disadvantage,[1] that it tends to focus attention on what appears to me to be the less important of the two assumptions on which the implicit contract theories of the labour market rest: the notion that workers are risk averse in respect of income fluctuations, i.e. that the utility function $u(y, L)$ defined over income and hours of leisure is concave in y.

Applying this assumption alone, the implicit contact argument leads, of

---

[1] It also tempts the author to (wrongly) stress as being fundamental to the theory, a notion which seems to me rather suspect: that the problem derives from an inability by workers to insure themselves against unemployment because such an arrangement would be in some way based on the contracting of their future labour services, in violation of the 'prohibition of slavery'. I don't see how this is so. Imagine workers making payments to an insurance scheme while employed, and deriving payments afterwards if and when they become unemployed. This is not only feasible at a microeconomic level, but remains so at the aggregate level, where the positive gross outflow from the insurance scheme at the downswing corresponds to the empirically familiar 'automatic stabiliser' provided by national insurance schemes.

course, at competitive equilibrium to the offer of a contract involving a fixed *real* wage and a fixed number of hours of employment per week—i.e. to a constant level of real income in the face of fluctuations in the marginal product of labour.

In order to account for what is observed empirically, that declines in demand are accompanied by wage inflexibility *and layoffs*, we require the crucial assumption that workers enjoy a positive level of utility while in the unemployed state. For the moment, we may assume that this is associated either with the 'value of leisure',[2] or the existence of unemployment compensation.

Once this is assumed, the central result follows readily: for, if the marginal product of labour, in some 'state of the world', falls below this 'value of leisure', or the level of unemployment compensation, then a firm can clearly offer a more attractive contract if it lays off workers in this 'state of the world'.

An aside is in order at this point: for some commentators have done less than justice to the implicit contract theories by arguing that this is 'just ordinary neo-classical voluntary unemployment', associated with workers having a positive reservation wage, and 'has nothing to do with implicit contracts'. One of the nice features of Azariadis's present exposition is that it neatly clarifies this point: that workers accept ex-ante a certain probability of lay-offs, does not necessarily imply that those actually laid off would not prefer to retain their jobs. The latter assertion depends crucially on what happens to the wage rate of those in employment. The question still remains however, as to whether this mechanism can generate what macroeconomists normally mean by 'involuntary unemployment'; this would require that the present model be imbedded into a convincing macroeconomic framework, a point we consider later.

What then is happening to wage rates? The firm, always assumed to be risk neutral, is interested only in the total wage bill, summed over all states of the world. It is at this point that we must distinguish carefully between the two candidate explanations for the positive utility enjoyed by unemployed workers.

Suppose firstly that one appeals to the 'value of leisure'. In that case, if we retain the assumption of risk aversion—concavity of $u(y, L)$ in y—then the optimal contract will involve the payment by the firm to its 'pool of workers' of a fixed wage *in all states*, i.e. both when they are employed and when they are not.

If we assumed instead that workers are risk neutral—that $u(y, L)$ is linear in y—then workers would be indifferent as to whether the same total payment was averaged out over periods of employment only, or over all periods—the result is indeterminate.[3]

[2] One way of justifying this was suggested in Azariadis (1975), where it was posited that workers prefer their leisure 'in lumps', evidencing the required convexity of $u(y, L)$ in L, as allegedly shown by their taking leisure in the form of weekends and annual holidays. Such a preference for short periods without work, however, does not necessarily imply an analogous preference for 'lumps' of the much longer duration typically associated with involuntary unemployment.

[3] One way out of this difficulty might be to point to the fact that the assumption of 'immobility' implicit in the models, i.e. workers remain 'attached' to the firm through successive periods of employment and unemployment, is too strong. A policy which involved the firm in paying a worker during periods of unemployment invites 'cheating'—in the form of his simultaneously holding a job with a different firm, so that he is not in fact necessarily available to his original employer in the next period. Such considerations might plausibly tilt the balance in favour of the 'payment only while working' option—but they would need to be cast in a rigorous form.

Turning however to the second notion, the existence of unemployment pay, *the fact that such payments are contingent on the workers not receiving income while unemployed* means that the desired result does indeed follow.

It would appear then that (i) the implicit contract approach does offer an explanation of why fixwage/layoff contracts are optimal, in the presence of unemployment compensation, whose prior existence is assumed, and (ii) the subsidiary assumption of risk aversion on the part of workers is not necessary to, and indeed works against, this effect—for it makes such contracts, involving as they do a fluctuation in real income, less attractive.

It is tempting to try and push the argument further, by observing that unemployment compensation, or unemployment insurance, is a natural concomitant of such contracts in that they involve real income fluctuations which workers, or the authorities, wish to reduce. But to try and explain the existence of unemployment pay along such lines would of course be to argue in a circle: the only reason why the fixwage/layoff contract is optimal is because of the assumed pre-existence of unemployment compensation.

This does however leave the theory vulnerable to objections that the pattern of wage-employment behaviour which it attempts to explain historically predates the introduction of unemployment insurance.

All that has been said so far concerns microeconomics. The implicit contract theories are concerned with analysing fluctuations in demand in an industry, embedded in a large stationary economy, whose role in the model is to define a 'general price level' in terms of which the implicit contracts are 'indexed'.

In order to extend the argument to deal with the empirical phenomenon which is to be explained, that wages and prices tend to display some degree of downward inflexibility in the face of declines in aggregate demand, we require two further elements.

Firstly, the analysis must be extended to apply to money wage rates, rather than real wages. The most convincing candidate here is the argument that possible fluctuations in the price of the firm's product, relative to the price level of the workers' 'consumption bundle', renders an agreement on a mutually satisfactory price index difficult to achieve.

Secondly, we require a model of pricing. Azariadis follows the usual course here in assuming perfect competition in product markets. This of course would imply a countercyclical variation in real wage rates; empirically however, real wage rates are approximately constant over the cycle.[4] To deal with this, the author suggests an explanation based on the notion that real wages are higher in those industries more prone to cyclical fluctuations, as the implicit contract theory would suggest. An upswing in activity then means a growth in the fraction of employment accounted for by these high wage industries, thus offsetting the tendency for real wages to fall on average, in the economy as a whole.

[4] Azariadis cites the view, which appears to be widely held, that real wages actually vary pro-cyclically. This assertion is based on studies of wage rates deflated by a consumer price index, the measure relevant to workers' welfare, and to the size of the multiplier. In the present context it is the product wage which is relevant, and here a wholesale price index is more appropriate. Careful scrutiny of the results in the extensive survey by Bodkin [1969] indicates that real wages, thus measured, are constant, or slightly falling, at the upswing. This is consistent with the very weak, but positive, responsiveness of prices to demand fluctuations noted later in the main text.

But this will not do. We have a wide body of statistical evidence to draw on here, which includes not only direct studies of real wage rates at the aggregate level, but also the complementary and consistent evidence on the same question from the econometric studies of price determination at industry level (for US studies see the contributions of Nordhaus, and of Eckstein and Wyss, in Eckstein and Wyss [1972], and for an eight industry study of the UK, Stromback and Trivedi [1976]). These indicate a weak responsiveness of prices to fluctuations in demand in all industries[5] and corroborate the evidence that wage-price relatives vary little over the cycle.

Thus there is no evidence that the near-constancy of real wage rates over the cycle is merely a 'composition effect' of the kind Azariadis suggests.[6]

A satisfactory passage to a macroeconomic analysis requires a convincing model of price behaviour. It has become increasingly clear in recent years that this requires that we relax the assumption of perfect competition in product markets, both for purely theoretical reasons (Arrow [1959], Hahn [1978]), as well as on empirical grounds (Keynes [1939]).

The implicit contract theories offer us a novel way of looking at labour market equilibrium. It is of the essence of the type of approach that wage contracts involve some kind of 'averaging out' of good times with bad, the fixed wage exceeding the marginal (revenue) product of labour at the downswing, and falling short of it at the upswing.

Now this, as it stands, explains too much. Wages are not rigid, but display typically a *limited* degree of inflexibility *in a downward direction* as demand fluctuates.

The now familiar response of contract theorists to the fact that wages respond asymmetrically to demand changes is to point to the obvious need to relax the assumption of 'immobility' used in the basic model, and to argue that some workers 'default' on contracts by accepting higher wage offers from rival employers at the upswing of the cycle. Now this is certainly plausible, though it is somewhat disturbing to find the most striking feature of the wage adjustment process accounted for by introducing a secondary argument of this kind. It is less easy to see how the fact that money wage rates do fall once aggregate demand declines sufficiently[7] might be reconciled with the implicit contract view, at least in a rigourous manner. This is unfortunate, for the obvious way in which we might test alternative views as to why wage rates are to some extent inflexible would be through a study of the varying conditions under which wages do, and do not, respond to demand changes.

There is a more old-fashioned view of these matters, however, the various elements of which are to be found in the traditional, and less formal, literature on the economics of the labour market. Firstly, there are (possibly small) adjustment costs which fall on both worker and firm in switching jobs, and

[5] With a negative response in the case of Eckstein's 'highly concentrated' industries in the USA.

[6] For similar reasons I remain unhappy with the present attempt to account for the behaviour of occupational wage differentials.

[7] For example, in US manufacturing between 1929 and 1930 a fall in employment of 15% led only to a negligible response in the average hourly wage rate (from 59.0c to 58.9c), in spite of a fall of 3.4% in the cost of living index. In the following three years, during which employment fell to 60% of its 1929 level, and the cost of living continued to fall, the average hourly wage rate fell markedly to a low of 53.9c (NICB, [1943], pp. 120, 132, 215).

secondly, workers are not usually indifferent between rival employers, so that a firm typically enjoys some degree of monopsony power. This implies some potential indeterminacy in the wage paid ex-post to workers once they have been hired, for a sufficiently small wage cut will not precipitate quits. On the other hand, workers can exert a sanction against such wage cuts by responding with a go-slow or strike, as the workforce can not be replaced costlessly at the prevailing wage. This view can in fact be cast in a quite rigourous form in which the outcome is characterised as a Nash Equilibrium in a repeated game between firm and workers (Sutton [1979]), and leads to a *downward* inflexibility of money wage rates in the face of falls in aggregate demand (or the general price level) *over a limited range.*

This more traditional view of labour market equilibrium in terms of an uneasy balance between opposing market agents, maintained, within bounds, from period to period, in the face of random exogenous disturbances, contrasts sharply with the characterisation offered by the implicit contract theories, of a mutually satisfactory arrangement based on an averaging procedure over a long horizon. It would seem to the present writer at least, that the older view still has much to recommend it.

REFERENCES

Arrow, K. J. [1959], 'Towards a Theory of Price Adjustment', in A. Abramovitz (ed.), *The Allocation of Economic Resources,* Stanford: University of California Press.

Azariadis, Costas [1975], 'Implicit Contracts and Underemployment Equilibria', *Journal of Political Economy,* Vol. 83, p. 1183.

Bodkin, Ronald G. [1969], 'Real Wages and Cyclical Variations in Employment: A Re-examination of the Evidence', *Canadian Journal of Economics,* Vol. 2, p. 353.

Eckstein, O., Wyss, D., (eds.), [1972], *The Econometrics of Price Determination,* Washington: Board of Governors of the Federal Reserve System.

Hahn, F. H. [1978], 'Keynesian Economics and General Equilibrium Theory: Reflections on Some Current Debates', in G. C. Harcourt (ed.), *The Microfoundations of Macroeconomics,* London: Macmillan.

Keynes, John Maynard [1939], 'Relative Movements of Real Wages and Output', *Economic Journal,* Vol. 49, p. 34.

National Industrial Conference Board [1943], *Economic Almanac for 1941-42,* Washington: NICB.

Sutton, John [1979], 'Individual Rationality and the Downward Inflexibility of Money Wage Rates', LSE Centre for Labour Economics Paper No. 57.

Stromback, C. T., Trivedi, P. K. [1976], 'The Determinants of Ex-works Price Changes', in Pearce, I. F., *et. al., A Model of Output, Employment, Wages and Prices in the UK,* Cambridge: Cambridge University Press.

Implicit Contracts and Related Topics: A Survey

COMMENT *by Martin Neil Baily* (Brookings Institute).

There is a lot of meat in Azariadis' survey of contract theory. The paper repays careful study. It provides a valuable analysis of many of the major issues and results in this area. Let me start my comments by dealing with points that troubled people at the conference.

Contract theory analyzes situations in which trading parties agree explicitly or implicitly to make transactions on terms that differ from those that would prevail in a myopic instantaneous market. The reason for such an agreement is that both parties are better-off in the long-run. The most important area of application of the theory is in the labour market. The most important neoclassical framework in which long-run gains create an incentive to deviate from short-run myopic market outcomes arises when firms act to reduce the wage risk—i.e., the human capital risk—faced by workers.

An immediate fruit of the contract theory approach is that it provides one explanation of an important labour market paradox. When there is a general fall in product demand, why do firms lay off workers but keep wages sticky? Under some fairly tight assumptions (discussed in the survey), one can show that a risk-reducing firm will not cut wages even though it has excess supply of labour. A sticky wage policy maximizes the firm's long-run or expected profits.

Contract theory does *not* by itself provide a behavioural basis for models with sticky money wages, but it may be a useful ingredient in a full model. For example, if workers prefer a wage contract that offers the insurance that their own wages will be maintained relative to the wages of other workers, this may lead to nominal wage stickiness in the macro economy. There are, of course, other assumptions that could be combined with a contract framework—incomplete information or 'adherence to the yardstick of the dollar.'

Contract theory as Azariadis surveys it does not deal with the product market at all, but, of course, a full macro model must tackle price adjustment as well as wage adjustment. My colleague Arthur Okun has applied the theory to prices as well as wages. He does not stress risk, but rather the less formal but appealing notion of fairness. Firms wish to maintain customer loyalty and cost-plus pricing is seen as fair by both sides. 'Exploiting' short-run demand fluctuations is seen as unfair. As he elegantly puts it, prices and wages are set by an invisible handshake, not by an invisible hand.

Let me return to the formal labour market models. Imbedded in the model that predicts wage stickiness is a criterion for layoffs. If there is a downturn in product demand, the privately efficient criterion is that temporary layoffs occur only when the value to the firm of the marginal product of a worker when employed is less than the value of unemployment insurance (U I) and leisure to

254

the worker if unemployed.[1] This finding has been used by some supporters of the theory to suggest that unemployment is voluntary and not terribly costly to the unemployed. It has been regarded by others as an unacceptable finding and hence a reason to reject the theory. Neither view is correct. First, an example: Suppose a young man from West Virginia decides to become a coal miner. A relative or perhaps another person of his acquaintance has had an accident or become sick as a result of being in the mines. But the availability of jobs and the relatively high wages overcome the young man's fears. Suppose he himself subsequently suffers illness or accident in the mine. Do we describe his misfortune as voluntary? It would be absurd to do so. But it would be equally absurd to suggest he did not know that mining was a dangerous occupation.

To continue the story: suppose the young man seeks out the best available medical care, thereby maximizing his probability of recovery. Does that bear on the severity of his illness? Again the suggestion is absurd.

If workers in cyclically sensitive industries know that their jobs are unstable and firms set wages and layoffs with this fact in mind, this does not say unemployment is voluntary. Thus, it implies nothing about the desireability of policy measures to mitigate recessions, i.e., to change the probability distribution over states of nature. Moreover, it does not tell us about the costs of unemployment. Let me explain.

During a recession something goes wrong in the product market. We do not have perfectly competitive product markets. Nor do we have perfectly flexible prices. When the US manufacturing sector reduced its employment of production workers from 14.8 million in November 1973 to 12.8 million in July 1975, it did so because the employers perceived that if employment and production had been maintained at their high levels, the marginal revenue product would have been very low—perhaps negative in many cases. To make layoffs in such circumstances does not imply that unemployment insurance and leisure are so valuable, but rather that the private value (not necessarily social value) of an increment to output was very low.[2] Thus, contract theory models do not need to make exaggerated claims for the value of UI or leisure in order to 'explain' layoffs.

Having said this, however, I should like to set the record straight by asserting that a short temporary layoff is not a disaster for the worker. A temporary layoff occurs, for example, when a plant closes for a week or a month or two. A production worker in manufacturing who finds himself collecting a weekly UI benefit check of $79 for this period rather than a weekly take-home check of about $175 doesn't like it, but it is not the end of the world (both figures are for 1977). Moreover the word 'leisure' is misleading. Many workers on layoff find stop-gap jobs, including untaxed casual employment. Of course, some layoffs last longer, and living on a reduced income gets tougher and tougher. But the great majority of temporary layoffs are over within two months.

The unemployed who really suffer are those with long spells. Some have

[1] Temporary layoffs are defined here to include all workers who are rehired, not just those with a recall date specified when they are laid off.

[2] An assumption frequently made is that firms are sales-constrained during downtimes. I am not terribly comfortable with this assumption. But if it were true, there would be no difficulty explaining layoffs in a contract model. The value of the increment to output would be zero.

difficulty entering the mainstream labour market because of low skills, inexperience or prejudice. Others have been laid off with no hope of recall. The phenomena of layoffs, rehires and wage stickiness are important ones empirically. But the bulk of unemployment weeks in a normal year do not come from temporary layoffs.

Another major question raised about contract theory concerns the importance of the assumed reputational effects on firms' behaviour. Simple models have to make simple assumptions. It is convenient to assume that workers know the layoff probabilities and that firms know this fact and then stick to implicit contracts. In practice both of these elements are shaded. Some workers ignore the chance of being laid off. Some firms pursue short-run gains with no regard for their reputations as employers.

But most executives and personnel managers that I talk to and read about express tremendous concern for their reputations as employers and the morale of their current work-forces. Indeed, they should. Albert Rees found that firms recruit new workers through their existing workers. The mechanism for transmitting reputational information is clear. Morale affects productivity and a disgruntled worker who feels the firm is behaving unfairly may drop a wrench into a million dollar machine—sometimes they do just that.

Now let me move from general points and make a few specific comments on the survey.

(a) The discussion of optimality with and without unemployment insurance was hard to follow. A fully efficient risk-sharing arrangement between risk-neutral firms and risk-averse workers requires side-payments to workers during periods of unemployment. The side-payments would provide full insurance to workers and in this case there is no inefficient over-employment. A fully experience-rated UI program with a benefit level high enough to provide full insurance (i.e. with $z = w - k$) mimics this solution and is efficient.

The same volume of employment during adverse states of nature can be achieved with less than full insurance, but with no experience rating, as Azariadis shows. But because workers are under-insured there is a dead-weight loss. Of course, in practice there are lots of reasons why firms would not offer full insurance to workers. Laid off workers might fail to search for new or stop-gap jobs or they might take the money and not return to the firm. Firms may be risk-averse and prefer to provide partial insurance. But Azariadis is not making his argument along these lines.

(b) A more fundamental objection to the welfare economics (and to other parts of the survey) is that it is too partial. If the adverse state of nature occurs because of sticky product prices or an erratic Federal Reserve Board, the socially optimal level of employment may well be full employment. The privately perceived marginal value product may have fallen, but the social value need not have. This is why there is a basic presumption that reducing employment fluctuations makes the economy better-off.

(c) The time dimension is missing from the discussion. Many of the findings do not require a particular time-horizon, but its absence tends to point the reader away from some key issues. How long do implicit contracts last and when do they break down? How do we get to a full theory of labour market dynamics with wage rate adjustment and quits and new hires as well as layoffs and rehires? In a multiperiod model the potential importance of savings is seen. Workers cannot eliminate wage-risk by saving, so the basic results hold. But they can smooth consumption and reduce their effective aversion to risk.

(d) The wage stickiness result is not just a corollary of Arrow-Borch. It drops out of a particular model where Von Neumann-Morgenstern expected utility 'separates' wage and employment risk. It is suboptimal to offer a risky wage even when employment varies. That finding was counter-intuitive to many people.

Risk Shifting, Unemployment Insurance and Layoffs*

Herschel I. Grossman
National Bureau of Economic Research

*The National Science Foundation and the John Simon Guggenheim Memorial Foundation have supported this research. Dale Mortensen provided a number of useful suggestions. Any opinions expressed are those of the author and not those of the National Bureau of Economic Research.

RISK SHIFTING, UNEMPLOYMENT INSURANCE AND LAYOFFS

1. A Market-Clearing Model of Layoffs

The observation that cyclical fluctuations in real variables such as aggregate employment appear to reflect predominately the effects of changes in aggregate demand for output poses two critical questions for macroeconomics. First, what are the causes of fluctuations in aggregate demand? Second, why do these fluctuations produce cycles in real variables, rather than being absorbed by price and wage adjustments as would be the case in a Walrasian model of general equilibrium?

A broad concensus, which emerged at least a decade ago, seems presently to prevail about the many issues associated with the first question, concerned with the determinants of aggregate demand. For example, there seems to be little active current discussion about the relative influence that monetary factors, fiscal actions, and endogenous phenomena have on aggregate demand. Recent years, however, have seen intense research interest and associated controversy directed towards the second question, concerned with identifying the characteristics of the actual economy that are responsible for the non-Walrasian responses of real variables to cycles in aggregate demand.

One popular approach, describable as Keynesian, has been to attribute the causal relation between aggregate demand and aggregate employment to a failure of wages and prices to adjust to equate quantities demanded and supplied in labour and product markets. An essential aspect of this interpretation of the process of employment fluctuation is that a contraction in employment resulting from a reduction in aggregate demand involves a situation in which perceived gains from trade are foregone. A frequent criticism of this non-market-clearing paradigm has been that the theoretical development in the existing literature provides no convincing rationale, based on neo-classical premises, for such a persistent failure to realize perceived gains from trade. For example, in the book by Barro and myself, the determination of the vector of wages and prices at which buyers and sellers are constrained to transact is based on ad hoc gradual adjustment processes. The choice-theoretic analysis is concerned mainly with the implications of such essentially arbitrarily specified wage-price vectors for the determination of employment. Some other models rationalize gradual wage and price adjustment on the basis of adjustment costs, which is logically adequate, but convincing stories about the precise nature of these costs do not seem to exist.

Despite this problem, the non-market-clearing paradigm has remained popular primarily because it has seemed to be realistic. The analysis in the present paper questions the accuracy of this impression. It suggests that the prevalence of layoffs as a mode of employment separation does not provide evidence of chronic failure of labour markets to clear and that the conventional view that in cyclical contractions workers typically confront excess supply in labour markets and are unable to obtain desired employment may involve a misinterpretation of the facts.

The basis for this revisionist argument is the recent theoretical development of the hypothesis that actual labour market transactions typically involve implicit contractual arrangements that stabilize worker income by shifting risk from workers to employers. This hypothesis suggests the possibility of rationalizing stickiness of wage rates and explaining the alleged symptoms of non-wage rationing of employment, such as layoffs, without invoking the failure of markets to clear.

The main specific objective of the present paper is to develop an analysis of labour markets in which the use of layoffs to effect employment separations does not imply that the amount of employment is suboptimal relative to current perceptions. This analysis suggests that the non-Walrasian causal relation between aggregate demand and aggregate employment results not from the failure of markets to clear, but from misperceptions of the terms of trade between labour services and consumption goods, as hypothesised by Friedman [1968], Lucas [1975], and others, and integrated into a model of risk shifting by Azariadis [1968]. Having focussed on these alternative explanations, it is worth stressing that non-Walrasian fluctuations in employment in either case are wasteful and undesirable, whether they result from the failure to realise perceived gains from trade or from the failure to perceive gains from trade correctly.

The risk-shifting hypothesis plays a critical part in the present analysis, but by itself does not provide a full account within a market-clearing framework of the diverse phenomena associated with layoffs. An adequate analysis of layoffs seems to require, in addition, explicit allowance for the consequences of tax-financed unemployment insurance.

A second specific objective of this paper is to use the model that incorporates both risk shifting and unemployment insurance to reconsider previous analysis of the effects of risk shifting on the magnitude of employment fluctuations. The present analysis shows that the quantitative effects of risk shifting and unemployment insurance are not additive. When analysed separately, both risk-shifting arrangements and unemployment insurance seem to magnify employment fluctuations by increasing the responsiveness of labour supply to shifts in labour's perceived real compensation. However, in the analysis below, the introduction of risk shifting into a model that allows for unemployment insurance has the opposite effect of reducing employment fluctuations.

2. Layoffs as a Mode of Employment Separation

Before reviewing recent analyses of risk shifting and unemployment insurance, it will be useful to have clearly in mind the characteristics of layoffs as a mode of employment separation. Layoffs involve the following four phenomena:
(P1) Employers follow the administrative procedure of assigning workers to the status of unemployment. Thus, the term 'layoff' in the present discussion

refers broadly to any separation, i.e., suspension or termination of employment, that the employer initiates. In other words, the status of being laid off denotes a proximately passive role for the worker in becoming unemployed. For simplicity, the analysis below also implicitly assumes that a worker who is laid off is available to return to work whenever his employer recalls him. However, extending the analysis to allow workers to choose to change jobs would not alter the main conclusions.

(P2) When employers lay off some workers, presumably indicating a decrease in the demand for labour services, they typically do not reduce wage rates for those other workers who continue to be employed. This practice seems inconsistent with the neo-classical inclination to view wage rates as changing to equate quantities of labour services supplied and demanded.

(P3) Workers who are laid off usually receive no income from their employers. In this respect, a layoff is not different from other modes of job separation.

(P4) Employers typically use seniority classification to determine which workers are laid off. In practice, a worker's seniority classification depends mainly on his length of service with a particular employer, but can also depend on other factors, a frequent one being his age. As the following discussion indicates, rationalizations for (P1) and (P4) have not been hard to invent, but no single approach has been able to account readily for both (P2) and (P3).

3. Summary of Recent Literature

The essential idea in the theory of risk shifting in labour markets is that a systematic difference between firms and their workers with regard to risk aversion leads to long-term commitments in which the firms absorb risk that would otherwise be borne by the workers. These commitments imply that actual relations between firms and workers implicitly involve two transactions. First, firms purchase from workers labour services for use in the production process and, second, firms sell to workers private insurance against undesirable income fluctuations. Workers engage in these transactions jointly with a single firm, instead of selling labour services to one firm and buying insurance from another, because the production relation between firms and workers mitigates the problems of monitoring and enforcement that arise in the insurance relation. As a result of these contractual arrangements, a worker's wage income equals either the value of his marginal contribution to output minus an implicit insurance premium or the value of his marginal contribution to output plus an implicit insurance indemnity, depending on whether the perceived real value of labour's marginal product, which is a stochastic variable, is high or low.

Risk shifting in effect credits part of the value of product when it is high to an implicit premium that yields an implicit indemnity when the value of product is low. This arrangement enables the worker to use product generated in states in which consumption would otherwise be high to boost consumption in states in which consumption would otherwise be low. Consequently, risk shifting increases the attractiveness of working when the value of product is high and decreases the pressure to work when the value of product is low relative to what would be the case if income and consumption in each state were equal to the value of product in that state. This reasoning explains the result, derived in Azariadis [1978] and Grossman [1978], that risk shifting makes the level of employment more variable.

Turning to the characteristics of layoffs, the idea that labour market transactions involve risk shifting has provided what seems to be only choice-theoretic explanation for (P2), the surprising wage rate stickiness associated with layoffs. The basic observation is that the insurance aspect of labour contracts serves to stabilise worker income and, thus, explains why reductions in the quantity of employment typically do not also involve reductions in wage rates.

The relation between risk shifting and productive efficiency also suggests a simple explanation for (P1), the administrative procedures associated with layoffs. Efficiency requires that a worker be employed in a particular state of nature if the utility associated with being employed and receiving the value of his marginal contribution to total product equals or exceeds the utility associated with not being employed. However, with risk shifting in effect, a worker's wage income does not equal the value of his marginal contribution to total product. As a result, his wage income cannot serve, as would the wage rate in a spot market, to signal the worker as to whether it is efficient for him to accept or to reject employment. Consequently, in order to achieve efficiency, the implicit labour contracts must specify each worker's employment status as a function of the perceived real value of his marginal product. Moreover, in order to economise on the costs of acquiring and processing information, the contracts delegate to the employer the administrative function of assigning workers to employment or unemployment.

Despite the essential nature of these insights, the basic analysis of risk shifting has the problem that it seems to imply too much. Specifically, it does not allow for (P3) and (P4), the failure of employers to provide a constant, fully insured income for all workers.

The model in Grossman [1978] attempts to remedy this problem by allowing for incompleteness and inter-worker differences in risk shifting. This extended model rationalizes (P4), the role of seniority in determining the incidence of layoffs by assuming that worker productivity increases with age and with length of service with a particular employer. In addition, in an attempt to account for (P3), the fact that laid-off workers typically receive no indemnity income from their employers, this model assumes that worker reliability is related to seniority. The problem of worker unreliability results from the possibility that the prospect of short-run gains, when the value of their marginal contributions to output are high, can induce workers to quit their jobs. Differences between more and less senior workers in their reputations for reliability, which relate to their behaviour when the perceived real value of marginal product is high, produce differences in the terms at which they can obtain income when the perceived real value of marginal product is low. Specifically, less senior workers, whose average reliability is low, contract for less stable incomes.

Whatever the actual importance of reliability considerations, the correspondence between the implications of this model and (P3) is unfortunately less than completely tight. Specifically, the model provides no reason why lower seniority classes should purchase from their employer exactly zero insurance against reduced income in those instances when productive efficiency dictates that they be unemployed.

The effects of tax-financed unemployment insurance on the variability of employment are similar to the effects of risk shifting. The existence of unemployment insurance increases the attractiveness of working when the value of product is high because a worker both earns his wage income and becomes eligible for unemployment insurance benefits and decreases the attractiveness of working when the value of product is low because benefits make unemployment more tolerable.

With regard to the characteristics of layoffs, the key characteristics of unemployment insurance are that an unemployed worker can receive benefits only if his unemployment is 'involuntary' and that the amount of these benefits are reduced by the amount of any other income that the worker receives when unemployed. These eligibility rules provide inducements for (P1), by which firms take proximate responsibility for job separations, and for (P3), the discontinuance of income payments by firms to laid off workers. In addition, in this context, as in the analysis of risk-shifting arrangements, the association of productivity with seniority can readily account for (P4), the role of seniority in determining the incidence of layoffs.

The existence of unemployment insurance, however, provides no explanation for (P2), the constancy of wages for employed workers. Existing theoretical models of the effects of unemployment insurance—for example, Baily [1977] and Feldstein [1976]—simply introduce (P2) as a realistic assumption. However, (P2) is the only qualitative economic feature of layoffs that is clearly distinctive. In contrast, (P1) is only an administrative procedure and (P3) and (P4) are not peculiar to layoffs as a mode of job separation. Thus, the inability to account for (P2) is a critical problem.

Another possible objection to focusing on unemployment insurance is that the use of the layoff mode to effect employment separations has not been historically associated with the advent of the current centrally administered programmes of income maintenance for the unemployed. However, this objection is not serious if the eligibility rules and financing arrangements of earlier privately and locally administered income-maintenance programs generated the same incentives as current programs.

To summarise, existing analysis suggests that both risk shifting and tax-financed unemployment insurance increase the variability of employment. However, neither models of risk shifting nor models of unemployment insurance can readily explain the full set of phenomena associated with layoffs as a mode of employment separation. The following sections show that analysis of the interaction between risk shifting and unemployment insurance both alters this conclusion about the effect of risk shifting on employment fluctuations and also produces a more satisfactory theory of layoffs.

4. Analytical Framework

The simple economy analyzed in this paper differs from the set-up in Grossman [1978] by allowing for unemployment insurance but abstracting from reliability considerations. In this economy, there are two large groups of individuals that differ in their attitudes to risk. One large group of identical individuals behaves in a less risk averse, or even risk neutral, manner. These individuals choose the role of entrepreneurs, who organize production by forming firms and employing inputs, including labour services.

The second large group of individuals behave in a more risk averse manner. These individuals choose the role of employees, who work for the firms and provide labour services. As indicated above, this difference between the attitudes toward risk of entrepreneurs and workers provides the basis for risk-shifting arrangements.

The analysis assumes, for simplicity, that all workers have the same utility function, and that this utility function is additively separable in consumption and the amount of time devoted to employment. Consumption here refers to consumable commodities purchased in the market place and employment refers to working as an employee of a firm. Individuals can use time not devoted to employment for home production of other consumable commodities.

The analysis also assumes that labour services are homogeneous and that each worker has only a single unit of time to devote to employment. It would seem fairly straightforward, although not essential for present purposes, to extend the analysis to take explicit account of variable hours of work.

A more important assumption is that individual workers differ with respect to the number of units of labour services that they provide per unit of employment time. The analysis assumes that the classification of potential workers according to age and length of service with a particular employer yields classes of increasing average productivity. It is convenient to index these seniority classes according to increasing seniority. Let the nonnegative variable k_i denote the average productivity of the ith class of workers, where k_i measures the average number of units of labour services provided by individuals in this class per unit of employment time. Thus, the lowest seniority class has the lowest k_i and the highest seniority class has the highest k_i.

Workers exchange their labour services for consumption goods through a network of markets. Let w denote the basic real wage rate, which is the perceived exchange ratio between consumption goods and a unit of labour services. Changes in w represent perceived 'real' disturbances, which is important because, as Barro [1977] has stressed, the productive efficiency of competitively determined contracts implies that in a contractual labour market, as in a spot market, disturbances perceived to be 'monetary' would not affect employment. Competition in the contractual labour market insures that w equals the perceived value of the marginal product of a unit of labour services. See Grossman [1978] for a derivation of this result. Whether or not the relevant perceptions are accurate does not matter for the present analysis.

From the standpoint of the workers, the variable w is stochastic and is determined at periodic intervals by serially independent drawings from an exogenously determined population. The interval between these drawings defines a unit of time. The population of w is such that

$$w = \begin{cases} w_1 \text{ with probability } \alpha_1 \\ w_2 \text{ with probability } \alpha_2, \end{cases}$$

where $w_2 > w_1 > 0$ and $\alpha_1 + \alpha_2 = 1$. Thus, w_2 characterizes a good state of nature and w_1 characterizes a bad state of nature. The assumption that there are only two states is a convenient simplification. See Grossman [1977] for a more general set-up. In the rest of the paper, the subscripts 1 and 2 denote the values of each relevant variable in the two states.

The analysis abstracts from the holding of assets—including investment goods, commodity inventories, and financial assets—by individuals. Allowing for the holding of either real or financial assets would make the analysis both more realistic and more complex, but would not seem to change the main conclusions. The key observation in this context is that, because the accumulation of assets involves foregoing consumption and because the probability is always positive that the next state will be bad, optimal worker or firm asset management would not involve using stocks of assets to achieve complete stability of worker consumption.

5. Employment Without Risk Shifting and Without Unemployment Insurance

In order to appreciate the significance of risk shifting and unemployment insurance and their interaction, this section begins the analysis by abstracting from these arrangements. This section and the next section, which allows for risk shifting, review relevant aspects of the analysis presented in Grossman [1978]. Subsequent sections extend the analysis to consider unemployment insurance and the interaction between risk shifting and unemployment insurance.

As indicated above, competition generates a vector of basic real wage rates, denoted by (w_1, w_2), that are equal to the perceived value of the marginal product of a unit of labour services. Moreover, the standard theory of human capital tells us that in the present context, which among other things abstracts from training costs, employers could not take advantage of the firm specificity of their senior workers' productivity without impairing their long-run ability to attract employees. Consequently, income possibilities for workers in the ith class in the two possible states of nature are $w_1 k_i$ and $w_2 k_i$.

Given these income possibilities, each worker selects the vector of employment and wage income that maximizes his expected utility. In formulating this problem, the present analysis assumes that workers take a myopic view that abstracts from the dependence of productivity on the length of service. Thus, suppressing the subscript i, the worker's implicit problem is to choose the vector $(l_1, l_2, \Omega_1, \Omega_2)$, where l measures units of employment time and Ω measures wage income, so as to maximise

$$E(u-v) = \alpha_1 [u(c_1) - v(l_1)] + \alpha_2[u(c_2) - v(l_2)],$$

where c measures worker consumption, $u(\cdot)$ is increasing and concave, and $v(\cdot)$ is increasing and convex, subject to the constraints,

$$l_1 = \{0, 1\}, l_2 = \{0, 1\}, c_1 = \Omega_1, c_2 = \Omega_2,$$
$$\Omega_1 = w_1 k l_1, \text{ and } \Omega_2 = w_2 k l_2.$$

These constraints say that in each state consumption equals wage income and that wage income equals either the product of the basic wage rate and productivity if the worker chooses employment or zero if he chooses unemployment.

Depending on $\alpha_1, \alpha_2, w_1, w_2$, and k, the solution to this problem can prescribe for a particular worker employment either in both states, only in the good state, or in neither state. In choosing among these options, the worker selects the largest of the following possible values of $E(u-v)$:

For employment in both states,
$$E(u-v) = \alpha_1 u(w_1 k) + \alpha_2 u(w_2 k) - v(1) \equiv A(1, 1).$$

For employment only in the good state,
$$E(u-v) = \alpha_1 u(0) + \alpha_2 u(w_2 k) - \alpha_1 v(0) - \alpha_2 v(1) \equiv A(0, 1).$$

For employment in neither state,
$$E(u-v) = u(0) - v(0) \equiv A(0, 0).$$

Comparison of these expected values reveals the following:

$A(1, 1)$ is largest *iff* $w_1 k > z$,
$A(0, 1)$ is largest *iff* $w_1 k < z < w_2 k$, and
$A(0, 0)$ is largest *iff* $z > w_2 k$,

where z satisfies $u(z) = u(0) - v(0) + v(1)$.

This solution implies that a worker desires employment in a particular state of nature if his possible income in that state is sufficiently high to make the net utility associated with being employed and consuming this income at least as large as the net utility associated with not being employed and not consuming market goods.

The determination of which classes of workers are employed in each state of nature requires assumptions about the distribution of the k_i. Specifically, if k_a is such that $w_2 k_a = z$ and k_b, where $b > a$, is such that $w_1 k_b = z$, workers in class b and higher classes are employed in both states of nature and workers in classes a through $b-1$ are employed only in the good state of nature. Individuals whose productivity is less than k_a are not employed in either state.

An important aspect of this analysis that ignores risk shifting and unemployment insurance is that the basic wage rate varies from state to state in such a way that, in any state of nature in which a worker is employed, his income is equal to the value of his marginal contribution to output. Thus, each worker's income and consumption, whether or not he is employed in both states, is lower in the bad state than in the good state. In addition, the basic wage rate in each state of nature, which together with his productivity determines his potential income in each state, signals the worker as to whether or not the utility associated with being employed and receiving the value of his marginal contribution to output in that state equals or exceeds the utility associated with not being employed. In other words, the active decisions of workers to accept or reject employment lead to productive efficiency Consequently, there is no need for the labour contracts to specify each worker's employment status as a function of the state of nature and, hence, no need for employers to take on the administrative task of assigning workers to employment or unemployment. In this context, adjustments in employment reflect solely wage-induced movements along the supply schedule of labour services and, except for the relation between employment and seniority, exhibit none of the characteristics associated with layoffs.

The observation that each worker, whether he is employed in both states or only in the good state, has higher consumption in the good state than in the bad state also suggests that the labour market in this analysis does not share risk in an efficient way. Specifically, the risk averse workers would prefer more predictable and stable consumption and the less risk-averse firms might be prepared to offer their workers a more predictable and stable income schedule.

6. Risk Shifting

This section introduces risk shifting, but continues to abstract from unemployment insurance. Risk shifting allows each worker's wage income in a particular state of nature to differ from the value of his marginal contribution to output in that state. As a result, efficient risk shifting can produce increased expected utility for the workers while at the same time producing an increase or no decrease in expected utility for the entrepreneurs.

Competition in the market for labour contracts that implicitly involve risk shifting generates, in addition to the basic real wage rates, an exchange ratio, denoted by p, at which workers give up income in the good state in return for income in the bad state. Risk shifting in effect provides the worker with additional income in state one equal to $(\Omega_1 - w_1 kl_1)$ in exchange for a reduction in income in state two equal to $(w_2 kl_2 - \Omega_2)$. The price of risk shifting, p, is the ratio of the expected value of the reduction, $\alpha_2(w_2 kl_2 - \Omega_2)$, to the expected value of the addition, $\alpha_1(\Omega_1 - w_1 kl_1)$.

A hypothetical value of p equal to unity would characterized an actuarially 'fair' price for risk shifting and would imply that workers could obtain a constant income at no cost to themselves in average income. Actually, we seem to observe that risk shifting reduces but does not eliminate income variability, even for workers who are employed in all states of nature. Specifically, although wage rates are sticky, they are not fixed. In addition, although not explicitly modelled in this paper, worker incomes vary with changes in hours of work.

These observations suggest that in fact p exceeds unity, but is not so large as to make risk shifting unattractive. According to the analysis in Grossman [1977; 1978], a value of p above unity implies either that entrepreneurs are risk averse, or that w_2 is much larger than w_1, or that workers sometimes behave unreliably.

With risk shifting, the worker's problem is to choose the vector $(l_1, l_2 \leq, \Omega_1, \Omega_2)$ so as to maximize $E(u - v)$, subject to the constraints

$$l_1 = \{0,1\}, l_2 = \{0,1\},$$
$$c_1 = \Omega_1, c_2 = \Omega_2, \text{ and}$$
$$p\alpha_1(\Omega_1 - w_1 k l_1) = \alpha_2 (w_2 k l_2 - \Omega_2).$$

This last constraint describes the terms of risk shifting. For example, for the special case of p equal to unity, it would say that the worker can exchange with his employer income in the good state for income in the bad state subject only to the condition that the expected value of his income equals the expected value of his marginal contribution to output, which is equivalent to the expected value of the product of the basic wage rate, his productivity index, and his employment status.

We can describe the solution to this problem in two parts. One part says that, given his choice of employment in each state of nature, the worker allocates his income between the two states to satisfy the first-order condition

$$u'(c_1) = pu'(c_2),$$

where $u'(\cdot)$ is the marginal utility function. For the special case of p equal to unity, this condition would imply that the worker sets Ω_1 equal to Ω_2, so that c_1 equals c_2, which means that his consumption is perfectly stable and predictable.

To obtain solutions for Ω_1 and Ω_2 for the case of p greater than unity, consider a family of $u(c)$ functions that exhibit constant relative risk aversion. The members of this family are $u = (1-r)^{-1} c^{1-r}$ for $r \neq 1$ and $u = \ln c$ for $r = 1$, where r measures relative risk aversion. For this family, the above first-order condition becomes

$$c_2 = p^{1/r} c_1,$$

which, when substituted into the constraints, implies

$$\Omega_1 = \frac{p\alpha_1 w_1 k l_1 + \alpha_2 w_2 k l_2}{p\alpha_1 + p^{1/r} \alpha_2}$$

and
$$\Omega_2 = p^{1/r} \Omega_1.$$

The second part of the solution to the worker's problem says that, given the criterion for allocation of consumption between the two states, the worker

determines his employment in each state. Depending now on α_1, α_2, w_1, w_2, k, and p, the worker again can choose employment in both states, only in the good state, or in neither state. In deciding among these options, the worker now selects the largest of the following possible values of $E(u-v)$:
For employment in both states,

$$E(u-v) = \alpha_1 u \left(\frac{p\alpha_1 w_1 k + \alpha_2 w_2 k}{p\alpha_1 \times p^{1/r}\alpha_2}\right) + \alpha_2 u\left(p^{1/r} \frac{p\alpha_1 w_1 k + \alpha_2 w_2 k}{p\alpha_1 + p^{1/r}\alpha_2}\right) - v(1) \equiv S(1)$$

For employment only in the good state,

$$E(u-v) \; \alpha_1 u \left(\frac{\alpha_2 w_2 k}{p\alpha_1 + p^{1/r}\alpha_2}\right) + \alpha_2 u \left(\frac{p^{1/r}\alpha_2 w_2 k}{p\alpha_1 + p^{1/r}\alpha_2}\right) - \alpha_1 v(0) - \alpha_2 v(1)$$
$$\equiv S(0,1).$$

For employment in neither state,

$$E(u-v) = u(0) - v(0) \equiv S(0,0).$$

In comparing the worker's options with and without risk shifting, observe that $S(0,0)$ is identical to $A(0,0)$, but that concavity of $u(\cdot)$ implies that $S(0,1)$ is larger than $A(0,1)$ and that $S(1,1)$ is larger than $A(1,1)$. Moreover, concavity of $u(\cdot)$ also implies that the value of $w_1 k$ that is necessary and sufficient for $S(1,1)$ to be larger than $S(0,1)$ is larger than z and is an increasing function of $w_2 k$.

These results mean that risk shifting increases the range of combinations of $w_1 k$ and $w_2 k$ for which the worker chooses employment only in the good state and decreases the ranges of combinations of $w_1 k$ and $w_2 k$ for which the worker chooses employment in both states and neither state. Because risk shifting allows the worker to use the value of his marginal contribution to output in the good state to supplement his actual income and consumption in the bad state, the value of working in the good state is larger and he desires not to be employed in the good state only if $w_2 k$ is sufficiently less than z. In addition, because risk shifting allows the worker to consume market goods in the bad state without working in the bad state, he desires to be employed in the bad state as well as in the good state only if $w_1 k$, is sufficiently more than z. Moreover, the larger is $w_2 k$, the larger has to be $w_1 k$ for the worker to desire employment in both states.

As before, the determination of which workers are employed in each state of nature depends on the distribution of the k_i. Again, the higher productivity classes of workers choose contracts that specify employment in both states of nature, whereas lower productivity classes of workers choose contracts that specify employment only in the good state of nature, and the lowest productivity individuals are not employed in either state of nature. However, this analysis confirms that with risk shifting fewer classes of workers are employed in both states of nature and more classes of workers are employed in at least one state of nature. Both of these changes mean that more individuals now experience variable employment.

The most important implication of this section relating to phenomena associated with layoffs is that risk shifting gives all workers, including those who are employed in both states or only one state, less variable wage income. In addition, as noted above, an essential consequence of the shifting of risk from workers to firms is that a worker's contractual income does not equal the value of his marginal contribution to total product, and, hence, it does not serve, as would the wage rate in a spot auction market, to signal the worker as to whether or not it is efficient for him to accept employment. Thus, this analysis confirms that allowing for risk shifting readily accounts for (P1) and (P2) and is consistent with (P4), but that the implications of risk shifting at the same time seem to be inconsistent with (P3), the fact that workers who are laid off usually receive no income from their employer.

7. Unemployment Insurance

This section introduces tax-financed unemployment insurance, but abstracts from risk shifting. The analysis assumes that the unemployment insurance works as follows: A fund is financed by taxes and pays benefits to unemployed workers. The net transactions of this fund are the only difference between the aggregate value of current consumption and the aggregate value of current output. Only workers who are not proximately responsible for the change in their own status from employed to unemployed can receive benefits. Use of the administrative procedure (P1) satisfies this restriction.

The amount of the benefits received by an unemployed worker depends directly on his earnings when employed. For the United States, the average replacement ratio of benefits, which until recently have not been taxable, to after-tax income seems to be slightly larger than one-half—Feldstein [1978]. For simplicity, the analysis assumes that average and marginal replacement ratios are equal. However, the analysis specifies that the amount of benefits would be reduced by the amount of any income that the unemployed worker received from his usual employer. This provision is apparently realistic and is crucial for the interaction, analysed in the next section, between unemployment insurance and risk shifting.

For unemployment insurance to be actuarially 'fair', the expected value of the taxes effectively paid to the unemployment insurance fund by each worker would have to equal the expected value of the net benefits he receives from the fund. It is possible that such an outcome would obtain if there were full experience rating in the calculation of each firm's contribution to the fund and benefits were taxed like other income. Actual unemployment insurance does not satisfy these conditions and apparently is actuarially favourable to workers who receive positive benefits and actuarially unfavorable to workers who do not receive benefits—Feldstein [1976]. For simplicity, the analysis abstracts from taxes, except for the financing of the unemployment insurance fund.

The worker's problem now is to choose the vector $(l_1, l_2, \Omega_1, \Omega_2)$ so as to maximize $E(u-v)$, subject to the constraints

$$l_1 = \{0, 1\}, l_2 = \{0, 1\},$$

$$c_1 = (1-\tau)\Omega_1 + b, \; c_2 = (1-\tau)\Omega_2,$$

$$\Omega_1 = w_1 k l_1, \quad \Omega_2 = w_2 k l_2,$$

$$b = \begin{cases} \beta\Omega_2, \text{ if } \alpha_2 = 1 \text{ and } \alpha_1 = 0 \\ 0, \text{ otherwise,} \end{cases}$$

$$\tau = \begin{cases} g, \text{ if } b = 0 \\ h, \text{ otherwise,} \end{cases}$$

where τ is the effective tax rate on wage income for the unemployment insurance fund and b is the amount of the unemployment benefit. According to these specifications, if an individual works only in the good state, b equals $\beta\,\Omega_2$ and τ equals h. Otherwise, b equals zero and τ equals g. Consumption in state two equals after-tax wage income. Consumption in state one equals either after-tax wage income or b.

Actuarially fair unemployment insurance would have g equal to zero and h equal to $\beta\alpha_1/\alpha_2$. As suggested above, it is probably more realistic to suppose that g is positive and that h is less than $\beta\alpha_1/\alpha_2$, which makes the system actuarially unfavourable to workers who are employed in both states and actuarially favourable to workers who are employed only in the good state.

The net replacement ratio is equal to $\beta/(1-h)$. We can easily calculate that unemployment insurance that was actuarially fair and complete, which would mean a net replacement ratio equal to unity, would have g equal to zero, h equal to α_1, and β equal to α_2.

Depending now on α_1, $\alpha_2, w_1, w_2, k, g, h$, and β, the solution to the worker's problem again can prescribe employment either in both states, only in the good state, or in neither state. In choosing among these options, the worker now selects the largest of the following possible values of $E(u-v)$:
For employment in both states,

$$E(u-v) = \alpha_1 u[(1-g)w_1 k] + \alpha_2 u[(1-g)w_2 k] - v(1) \equiv I(1,1).$$

For employment only in the good state,

$$E(u-v) = \alpha_1 u(\beta w_2 k) + \alpha_2 u[(1-h)w_2 k] - \alpha_1 v(0) - \alpha_2 v(1) \equiv I(0,1).$$

For employment in neither state,

$$E(u-v) = u(0) - v(0) \equiv I(0,0).$$

In comparing the worker's options with and without unemployment insurance, observe that $I(0,0)$ is identical to $A(0,0)$ and $S(0,0)$, and that, for actuarially fair and complete unemployment insurance and actuarially fair risk shifting, $I(0,1)$ is identical to $S(0,1)$ and larger than $A(0,1)$, and $I(1,1)$ is identical to $A(1,1)$ and smaller than $S(1,1)$. These relations mean that fair and complete unemployment insurance implies a range of values of w_2k for which the worker chooses employment in neither state that is the same as with fair risk shifting, a range of combinations of w_1k and w_2k for which the worker chooses employment only in the good state that is larger than with fair risk shifting, and a range of combinations of w_1k and w_2k for which the worker chooses employment in both states that is smaller than with fair risk shifting. These results mean that the introduction of fair and complete unemployment insurance would cause fewer classes of workers to be employed in neither state of nature, more classes of workers to be employed in only one state of nature, and fewer classes to be employed in both states of nature, and that the latter two effects are larger than would result from the introduction of fair risk shifting.

Extensions of these results are straightforward. Given actuarially fair unemployment insurance, making the net replacement ratio less than unity—which would mean $\alpha = 0, h = \beta\alpha_1/\alpha_2$, but $h < \alpha_1$ and $\beta < \alpha_2$—would reduce $I(0,1)$ and, hence, reduce the increase in the variability of employment. Alternatively, given complete unemployment insurance, making taxes actuarially favourable to individuals whose employment is variable—which would mean $\beta = 1-h$, but $h < \alpha_1$ and $\beta > \alpha_2$—would raise $I(0,1)$, and making taxes actuarially unfavourable to individuals whose employment is constant—which would mean $g > 0$—would reduce $I(1,1)$. Both of these changes would boost the increase in the variability of employment.

It is worth noting that the effect of actuarially fair unemployment insurance on the variability of employment depends on workers being risk averse. If workers were not risk averse, unemployment insurance would make employment more variable only if it were actuarially favourable to workers who are employed only in the good state, as in Feldstein [1976], or actuarially unfavourable to workers who are employed in both states.

This analysis also confirms that focusing only on unemployment insurance does not provide an adequate model of layoffs, because, although it is consistent with (P1), (P3), and (P4), this analysis cannot account for (P2). Specifically, in this section, the actual wage rate and income received by a worker who is employed in both states varies with the value of his marginal contribution to output.

8. Risk Shifting and Unemployment Insurance

This section combines the analyses of the previous two sections to consider the interactions between risk shifting and unemployment insurance. With both risk shifting and unemployment insurance available, the worker's problem is to choose the vector $(\alpha_1, \alpha_2, \Omega_1, \Omega_2)$ so as to maximize $E(u-v)$, subject to the constraints

$l_1 = \{0,1\}, l_2 = \{0,1\},$

$c_1 = (1-\tau)\,\Omega_1 + b, c_2 = (1-\tau)\,\Omega_2$

$p\alpha_1(\Omega_1 - w_1 k l_1) = \alpha_2(w_2 k l_2 - \Omega_2),$

$$b = \begin{cases} \beta\Omega_2 - \Omega_1, & \text{if } l_2 = 1 \text{ and } l_1 = 0 \\ 0, & \text{otherwise,} \end{cases}$$

$$\tau = \begin{cases} g, & \text{if } b = 0 \\ h, & \text{otherwise.} \end{cases}$$

This set of constraints creates the complication that a worker who chooses employment in the good state and unemployment in the bad state has the alternative of receiving income in the bad state either from risk-shifting arrangements with his employer or from unemployment insurance benefits. Note that, because benefits are paid only to replace lost income, this worker has no motivation to choose a combination of risk shifting and unemployment insurance benefits. If he chooses risk shifting, his net income is $(1-g)\,\alpha_2 w_2 k/(p\alpha_1 + p^{1/r}\alpha_2)$ in the bad state and $(1-g)\,p^{1/r}\alpha_2 w_2 k/(p\alpha_1 + p^{1/r}\alpha_2)$ in the good state. If he chooses unemployment insurance, his net income is $(1-h)\,w_2 k$ in the good state and $\beta w_2 k$ in the bad state.

If risk shifting were actuarially fair—i.e., $p = 1$—and unemployment insurance were actuarially fair and complete—i.e., $g = 0$ and $h = \beta\alpha_1/\alpha_2$—these alternatives would both provide constant net income equal to $\alpha_2 w_2 k$ and would be equally attractive. However, as discussed above, p actually seems to exceed unity, which makes risk shifting less attractive, and actual unemployment insurance is incomplete but seems to be actuarially favourable to unemployed workers, characteristics that have offsetting effects on its attractiveness. These considerations suggest that it is reasonable to suppose that workers who choose employment only in the good state find unemployment insurance to be preferable to risk shifting. Note, however, that even if such workers find risk shifting unattractive relative to unemployment insurance, risk shifting remains attractive in reducing income variability for other workers who choose to be employed in both states.

Under these conditions, the worker now selects the employment status that corresponds to the largest of the following possible values of $E(u-v)$:

For employment in both states,

$$E(u-v) = \alpha_1\, u\left[(1-g)\,\frac{p\alpha_1 w_1 k + \alpha_2 w_2 k}{p\alpha_1 + p^{1/r}\alpha_2}\right] + \alpha_2\, u\left[(1-g)p^{1/r}\frac{p\alpha_1 w_1 k + \alpha_2\, w_2 k}{p\alpha_1 + p^{1/r}\alpha_2}\right]$$

$$- v(1) \equiv SI(1,1)$$

For employment only in the good state,

$$E(u - v) = \alpha_1 u(\beta w_2 k) + \alpha_2[(1-h)w_2 k] - \alpha_1 v(0) - \alpha_2 v(1) \equiv SI(0,1).$$

For employment in neither state,

$$E(u-v) = u(0) - v(0) \equiv SI(0,0).$$

In evaluating the worker's options with both unemployment insurance and risk shifting, observe that $SI(0,0)$ is identical to $I(0,0)$, that $SI(0,1)$ is identical to $I(0,1)$, and that $SI(1,1)$ is larger than $I(1,1)$. These observations imply that the range of values of $w_2 k$ for which the worker chooses employment in neither state is the same with both unemployment insurance and risk shifting as with only unemployment insurance, but that the range of combinations of $w_1 k$ and $w_2 k$ for which a worker chooses employment in both states is larger with both unemployment insurance and risk shifting than with only unemployment insurance.

These results enable us to draw the following two conclusions. First, although the introduction of risk shifting into a model without unemployment insurance would tend to magnify employment fluctuations, the actual effect of risk shifting in economies that have unemployment insurance is probably to make employment less variable. This result obtains as long as unemployment insurance is more attractive than risk shifting for most workers as a way to obtain income during states of unemployment. Under these conditions the availability of risk shifting does not make unemployment any more tolerable, but it does make stable employment more attractive.

Second, allowing for the effects of both risk shifting and unemployment insurance enables us to account for the full set of diverse phenomena associated with layoffs. The administrative assignment of workers, (P1), results from the fact that risk shifting makes wage income unequal to the value of product and/or from the eligibility rules of unemployment insurance benefits. The constancy of wages for employed workers, (P2), directly reflects risk shifting. The fact that workers who are laid off usually receive no income from their employer, (P3), results from the attractiveness to them of unemployment insurance relative to risk shifting. Finally, the role of seniority in determining the incidence of layoffs, (P4), reflects the relation between age and length of service and productivity.

9. General Implications

As indicated by the preceding paragraph, this paper has developed explanations for the phenomena associated with layoffs without reference to a failure of labour markets to clear and a loss of perceived gains from trade. This analysis implies that, although a laid-off worker might want to work if offered either the wage rate he received when he was employed or the wage rate inclusive of insurance indemnity received currently by more senior workers who are employed, he would typically not want to work at the wage rate equal to the perceived value of his marginal product. Thus, the use of layoffs to effect employment separations does not imply that the amount of employment is suboptimal relative to current perceptions.

This interpretation of layoffs suggests that, as mentioned above, it may be realistic to attribute the causal relation between aggregate demand and aggregate employment to misperceptions of the exchange ratio between consumption goods and labour sevices, resulting from the limited ability of economic agents to distinguish aggregate disturbances from relative disturbances, rather than to an alleged failure of markets to clear. Other recent work incorporating risk shifting arrangements into the paradigm of incomplete information supports this point of view. For example, Grossman [1979] shows that the existence of risk-shifting arrangements in labour markets strengthens the substitution effects that influence the choice of the efficient level of employment, implying that only weak restrictions on worker utility functions are necessary for changes in current nominal marginal products relative to perceived prices or expected future marginal products to have a strongly positive effect in employment. Finally, it is worth stressing again that emphasising the failure to perceive gains from trade correctly does not mitigate in any way the wastefulness of non-Walrasian fluctuations in aggregate employment and the undesirability of monetary and fiscal policies which produce fluctuations in aggregate demand.

REFERENCES

Azariadis, C. [1978], 'Escalator Clauses and the Allocation of Cyclical Risks,' *Journal of Economic Theory*, 18, June, 119–155.

Baily, M. N. [1977], 'On the Theory of Layoffs and Unemployment,' *Econometrica*, 45, July, 1043–1063.

Barro, R. J. [1977], 'Long-Term Contracting, Sticky Prices, and Monetary Policy,' *Journal of Monetary Economics*, 3, July, 305–316.

Barro R. J., and Grossman, H. I. [1976] *Money, Employment, and Inflation*, (New York: Cambridge University Press).

Feldstein, M. [1976], 'Temporary Layoffs in the Theory of Unemployment,' *Journal of Political Economy*, 84, October, 937–957.

Feldstein, M. [1978], 'The Effect of Unemployment Insurance on Temporary Layoff Unemployment,' *American Economic Review*, 68, December, 834–846.

Friedman, M. [1968], 'The Role of Monetary Policy,' *American Economic Review*, 58, March 1–17.

Grossman, H. I. [1977], 'Risk Shifting and Reliability in Labor Markets,' *Scandinavian Journal of Economics*, 79, no. 2, 187–209.

Grossman, H. I. [1978], 'Risk Shifting, Layoffs, and Seniority,' *Journal of Monetary Economics*, 4, November, 661–686.

Grossman, H. I. [1979], 'Incomplete Information, Risk Shifting, and Employment Fluctuations,' unpublished manuscript, April.

Lucas, Jr., R. E. [1977], 'Understanding Business Cycles,' in K. Brunner and A. Meltzer, eds., *Stabilization of the Domestic and International Economy*, (New York: North Holland), 7–29.

Risk Shifting, Unemployment Insurance and Layoffs

COMMENT by Harvey S. Rosen (Princeton University)

Unemployment is characteristic of the economies of both the UK and the US in the view of many economists, unemployment is a disequilibrium phenomenon. In a typical disequilibrium model, for some (usually unspecified) reason, the wage fails to equate supply and demand, and therefore there exist unexploited opportunities for mutually beneficial trade.

The literature on implicit labour contracts provides a choice-theoretic explanation for wage inflexibility. The basic idea is that risk-averse employees and risk neutral employers can both benefit if the employers provide workers with wage insurance. Workers are willing to accept a wage lower than their marginal product in 'good times' in exchange for a wage higher than their marginal product in 'bad times'—hence, wage inflexibility.

Unfortunately the simple model appears to do its work too well, because it implies that at the optimum the individual will receive a 'guaranteed' wage in all states of nature. Grossman introduces unemployment insurance into the implicit contract framework in order to provide a rationalization for layoffs without pay. In effect, due to the absence of complete experience rating, it benefits both employer and employee if the employee is periodically laid-off and the government provides income. The basic idea is similar to one introduced by Feldstein [1976] several years ago.

Thus, Grossman's paper moves the implicit contract literature in the direction of greater realism. A few problems remain, however. The theory seems to provide rationalization for rigidity in *real* wages, although *nominal* wage stickiness seems to be quite important. Furthermore, there may be a moral hazard problem in the model. Presumably, employers have better information about the true state of the world than employees as well as an incentive (in Grossman's model) to tell employees that the state of the world is 'good' even if this is not true. Although it may be the case that firms will not lie because a reputation for honesty is very valuable in the market place, such considerations should be incorporated in the model explicitly and not added in an *ad hoc* fashion.

Before proceeding further, it may be useful to introduce a simple diagram that often accompanies discussions of non-market clearing labour markets. In figure one, the real wage (W) is measured on the vertical axis, manhours (L) on the horizontal, and DD and SS indicate demand and supply schedules, respectively. W_e is the market clearing wage, but because of 'rigidities,' wage $\bar{W}$, prevails. At $\bar{W}$, supply of labour L^S exceeds demand L^D, leading to involuntary employment of $(OL^S - OL^D)$.

Figure 1

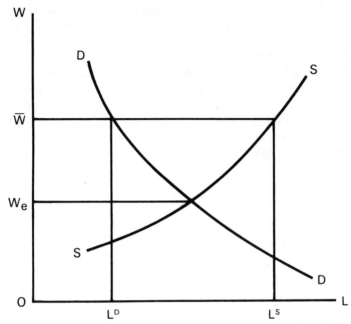

Mathematically, the situation can be characterized by these equations:

(1) $\qquad L^D_t = f(W_t, X_t)$

(2) $\qquad L^S_t = g(W_t, Z_t)$

(3) $\qquad L_t = \min(L^D_t, L^S_t),$

where the t subscript denotes time period $t, f(\cdot)$ and $g(\cdot)$ are the demand and supply functions, respectively, and X_t and Z_t are vectors of shift variables. This system is often augmented by a wage adjustment equation:

(4) $\qquad \dfrac{6dw}{dt} = \gamma \times (L^D_t - L^S_t),$

where $\gamma > 0$. In words, the real wage moves according to excess demand.

Now, the implicit contract literature can be viewed as a criticism of this view of the world. Researchers like Grossman believe that situations in which L^S_t exceeds L^D_t are not consequences of disequilibrium. Rather, such phenomena are *ex post* consequences of situations that are *ex ante* in equilibrium. 'Min conditions' like equation (3) are criticized as *ad hoc* constructs because there is no optimizing story behind them.

However, Eaton and Quandt [1979] have recently shown in an implicit contract theory framework that disequilibrium in a market need not rest on an *ad hoc* assertion of price rigidity, but may emerge as a result of optimizing by

279

firms subject to stochastic variation of their production functions. Non-market clearing theories thus cannot be dismissed as lacking choice-theoretic foundations. Perhaps, then, effort should be devoted to econometric tests of which view of the economic environment in which implicit contracts are formed better corresponds to reality.

Finally, I would like to comment briefly on the relationship between the Grossman paper and equation (4). Such wage adjustment equations have also been criticized—and appropriately so—for lacking choice-theoretic foundations. Economists appear to know very little about how prices move between equilibria. Implicit contract theory is mostly silent on this dynamic issue, which surely deserves serious attention.

REFERENCES

Eaton, Jonathan and Quandt, Richard E. [1979], 'A Quasi-Walrasian Model of Rationing and Labor Supply: Theory and Estimation,' mimeo, Princeton University.

Feldstein, Martin S., [1976], 'Temporary Layoffs in the Theory of Unemployment,' *Journal of Political Economy*, October, pp. 937–58.

Forecasting Employment and Unemployment*

S. G. B. Henry
National Institute of Economic and Social Research

* Thanks are due to Hassan Feisal and Leigh Roberts for valuable research assistance in preparing this paper.

FORECASTING EMPLOYMENT AND UNEMPLOYMENT

(1) Introduction

This paper describes the models used by the major forecasting teams in the UK in forecasting employment and unemployment. Then, using a common data set for the manufacturing sector, the paper investigates the properties of a number of alternative models of employment determination. Under this second heading the consistency of the proposed models with the changes in the labour market and their robustness, or structural stability, over different sample periods is emphasised. The reason for this concentration on a relatively aggregate measure of employment in the regression work is that, as described later, a good deal of the uncertainty about the labour market arises from the actual behaviour of employment, particularly in the manufacturing sector. A further reason is that disaggregate models of employment typically use equations originally developed and tested on aggregate manufacturing data (e.g. Wilson [1979]). Finally there has been a paucity of empirical studies on unemployment, so that a comparative study of the kind already indicated, is not possible for this.

(2) The problems of Employment and Unemployment Forecasting

The forecaster is confronted with immense problems in the dual task of providing an account of labour market behaviour and in predicting movements in aggregates like employment and unemployment. The reasons for this are the substantial changes that have apparently taken place in the behaviour of employment and unemployment since the mid 1960s. Unemployment, typically hovering around 200–300,000 in the early 1960s, rose to the 800,000 level by 1972 and then to approximately 1.4 million by 1978. Such levels as often pointed out, were unthinkable in the 1950s and early 1960s. Employment has also proved difficult, perhaps more difficult, to explain. Two developments are often commented on, and indeed will figure in later discussion in this paper. In the late 1960s employment was generally less than predicted. It was common to hear this referred to as 'shake-out', this expression conveying the belief that firms had moved to a less employment intensive technology, with supposed advantageous improvements in labour-productivity. Since there was little independent testing of this interpretation, 'shake-out' now appears to be a rationalisation undertaken after the event.[1]

After 1973–4 a similar, but reverse, phenomenon occurred. That is to say, employment was actually higher from this time than had been the case of earlier periods when demand (as measured by output) had been at similar

[1] One exception was the work by Taylor [1972].

levels. Again, as in the 1960s, this engendered the view that the underlying productivity performance of the economy had undergone a structural change. Certainly the trend movement in output per head apparently changed as chart 1 below shows, and it was observations such as this that led to the proposal that changed employment behaviour was due to changes in (labour) 'productivity trends'. I will discuss the empirical usefulness of such interpretations in section 4 below.

Figure 1   Source: Financial Statement [1979]

It is worth adding that this is not a problem peculiar to the U K. George Perry, in his paper on Potential Output and Productivity, notes what he terms the weakness of productivity in the US since 1973. The Council of Economic Advisors interpreted this as reflecting low rates of capital accumulation and the rise in energy prices, and consequently revised down projected potential growth to 3½ per cent through to 1980. (CEA 1977)

In the sections that follow I intend to give an account of how the main forecasting teams have approached these problems of modelling employment and unemployment, and give an outline of the problems encountered by their models. I will also describe a number of proposals that have been made, aimed at improving both the understanding of labour market behaviour and forecasting performance. In both of these areas I will restrict myself to published models and research papers, since other model proprietors no doubt have their own strategies for dealing with the problems I have described, and will describe these elsewhere in this conference. The topics I am to cover will not, I hope be unhelpful to modellers though. However, although this paper will tend towards being a survey of labour market modelling it will soon be clear that it is an extremely selective one. This is perhaps inevitable in a paper of this kind. One omission is the absence of any full discussion of the role of different assumptions about technology in employment models, and possible extensions that might be made here to current practices. I do this with the belief that, whilst important, our failure to model the firms' technology in a more realistic way is not at the root of our failure to forecast employment. I hope to be able to show that some progress in modelling employment for example may be made using fairly simple assumptions about the firms' technology. Others perhaps will take a different view.[2]

(3) Current models of employment and unemployment

Here the main lines of the models currently being used by the major UK forecasters are sketched out. Details of the sources used are given in the bibliography.

(i) *Employment*

In employment forecasting there is a considerable degree of agreement over the basic approach among the main forecasting teams. The group standing somewhat outside the description that follows is the MRG at Warwick, and I will discuss this separately later. The rest deal with employment forecasting using an equation which may be loosely referred to as a demand for labour equation. The Bank, HMT and NIESR adopt an equation derived from the assumption of a cost minimising firm attempting to meet given output objectives. The minimising is assumed to be with respect to a single factor, that of labour, and the usual practice is to treat labour simply as numbers employed. Thus in these equations employment depends on output, which is treated as predetermined, with a lagged adjustment. The capital stock is either substituted out, or subsumed—together with exogenous technical progress—into a time trend. Seminal papers on which this approach is based are those of Ball and St. Cyr [1966] and Brechling [1965]. There are differences between the forecasting models, for example over the degree of disaggregation used, but these are not matters of any controversy and I do not propose to discuss them any further in this section.

The LBS equation is somewhat different from the others as it relates employment to the real wage (defined as average earnings in real terms including employers' contributions and the NI surcharge, and adjusted for cyclical output per head changes), and output. This may be derived from the first order profit-maximising condition with respect to labour, i.e.

(1) $\qquad w = f_N' (N, K, t)$

where w is the real wage, N is employment, K is the capital stock and t a time

---

[2] Interesting work using vintage capital assumptions in employment modelling has been reported in Hutton *et. al.* See also Peterson [1976].

trend. Substituting out K by using the production function

(2) $\qquad Q = f(N, K, t)$

and solving the resulting equation for N, the equation is a straightforward demand for labour function (see (3) below). One convenient simplification (or perhaps it should be called a convenient fiction) disappears in this formulation compared with that of the cost-minimising model described in the previous paragraph. Relative factor prices are, along with output, taken as given by the firm in the cost minimising exercise. In the profit maximising one, the real wage is jointly determined along with labour. I will discuss this point further in Section 5 on full market models. At this point it should merely be noted that in the LBS model the immediate problem of estimating the equation

(3) $\qquad N^D = N(Q, w, t)$

is approached by lagging the real wage and estimating the equation by OLS.

Since the CEPG has an interdependent employment and unemployment model, I will first move on to discuss general practice in modelling unemployment before returning to their model.

(ii) Unemployment

If the papers by Ball and St. Cyr and Brechling are essential reading to appreciate the methods used by UK model builders to model employment, then the work by Godley and Shepherd [1964] on unemployment, employment and productive potential is the intellectual antecedent of a good deal of current practice in modelling unemployment. It is worth recalling briefly. Given a forecast of employment, the Godley and Shepherd equation provides a simple empirical scheme for mapping this into a level of unemployment allowing for two additional influences: the changes in the potential workforce due to population changes and participation rates, and estimated cyclical variations in the registration rate. Thus the total labour force is F where

(4) $\qquad F = N + U + U_n,$

where U is registered unemployment and U_n is the number of unemployed who do not register. The hypothesis concerning U_n is that it is a non-linear function of the level of unemployment, where more workers register as unemployment rises, thus

(5) $\qquad U_n = g(U)$, with $g' > 0$

Further they assume

(6) $\qquad F = D + f(t)$

286

where D is the 'demographic contribution to the work-force', or the working population at given (mid 1961) participation rates, so that $f(t)$ is meant to measure the trend change in participation rates. Combining (4), (5) and (6) gives the equation

$$(7) \qquad E - D = U + g(U) + f(t)$$

where the functions $g(.)$ and $f(.)$, were determined by Godley and Shepherd by computing regression for (7) over a few simple alternative forms for these functions.

Current practice amongst U K modellers has not added much to the Godley and Shepherd equations (equation 7), either by developing a model on a firmer theoretical base or using noticeably more elaborate estimation methods than they did. It is particularly significant that none of the forecasting models described so far (HMT, LBS, NIESR and the Bank of England) use an estimated model for unemployment. (The CEPG does not quote summary statistics for the regression results of any of its equations, so it is impossible to judge the adequacy of their formulation on statistical grounds.) The LBS, for example, uses the most simplified form of unemployment equation, linking the change in employment to changes in unemployment with an imposed coefficient of -0.89063. The Treasury's version is perhaps the most sophisticated, with an imposed logistic function to model the non-linear rate of non-registration, although in all other essentials it is a direct descendent of the original Godley and Shepherd model.

The CEPG, though a near relative, has some important differences compared with models already discussed. Employment is given by the orthodox partial adjustment scheme, i.e. in logs.

$$\Delta N = \lambda \{N^* - N_{-1}\}$$

where, however, desired values are

$$(8) \qquad N^* - L = a_0 + a_1 t + \beta_1 \{Q - \beta_2 L\}$$

(technical manual p. 44). Here the variable L represents the total labour force less an exogenous component for public service employment, (n.b. employment is measured in terms of a full time equivalent, so L is adjusted for this also). The term in brackets in (8) represents 'productive potential', and I will have more to say about this in the next section. The CEPG's model of unemployment also allows for variations in registrations due to changes in the level of unemployment.

(iii) Warwick Group

The MRG at Warwick present disaggregated projections for employment and unemployment over a medium term forecasting horizon (1977–82). In modelling the labour demand side the Group appear to rely on models like those described here and in the next few sections for aggregate employment. (See Section 4 below especially the discussion of the model produced by Hazledine [1978]). The problems of deriving a statistically robust account of the demand side which I will continue to emphasise in discussion of the aggregate models apply here also, perhaps with greater force since their forecast period is longer. Assessment of their performance on this score is however difficult since although they project employment, for a large number of different employment categories, the equations used for these calculations are not quoted. (See Lindley [1978] p. 120 which promises a full explanation of the (employment) model eventually). Wilson summarises work done at Warwick which compares the forecasting performance of the Hazledine model as compared with the Ball-St. Cyr model among others, and further tests and comments on Hazledine's model are given in the present paper (section 4 below).

On the supply side, the MRG base their forecasts on DE projections disaggregated using population accounting matrices. Apart from the disaggregation, the approach is similar to that adopted by other forecasting teams, and my remarks on the aggregate models are intended to apply equally to this work also.

(4) Some Problems in the Current Models

This section summarises what have appeared as the major problem areas in both the theoretical and empirical features of the employment and unemployment models. For brevity these are simply listed with short accompanying notes below.

(i) The first and obvious problem is an empirical one, namely the failure by most teams to find reliable and technically stable functions to forecast with. In the case of unemployment, the absence of fitted equations is evidence of obvious failure here. In the case of employment it is well known that when estimating employment-output relationships with simple dynamics, quite radically different parameter values are obtained when the employment equation is estimated over different sample periods. This failure implies two things. First, that it is difficult to forecast either employment or unemployment, sometimes even over relatively short periods of time. Second, policy implications for the medium term become highly uncertain.

The equation in Table 1 illustrates the problem of obtaining a technically stable relationship for employment. It is a re-estimate of the original Ball and St. Cyr model, and I have taken this as an illustration since it is sufficiently closely related to models currently used to make the results of some interest, while avoiding the invidious choice of selecting a particular forecasting model to illustrate a common failing.

Seasonal dummy variables are not quoted. Figures in parenthesis are 't' statistics. $\chi_1^2 (8)$ is a test of post fitting parameter stability based on the one step forecast errors. $\chi_2^2 (12)$ is the Box-Pierce random residual correlogram test with twelve degrees of freedom, and $\chi_3^2 (1)$ is a likelihood ratio test of the unrestricted reduced form of a first order autoregressive version of the model versus an ordinary least squares version.

Table 1 Ball and St. Cyr model, $ln\ N = a_0 + a_1\ ln\ Q + a_2\ ln\ N_{-1} + a_3 t$
(Data Manufacturing Industry, not seasonally adjusted)

Sample	a_0	a_1	a_2	a_3	$\chi_1^2(8)$	$\chi_2^2(12)$	$\chi_3^2(1)$	R^2
1964 Q1–	0.250	0.121	0.824	−0.002	49.85	26.165	3.204	0.99
1976 Q4	(1.254)	(5.102)	(18.915)	(6.065)				

This model is estimated up to 197604, and a further eight sample points are retained to test the post sample stability of the equation. The test shows a failure by the model by a considerable margin (the cut-off value at the 5% level is 15.5). The other feature of this equation that is worth bringing out concerns the perennial question of the implied returns to labour. The estimation in Table 1 gives a long run value for this parameter of 1.4545 $[a_1/(1-a_2))^{-1}]$ An earlier study by Hornstein and Tarling [1976] computed regressions for the manufacturing sector and obtained a value of 1.662 for the period 1954–1966, but a value of 0.810 for the period 1966–73.

(ii) The Ball-St. Cyr model is a convenient one for illustration, but, as will be described in the next section, other models which are commonly used reveal a similar instability. This instability raises problems in forecasting, particularly over the medium term, since as the example illustrates, projections based on supposed firm relationships between employment and output must be subject to great uncertainty since these relationships apparently have undergone substantial change over the last decade or so.

(iii) On the supply side, it is clear that common practice is to treat labour supply as being effectively exogenous. Most forecasting teams use total labour force predictions based on the Department of Employment projections. These use estimates of the population derived from population surveys and related information, and predictions are based on extrapolated activity rates for the different age-sex groups comprising the labour force. In very short-run studies the errors involved in these predictions need not be substantial. For medium term projections they may be very serious, and involve substantial changes in both the level and the composition of the workforce. On the latter point for example, a recent Department of Employment appraisal notes the sharp rise in female activity rates from 1971 to 1975, [1977], and attributes, these changes to a declining birth rate which released a larger proportion of females for work, the possibility of equal pay and job opportunities encouraging additional female workers, and finally, the growth in part-time work. Unemployment forecasts are made therefore, with the labour force variable treated as effectively exogenous, and the evidence is that there are serious errors in the forecast values. There has been very little time series work on endogenous labour supply, even in medium to long-run studies, which is a serious gap, though given the dearth of published work in this area of forecasting, I will not give much space to this topic in later sections.

[1] This equation was estimated on GIVE, a program developed by D. Hendry and F. Srba. LSE. All reported results use this programme unless otherwise stated.

(iv) Finally these points together should introduce extreme caution in the treatment of calculations of 'productive potential'. This is usually gauged from trend movements in output per head, with working population figures at extrapolated participation rates substituted in for employment to represent 'supply' side influences. (See for example the CEPG model, equation (8) above, which has this feature).

In the next section, I will be reviewing some amendments to employment and unemployment modelling that have been suggested in the light of some of the problems noted in the present section. These may broadly be thought of as attempts to improve the properties of employment and unemployment equations in a piecemeal way. More elaborate possibilities are described in section (6).

(5) Possible re-specification of existing models

(a) *Employment*

(i) One attempted rationalisation of supposed increasing returns to labour was that it indicated a mis-specification due to the assumption of full utilisation of capital stock in the short-run. This view was advanced by Smyth and Ireland [1976], who argued that both the rates of utilisation of the capital stock and the labour force are decision variables in the short-run. Assuming a CES production function, the resulting employment equations merely involve a re-parameterisation of that advocated by Ball and St. Cyr. The ratio of coefficients $a_1/(1 - a_2)$ (See Table 1 above), instead of identifying long-run responses of employment to output (the inverse of returns to labour), now identifies the returns to scale in the CES function. Therefore, the argument goes, this could be greater than one without offending the short-run maximising requirement that returns to factors be diminishing. Such a re-interpretation must be treated with scepticism in the light of the regression results given earlier, since it implies, if true, that returns to scale have been fluctuating quite substantially over different sample periods.

(ii) It may be argued that the underlying trend behaviour of the economy has altered, and a re-specification of the Ball and St. Cyr model which took this into account would produce a more successful forecasting equation. A view of this sort might be suggested from the inspection of trend movements of output per head in Chart 1 above, where there is clearly a structural break around 1973–74. Clearly such a step aims at improving the equation on a purely post-hoc basis. As such it is a prime example of evidence without theory, but it may nonetheless be a successful ploy. I have attempted to test such a view by re-estimating the Ball and St. Cyr model with an additional dummy variable T which is a time trend initiated in 1974 Q1. The results are shown in Table 2. Whilst the use of this dummy variable results in a reduction of post fitting error variance, clearly the experiment is not a success. The χ_1^2 (8) is still significant at the 5% level, and the implied returns to labour have jumped to 2.121. This latter result depends partly on the coefficient in the lagged dependent variable getting dangerously close to unity.

290

(iii) Another, wholly more challenging view than the two proposals discussed so far is by Nickell [1979], who suggests that a combination of increased cost of acquiring and firing workers (due to employment protection legislation) and growing pessimism of future output

Table 2 $lnN = \beta_0 + \beta_1 \, lnQ + \beta_2 \, lnN_{-1} + \beta_2 t + \beta_4 T$
(Data Manufacturing Industry, not seasonally adjusted)

Sample	β_0	β_1	β_2	β_3	β_4	$\chi_1^2 (8)$	$\chi_2^2 (12)$	$\chi_3^2 (2)$	R^2
1964 Q1	−0·0481	0·193	0·909	−0·001	0·002	25·592	16·96	3·009	0·992
1976 Q1	(1·722)	(6·433)	(19·641)	(7·576)	(3·402)				

trends are important to understand recent employment behaviour. His analysis indeed aims to show that both the variations in estimated returns to labour and the structural instability already noted can be explained.

The essential new ingredient in the analysis is the introduction of adjustment costs due to changes in the size of the work force. Such an assumption of adjustment costs is often used in both investment and employment models, and since this assumption will occur in other parts of this paper I will give a short account of it here to establish its main features. In a single factor intertemporal case the firm is assumed to maximise

$$(9) \qquad \Phi = \int_0^\infty e^{-rt} f(N, \dot{N}, t) \, dt$$

given initial conditions. The first order conditions of importance produce a second order differential equation in N (the Euler condition), i.e.,

$$(10) \qquad f_{\dot{N}\dot{N}} \ddot{N} + f_{\dot{N}N} \dot{N} + f_N - rf_{\dot{N}} = 0$$

and the transversality conditions

$$(11) \qquad \lim_{t \to \infty} e^{-rt} f_{\dot{N}} = 0$$

Next the non-linear equation is linearised around an equilibrium path $N^*(t)$ (supposing one can be found, which is no easy matter, see Tinsley [1971]), giving

$$(12) \qquad A\ddot{N} + B\dot{N} + C(N - N^*) = 0$$

where the terms A, B and C are dependent on derivatives all evaluated on the equilibrium path. Finally to obtain an explicit solution path for $N(t)$, the characteristic roots of (12) are extracted. These roots are symmetric with $\mu_1 <$

$0 < \mu_2$, where $\mu_i (i = 1, 2)$ are the roots. Thus a solution consistent with the transversaility conditions (11) rules out the positive root μ_2, and then

$$N(t) = Ae^{\mu_1 t} + N^*$$

with A dependent on initial conditions. Such a formulation has been used for employment studies by Tinsley [1971], Wickens [1974], Henry [1979] and Nickell [1979].

Nickell introduces expected movements in output and the possibility of policy-induced movements in adjustment costs explicitly into this framework. His analysis is in discrete time, but apart from that the analysis follows that indicated above, with extensions as I shall note presently. The production function is assumed to be (where Q^e is expected output)

(13) $$Q_t^e = g(N_t)H_t e^{Bt}$$

Then the dynamic equation for $N(t)$ (the discrete version of equation 10 above) may be linearised around N^* (a fixed value) which is the solution of the static problem

$$\underset{N}{\text{Min }} W(\dot{H}) N \, s.t \, \bar{Q} = g(N)H$$

where $\bar{Q}$ is the mean value of Q^e. The solution of the resulting linear equation may be written

(14) $$lnN - \mu_1 \, ln \, N_{-1} = \alpha + \epsilon(1-\mu_1)(1-\alpha_1\mu_1) \overset{\infty}{\underset{s}{\Sigma}} (\alpha_1\mu_1)^{s-t} \, ln \, N^*(s) + \epsilon(1-\mu_1)Bt$$

where $g(\cdot) = AN^{1/\epsilon}$, and N is assumed to be in the region of N^* defined above. In this formulation μ_1 is the stable root of the linearised characteristic equation of the Euler equation, and, as can be readily established, is a bounded optimal solution to the minimising problem posed. Further, $1/\epsilon$ may be identified as the output elasticity of employment, α_1 is the rate of discount $\{(1 + r)$ in the discreet case$\}$, and it may be established that μ_1 (the stable root) increases as adjustment costs increase [see Nickell, p. 10]

Next, following Sims [1974] if the firm forms its expectation about future output movements according to the rule

$$Q(s) = e^{-\gamma s} \bar{Q}(1 + \phi^{s-t}(\frac{Q}{Q_e}\gamma t - 1))$$

where $0 \leqslant \phi \leqslant$, and $\bar{Q}$ is a known deterministic trend in output, then, on substituting this expression into equation (14), the resulting first order equation resembles the Ball and St. Cyr type we have used so far, i.e.,

(15) $$ln \, N = \beta_0 + \frac{(1 - \mu_1)(1 - \alpha_1\mu_1)}{(1 - \alpha_1\mu_1\phi)} ln \, Q + \mu_1 \, ln \, N_{-1} + \beta_1 t.$$

In the absence of an independent estimate of ϕ, the equation is underidentified, but it nonetheless may be used to suggest possible reasons for the apparent changes already noted. The coefficient on $ln\ N_{-1}$ increases with adjustment costs, so there is an a priori case for expecting a significant change in this coefficient post 1966. Secondly, this coefficient may be expected to change yet again post 1972, due to the various measures aimed at protective employment introduced from that date.

The coefficient of $ln\ Q$ is not equal to ϵ, where $1/\epsilon = \delta ln\ Q/\delta ln\ N$, unless ϕ, the adjustment parameter in (15) above, equals unity. That is, the more *slowly* Q approaches $Qe^{\gamma t}$, the closer the estimated coefficient on $ln\ Q$ in (16) above approximates ϵ.

Thus increases in hiring and firing costs will tend to push up the coefficient on the lagged dependent variable, while growing pessimism about output growth ($\phi \to 1$) will increase the coefficient on Q in the equation. The effects of each will be to push up the ratio of coefficients $a_1/(1 - a_2)$, and lower the long-run elasticity of output with respect to employment. However, the results quoted on p.8 earlier do not support this hypothesis of a monotonic change in the implied elasticities. The Hornstein and Tarling results show the elasticity $(a_1/(1 - a_2))^{-1}$ falling, but Table 1 shows that this rises when additional data points (1974–1976) are added, which result conflicts with the explanation put forward by Nickell. Further, equation (15) is a first-order type which is known not to forecast well, so Nickell's suggestion, interesting though it is, would not appear to help the forecaster much.

(iv) Special employment measures, e.g., TES, Job Release Scheme etc., whilst important for the modeller to take into account, are not likely to account for the problems in relating employment to measures of output, factor prices and the like. I say this because

(a) these affect only a relatively small number of employees; the DE calculated the maximum number covered by all the schemes were 320,000 in November 1977 for example,

(b) their effects are concentrated in certain industries, e.g. Clothing and Textiles, and these show a similar productivity change to that noted above.

(v) Dynamic modelling of BSC model. Initially, Sargan, and more recently Hendry, have exposited techniques aimed at the empirical determination of distributed lags in economic relationships (Sargan [1980], Davidson *et. al.,* [1978] and Hendry and Mizon [1980] are useful references here). The techniques are in some contrast to that usually undertaken in applied studies which begin from a restricted model and then consider, in the light of the empirical results, whether a more general model is required (e.g., interpreting a significant DW statistic as evidence pointing to additional first order lags in the systematic model). Instead the analysis proceeds from a general unrestricted dynamic model, and seeks to provide systematic testing procedures for simplifying the model in the light of the results. In order to implement these techniques, and to investigate whether a tolerably successful short-run forecasting equation can be developed, I have taken a model suggested by the Ball and St. Cyr study described at length already. That is, I have taken as the steady state growth path a relationship of the form,

$$\left(\frac{Q}{N}\right) = A_0 e^{\gamma t}$$

As argued earlier, however, there is considerable evidence that long-run productivity (output per head) levels have changed significantly since 1974, so a dummy variable was used in the model to give this effect, as described earlier. These dynamics, or out of equilibrium behaviour, of the N variable were not specified a priori (as it is, for example, in Table 6) but were investigated using the techniques alluded to earlier. In general form the model proposed is

$$(16) \qquad \Delta ln\ N = \theta(L)\ \Delta ln\ N + \psi(L)\ \Delta lnQ + \delta(L)\ \left(ln\tfrac{Q}{N}\right)_{-1}$$
$$+ \Sigma_i\ ln\left(\tfrac{Q}{N}\right)_{-i} + \epsilon t$$

where L is the lag operator and $ln\left(\tfrac{Q}{N}\right)$ and $\Sigma(.)$ are error correction mechanisms of proportional and integral form respectively. Up to fourth order lags were used on the variables and the implied parameterisation was a fourth period difference (Δ_4) on N and Q and a single proportionate error correction term. This appeared to be the most parsimonious form given the tests described earlier. The eventual preferred equation is contained in Table 3.

The steady-state solution of the model is

$$\left(\frac{Q}{N}\right) = A\ K_0 e^{0.0096t}\ , \text{ where}$$

$$A\ = \text{unity pre 1974 Q1}$$

$= 0.0886$ post 1974 Q1 due to the operation of the dummy variable D. In other words, the steady state solution is constrained to produce a switch in output per head at 1974 Q1, so that the correction mechanism is aimed at a lower trend movement in output per head after that date. As I have emphasised, this is a post-hoc device aimed to produce improved forecasts, and is not to be confused with an explanation of why the changes in these trend movements in $\tfrac{Q}{N}$ took place. Unlike the examples quoted earlier, the one step forecasting performance of this equation is fairly good, and though it does not suggest reasons for the changes in employment behaviour over the last decade, it is relatively coherent with the data. In Section 5 below I will discuss this more fully, and compare the performance of this equation with others developed in that section.

Before leaving this section I would point out the resemblance of the line of argument in this section (and the example in Table 3 and the model of employment and hours provided by Hazledine. His analysis of the employment function also contains a considerable amount of rationalising of known changes in trends, being linked to peak to peak extrapolations in output per head. A

Table 3

$$\Delta_4 ln\, N = \theta_1 \Delta_4 ln\, N_{-1} + \psi_1 \Delta_4 ln\, Q + \delta_1 ln \left(\frac{Q}{N}\right)_{-1} + \epsilon_0 t + \epsilon_1 D + \epsilon_2$$

Sample	θ_1	ψ_1	δ_1	ϵ_0	ϵ_1	ϵ_2	$\chi_1^2(8)$	$\chi_2^2(16)$	$\chi_3^2(3)$	R^2
1965 Q3 1976 Q4	0·789 (13·796)	0·171 (5·501)	0·104 (2·480)	−0·001 (2·715)	0·013 (3·217)	0·000 (0·02)	12·246	21·017	4·738	0·9299

Table 4

$$ln\, N = \delta_0 + \delta_1 ln \left(\frac{Q}{Q^+}\right)^{(+)} + \delta_2 ln \left(\frac{Q}{Q^+}\right)^{(-)} + \delta_3 ln\, E^+ + \delta_4 ln\, N_{-1} + \delta_5 ln\, H_{-1} + \delta_6 t$$

Sample	δ_0	δ_1	δ_2	δ_3	δ_4	δ_5	δ_6	$\chi_1^2(8)$	$\chi_2^2(4)$	$\chi_3^2(3)$	R^2
1964 Q2 1975 Q4	−1·723 (2·099)	−0·030 (0·222)	−0·162 (5·577)	0·016 (1·932)	0·932 (23·252)	0·087 (1·603)	0·003 (1·830)	89·67	1·862	2·949	0·993

where $\dfrac{Q}{Q^+}{}^{(\pm)}$ is the ratio of output to 'normal', for $Q \gtrless Q^+$

and E^+ is employment at peak productivity.

295

further account of its derivation is contained in Henry [1979] together with details of the result quoted in Table 4. It should be emphasised, however, that the model is based on the incorporation of past trends in productivity movements, and so, like the example in Table 3, does not provide a explanation of changes in these trends. This point is particularly damaging to medium term projections of employment based on this approach. (As is recognised by Wilson for example. See Wilson p.29). Also the results of table 4 show that the model exhibits unacceptably large prediction errors outside the sample for which it was fitted, even over the short-run

(b) *Unemployment*

Unlike the case of employment equations, there appears to have been little activity on modelling unemployment equations. The following is a selection of some of the main proposals over the last few years.

(i) Direct influences on unemployment have been investigated by a number of people. Bray [1971] in an attempt at a time series study of the Treasury employment/unemployment and output linkages, suggested a direct approach. Modelling a dynamic relationship between unemployment and output was desirable since he believed employment did not convey useful information when introduced into an unemployment output equation (p.177). Although such a view may sound unusual to an economist's ears, it may still be the case that a reliable statistical relationship between unemployment and output could be identified, and clearly such a result would be very useful. Unfortunately, the equation developed by Bray had a number of shortcomings as was pointed out by Box (see p. 214) including over-parameterisation (i.e., a non-parsimonious representation) and a corruption of the noise process produced by the use of arbitrary lagged averages of the data. In discussion of the Bray paper, Jenkins (p. 212) produced a more refined estimate of an unemployment and output equation, using the transfer function formulation estimated using Box-Jenkins methods, i.e.

$$\Delta U = c + \frac{\chi_1 + \chi_2 L}{(1 - \theta_1 L + \theta_2 L^2)} \Delta Q + (1 - \epsilon_0 L) u$$

Where L is the conventional lag operator, and u is white noise. However, this model does not yield any steady state solutions which could be interpreted in terms of static economic theory. Secondly, the moving average error process is a disturbing feature of the equation and could imply possible dynamic mis-specification (see Sargan [1980]).

(ii) One other strand of analysis of the labour market has concentrated on the existence or otherwise of a (structurally) stable u-v relationship. Cheshire *et. al.*, [1972] investigate the principal changes in this relationship, and investigate the evidence for a structural break in the relationship in the mid-1960s.

Clearly, however, the equation 'explaining' the variable should be interpreted as a reduced form relationship from a structural model where employment, unemployment and vacancies are being determined. For the moment we may note that exchanges such as that undertaken by Gujarati [1972] and Taylor [1972], which sought to assign the explanations of a shift in the u-v relationship to either supply side changes (produced by changes in unemployment benefits including earnings related benefits [1966] and the lump sum benefits due to redundancy payments [1965]) as argued by Gujarati, or demand side shifts due to 'shake-out' as argued by Taylor, were simply mistaken. Either factor could be true, both could operate simultaneously, and the appropriate way to identify their likely effects is in a complete (demand and supply) model.

More recent work was concentrated on modelling the unemployment register, and influential work has been published by Nickell [1978], for example. Much of this research uses cross-section data, but with the production of time series on inflow and outflow data from 1967 the possibility of having a related approach to time-series modelling of the unemployment register now exists. An early attempt to use this was made by Leicester[1]. One conspicuous feature of the disaggregation of unemployment into stock-flow magnitudes is the relative stability of the gross inflow, over the 1967 to 1978 period, despite an effective doubling of the level of unemployment over the same period. This suggests that a concentration on the average duration component of unemployment will probably be most rewarding. Two useful aspects of the work already undertaken, however, may be noted.

(a) The possibility of extending models of the labour market to include inflow-outflow equations (with therefore implied durations) and the appendage of this to an explicit model of turnover in the firm (see Wickens [1974]). This would allow for supply factors in inflows (including voluntary separations), and outflows (workers leaving the workforce) and demand factors in inflows (decreases in demand producing involuntary separation) and outflows (new hires).

(b) The extension to modelling the register has shed revealing light on the more extravagant claims of the relative importance of supply factors in the changes in unemployment. Nickell [1979] for example, on the possible relation of unemployment and related benefits on the duration of unemployment, notes that the argument that these increased benefits produced the relatively high rates of unemployment has two non-exclusive strands. The first increases the flows into the register—because increased benefit rates cet-par increase the willingness of the individual to enter unemployed status voluntarily. The second increases the average duration of the individual on the register, because the individual may be more selective about taking a new job. Given the stability of the inflow, the former argument may be discounted, and consequently, if this argument is correct, the effects of increased benefits must be anticipated to fall on average duration. His results for 1964/5 compared with 1973 attributes some 14% of the change in unemployment (the change in unemployment between the dates was 98%) to the impact of increased benefit rates. Since 1973 estimates of the replacement ratio show that it hardly changes at all, and consequently little of the changes in unemployment can be attributed to this factor.

---

[1] His analysis was quite simplified, however, relating summary flow statistics to u-v measures.

(5) Possible lines for future development.

(a) *Whole market models.*

This section is a section on conclusions, since I want to pull together some threads from earlier discussion and draw some tentative conclusions regarding work in the future. The main point of my conclusion, that the time is long overdue for modelling of the labour market which is both more detailed and comprehensive than that typically used in forecasting, is perhaps unsurprising. The arguments for the simple output-employment and unemployment-employment relationships depend essentially on their success in forecasting. Whilst not unrealistic, they are not rich in structural detail, and most users would interpret them as oversimplified but nonetheless useful caricatures of an essentially complicated world. In earlier sections I have illustrated the failings of these models to deliver even a modest menu of success in terms of forecasting performance and structural stability. More important, perhaps, is that this feature has been known and commented on for at least ten years, so change is long overdue. Perhaps the deficiencies in current practices are most manifest in a medium or long term horizon where, as I indicated in Section 3, the structural instability in demand side equations (and ergo, in projected output per head trends) and the deficiencies in modelling supply side decisions make long-run predictions highly imprecise. Hopefully we could aim for short-run forecasting models which are sufficiently reliable to engender a greater sense of confidence when they were used to forecast over a longer period. The question is, what sort of modelling would this be. One possible approach, that of a complete market model, is described now. Here I will link my remarks to a recent paper by Beenstock and Warburton [1979].

One way of developing a whole market approach is to explicitly model both demand and supply in an overtly neoclassical manner, determining both employment and real wage rates. Beenstock and Warburton adopt this approach. Their model is the very simplified one

(17) $$L^d = \alpha_0 + \alpha_1 Q + \alpha_2 W$$
$$L^s = \beta_0 + \beta_1 POP + \beta_2 W$$

where W is the real wage, POP the working population and L is defined as $E + H$ with E being employment and H being hours (all variables in logs). This represents a long-run model, since they note a long-run proportionate relationship between employment and the population of working age, indicating that the labour market is inherently stable, a property which their model is designed to capture. One might note in passing that their diagram illustrating this proportionate relationship shows that there may be substantial divergences between employment and POP for as long as twenty years (p. 2, for the period 1921–1941).[1] They estimate a dynamic version of this model, indicated by the

[1] They also claim support for their theory from a highly idiosyncratic reading of the economic history of this period. Thus according to them 'real wage rates fell especially during the recession in the early thirties.' In fact from the mid-twenties onwards real wage rates were rising, and they rose especially fast from 1929–1933. The recovery of both output and employment was well underway before the rise in real wage rates was halted. (p. 23 Economic Outlook, vol 3, No 9 and 10, LBS Centre for Economic Forecasting.)

Hendry methodology already described. This dynamic model (with dynamic adjustment around the reduced form of 17 above) is

(18)

$$\Delta L = \gamma_0 + \gamma_1 \Delta W + \gamma_2 \Delta Q + \gamma_3 \Delta POP_{-1} + \gamma_4 (\frac{L}{Q})_{-1} + \gamma_5 (\frac{Q}{POP})_{-2} + \gamma_6 Q_{-2} + \gamma_7 t$$

$$\Delta W = \epsilon_0 \Delta L + \epsilon_1 \Delta W_{-1} + \epsilon_2 \Delta Q + \epsilon_3 (\frac{W}{Q})_{-1} + \epsilon_4 W_{-4} + \epsilon_5 Q_{-2} + \epsilon_6 POP + \epsilon_7 t + \epsilon_8$$

I do not propose to discuss their results in any detail. There are a number of general points which I would like to comment on, however.

(i)   They suggest that their estimation strategy 'tests the long-run restrictions' of the theory, while modelling short-run dynamics in an effective data coherent way. The proper description is that they derive a data coherent dynamic equation conditional upon their assumed steady-state solution for employment and real wages. This steady-state solution is not tested against any alternative in any way.

(ii) The estimated model is treated as a reduced form, yet as (18) shows it contains endogenous regressors so the estimates are subject to simultaneous equations bias.

(iii) The real wage variable does not distinguish between the demand price (in the aggregate the real wage inclusive of fixed employment costs) and supply price (net of direct tax payments) in their exactly identified case.

(iv) The measurement of labour does not allow for vacancies or unemployment to appear in the market.

Thus, whereas I believe a useful development may be to model the complete labour market, either as a clearing market with lagged adjustment as the earlier example attempts, or as an explicitly disequilibrium model as Quandt and Rosen [1978] do, for example, little progress has yet been made.

It remains to describe possible improvements to forecasting and analysis of employment using a more detailed modelling of the demand side. To reiterate, this may be interpreted as a short-run approach, where supply factors are taken to be approximately constant. This I understand to be the central assumption of many existing models. The question for forecasters is, can any improvement be made compared with, say, the models described by Tables 1 and 2 above? The aspect I wish to comment on in the rest of this section is interrelated models of factor demand. I hope to show that they indicate that a more successful record in forecasting is possible.

(b) *Interrelated models of factor demand*

Important early articles were provided by Nadiri and Rosen [1969], and Brechling and Mortensen [1971], and applications using related approaches have been made to US data by Tinsley [1971], and to the UK by Peterson [1978] and Henry [1979]. Work here has retained the cost minimising approach noted in the section on single factors, so output and factor prices are treated as predetermined. One important difference between the studies, however, has been the effective choice of factors for which the firm makes optimal decisions. Brechling and Mortensen, for example, consider the joint decision to be between capital and labour services; Nadiri and Rosen on the other hand consider a full model with vectors of input stocks, together with their utilisation rates, being choice variables. The other remaining difference, which is important from the theoretical point of view, concerns dynamic assumptions. Nadiri and Rosen take the vector equivalent of the single equation partial adjustment model, i.e.,

$$\Delta Y_i = \overset{4}{\Sigma} B_{ij}\big(G_j(X, R) - Y_{jt-1}\big) \qquad i = 1, 4$$

where $G_j(\ )$ are steady-state or equilibrium relations for each of the decision variables Y_i (they take employment, hours per man, capital and the flow of capital services per unit of capital), depending on output and the relative price vector (R). The adjustment matrix $\underline{B}$ then assumes that, in principle, disequilibrium in any element Y_j could affect the adjustment of each factor and its level of utilisation.

A general model of dynamic factor adjustment may be developed by extending the single equation model subject to adjustment costs, given in equations (9) to (12). Brechling and Mortensen [1971], Brechling [1965] and Wickens [1974] have provided examples. The principle features of the analysis are, in very summary form, that the firm minimise the vector cost functional

$$L = \int^{\infty} e^{\rho t} G(\underline{Y}, \underline{\dot{Y}}, \underline{X}) \, dt$$

given $y(0) = Y_0$, where Y is a vector of decision variables, which are variables in levels, e.g. employment, the capital stock, average hours, and X is a vector of exogenous variables. Then the vector equivalent to equation (10) earlier is the vector second order differential equation

(19) $\qquad G_{\dot{Y}\dot{Y}}\ddot{Y} + G_{\dot{Y}Y}\dot{Y} - G_Y - \rho G_{\dot{Y}} = 0$

Conventionally, these non-linear equations are linearised around a static optimising solution (see Brechling p. 475). Given this linearisation is made, an equation of the form

(20) $\qquad G^*_{\dot{Y}\dot{Y}}\ddot{Y} - \rho G^*_{\dot{Y}\dot{Y}}\dot{Y} - (G^*_{YY} + G^*_{\dot{Y}Y})(Y - Y^*) = 0$

results, where derivatives are evaluated at the static solution (Y^*) and we also assume that all expected movements of exogenous variables are formed using static expectations (see Tinsley [1971]). Proceeding in the same way as for the single factor case, the positive roots of the characteristic equation to (20) above are ruled out by the transversality condition. Hence the solution is of the form

$$Y = Y^* + \underline{m}e^{\Lambda t}$$

with e^{Λ} the vector of stable roots $(e^{\Lambda_i t})$ and with eigenvectors given by the initial conditions. Thus

(21) $\dot{Y} = A(Y^* - Y)$

where $A = M\Lambda M^{-1}$ and Λ is the diagonal matrix (Λ_i) composed of stable roots.

One problem, however, to which I drew attention in an earlier paper, is the loss of some structural information in deriving the first-order system (21) above. Although, as the derivation makes clear, the adjustment matrix and the equilibrium terms resemble the familiar partial adjustment models as used by, e.g., Ball and St. Cyr in modelling employment functions, this is appearance only. The adjustment term embodies a priori restrictions involving the discount rate, and the equilibrium term is a moving trajectory of weighted terms involving relative rentals, the weights being the roots of the characteristic equation (20). However it is not practicable to embody these restrictions in the equilibrium equation. In a later paper for example, Brechling takes the equilibrium terms to be simply the static optimising conditions for the firm's factor demands. Tinsley [1971] provides a fuller and more provoking analysis based on forming 'pseudo-myopic' approximations to the equilibrium trajectory. In all cases I have seen, the adjustment parameter(s) are simply estimated. Mainly for this reason—loss of potential structural information—I suggested that the second-order equation (19) above, although only part of the necessary conditions for optimising factor demands and therefore not giving a unique path for the $Y(t)$'s, be used as a basis for determining econometric or empirical demand equations (see Henry [1979]). This was suggested as an expedient, and indeed there seems to be some empirical support for such a step. A more satisfactory procedure which might prove to be as empirically useful is provided by Wickens [1974]. He notes that the optimising problem may be re-specified as the fixed end point problem, with terminal time T, and the end point condition

$G(\dot{Y}(T), Y(T), T) = 0$

This, together with the necessary conditions, then gives a unique optimal path for $Y(T)$ (assuming $Y(0) = Y_0$). The system produced by the two conditions may then be estimated by using a sample $S(>T)$, estimating the second order structural relationship in $\ddot{Y}$ and $\dot{Y}$, etc., by using the entire sample S, and also using $S - T$ sample points to determine the end point equation above. This obviously introduces an arbitrary element into the estimation due to the enforced choice of the variable T, but presumably this would be less important the longer the sample was, and a sensitivity analysis is, in any event, possible using different values of T.[1]

A selection of results is given below to assess the usefulness of some of the suggestions made above. The first is a simple first order pair in employment and average hours using the formulation described by Brechling and Mortensen

[1] The resemblance of this to rational expectation models which seek to exploit the terminal or end-point conditions is very close. See, for example, Minford and Matthews.

quoted above. (See also a more recent study by Brechling [1965]). Then Table 6 shows the results of a model I developed in an earlier paper. Finally, results of a joint employment hours model by Peterson [1978], which explicitly allows for variations in capital expenditure, is given.

In preparing these regressions I have used non-restricted estimation methods, which do not use the production function parameters embedded in the static equilibrium solutions of the equations where these occur. The main reason for this is the lack of an appropriate non-linear estimation programme, though I would add that there are theoretical problems in imposing these constraints. The equilibrium solution to the model with adjustment costs is a moving equilibrium, so this becomes time dependent. Second, the symmetry assumption of own and cross price effects applies only when adjustment costs are separable (see Peterson [1978], p. 3 on this point). However it must be recognised that the estimates provided below are not efficient.

The first set of models is suggested by the results of Brechling and Mortensen. They take the interdependent system to be

$$\Delta Y = M(Y_{-1} - AZ) + u$$

where Y is the set of inputs and their utilisation rates, Z the set of predetermined variables and we have allowed for an equilibrium relationship in these partial adjustment equations

$$Y^* = AZ$$

In their model Brechling and Mortensen noted that stocks depend on relative factor prices and output (plus a time-trend modelling exogenous technical charge), whereas utilisation rates depend on relative prices only. Table 5 presents estimates of this model and tests this property for N and H.

In the second example, hours are assumed to operate as a buffer variable and output changes filter through to employment via their effect on hours. The basis of this model is contained in my earlier paper (Henry [1979]). Essentially it is the system contained in the conditions

(22) $$\frac{FH}{FK} = \frac{PH}{PK} \quad \text{and}$$

(23) $$\frac{\partial \Phi}{\partial N} - \frac{d}{dt}\left(\frac{\partial \Phi}{\partial N} \right) = 0, \text{ or}$$

(24) $$\ddot{N} = \frac{1}{\gamma}\left[r \frac{\partial}{\partial N} \gamma \; (\cdot) - PH + PH \; \frac{FN}{FH} \right]$$

where $PH \; (= (W + W'H)N)$ is the incremental cost of additional hours, $PN (= H.W)$ the flow cost of an additional worker including recurrent fixed labour charges, and FK is the Jorgenson user cost of capital with no taxes.

Equation (22) is solved using the production function to give an equation in Q, N, PH/PK and t, and the ratio of marginal products in (24), expressed in terms of H/N. Estimating a system like this is clearly incomplete for the reasons discussed on p. 29, but as shown in an earlier paper there is some support for it, though tests of the dynamic specification following that described in section 3, showed that N did not enter the H equation, Q entered in (fourth) difference form and PH/PK with a third order lag. The dynamic equation for N (second order due to the assumption of quadratic adjustment costs) received support, and longer lags on N did not seem warranted.

Finally, a recursive model developed by Peterson [1978] is re-estimated, and the results shown in Table 7. He argues that the hours worked, employment model is recursive. For hours, adjustment is to standard hours (HN) according to a partial adjustment scheme, and that there is also an increased pressure to shorten actual hours when unemployment is higher (demand is low). Thus

$$(25) \qquad \Delta lnH = b_0 + b_1 \Delta ln \, HN + b_2 \, (ln \, HN_{-1} - ln \, H_{-1}) + b_3 \, ln \, U$$

For employment, from the inverted CD production function

$$\Delta ln \, M = a_1 + a_2 \Delta ln \, Q + a_3 \Delta ln \, K,$$

where M is 'labour' input, and since

$$\Delta ln \, K = \alpha(t) . \, I/Q - \delta(\gamma)$$

where $\alpha(t)$ is the K/Q ratio at t, and δ the proportionate level of replacement investment, then if $\alpha(t) = \alpha_0 + \alpha_1 t$, and $\delta(\, . \,)$ is assumed constant at δ,

$$(26) \qquad \Delta ln \, M = (a_1 + a_3 \delta) + a_2 \Delta ln \, Q + a_3 (\alpha_0 + \alpha_1 t) \frac{I}{Q}$$

Finally, from the definition

$$M \equiv N . H . J$$

where J is an unobservable utilisation or intensity of effort variable assumed to be inversely related to the unemployment,

$$\Delta ln \, J = \beta \Delta ln \, U,$$

the employment equation is

$$(27) \qquad \Delta ln \, N = C_0 - \Delta ln \, H + C_2 \Delta ln \, Q + (C_3 + C_4 t) \frac{I}{Q} + C_5 \Delta ln \, U$$

The results for these three models are shown on the following tables.

Table 5[1]

(A) $\Delta \ln N = \gamma_0 + \gamma_1 \ln N_{-1} + \gamma_2 \ln H_{-1} + \gamma_3 \ln \left(\frac{PN}{PH}\right) + \gamma_4 \ln Q + \gamma_5 t$

	γ_0	γ_1	γ_2	γ_3	γ_4	γ_5	R^2	$\chi_1^2(8)$	$\chi_2^2(16)$	$\chi_3^2(3)$
Sample 1964 Q3 1976 Q4	-0.731 (1.605)	-0.109 (1.73)	0.166 (2.39)	-0.068 (1.319)	0.107 (4.036)	-0.001 (2.183)	0.706	31.07	28.451	3.527

(B) $\Delta \ln H = \gamma_0 + \gamma_1 \ln N_{-1} + \gamma_2 \ln H_{-1} + \gamma_3 \ln \left(\frac{PH}{PN}\right) + \gamma_4 \ln Q + \gamma_5 t$

	γ_0	γ_1	γ_2	γ_3	γ_4	γ_5	R^2	$\chi_1^2(8)$	$\chi_2^2(16)$	$\chi_3^2(3)$
Sample 1964 Q3 1976 Q4	2.955 (3.284)	-0.004 (0.03)	-0.814 (0.45)	-0.172 (1.689)	0.252 (4.849)	-0.002 (3.817)	0.734	64.927	28.749	9.219

(1) All the results use unadjusted data for the manufacturing sector

Table 6

(A) $\Delta N = \epsilon_0 + \epsilon_1 PN + \epsilon_2 PH \dfrac{H}{N} + \epsilon_3 \Delta N_{-1}$

Sample	ϵ_0	ϵ_1	ϵ_2	ϵ_3	R^2	$\chi_1^2(8)$	$\chi_2^2(12)$	$\chi_3^2(2)$
1964 Q3	$-2{\cdot}189$	$-2{\cdot}235$	$5{\cdot}439$	$0{\cdot}632$	$0{\cdot}839$	$13{\cdot}587$	$17{\cdot}58$	$0{\cdot}203$
1976 Q4	$(2{\cdot}523)$	$(3{\cdot}376)$	$(3{\cdot}422)$	$(6{\cdot}951)$				

PN is the gross weekly compensation per worker in real terms. PH is taken to be the basic hourly wage rate.

(B) $\ln H = f_0 + f_1 \Delta_4 \ln Q + f_2 \left(\dfrac{PH}{PK}\right)_{-3} + f_3 t$

Sample	f_0	f_1	f_2	f_3	R^2	$\chi_1^2(8)$	$\chi_2^2(16)$	$\chi_3^2(2)$
1964 Q1	$4{\cdot}684$	$0{\cdot}212$	$-0{\cdot}0115$	$-0{\cdot}001$	$0{\cdot}838$	$13{\cdot}975$	$12{\cdot}05$	$5{\cdot}96$
1976 Q4	$(118{\cdot}84)$	$(5{\cdot}700)$	$(2{\cdot}121)$	$(8{\cdot}618)$				

Table 7

(A) $\Delta \ln H = g_0 + g_1 \Delta \ln HN - g_2 (\ln HN_{-1} - \ln H_{-1}) + g_3 \ln U$

Sample	g_0	g_1	g_2	g_3	R^2	$\chi_1^2(3)$	$\chi_2^2(16)$	$\chi_3^2(2)$
1964 Q2	$0{\cdot}264$	$2{\cdot}282$	$0{\cdot}650$	$-0{\cdot}026$	$0{\cdot}341$	$2{\cdot}668$	$19{\cdot}429$	$5{\cdot}593$
1976 Q4	$(3{\cdot}456)$	$(1{\cdot}809)$	$(4{\cdot}843)$	$(3{\cdot}116)$				

(B) $\Delta \ln N = h_0 + h_1 \Delta \ln H + h_2 \Delta \ln Q + h_3 \dfrac{I}{Q} + h_4 t \dfrac{I}{Q} + h_5\ \Delta \ln U$

Sample	h_0	h_1	h_2	h_3	h_4	h_5	R^2	$\chi_1^2(8)$	$\chi_2^2(16)$	$\chi_3^2(5)$
1964 Q2	$-0{\cdot}040$	$-0{\cdot}147$	$0{\cdot}050$	$0{\cdot}001$	$-0{\cdot}000$	$-0{\cdot}016$	$0{\cdot}232$	$12{\cdot}123$	$70{\cdot}64$	$29{\cdot}34$
1976 Q4	$(1{\cdot}423)$	$(1{\cdot}906)$	$(2{\cdot}435)$	$(1{\cdot}457)$	$(2{\cdot}121)$	$(1{\cdot}215)$				

Each of the models in tables 5–7 derive a measure of empirical support. The Brechling-Mortensen model shown in table 5, has a rather mixed fortune. It is based on the assumption that average hours are unaffected by output and employment, but the results in table 5(B) reveal a significant effect for output at least. In both the employment and hours equations, the cost term is insignificant. Perhaps the most surprising result with this model is that the lagged dependent variable in the employment equation (5A) is insignificant. Finally, according to these results, changes in output have a direct impact on both employment and hours, a feature not shared with the next example (table 6), though it should be emphasised that the empirical results for this model are not good enough for much reliance to be placed on this finding (the hours equation B, for example, is dynamically misspecified).

The results in table 6 refer to the model of employment and hours I developed in an earlier paper (Henry [1979]). This model incorporates an indirect influence of changes in output on employment, the effect operating via changes in the average number of hours worked. Also, dynamic adjustment in employment is dictated by a second order process in N, this being the direct result of assuming a quadratic adjustment cost function for employment. The model as a whole obtains empirical support from these results in terms of predicted signs of coefficients, significance of these, and apparent absence of serial correlation in the errors. Also the post-fitting performance of the model is acceptable, with a $\chi_1^2(8)$ of 13·587 compared to a cut-off value of 15·5. This is comparable with the performance of the model illustrated in table 3 earlier, though, as I have stressed, that model was based on a post-hoc change in the observed trend of output per employee. It might also be noted that the dynamic specification of the employment equation, in particular, appears to be upheld by the result ($\chi_3^2(2) = 0·203$). This is evidence in favour of the choice of a second order model such as this, and also evidence supporting, indirectly, the assumption of quadratic adjustment costs.[1]

The unrestricted version of the Peterson model also does fairly well, (table 7), although the obvious problem here is the low level of explanation of each equation, no doubt due to the absence of any explicit dynamics in either equation. Regarding this point, the employment equation is clearly dynamically misspecified, and this, together with the result in table 5 showing an insignificant value for lagged levels of employment, is further evidence in favour of the dynamics I adopted in the example shown in table 6. The role of the investment-output ratio is now well determined in this model, but this may indicate empirical problems in approximating the capital-output ratio in the way that Peterson did. Given the well known problem of deriving reliable measures of the capital stock, there does not seem any obvious way of dealing with this problem, except possibly by more refined modelling of the equations linking capital variables to gross investment. Finally, the apparent success of the equations in the post-fitting sample period is misleading, since given that the standard errors of the equations are so large, substantial forecasting errors appear to be trivial.

[1] More general lagged versions of the model were estimated and tested as a 'general to specific' sequence. This showed that the second-order model of table 6 was clearly the preferred dynamic specification.

Given the very preliminary nature of some of these results, e.g. Peterson's model has not been estimated using an efficient estimation method, I do not think it appropriate to embark on any extensive testing of the relative statistical performance of these models. Some broad features, however, are suggested by these results. The first is that there is evidence in these results in favour of the treatment of hours as a buffer variable, so that the effects of output changes work their way through indirectly to employment changes (table 6). The way in which this develops is illustrated below in table 8, which simulates the model of table 6 allowing for a growth in output, 2% higher per annum than the actual rate, for the period 1976–77.

Table 8: Simulated employment/hours from table 6 above (measured as deviations from base run). Output growth 2% p.a. greater than historical value.

	1974 Q1	Q2	Q3	Q4	1975 Q1	Q2	Q3	Q4
N	0·072	0·170	0·349	0·533	0·682	0·889	1·148	1·407
H	1·338	1·051	2·276	2·768	2·558	2·054	2·359	1·711

	1976 Q1	Q2	Q3	Q4	1977 Q1	Q2	Q3	Q4
N	1·623	1·768	1·84	1·86	1·85	1·86	1·88	1·92
H	0·928	0·006	−0·331	−0·568	−0·488	0·361	0·345	0·256

As the table illustrates, the increase in output produces increases in hours, which then filter through to produce changes in numbers employed. Numbers employed continue to increase fairly steadily but by the end of 1977 have levelled out. In turn hours have increased, stabilised and eventually started to decrease as employment increases, which pattern seems plausible. It suggests that overtime working is undertaken to meet output increases, and if these increases are maintained eventually employment is increased with hours tending then to decline.

If output does not grow fast enough, the model also implies that employment will then tend to be stationary since all output fluctuations may be met by varying average hours. Such a feature is consistent with recent employment sluggishness, which the Ball-St. Cyr model for example does not explain and would typically imply significant falls in employment at recent recorded growth rates in output. The second feature to emerge from these results is the usefulness of a second order process for modelling employment. Although the assumption of quadratic adjustment costs is often criticised as being oversimplified, the results of tables 5–7 indicate that, as an empirical approximation, it does remarkably well.

(7) Conclusions

This paper has reviewed recent practices in modelling employment and unemployment relationships for use in short and medium term forecasting. The problems of deriving plausible equations for these key variables which prove to be technically stable has been illustrated, in detail with reference to employment relationships for the manufacturing sector. Here it has been argued that it is possible to make progress in modelling employment basically as demand determined in conjunction with average hours worked. It is not possible to be equally optimistic about the supply side. Little progress has been made in deriving and testing detailed structural models of unemployment such as that already done using cross section samples. It still remains a major objective for forecasters to test models of the stock and flows of the unemployment register for example, using the more demanding time-series techniques of dynamic specification and structural stability now at their disposal.

Data used in comparative study: definitions
(Manufacturing: not seasonally adjusted)

N = Employees in employment

H = Average hours worked

HN = Normal hours

Q = Output

PH = Factor price of hours. Approximated by basic hourly rates.

PN = Price per worker. Approximated by average earnings.

PK = User cost of capital. Approximated by PI $(r + \delta - \Delta PI)$ where r is minimum lending rate, $\delta = 0.006$, and PI the implicit deflator of investment goods.

U = Unemployment (aggregate GB excluding school leavers).

REFERENCES

Ball, J., St. Cyr, E. [1966], 'Short-term Employment Functions in British Manufacturing Industry'. *Review of Economic Studies.*

Barker, T. S. [1976], *Economic Structure and Policy.* Chapman and Hall.

Beenstock, M., Warburton, P. [1979], 'A Neoclassical Model of Employment and Wages'. London Business School mimeograph.

Bowers, J., Cheshire, P. C., Webb, A. E., Weeden, R. [1972], 'Some Aspects of Unemployment and the Labour Market 1966–71'. *National Institute Economic Review.*

Bray, J. [1971], 'Dynamic Equations for Economic Forecasting with the GDP—Unemployment Relation and the Growth of GDP in the UK as an Example'. *Journal of the Royal Statistical Society.* Series A.

Brechling, F. [1965], 'The Relationship between Output and Employment in British Manufacturing Industries'. *Review of Economic Studies.*

Brechling, F., Mortensen, D. [1971], 'Interrelated Investment and Employment Decision'. Paper presented to 1971 AUTE conference at Kent.

Brechling, F. [1974], 'Monetary Policy and Neoclassical Investment Analysis' in *Issues in Monetary Economics* ed. H. Johnson and R. Nobay.

Davidson, J., Hendry, D., Srba, F., Yeo, S. [1978], 'Econometric Modelling of the Aggregate Time Series Relationship between Consumers' Expenditure and Income in the UK'. *Economic Journal.*

Department of Employment Gazette. [1977], 'New Projections of Future Labour Force'.

Godley, W., Shepherd, J. [1964], 'Long Term Growth and Short Term Policy'. *National Institute Economic Review.*

Gujarati, D. [1972], 'The Behaviour of Unemployment and Unfilled Vacancies'. *Economic Journal.*

Hazledine, T. [1978], 'New Specifications for Employment and Hours Functions for UK Manufacturing Industries'. *Economica.*

Hendry, D., Mizon, G. [1980], 'An Econometric Application and Monte Carlo Analysis of Tests of Dynamic Specification'. *Review of Economic Studies.*

Henry, B. [1979], 'Employment Equations for the UK'. Paper presented to the SSRC Econometric Modelling Group.

Hornstein, Z., Tarling, R. [1976], 'Labour Hoarding and Employment in UK Manufacturing'. Department of Employment mimeograph.

Hutton, J., Stamler, V. H., Stern, J. [1978], 'Employment in Manufacturing Industry in a Vintage Capital Model'. *GES Working Paper No. 10.*

Leicester, C. [1976], 'The Duration of Unemployment and Job Search', in Worswick *op. cit.*

Lindley, R. [1978], *Britain's Medium-term Employment Prospects.* MRG Warwick.

Minford, A. P., Matthews, P. [1979], 'Terminal Conditions, Uniqueness as the Solution of RE models'. *SSRC, University of Liverpool, Working Paper.*

Nadiri, M., Rosen, S. [1969], 'Interrelated Factor Demand Functions'. *American Economic Review.*

Nickell, S. [1979], 'The Effects of Unemployment and Related Benefits on the Duration of Unemployment'. *Economic Journal.*

Nickell, S. [1978], 'Unemployment and the Structure of Labour Costs'. London School of Economics Mimeograph.

Perry, G. [1977], 'Potential Output and Productivity'. *Brookings Papers* No. 1.

Peterson, W. [1978], 'A Recursive Model of Employment and Hours Worked'. Cambridge D. A. E. Mimeograph.

Peterson, W. [1976], 'Employment' in Barker *op.cit.*

Rosen, H., Quandt, R. [1978], 'Estimation of a Disequilibrium Aggregate Labour Market'. *Review of Economics and Statistics.*

Sargan, D. [1980], 'The Consumer Price Equation in the Post-war British Economy'. *Review of Economic Studies.*

Shepherd, J. [1968], 'Productive Potential and the Demand for Labour'. *Economic Trends.*

Sims, C. [1974], 'Output and Labour Input in Manufacturing'. *Brookings Papers* No. 3.

Smyth, D., Ireland, N. [1970], 'The Specification of Short-Run Employment Models'. *Review of Economic Studies.*

Taylor, J. [1972], 'The Behaviour of Unemployment and Unfilled Vacancies'. *Economic Journal.*

Tinsley, P. [1971], 'A Variable Adjustment Model of Labour Demand'. *International Economic Review.*

Wickens, M. [1974], 'Towards a Theory of the Labour Market'. *Economica.*

Wickens, M. [1974], 'An Econometric Specification of a Dynamic Model of the Interrelated Decisions of the Firm'. Mimeograph.

Wilson, R. [1979], 'Comparative Forecasting Performance of Disaggregated Employment Models'. *Discussion paper no. 3, Manpower Research Group.* University of Warwick.

Worswick, D. (ed). [1976], *The Concept and Measurement of Involuntary Unemployment.* Allen and Unwin.

Sources of models cited in the text: Bank of England, 'Short-term Economic model of the UK Economy', 1978
CEPG, 'Technical Manual' 1978
HM Treasury, 'Technical Manual' 1978
LBS, 'Quarterly Model of the UK Economy.' 1976
NIESR, 'A Listing of National Institute Model III'

Forecasting Employment and Unemployment

COMMENT *by Colin Leicester* (Institute of Manpower Studies, University of Sussex)

The dual objectives of this paper are quite ambitious. On the one hand, Henry presents us with an extensive (if admittedly selective) review of the empirical estimation of employment and unemployment functions. On the other hand, to illustrate many of his main arguments, he provides us with fresh estimates of different equations, based albeit on the manufacturing sector of the UK economy only, and covering at least 14 to 16 years of the historical past. Both the bibliography and the results given provide a solid basis for an evaluation of work in this area.

The conclusions we may draw from this paper may, however, be different from those of his own, even if we restrict ourselves to the two criteria he himself uses. Is the failure of past employment and unemployment models to produce reasonably accurate forecasts an indictment of them? Unlike those who work in the natural sciences, economists are less inclined to view the lack of predictive power of their theories as a signal that perhaps those theories should be revised. More explicitly, is the economic rationale of the models described sufficiently realistic? Henry himself, speaking apparently on behalf of most forecasters, states that they would prefer 'a model which provides a reasonably intelligible account of economic behaviour'.

Two general comments may be made. First, arguably, a good model depends on having a good economic hypothesis, and this may or may not be drawn directly from theory. We note that an exception to the use of a theoretical justification for modelling employment is already provided by those models which explicitly treat the future growth or decline of public sector employment as the outcome of decisions taken on the relevant items of government expenditure. It is only a small extension of this practice to argue that logically the modelling of employment elsewhere in the economy should reflect the kinds of decisions taken, and the nature of the decision processes, appropriate to employers in different industrial sectors. It is not obvious that this would not eventually imply that a different employment model is appropriate to manufacturing as opposed to service industries; or, furthermore, that a workable hypothesis for a specific industry in the production sector may not differ in substantial detail from that implied by neo-classical theory. In brief, there is a case for direct observation of how employers in different economic sectors go about altering the size and composition of their work-force, if only to check whether an alternative to the conventional hypotheses drawn from theory does or does not exist.

Taking that step is both desirable and feasible, and may satisfy the need for a 'reasonably intelligible account of economic behaviour'. But a second comment must be made. In all humility, we should as economists accept the possibility that our conceptual framework and postulated relationships may have limitations. If so, we ought perhaps to be prepared to cross certain inter-disciplinary boundaries. To indicate what is meant by that, three specific illustrations may be given.

One example follows from the assumption of the homogeneity of labour in the production function we normally make. Employment functions used to explain the past and to forecast the future usually have total aggregate employment as their dependent variable. Yet, apparently, as a casual scrutiny of the data suggests, a significant proportion of the work-force in an establishment or industry does not enter directly into the production process: that is, these workers may not be a direct factor of production. This proportion of indirect labour (as opposed to direct labour) is different for different industries and furthermore it appears to be increasing over time. If such workers serve other purposes than as a direct factor of production, then their numbers are less variant (if not totally invariant) with respect to changes in production. Their inclusion in the total level of employment, which is then related to independent variables in the employment function, may be one good reason for estimating the elasticity of employment with respect to output as a value lying between zero and unity. To accommodate the non-homogeneity of labour, we may need to learn one or two lessons from elsewhere in the literature e.g. the sociology of work in business organisations.

A second example is our treatment of employment as a stock, and as net changes in that stock, without an explicit treatment of the behaviour of flows into and flows out of that stock. Similar remarks apply to the usual treatment of unemployment. Yet a casual inspection of the data (Leicester [1976], Leicester et. al. [1975a]) indicates that the net inflows and the net outflows for both the stocks of employment and unemployment rise and fall when the stocks themselves rise and fall. For this reason alone, the adjustment of the stock levels to the impact of the relevant casual factors may be slower than otherwise expected. Furthermore, the impact coefficients of the same causal factor on the inflow and on the outflow may be different; but most important of all the magnitude of the inflow is related to successive components of the outflow over different time periods by a statistical probability distribution. Hence, the behaviour of the stock would more realistically be modelled by paying explicit attention to its structure, classified by duration (Leicester et.al. [1975b]). This is another way of saying that lessons may be learnt from another section of literature i.e. that on statistical models of the survivor function.

A third example of where our previous practices may be improved upon is the rather cavalier manner in which technological change is treated in economic models. This is not to say that we have not drawn distinctions between embodied and disembodied technological change, labour augmenting and capital augmenting improvements in techniques, neutral and non-neutral shifts in the production function. But we understand little about the causes of these changes; and, arguably, the concepts by which we represent these distinctions may be too imprecise. To improve on this situation would require the crossing of yet another disciplinary boundary i.e. to understand, accept and incorporate the research findings of those with an engineering and natural science background, within (hopefully) an expanded economic conceptual framework.

On reflection, this third specific proposal may be the most important. Unlike Henry, I am less sanguine that the failure to model technology at the level of the firm has not been a major cause of previous forecasting failure. More significantly, the refusal by economists to work with technologists on the determinants of work opportunities may lead to their being able to say very little that is relevant on the future trends in either the level or the composition of employment in Britain. In brief, such a refusal may be seen by our critics as a denial of professional responsibility and a source of professional impotence.

REFERENCES

Leicester, Colin. [1976], 'Analysing the labour market', in W. L. Price (ed). *Readings in Manpower planning*, Canadian Operational Society.

Leicester, Colin, *et. al.* [1975a], *Flows of Unemployment and Flows of Vacancies*, Research Report prepared for the Manpower Services Commission.

Leicester, Colin, *et. al.* [1975b], *Short-term Forecasts of Unemployment in Britain: experience and possibilities*, Research Report prepared for the Manpower Services Commission.

Forecasting Employment and Unemployment

COMMENT *by R. J. Tarling* (Department of Applied Economics, Cambridge).

The evolution of the methods adopted for forecasting employment and unemployment in the post-war period are well summarised by Henry in his paper. His conclusion, that there is hope of achieving a better understanding on the demand side, is one which I share. What worries me is that such progress, whilst being a valuable contribution, may not be enough to cope with forecasts made under changing economic conditions. The ad hoc amendments of the past, such as bending productivity trends, changing lag structures and adding new variables, have all been short-lived. I do not think we should be satisfied until we have made progress on a full model.

Attempting to summarise Henry's paper, perhaps with too much brevity, I would see the evolution of method as having taken place in the early 1960's. After inverting a production function and adding a simple proportional adjustment process, Brechling and then Ball and St. Cyr introduce the endogeneity of wage cost per hour, which, together with cost minimising behaviour, gives theoretical underpinning to the formulation we have all used for so long. Even the most recent promising area of development, recursive models of employment and hours worked, has in essence the same theoretical basis. The major advances in recent years have not been in the economic theory but are those of Sargan and Hendry, allowing more specific testing of structural and dynamic specifications. That is, the advances have improved our ability to apply discriminatory tests, but we are limited in the alternative hypotheses which we can specify.

In my opinion, our limitation is two-fold. First, the tenacity with which we hold on to the assumption of an atomistic market with homogeneous labour limits the incorporation of theories and empirical results of studies of labour market segmentation. More importantly, the theory behind the short-run employment function only supports the derivation of short-run employment demand: it is only because we think of a representative firm in an atomistic market that we can immediately translate that demand into actual employment levels. Second, the data at our disposal are strictly limited, particularly in aggregate. The absence of flow data makes empirical testing of any specification of the dynamics of the labour market very difficult: the reduced form used to test each hypothesis is limited by the evidence available and hence it is difficult to find discriminatory tests.

In a structural model of the labour market, it is necessary to specify the following:
1. The relationship between the demand for output, market structure, technology employed and the demand for labour services.

2. The relationship between the demand for labour services and the demand for employees: this is principally concerned with the restrictions imposed by technology and the buffer adjustments made through average hours of work. In fact, it is easiest to think of this relationship as that part of the adjustment to meet the aggregate demand for labour services that can be achieved by a single firm—an internal adjustment mechanism, by which each firm has a desired recruitment or redundancy flow.

3. The behaviour of that part of the labour market external to individual firms. The gross demands for employees, which comprise desired net stock changes and replacement of voluntary quits, are matched in whole or in part by the gross supply, which includes the voluntary quits, the unemployed and the new entrants: what is important is how people choose to apply for jobs, how employers choose among applicants and how much discrimination there is affecting these choices.

4. The determinants of the supply of labour and extent of concealed unemployment (potential employees) outside the observed labour force.

Although such models are not easy to specify, especially if they are to be tractable and give rise to useful results for dynamic analysis, they do provide a wider framework through which to discuss the workings of the labour market.

Conventional models of aggregate employment cover only (1) and (2) above: that is, they include a production relationship and, through the representative firm assumption, an internal adjustment mechanism. The short-run employment function derived is strictly speaking an input to (3) and not the reduced form of a structural model. Use of search theoretic models with discrete time may be included under (3) to justify some external adjustment but more complete specifications of mechanisms (3) would not in general be ones which guarantee that desired changes in employment are realised.

There is a considerable body of evidence on the existence and nature of labour market segmentation. Despite the descriptive and static nature of the dual labour market analysis of Doerringer and Piore, and the rather imprecise way in which employers' responses are governed by uncertainty, the analysis provides some insights into the division of adjustment between (2) and (3) above. The more general distinction between primary and secondary jobs, although rather stark, is important in indicating the variability of adjustment on average to the composition of jobs filled.

In terms of the framework of areas of analysis (1) – (4) outlined above, segmentation theory suggests the need to modify the theoretical basis of the conventional model. Under (1), the relationship between demand for output and the demand for labour services is affected by the degree of market control exercised by firms and their ability to shift the burden of costs of output variation onto the consumer or onto labour. Under (2), the extent to which firms can adjust the average utilisation of existing labour stocks on the technology employed and the degree of labour cost fixity, is comparable in many respects to the degree of penetration of internal labour market structures. Firms, in order to minimise costs, attempt to shift the burden of costs and employers devise strategies to achieve such shifts: labour in general has a conflict of interest with the employer and the degree of resistance depends on the cohesion of employed labour. Under (3), choices made by individuals and by firms may be substantially affected by actual and statistical discrimination. Under (4), new entry of significant numbers of unskilled labour of new minority groups, such as migrant labour, may have important effects on the recruitment policies of firms.

Thus, at each stage, segmentation theory can make a contribution. To construct such a model is a very demanding exercise—but the alternative for macro-economic modellers may be to reduce their role in the context of the labour market to that of manipulating residuals. Given the current economic situation and the move away from forecasts of no policy or limited policy change towards the need to examine alternative scenarios under a wide range of policies, manipulation of residuals is a very dangerous method so that it is crucially important to define a model of labour market behaviour with which we can satisfactorily model a wide range of labour market behaviour.

Forecasting Employment and Unemployment

COMMENT *by Michael Beenstock* (London Business School)

Brian Henry rightly draws attention to the almost universal failure to integrate labour supply and demand in the econometric modelling of employment (and wage rates). Indeed, even at this conference the treatment of supply and demand has proceeded more or less along parallel lines. While the failure to achieve this integration is particularly serious in the context of the medium- to long-term, it certainly cannot be taken for granted that in the short-run supply effects do not matter.

This raises the general problem of how to specify whole market models that are appropriate for both short- and long-run analysis. In Beenstock and Warburton [1979] the short-term dynamics were determined on purely empirical grounds so that at any moment in time actual employment is a weighted average of long-run labour supply and demand. This approach differs from that of Rosen and Quandt [1978] in that the sample is not split into purely supply or demand constrained periods. It seems more reasonable to assume that short-term realizations are a mixture of both supply and demand considerations.

Nevertheless, it seems undesirable that this mixture should be determined on purely empirical grounds, especially when recent developments in economic theory suggest how the long-run neo-classical model might be extended into the short-term domain in a way that avoids the conceptual problems associated with non-market clearing. The gist of this extension may be understood if Henry's equations (17) are expanded to include expectational arguments about real wage movements:—

$$L^d_t = \alpha_0 + \alpha_1 Q_t + \alpha_2 W_t + \alpha_3 ({}_t E W_{t+1} - W_t) + \alpha_4 {}_t E Q_{t+1}$$

$$L^s_t = \beta_0 + \beta_1 POP_t + \beta_2 W_t + \beta_3 ({}_t E W_{t+1} - W_t)$$

where e.g. ${}_t E W_{t+1}$ is the current expected value of real wage rates in the next period. The first equation states that in the short-term the labour demand schedule shifts with expectations about output and wage rates. For example, if wage rates are expected to rise employers will try to contract labour now rather than later. The second equation suggests that the short-term labour supply schedule is also shifted by expectations so that, if wage rages are expected to rise, labour contracting will be delayed from the supply side.

This speculative model of the labour market implies that labour contracts typically last longer than one period in recognition of the numerous adjustment costs to the hiring and firing of labour from the employers' side and of job search from the employees' side. In the steady-state, when expectations equal out-turns, the model reverts to its long-term mode. Since the real wage is defined as

$$W_t = w_t - P_t$$

where w represents nominal wage rates and P the price level we may write the reduced form for employment (and w) as

$$L_t = L^*(Ew_{t\,t+1}, EP_{t\,t+1}, P_t, EQ_{t\,t+1}, Q_t, POP_t)$$

This specification implies short-term labour market clearing in the ex ante sense. Ex post expectations may be wrong for a variety of reasons. Firms may have too little labour, while workers may feel involuntarily unemployed.

A gloss on this specification is to consider the split between hours and people employed, as Henry suggests, but in this case too it would be necessary to integrate the supply effects. We cannot take it for granted even in the short-term that firms have complete control over the amount of overtime.

Finally, the whole market analysis enables us to detect long-term shifts in labour demand and supply caused by changes in national insurance contributions, taxation and unemployment benefit, etc. which may be included as explanatory variables in the reduced form for employment. But it should not be forgotten that the employment function has a corresponding wage function implied by this kind of labour market analysis.

Forecasting Employment and Unemployment

COMMENT *by R. M. Lindley* (Manpower Research Group, University of Warwick

Brian Henry's paper deals with short-term aggregate employment forecasting, concentrating upon manufacturing, and adds a few observations on forecasting labour supply and unemployment and an occasional reference to the medium term. It is therefore rather narrowly conceived—in fact its substance relates mainly to the earlier session on the short-run determinants of employment and hours.

At a conference on the labour market, perhaps we could, nonetheless, agree to see the forecasting problem in terms of modelling the labour sector as a whole rather than the selection and testing of alternative specifications of the output-employment relationship and the ingenuity with which we try to negotiate data problems on the supply side. This means deciding how we should try to represent the labour market, or multitude of labour markets, and what is the appropriate strategy for endogenising certain elements, which have been covered already in previous sessions, for example, labour supply, and other elements which have not been covered—surprisingly enough for a conference on the labour *market*, the latter include the aggregate wage and the wage structure. Thus, apart from the actual specification of equations embodied in the sub-model of the labour sector, I would raise the following issues for discussions:

(i) the interplay between the labour sector and other sectors in the model,
(ii) the level of disaggregation thought desirable, and
(iii) the scope for evaluating policy—are the relevant instruments identified? In particular, bearing in mind the many specific industrial and employment policies introduced during the 1970s, does the degree of disaggregation allow for some analysis of the potential effects of new instruments for which there is no econometric track-record on which to rely? The author's remark that 'differences between the forecasting models . . . over the degree of disaggregation used . . . are not matters of any controversy' seems to sweep to one side an important issue, especially for the study of medium-term employment prospects. This concerns both the industrial disaggregation of employment, output, wages, etc. and the further disaggregation of labour input into broad occupational groups, with or without corresponding disaggregations of other variables (e.g. wages).

This brings me to another general point before making one or two more detailed remarks. The author explains the absence of much discussion of the treatment of technology by asserting his belief that 'whilst important, our failure to model the firm's technology in a more realistic way is not at the root of our failure to forecast employment'. This reflects the aggregate short-term

318

perspective adopted. If, instead, the objective were to forecast employment in different industries, then the demands of consistency would dictate some recourse to input-output analysis and an appropriate technology matrix. With an eye more for the medium-term the need to allow for exceptional behaviour in changes in capital stock and capital utilisation would warrant more direct attention to the technology of production than is given in neo-classical models. The effects of the oil crisis and its aftermath on industrial cost structures and investment etc. provide sufficient incentive to move in this direction.

The employment function field is one desperately waiting for a few nails to be hit firmly on the head. From that point of view I find Brian Henry's discussion of alternative ideas and estimated equations somewhat inconclusive. Models estimated on quarterly data for 1964–76 or thereabouts and tested for one-step forecasting errors for 1977–78 may well display different performance rankings when estimated on annual data for 1948–70 and tested for forecasting errors over 1971–76 by supplying actuals of all the independent variables concerned and estimates for lagged dependent variables (see Wilson, [1979]). Those successfully applied to manufacturing in aggregate may not produce satisfactory results for its constituent industries. Without wishing to start the usual methodological debate this does raise questions about our interpretation of the aggregate model and its implications for policy when embedded in a full-scale macroeconomic model. I would also mention that (i) both the MRG and the Cambridge Growth Project use estimates of *gross* output rather than net output and (ii) before testing Hazledine's model it is necessary to decide upon the rule for extrapolating optimal productivity and hours outside the first and last peaks recorded in the sample period—no mention of this is made in the paper.

A summary of the approach taken by the Manpower Research Group (MRG) is given in Lindley [1978], and Wilson [1979] provides a comparison of the forecasting performance of several employment equations. Our general conclusion so far is that a version of the Hazledine model is particularly useful in medium-term assessment situations where judgments are inevitably being made about the general trend of productivity. The concept of optimal productivity provides a device through which exogenous assumptions about productivity can be imposed in circumstances where a satisfactory model of what determines changes over the medium term is lacking. Conceptually we should like to integrate the vintage explanation of the technical optimum with a bargaining model by which this technical optimum is modified in practice, since productivity, like wages, is the subject of collective negotiation. Within that theoretical framework one would then have a short-run employment-output relationship emerging from decision rules for the utilisation of capital and labour. But it is much easier to state the idea than give it empirical support. However, it must surely be the model-builder's objective to dispense with the time trend which creeps into virtually all employment equations, meaning that the contribution of the equation is largely to track cyclical (and seasonal, in quarterly models) fluctuations around an unexplained trend in a conceptual mishmash of gains in capital stock and Hicks-neutral technical progress. Hazledine's formulation recognises this problem very clearly: it can obviously be criticised for relying upon peak-to-peak variables but to describe his approach as containing a 'considerable amount of rationalising of known changes in trends' seems to me to miss the point of his overall modelling strategy.

Turning to Brian Henry's own experiments with models of interrelated factor demands concentrating upon employment and hours: these certainly show promise for short-term forecasting. However, the introduction of further independent variables (e.g. the incremental cost of additional hours and the user cost of capital, when compared with simpler specifications, leaves the ultimate empirical question unanswered: how will forecast performance compare with that of other models when the independent variables themselves need to be predicted? And the presence of the time trend in both employment (implicitly) and hours equations (Table 6) undermines my confidence in their value for *medium*-term forecasting. Nonetheless it is time someone paid more attention to the specification of lags in employment models and Brian Henry's paper is a useful contribution to empirical work for the UK.

As for labour supply and unemployment I would agree that certain developments, notably by Nickell, have already yielded useful results. But I do not think that the solution to the problem of forecasting unemployment, certainly not over the medium-term, resides in building models of labour turnover and flows through the unemployment register. Such work is important because there are many policies which affect a multitude of short-run movements in the labour market but forecasting the main changes in unemployment requires the modelling of population and manpower flows in a broader context. I have in mind the construction of a population accounting framework [1] within which one might chart flows between the labour force, education and training, and the rest of the population. This would be a step towards modelling supply at the disaggregated level, concentrating on those gross flows into and out of the labour force which are large and particularly variable over time. From this perspective I would stress much more the problems of inadequate data than does the author. It seems to me that the last sentence of the paper reflects a preoccupation with the technical immaturity of labour supply research when a blast or two in the direction of those allocating resources for the collection of household-based statistics would be more appropriate.

My final remark concerns the general approach to modelling the labour market and the value we place on different types of evidence about its operations. In addition to research on the labour market carried out at the aggregate industrial level, the MRG is engaged on several studies of specific labour markets where their significance for policy and the availability of data suggest that more detailed analysis would be worthwhile. It is unrealistic to expect the estimation of aggregate neo-classical models to provide the main basis for policy evaluation. Research findings for many industrial-occupational labour markets do not support neo-classical theory, however hedged around with judiciously chosen supplementary hypotheses. This is not to deny the

[1] Rough estimates of 'population accounting matrices' are given in Lindley [1978] together with some indication of the usefulness of these matrices in discussing labour supply.

presence of wage and price responses but merely to underline the strength of other forces which impede the process of market adjustment over long periods of time. Whilst I am in favour of experimenting with aggregate models of labour supply and demand, using either equilibrium or disequilibrium formulations, I would agree with Brian Henry that little real progress has yet been made. Strong assertions about the nature of the labour market derived from such models would seem to be out of keeping with their present stage of development and with other evidence at both industrial and more disaggregate levels.[2]

REFERENCES

Lindley, R. M. [1978] (ed.), *Britain's Medium-Term Employment Prospects*. Coventry: Manpower Research Group, University of Warwick.

Lindley, R. M. [1980], 'Approaches to Assessing Employment Prospects'. *Economic Change and Employment Policy*. Ed. R. M. Lindley. London: Macmillan.

Wilson, R. A. [1979], 'Comparative Forecasting Performance of Disaggregated Employment Models'. MRG Discussion Paper no. 3. Coventry: Manpower Research Group, University of Warwick. (mimeographed).

[2] See Lindley [1980] for an elaboration of this point of view as well as a comment on the Beenstock and Warburton model mentioned in the paper.

INDEX OF NAMES

Printed in England for Her Majesty's Stationery Office, by Tonbridge Printers Limited,
Shipbourne Road, Tonbridge, Kent
Dd 696896 K16